SIX MODERN

AMERICAN PLAYS

MODERN LIBRARY COLLEGE EDITIONS

SIX MODERN AMERICAN PLAYS

INTRODUCTION BY
ALLAN G. HALLINE

THE MODERN LIBRARY · NEW YORK

THE MODERN LIBRARY

is published by RANDOM HOUSE, INC.

Manufactured in the United States of America

CONTENTS

INTRODUCTION

By

ALLAN G. HALLINE

Though the history of American drama dates from pre-Revolutionary days, our playwriting has achieved major significance only in the last three decades. The striking emergence of American drama into world recognition after World War I is explained in various ways: the victory America helped effect not only stimulated but also spotlighted our writers; the waxing and maturing nation inevitably produced an important theatre; the lashing by our own and foreign critics prodded us to greater effort; technical stage advances, growing audiences, and a flourishing English and continental drama posed a challenge to our native writers. These were undoubtedly factors in the upthrust of our drama, but one must not overlook the inexplicable insights and powers which dwell in the creative mind—these are often the real determining forces. Eugene O'Neill possessed these insights and powers in a superlative degree, and when they functioned under the stimulus of an exciting world, a new drama was born. The burgeoning of O'Neill's genius through succeeding decades produced the greatest single contribution to that new drama; it also charged the native theatre with such energy that other creative minds were impelled to significant activity. This does not mean that O'Neill became the leader of a school, for he had no actual imitators; but his daring and informed craft and his imaginative power stirred the American theatre as nothing else had. From this deep provocation came other playwrights in the twenties who expanded O'Neill's challenge to a national achievement: Maxwell Anderson initiated his brilliant career with *What Price Glory?* in 1924; Philip Barry inaugurated his long line of expert social comedies with *You and I* in 1925; Elmer Rice experimented boldly in *The Adding Machine* (1923); Sidney Howard first gained recognition for his dramas of character with *They Knew What They Wanted* (1924); and George S. Kaufman vaulted into prominence as a comic satirist with *Dulcy* (1921).

Although the greatest excitement and expectancy, as well as a measure of fulfillment, came during the twenties, it was during the thirties that the most extensive and representative contribution to American drama was made. In that decade, characterized by range and maturity, the dramatists just named, together with S. N. Behrman, Robert E. Sherwood, Paul Green, and Lillian Hellman, fashioned new concepts in characterization, poetic drama, philosophic approach, expressionism, and comedy. These dramatists not only worked within traditional forms, but they also responded perceptively to European experiments in technique, often with variations that amounted to originality.

During the forties a notable and natural phenomenon occurred: World War II took immediate possession of our serious dramatists and relinquished them only gradually after the end of the war. This was in striking contrast to the situation during World War I, when our drama failed almost completely to respond to the crisis either during the conflict or in the years immediately following. The spirit of American drama had changed by the time of Munich: our playwrights were more alert to see significant dramatic material in the burning issues of the day. One phase of this phenomenon was that, though the serious drama was dominated by the war, the comic drama largely avoided the topic until the end of hostilities: the war was too close and too terrible for light treatment. The latter part of the forties saw a spate of war comedies and the emergence of new writers of tragedy, notably Tennessee Williams and Arthur Miller. The theatre at the beginning of the fifties appears to be dominated by the success of the expert musical comedy; but a few of the older playwrights have held the attention of the public, and the younger writers of tragedy are fulfilling their early promise.

O'NEILL

Though O'Neill has had only one play on Broadway in the last fifteen years, he has not been superseded as America's foremost playwright. Even if he produces nothing more, he will not be dislodged from this position in the foreseeable future. The phenomenon of O'Neill cannot easily be explained. Several factors have already been cited which were conducive to the sudden upswing in American drama; other more specific factors which helped to shape O'Neill in particular are apparent when one considers his career. Spending his boyhood touring with his famous actor-father, James O'Neill, the youth early imbibed the magic of the theatre, though he did not at once go into the "profession." Following a Catholic schooling and a curtailed career at Princeton, O'Neill, under the spell of Conrad and Jack London, spent two years as a seaman on the far reaches of the Atlantic, an adventure which undermined his health and stocked his imagination. A brief stay in a sanitarium precipitated the decision to write plays; a year in Professor Baker's Workshop 47 at Harvard, followed by residence in Greenwich Village and in Provincetown, provided the training and outlets which launched him on his career. Science and realism, European tradition and American pressures were ubiquitous and insistent. These were the external influences which played upon O'Neill, but more impressive in his work was the transfiguring operation of genius.

In the forecastles of freighters and in the back rooms of "Jimmy the Priest's," suffering and brutality, dissipation and despair flowed before the eyes of the sensitive writer, and much of what he saw entered into his soul. Whether this initial experience with sorrow and anguish was deepened by subsequent biographical events is not here inquired into; but it is clear that the large majority of O'Neill's plays, from apprentice one-acters to mature trilogy, are marked by brooding concern with the griefs and tortures of life.

It may be said that the most notable characteristics of O'Neill's work are: (1) an absorption in character, implemented by skill in subtle psychological analysis and a perception of a wide range of emotions; (2) a creative capacity for incorporating these analyses and perceptions into expressive human beings; (3) a constructive talent for leading these characters through intense conflicts; (4) a bold imaginativeness not only in using conventional dramatic devices in new ways but also in inventing devices to convey the values intended, with the result that most of his dramas are in part experimental; (5) a tendency to dwell upon the extremes of unhappiness; (6) an effort to interpret life in consonance with the findings of science, especially Freudian psychology, and at the same time a longing to find cosmic release in a mystical universe. These characteristics will be seen in a brief review of O'Neill's plays.

O'Neill's first full-length drama, *Beyond the Horizon* (1920), though mainly realistic, is experimental in its alternation of indoor and outdoor scenes to suggest a rhythm in the lives of the characters. In this play, suggested by the life story of a sailor O'Neill had known, the frustrations which beset the characters are ravaging and final; the victims have no chance of overcoming their own natures and the environmental forces which press them down.

The inclusion of *The Emperor Jones* in this volume reflects the high favor in which the public has held this play since its first production in 1920. This success may be attributed to the combination of suspenseful plot and startling dramatic device: add to the basic story of flight and pursuit the pulse-compelling throb of the drum, the weird pantomimic imagery, the unfolding of personal and race memory through symbolistic monologue, and it is easily seen why *The Emperor Jones* has had many productions and has been widely acclaimed as a reading play.

In *Anna Christie* (1921) the realistic technique is chiefly employed, but the experimental approach appears in the personification of the sea as a means of vivifying an irony in the story: blame is placed on the sea whereas it is the land that has wrought the harm. Anna's improvement in character is brought about, to be sure, not simply by the influence of the sea, but by the devoted love of a man who is a product of the sea.

In considering *The Hairy Ape* (1922) it is pertinent to define the term *expressionism,* for this play is the purest example of the type that O'Neill wrote. Expressionism is a dramatic form which articulates ideas and emotions not normally expressed in the given situation; it employs such devices as soliloquies, heightened language, asides, masks, pantomime, choruses, suggestive scenery, lighting, costume, sound effects—all for the purpose of giving outward expression to thoughts and emotions (of characters or author) which are normally unexpressed. In *The Hairy Ape* the feelings and attitudes of the characters, as well as the intent of the author, are brought out by heightened language, choral treatment of characters, distorted and symbolic sets, stylized acting. A majority of O'Neill's plays, it may be noted, are expressionistic in one degree or another.

O'Neill's interest in character is stressed in most of his plays. Character in relation to environment is treated in *Desire Under the Elms* (1924) in which the earthiness of the farm seems to permeate the characters. Expressionism is present in the cross-sectional set and in the embracing elms. One of O'Neill's two most searching studies of character is *The Great God Brown* (1926). In this play the approach is the idea that most persons change their characters according to the company they are in; the employment of masks in this play to mark the shift in basic character makes possible an unusually subtle analysis of both static and changing characters. The major theme of the play is the conflict between the introvert artist and the extrovert business man as they struggle for supremacy in love and occupation. The other play which is outstanding as a study of character is *Strange Interlude* (1928); this drama is noteworthy for three reasons: its probing analysis of emotion and thought; its tracing of character change through three decades; and its dramatization, by the use of asides, of the divergence between what we think and what we say. This portrayal of character duality gives the play its particular power. Less impressive with respect to character in dissection but more suspenseful with respect to character in action, *Mourning Becomes Electra* (1931) tells the Agamemnon-Clytemnestra-Electra-Orestes story in terms of a Civil War homecoming, with character rather than fate as the shaping force. For sheer excitement of narrative *Mourning Becomes Electra* is unsurpassed in O'Neill and seldom equaled by other playwrights. Character is subordinate to philosophy in O'Neill's last play, *The Iceman Cometh* (1947), for the main stress is on the necessity of illusion in the lives of disintegrated characters. The differentiation of character in the habitués of Harry Hope's place is arbitrary and serves merely to demonstrate the universal utility of illusion. Though described as one of O'Neill's greatest plays by some critics, *The Iceman Cometh* is inferior in character analysis, emotional power, and dramatic effectiveness to *The Great God Brown, Strange Interlude,* or *Mourning Becomes Electra*.

Other plays of O'Neill's which illustrate his general qualities are the poetic, buoyant *The Fountain* (1926), the satiric *Marco Millions* (1927), the symbolic *Lazarus Laughed* (1927) and *Dynamo* (1929), the religious *Days Without End* (1934), and the entertaining *Ah, Wilderness!* (1933). These plays are not of equal importance, but they all reveal new facets of O'Neill's wide understanding and versatile art. His combination of character analysis, emotional power, masterly technique, and imaginative experimentation has made O'Neill not only America's greatest playwright but one of the two or three most important in the modern world.

ANDERSON

Maxwell Anderson, the playwright next in stature to O'Neill, has already produced a long sequence of significant plays and is still adding to his achievement. His dramas may be viewed as falling into five groups: (1) comedy and satiric drama; (2) historical tragedy; (3) contemporary drama and tragedy; (4) fantasy; and (5) musical drama. Though Anderson has achieved sufficient success in each of these fields to establish his versatility, his accomplishment is not equal in each group; to date his contributions to either the second or the third group are more important than his work in the other three combined.

Although his first produced drama, *White Desert* (1923), was a tragedy of pioneer life, Anderson came into prominence as the coauthor with Laurence Stallings of *What Price Glory?* (1924), a play which came to have a reputation of debunking war but which actually is more of a lustily realistic account of a curse-flinging friendship. It is true that the soldiers represented in the play are disillusioned about "fighting for democracy" and that the ugly aspects of war are exposed, but the dramatic interest centers in the personal feud between a captain and a sergeant, both professional soldiers, who revile each other off duty but who hold fast to each other under fire. Another satiric play was *Outside Looking In* (1925), based on Jim Tully's account of the tramp world, *Beggars of Life*. Anderson's domestic comedy, *Saturday's Children* (1927), is partly a conventional account of the bickering during the "first year" of married life and partly a toying with the idea that love succeeds best when the couple is unmarried. Although this was a popular play, Anderson did not write in the same vein again. Anderson's best satire, *Both Your Houses* (1933), is a somewhat pedestrian but nevertheless effective account of how the Washington lawmakers promote special interests and their own reëlection by a variety of dishonest practices; the central action concerns a young and idealistic Congressman who hopes to defeat a pork-barrel bill by so loading it with preposterous appropriations that it will fall of its own weight—but the bill passes. The simplicity of the play's construction secures focus, and the plausibility of the speeches and action assures cogency.

In the field of historical tragedy, Anderson has made a notable contribution. The distinctive qualities of these plays are: their presentation of historical personages in psychological terms that give the sense of present reality without destroying the illusion of the past; their skillful stagecraft which effectively makes use of conventional forms and introduces a few innovations; their frequent employment of blank verse; and their embodiment of Anderson's theory of tragedy which includes (a) the portrayal of an inner conflict between good and evil, (b) a protagonist of exceptional qualities who represents the forces of good and who wins, and (c) a protagonist who is not perfect at the beginning and who is ennobled in the course of the action. Anderson's first play in this group, *Elizabeth the Queen* (1930), is an account of the love-ambition contest between Elizabeth and Essex, done with the rapierlike precision of a courtier's duel; add to this the swift etching of the minor characters, and the result is a tense, polished drama. *Mary of Scotland* (1933) is the fullest expression of Anderson's theory of tragedy in its sympathetic portrayal of forbearing, sweet-tempered Mary who is ennobled in the face of death by her faith that she will in time's estimate be esteemed above the triumphant but treacherous Elizabeth. Though *The Wingless Victory* (1936) is historical in its treatment of the New England Puritan period, it falls short of true tragedy, for its central figure is neither an exceptional nor a sympathetic character. Included in the category of historical tragedy are also *The Masque of Kings* (1936), *Joan of Lorraine* (1946), and *Anne of the Thousand Days* (1948). *Joan of Lorraine* embodies an Anderson innovation in its use of a rehearsal to dramatize two divergent interpretations of Joan's essential nature; alternation of rehearsal scenes with playing scenes gives rise to a stirring analysis of the religious problem involved. *Anne of the Thousand Days* adds to the conventional picture of the lustful Henry a brief account of his childish compositions in poetry and music, but its most memorable portrait is of Anne, who excitingly rebukes the royal pursuer while her own lover lives and who unflinchingly insists upon her rights until her influence with the king has expired. The drama fits Anderson's concept of tragedy in representing ennoblement of character: just before her execution Anne tells Henry that *he* is going to his death, and she to her expiation: "It involves dying to live." Henry is left in life to lug his bag of horrors behind him.

In the field of contemporary drama and tragedy Anderson's *Winterset* (1935) has remained the best known. This story of an American youth's effort to avenge his father's death, ending in the irony of his own death at the hands of the antagonists, invites comparison to Hamlet: although in Anderson's play the tragic hero is redeemed through love from the necessity of revenge, and is thus closer to modern psychology, yet he has neither the emotional nor intellectual stature of his prototype. The remainder of Anderson's plays in this category have to do with war themes. *Key Largo* (1939) depicts the effort of an American youth, who has failed his cause and his comrades in the Spanish Civil War, to redeem himself by risking his life for others purely from principle and not from passion. *Key Largo* is one of Anderson's significant plays in its dramatization of moral values and cosmic concepts in terms of melodramatic action. *Candle in the Wind* (1941) tells a story of the Nazi occupation of Paris; the more successful *The Eve of St. Mark* (1942) conducts an American boy from his home, through training camp, to a moral crisis in battle similar to the first scene in *Key Largo*.

Storm Operation (1944) is a technically correct but dramatically ineffective account of a military landing during World War II.

Though Anderson's plays in the fields of fantasy and music are less important than the foregoing, they reveal the scope of his talent. Fantasy is the dominant characteristic of *High Tor* (1937), a story of Dutch settlers and legends on the Hudson River, and it is also predominant in *The Star Wagon* (1937), a picture of what we might do had we our lives to live over again. The former play combines history and broad humor with its imaginative elements, but the latter is pure fantasy in form. *Knickerbocker Holiday* (1938) is a musical comedy freely recreating Irving's pictures of early New York. Anderson's latest production, *Lost in the Stars* (1949), is a music drama of serious import, Kurt Weill contributing the music; it is based on Alan Paton's novel, *Cry, the Beloved Country*. The drama is a compassionate account of white-Negro relations in South Africa and celebrates a white man's forgiveness, through understanding, of the Negro who murdered his son.

The solid, comprehensive, and often imaginative achievement of Anderson, whose work is shaped by high ideals, places this craftsman and poet near the top of American dramatists.

KAUFMAN and HART

For nearly thirty years George S. Kaufman has been the leading writer of satiric comedy in America. With the exception of the last decade he has produced at least one show a year, sometimes more, and on one occasion he had four shows playing simultaneously on Broadway, a feat equaled only by Clyde Fitch three decades earlier. Most of Kaufman's shows have been successes and an unusually high percentage of them have been hits; he has also had widespread production on the semi-professional and amateur stage. The explanation of this phenomenal record seems to be that Kaufman gives fuller expression to the American comic spirit than anyone else; this spirit, as embodied in his plays, is a derisive but not bitter caricature, amplified by the ludicrous and spiced by sex. One is always aware in Kaufman's comedies that the objects of satire are deficient or aberrant in mental powers; yet there is a sympathy with them as human beings. Kaufman's caricature is grounded upon a detailed knowledge of human behavior, and by skillfully varying the degree of character distortion, the playwright secures the specific effect he wishes. Another of Kaufman's talents is an unflagging inventiveness in thinking up language, costumes, properties, sounds, pantomime, and situations that provoke humor.

Paradoxically, Kaufman is the most dependent and yet one of the most original of American playwrights. With one or two exceptions, all of his plays have been written in collaboration—a long-lasting reliance resorted to by no other American playwright. But in spite of the fact that he has had at least ten different collaborators, there is a recognizable dramatic quality common to every play. Only Kaufman could have supplied it. Although each of the collaborators must have brought markedly different talents and materials to the joint enterprise, yet it appears from Moss Hart's testimony that every word of their final creation passed through the alembic of Kaufman's original and disciplined mind.

Kaufman's work falls chiefly into two groups: satiric comedies and satiric musical comedies. He has written a few plays which do not fit these categories, viz., *The American Way* (1939) with Moss Hart, a patriotic panoramic play; *Merrily We Roll Along* (1934) with Moss Hart, a study of character disintegration, arranged in an inverted time sequence; *The Land Is Bright* (1941) with Edna Ferber, a survey of three successive family generations; *The Small Hours* (1951), with Leueen McGrath, an account of a distraught wife who comes to realize that the problems of the other members of her family are greater than her own. The satiric comedies stress either character, situation, or general idea. The first of Kaufman's character satires, written with Marc Connelly, was *Dulcy* (1921), so far the best stage portrayal of the "bromidic" mind; *The Royal Family* (1928) with Edna Ferber extends the character satire to a whole stage family, the Barrymores. *Dinner at Eight* (1932) with Edna Ferber applies the scalpel treatment to a pair of social climbers and an assortment of others; *First Lady* (1935) with Katharine Dayton ridicules scheming politicians; *Stage Door* (1936) with Edna Ferber is an unimpressive picture of actress life in a boarding house; *The Man Who Came to Dinner* (1939) with Moss Hart is the most brilliant of all the character satires and a masterpiece of invective. The flexibility of Kaufman's satiric skill may be seen particularly in *The Late George Apley* (1944) in which the author's characteristic boisterous manner is groomed down, no doubt by collaborator John Marquand, upon whose novel the play is based.

Kaufman's satiric comedies which stress situation include: *To the Ladies* (1922) with Marc Connelly, an American version of Barrie's *What Every Woman Knows; Merton of the Movies* (1922) with Marc Connelly, in which an actor who thinks he is a tragedian succeeds only in being a comedian; and *You Can't Take It With You* (1936) with Moss Hart, a potpourri of antic episodes. Several of the satiric comedies center about general ideas or conditions. The earliest of these plays, *Beggar on Horseback* (1925) with Marc Connelly, remains one of the best; ingenious and provocative, it employs a clever dream sequence in which a sensitive, aspiring composer finds himself in the clutches of materialism and mass production. Kaufman and Hart's first collaboration, *Once In a Lifetime* (1930), mocks the superficialities of Hollywood; *George Washington Slept Here* (1940), with Moss Hart, mildly satirizes pride in place and tradition.

The second major category of Kaufman's plays is satirical musical comedies; in some of these the satiric element is subordinated to the musical, but in one or two the biting sting of satire is as strong as in the straight plays. Included in this major category are: *Animal Crackers* (1928) with Morrie Ryskind; *Of Thee I Sing* (1931) with Morrie Ryskind, a brilliant political satire; *The Band Wagon* (1931), a revue written with Howard Dietz; *Let 'Em Eat Cake* (1933) with Morrie Ryskind, another political satire; *I'd Rather Be Right* (1937) with Moss Hart, a caricature of Roosevelt; and *Park Avenue* (1946).

Though stress has here been placed upon the career of Kaufman, the achievement of Moss Hart must not be underestimated. Of all Kaufman's collaborators he has been the most frequent and one of the most successful; it must be remembered that *Once In A Lifetime* was originally Hart's play and that the collaboration was in fact a rewriting. In their subsequent work Hart has been a full-fledged partner; Kaufman speaks of the prodigality of Hart's mind and calls him "forked lightning." As a writer independent of Kaufman, Hart has had a creditable career of his own. His *Lady in the Dark* (1941) is an ingenious dramatization of psychiatry in which deftly told story scenes alternate with flamboyant dream sequences set to music by Kurt Weill with lyrics by Ira Gershwin. The music drama had an unusually successful run. Hart's next play, *Winged Victory*

(1943), was a panoramic glorification of the Air Corps and enjoyed widespread acclaim as a war play. *Christopher Blake* (1946) was a study of the effect of divorce upon a child; *Light Up the Sky* (1948) was a brilliant satire on show people. With the exception of the latter play, the foregoing all reveal some dramatic qualities not evident in the collaborations with Kaufman and indicate the widening arc of Hart's talents. In such a play as *Christopher Blake*, for example, despite its specious psychic dreams, the fundamental purpose is to arouse sympathy for a child whose parents are being divorced—an emotional approach wholly foreign to Kaufman; in *Lady in the Dark* the probing of the emotional past is done in a non-Kaufman vein.

In the present editor's opinion Kaufman and Hart surpass Congreve and Wycherley in social satire; time may show that their achievement is as important as that of Molière or Wilde.

LILLIAN HELLMAN

If the foregoing are the elder playwrights, Lillian Hellman belongs to the group which came into prominence during the thirties. She has been a painstaking, somewhat non-imaginative, but nonetheless gripping writer; her mordant dramas have struck a responsive chord in contemporary audiences. Not strictly comedies or tragedies, her plays are serious dramas with sinister overtones; their significance lies in their frank portrayal of situations and people as Miss Hellman finds them—which is usually unpleasant. In all but her war plays and her last adaptation, the main purpose seems to be to exhibit the characters in all their rancor, selfishness, cruelty, and perversity, with little or no redemption from the forces of darkness. In one of her war plays, however, the miasma is offset by a faith that one side is in the right and will win. Miss Hellman is a scrupulous writer, arouses compressed emotion, and asks sharp questions; but her constricted imagination may anchor her to her period.

It was in 1934 that Miss Hellman established herself with *The Children's Hour* as a writer meriting serious attention. The analysis of character in the play is sharp, and the boldness in treating the theme of abnormality is balanced by a taste that keeps the story from being merely sensational; but the ending has been justly described as lacking an "Aristotelian purgation." *Days to Come* (1936) is a serious but only partially successful effort to dramatize a three-cornered struggle among capital, labor, and the unions; it is interwoven with a theme of family disintegration. The play had a poor reception, and it must be acknowledged that as a drama of labor-capital relations it is inferior to Galsworthy's *Strife*. With the production of *The Little Foxes* (1939) Miss Hellman achieved what seems to be her most representative work; it is here that her specialty in unmasking malice is exercised with balanced skill, and the play is notable as a picture of internecine family strife.

With the advent of World War II Miss Hellman was among the first of the dramatists to respond. Even before Pearl Harbor she had produced *Watch on the Rhine* (1941), an anti-Nazi play which revealed that the war was already being fought on our own shores in the activities of foreign agents. As a clear and foreboding exposé, *Watch on the Rhine* made a vivid impression on the tense American public. A more ingenious and subtle play, *The Searching Wind* (1944), scrutinized our pre-war foreign policies and blamed our statesmen for an equivocating, temporizing, and appeasing diplomacy that permitted the fatal growth of fascism during the twenties and thirties. The major theme of the play is echoed in an accompanying story of personal relationships, but the latter plot is not sufficiently clear-cut or integrated to produce a complete fusion of materials.

The end of the war released Miss Hellman from nationalistic themes and permitted her return to representative work in *Another Part of the Forest* (1946). The title indicates that the story is again of "The Little Foxes," twenty years earlier, at which time we get a picture of the "big fox." It is hard to tell whether the Hubbards of 1880 or those of 1900 are the worse cutthroats. In explaining her return to these people Miss Hellman spoke of her "graveyard affection for the Hubbards, whom I cherish as one would cherish a nest of particularly vicious diamond-back rattlesnakes, but it did make me feel that it was worth while to look into their family background and find out what it was that made them the nasty people they were." [1]

Miss Hellman's *Montserrat* (1949) is not in her characteristic vein; instead it is an adaptation of a foreign play dealing with a remote story, viz., the cruelty of Spanish rulers in their effort to capture the rebel Bolivar in Venezuela. The melodrama of which Miss Hellman had earlier been accused is evident in this play. The author's latest production, *Autumn Garden* (1951), concerns a group of summer boarders in a Gulf Coast mansion who are laboring under various delusions about themselves; a spate of self-analysis toward the end of the play has its beneficial effects. This play is in a mellower mood than is customary with Miss Hellman.

All of Miss Hellman's representative plays are acknowledgedly moralistic and serious; and they are sombre without being classically tragic. Miss Hellman's technique is conventional but sure; her language familiar but vital, thus providing a natural vehicle for the actor. She chronicles and exposes vicious aspects of our national scene and character; but she does not cheer her age.

[1] Burns Mantle, *The Best Plays of 1946-47*, New York, 1947, p. 163.

WILLIAMS

Among the younger American playwrights of importance Tennessee Williams was the first to emerge and has retained an edge in leadership. He represents a new spirit in local color tragedy: the concern with a fragile character who is beset with an obsession born of frustration and who is engulfed by a callous or cruel world, usually localized in the lower Mississippi region. It is natural for Williams to write of the locale which flowed in upon his youthful mind, and in so doing he achieves an authentic tone in his plays; but his forte is a sensitive insight into frail characters who find life too much for them. Williams' language is responsive to the demands of the situation; he employs striking contrasts; and he uses a partially expressionistic technique to enforce emotional effects.

Williams first drew attention with *The Glass Menagerie* in 1944. It is worth noting that during a period when serious drama was preoccupied with war themes, this delicate, irrelative story should captivate the theatre-going public. The indication is that distinctive drama with universality always appeals. The account in this play of the shy, crippled girl, who is crossed in her youthful love and who turns to her menagerie for solace, strikes a responsive note in all who have been wounded by the world and who try to carry their pain in silence; add to this the psychic nostalgia of the mother who dwells upon her happiness in the past, and the wistful quality of the play is deepened further. Produced unsuccessfully the following year, *You Touched Me* (1945) told again the story of a fragile girl, having the "almost transparent quality of glass," who daydreams amid delicate ornaments and shrinks from an intimidating environment.

Williams' most successful play, *A Street Car Named Desire*

(1947), is a tragic drama of the same major design as *The Glass Menagerie* (a critic has said that it might be called *Another Part of the Glass Menagerie*), but it is more intense and violent. There is a delicate, cultured central character, driven to neurasthenia by frustration; she finds herself in a harsh world, here localized in New Orleans. Blanche du Bois of *A Street Car Named Desire* is, to be sure, a different person from Laura Wingfield in *The Glass Menagerie;* the former is excitable and frenzied whereas the latter is reserved, even ingrown; Blanche seeks compensation for her frustrated love by frantically pursuing lovers, whereas Laura finds a measure of consolation in her silent glass animals. But the outlines of their stories are similar: each has suffered disappointment and disillusionment in a broken love affair preceding the action of the play; each converts a beguilement into an obsession; each experiences a moment of retrieved or new-found elation before the final resolution, which for Laura is relapse and for Blanche is insanity. In both plays the environment of the heroine is callous, depressing, or harsh: for Laura the tawdry tenement, the droning mother, the evanescent rekindled love; for Blanche the decaying house, the violent brother-in-law, the cruel commitment. Both plays make expressionistic use of setting, lights, properties, and music.

Summer and Smoke (1948), which failed to gain public support, tells the story of a delicate girl whose sense of propriety is so strong that she is driven to frustration by a scientist lover. Williams' last play, *The Rose Tattoo* (1951), represents a departure from the pattern that had dominated his previous plays. In an exuberant, partly comic mood he writes of a Sicilian woman on the Gulf Coast who passionately builds up an ideal of her departed husband, only to find that she has all along been deceived. The result is not unrelieved despair, however, but regeneration.

Tennessee Williams' major talent revealed so far is a dual ability to portray sensitive characters with lyric vitality and to depict elemental beings with naked power. He blends these and intermediate characters with structural skill and restrained expressionism. Unless he continues to develop new thematic patterns, as in his last play, he will be limited in range; but he works adroitly within his chosen area. Though his tragic dramas do not embody the concept of ennoblement as Anderson defined it, they are faithful to the modern spirit of unrelieved failure or disaster.

HEGGEN and LOGAN

As pointed out earlier, the response of serious drama to World War II was immediate and significant, whereas comedy largely avoided the subject until after the cessation of hostilities. Even then comedy was likely to shun themes of suffering and to concentrate on non-combat situations. Such was the most successful comedy about the war, *Mister Roberts* (1948). The authorship of this drama began in a short novel which Thomas Heggen wrote about his experiences on an assault transport in the Pacific; the play is a skillful adaptation by Joshua Logan.

The sensational three-year run of *Mister Roberts* invites inquiry as to the reasons for its popularity. There are at least four aspects of the play which have an immediate appeal for audiences of the day: its unabashed realism in language and character depiction; its hilarious typical episodes; its exploitation of the military "gripe"; and its underlying vein of moral idealism evinced in the crew's admiration for a man who will sidetrack himself for others. The ribaldry, the sizzle of invective, the comicality of requisite disillusion contribute to the surface humor of the play; the underlying appeal to the qualities of the heart fuses the materials into a moving drama.

Thomas Heggen's career began with a brilliant college record in journalism and soon led into four years in the Navy in the Pacific, where he saw the action that was absent in *Mister Roberts*. During the remarkable run of the play, Heggen was found dead in 1949 under unexplained circumstances in his apartment.

Prior to the adaptation of Heggen's novel, Joshua Logan had been a successful young Broadway director. Since his collaboration he has written another adaptation, *The Wisteria Trees* (1950), based on Chekhov's *The Cherry Orchard*. Nearly all the characters, episodes, and meanings of Chekhov's play are taken over by Logan and reset in Louisiana just before 1900, about the time of the original story. Opinion has been divided as to whether anything is gained in the retelling; clearly a sense of immediacy is achieved for Americans by placing the action in more recognizable surroundings and using more familiar character types; but the qualities of charm and pathos are diminished by a slangy idiom. In addition to writing this play, which Helen Hayes acted with success, Joshua Logan has continued his directing activities on Broadway.

The plays presented in this volume are all significant achievements in the modern American theatre, and their authors include leaders among the elder as well as among the younger playwrights; but this representation should not be interpreted as comprehensive, for the work of other important dramatists would have to be added to complete such a survey. The focused aims of this volume, together with copyright restrictions, have resulted in the particular selections here made.

BIBLIOGRAPHY

In this brief bibliography repetition of entry is avoided by dispensing with individual listings according to playwright.

Anderson, John, *The American Theatre*, New York, 1938.

Atkinson, Brooks, *Broadway Scrapbook*, New York, 1947.

Bentley, Eric, *The Playwright as Thinker*, New York, 1946.

Block, Anita, *The Changing World in Plays and Theatre*, Boston, 1939.

Brown, John Mason, *The Modern Theatre in Revolt*, New York, 1929.

———, *Upstage*, New York, 1930.

———, *Two on the Aisle*, New York, 1938.

———, *Broadway in Review*, New York, 1940.

———, *Seeing Things*, New York, 1946.

———, *Seeing More Things*, New York, 1948.

Clark, Barrett H., *Maxwell Anderson: the Man and His Plays*, New York, 1933.

———, *A Study of the Modern Drama*, New York, 1938.

———, *Eugene O'Neill: the Man and His Plays*, New York, 1947.

Clark, Barrett H., and Freedley, George, *A History of Modern Drama*, New York, 1947.

Gassner, John, *Masters of the Drama*, New York, 1940.

———, *A Treasury of the Theatre*, New York, 1950.

Halline, Allan G., *American Plays*, New York, 1935.

Krutch, Joseph Wood, *The American Drama Since 1918*, New York, 1939.

Moses, Montrose J., and Krutch, J. W., *Representative American Dramas*, Boston, 1941.

Nathan, George Jean, *The Theatre Book of the Year*, New York, 1942–43 and annually thereafter.

Quinn, Arthur Hobson, *A History of the American Drama from the Civil War to the Present Day*, New York, 1936.

————, *Representative American Plays*, New York, 1938.

Skinner, Richard Dana, *Eugene O'Neill, a Poet's Quest*, New York, 1935.

Spiller, Robert E., *et al.*, *Literary History of the United States*, New York, 1948. Vol. II for discussion; Vol. III for bibliography.

Winther, Sophus K., *Eugene O'Neill: A Critical Study*, New York, 1934.

Young, Stark, *Immortal Shadows*, New York, 1948.

Eugene O'Neill

THE EMPEROR JONES

CHARACTERS

BRUTUS JONES   *Emperor*

HENRY SMITHERS   *A Cockney Trader*

             AN OLD NATIVE WOMAN

LEM   *A Native Chief*

SOLDIERS   *Adherents of Lem*

The Little Formless Fears; Jeff; The Negro Convicts; The Prison Guard; The Planters; The Auctioneer; The Slaves; The Congo Witch-Doctor; The Crocodile God.

The action of the play takes place on an island in the West Indies as yet not self-determined by white Marines. The form of native government is, for the time being, an empire.

SCENE ONE

SCENE—*The audience chamber in the palace of the Emperor—
a spacious, high-ceilinged room with bare, white-washed walls.
The floor is of white tiles. In the rear, to the left of center,
a wide archway giving out on a portico with white pillars.
The palace is evidently situated on high ground for beyond
the portico nothing can be seen but a vista of distant hills,
their summits crowned with thick groves of palm trees. In
the right wall, center, a smaller arched doorway leading to
the living quarters of the palace. The room is bare of furniture with the exception of one huge chair made of uncut
wood which stands at center, its back to rear. This is very
apparently the Emperor's throne. It is painted a dazzling,
eye-smiting scarlet. There is a brilliant orange cushion on
the seat and another smaller one is placed on the floor to
serve as a footstool. Strips of matting, dyed scarlet, lead
from the foot of the throne to the two entrances.*

*It is late afternoon but the sunlight still blazes yellowly
beyond the portico and there is an oppressive burden of exhausting heat in the air.*

*As the curtain rises, a native Negro woman sneaks in cau-
tiously from the entrance on the right. She is very old, dressed
in cheap calico, bare-footed, a red bandana handkerchief
covering all but a few stray wisps of white hair. A bundle
bound in colored cloth is carried over her shoulder on the
end of a stick. She hesitates beside the doorway, peering
back as if in extreme dread of being discovered. Then she
begins to glide noiselessly, a step at a time, toward the doorway in the rear. At this moment,* SMITHERS *appears beneath
the portico.*

SMITHERS *is a tall, stoop-shouldered man about forty. His
bald head, perched on a long neck with an enormous Adam's
apple, looks like an egg. The tropics have tanned his naturally
pasty face with its small, sharp features to a sickly yellow,
and native rum has painted his pointed nose to a startling*

3

red. His little, washy-blue eyes are red-rimmed and dart about him like a ferret's. His expression is one of unscrupulous meanness, cowardly and dangerous. He is dressed in a worn riding suit of dirty white drill, puttees, spurs, and weais a white cork helmet. A cartridge belt with an automatic revolver is around his waist. He carries a riding whip in his hand. He sees the woman and stops to watch her suspiciously. Then, making up his mind, he steps quickly on tiptoe into the room. The woman, looking back over her shoulder continually, does not see him until it is too late. When she does SMITHERS *springs forward and grabs her firmly by the shoulder. She struggles to get away, fiercely but silently.*

SMITHERS [*Tightening his grasp—roughly*]: Easy! None o' that, me birdie. You can't wriggle out now. I got me 'ooks on yer.

WOMAN [*Seeing the uselessness of struggling, gives way to frantic terror, and sinks to the ground, embracing his knees supplicatingly*]: No tell him! No tell him, Mister!

SMITHERS [*With great curiosity*]: Tell 'im? [*Then scornfully.*] Oh, you mean 'is bloomin' Majesty. What's the gaime, any 'ow? What are you sneakin' away for? Been stealin' a bit, I s'pose. [*He taps her bundle with his riding whip significantly.*]

WOMAN [*Shaking her head vehemently*]: No, me no steal.

SMITHERS: Bloody liar! But tell me what's up. There's somethin' funny goin' on. I smelled it in the air first thing I got up this mornin'. You blacks are up to some devilment. This palace of 'is is like a bleedin' tomb. Where's all the 'ands? [*The woman keeps sullenly silent.* SMITHERS *raises his whip threateningly.*] Ow, yer won't, won't yer? I'll show yer what's what.

WOMAN [*Coweringly*]: I tell, Mister. You no hit. They go— all go. [*She makes a sweeping gesture toward the hills in the distance.*]

SMITHERS: Run away—to the 'ills?

WOMAN: Yes, Mister. Him Emperor—Great Father. [*She touches her forehead to the floor with a quick mechanical jerk.*] Him sleep after eat. Then they go—all go. Me old woman. Me left only. Now me go too.

SMITHERS [*His astonishment giving way to an immense, mean satisfaction*]: Ow! So that's the ticket! Well, I know bloody well wot's in the air—when they runs orf to the 'ills. The tom-tom 'll be thumping out there bloomin' soon. [*With extreme vindictiveness.*] And I'm bloody glad of it, for one! Serve 'im right! Puttin' on airs, the stinkin' nigger! 'Is Majesty! Gawd blimey! I only 'opes I'm there when they takes 'im out to shoot 'im. [*Suddenly.*] 'E's still 'ere all right, ain't 'e?

WOMAN: Yes. Him sleep.

SMITHERS: 'E's bound to find out soon as 'e wakes up. 'E's cunnin' enough to know when 'is time's come. [*He goes to the doorway on right and whistles shrilly with his fingers in his mouth. The old woman springs to her feet and runs out of the doorway, rear.* SMITHERS *goes after her, reaching for his revolver.*] Stop or I'll shoot! [*Then stopping—indifferently.*] Pop orf then, if yer like, yer black cow. [*He stands in the doorway, looking after her.*]

[JONES *enters from the right. He is a tall, powerfully-built, full-blooded Negro of middle age. His features are typically negroid, yet there is something decidedly distinctive about his face—an underlying strength of will, a hardy, self-reliant confidence in himself that inspires respect. His eyes are alive with a keen, cunning intelligence. In manner he is shrewd, suspicious, evasive. He wears a light blue uniform coat, sprayed with brass buttons, heavy gold chevrons on his shoulders, gold braid on the collar, cuffs, etc. His pants are bright red with a light blue stripe down the side. Patent-leather laced boots with brass spurs, and a belt with a long-barreled, pearl-handled revolver in a holster complete his make up. Yet there is something not altogether ridiculous about his grandeur. He has a way of carrying it off.*]

JONES [*Not seeing anyone—greatly irritated and blinking sleepily—shouts*]: Who dare whistle dat way in my palace? Who dare wake up de Emperor? I'll git de hide fravled off some o' you niggers sho'!

SMITHERS [*Showing himself—in a manner half-afraid and half-defiant*]: It was me whistled to yer. [*As* JONES *frowns angrily.*] I got news for yer.

JONES [*Putting on his suavest manner, which fails to cover up his contempt for the white man*]: Oh, it's you, Mister

Smithers. [*He sits down on his throne with easy dignity.*] What news you got to tell me?

SMITHERS [*Coming close to enjoy his discomfiture*]: Don't yer notice nothin' funny today?

JONES [*Coldly*]: Funny? No. I ain't perceived nothin' of de kind!

SMITHERS: Then yer ain't so foxy as I thought yer was. Where's all your court? [*Sarcastically.*] The Generals and the Cabinet Ministers and all?

JONES [*Imperturbably*]: Where dey mostly runs de minute I closes my eyes—drinkin' rum and talkin' big down in de town. [*Sarcastically.*] How come you don't know dat? Ain't you sousin' with 'em most every day?

SMITHERS [*Stung but pretending indifference—with a wink*]: That's part of the day's work. I got ter—ain't I—in my business?

JONES [*Contemptuously*]: Yo' business!

SMITHERS [*Imprudently enraged*]: Gawd blimey, you was glad enough for me ter take yer in on it when you landed here first. You didn' 'ave no 'igh and mighty airs in them days!

JONES [*His hand going to his revolver like a flash—menacingly*]: Talk polite, white man! Talk polite, you heah me! I'm boss heah now, is you fergettin'? [*The Cockney seems about to challenge this last statement with the facts but something in the other's eyes holds and cows him.*]

SMITHERS [*In a cowardly whine*]: No 'arm meant, old top.

JONES [*Condescendingly*]: I accepts yo' apology. [*Lets his hand fall from his revolver.*] No use'n you rakin' up ole times. What I was den is one thing. What I is now 's another. You didn't let me in on yo' crooked work out o' no kind feelin's dat time. I done de dirty work fo' you—and most o' de brain work, too, fo' dat matter—and I was wu'th money to you, dat's de reason.

SMITHERS: Well, blimey, I give yer a start, didn't I—when no one else would. I wasn't afraid to 'ire yer like the rest was —'count of the story about your breakin' jail back in the States.

JONES: No, you didn't have no s'cuse to look down on me fo' dat. You been in jail you'self more'n once.

SMITHERS [*Furiously*]: It's a lie! [*Then trying to pass it *off by an attempt at scorn.*] Garn! Who told yer that fairy tale?

JONES: Dey's some tings I ain't got to be tole. I kin see 'em in folk's eyes. [*Then after a pause—meditatively.*] Yes, you sho' give me a start. And it didn't take long from dat time to git dese fool, woods' niggers right where I wanted dem. [*With pride.*] From stowaway to Emperor in two years! Dat's goin' some!

SMITHERS [*With curiosity*]: And I bet you got yer pile o' money 'id safe some place.

JONES [*With satisfaction*]: I sho' has! And it's in a foreign bank where no pusson don't ever git it out but me no matter what come. You didn't s'pose I was holdin' down dis Emperor job for de glory in it, did you? Sho'! De fuss and glory part of it, dat's only to turn de heads o' de low-flung, bush niggers dat's here. Dey wants de big circus show for deir money. I gives it to 'em an' I gits de money. [*With a grin.*] De long green, dat's me every time! [*Then rebukingly.*] But you ain't got no kick agin me, Smithers. I'se paid you back all you done for me many times. Ain't I pertected you and winked at all de crooked tradin' you been doin' right out in de broad day? Sho' I has— and me makin' laws to stop it at de same time! [*He chuckles.*]

SMITHERS [*Grinning*]: But, meanin' no 'arm, you been grab-bin' right and left yourself, ain't yer? Look at the taxes you've put on 'em! Blimey! You've squeezed 'em dry!

JONES [*Chuckling*]: No, dey ain't *all* dry yet. I'se still heah, ain't I?

SMITHERS [*Smiling at his secret thought*]: They're dry right now, you'll find out. [*Changing the subject abruptly.*] And as for me breakin' laws, you've broke 'em all yerself just as fast as yer made 'em.

JONES: Ain't I de Emperor? De laws don't go for him. [*Judicially.*] You heah what I tells you, Smithers. Dere's little stealin' like you does, and dere's big stealin' like I does. For de little stealin' dey gits you in jail soon or late. For de big stealin' dey makes you Emperor and puts you in de Hall o' Fame when you croaks. [*Reminiscently.*] If dey's one thing I learns in ten years on de Pullman ca's listenin' to de white quality talk, it's dat same fact. And when I gits a chance to use it I winds up Emperor in two years.

SMITHERS [*Unable to repress the genuine admiration of the small fry for the large*]: Yes, yer turned the bleedin' trick, all right. Blimey, I never seen a bloke 'as 'ad the bloomin' luck you 'as.

JONES [*Severely*]: Luck? What you mean—luck?

SMITHERS: I suppose you'll say as that swank about the silver bullet ain't luck—and that was what first got the fool blacks on yer side the time of the revolution, wasn't it?

JONES [*With a laugh*]: Oh, dat silver bullet! Sho' was luck! But I makes dat luck, you heah? I loads de dice! Yessuh! When dat murderin' nigger ole Lem hired to kill me takes aim ten feet away and his gun misses fire and I shoots him dead, what you heah me say?

SMITHERS: You said yer'd got a charm so's no lead bullet'd kill yer. You was so strong only a silver bullet could kill yer, you told 'em. Blimey, wasn't that swank for yer—and plain, fat-'eaded luck?

JONES [*Proudly*]: I got brains and I uses 'em quick. Dat ain't luck.

SMITHERS: Yer know they wasn't 'ardly liable to get no silver bullets. And it was luck 'e didn't 'it you that time.

JONES [*Laughing*]: And dere all dem fool, bush niggers was kneelin' down and bumpin' deir heads on de ground like I was a miracle out o' de Bible. Oh Lawd, from dat time on I has dem all eatin' out of my hand. I cracks de whip and dey jumps through.

SMITHERS [*With a sniff*]: Yankee bluff done it.

JONES: Ain't a man's talkin' big what makes him big—long as he makes folks believe it? Sho', I talks large when I ain't got nothin' to back it up, but I ain't talkin' wild just de same. I knows I kin fool 'em—I *knows* it—and dat's backin' enough fo' my game. And ain't I got to learn deir lingo and teach some of dem English befo' I kin talk to 'em? Ain't dat wuk? You ain't never learned ary word er it, Smithers, in de ten years you been heah, dough yo' knows it's money in yo' pocket tradin' wid 'em if you does. But you'se too shiftless to take de trouble.

SMITHERS [*Flushing*]: Never mind about me. What's this I've 'eard about yer really 'avin' a silver bullet moulded for yourself?

JONES: It's playin' out my bluff. I has de silver bullet moulded and I tells 'em when de time comes I kills myself wid it. I tells 'em dat's 'cause I'm de on'y man in de world big enuff to git me. No use'n deir tryin'. And dey falls down and bumps deir heads. [*He laughs.*] I does dat so's I kin take a walk in peace widout no jealous nigger gunnin' at me from behind de trees.

SMITHERS [*Astonished*]: Then you 'ad it made—'onest?

JONES: Sho' did. Heah she be. [*He takes out his revolver, breaks it, and takes the silver bullet out of one chamber.*] Five lead an' dis silver baby at de last. Don't she shine pretty? [*He holds it in his hand, looking at it admiringly, as if strangely fascinated.*]

SMITHERS: Let me see. [*Reaches out his hand for it.*]

JONES [*Harshly*]: Keep yo' hands whar dey b'long, white man. [*He replaces it in the chamber and puts the revolver back on his hip.*]

SMITHERS [*Snarling*]: Gawd blimey! Think I'm a bleedin' thief, you would.

JONES: No, 'tain't dat. I knows you'se scared to steal from me. On'y I ain't 'lowin' nary body to touch dis baby. She's my rabbit's foot.

SMITHERS [*Sneering*]: A bloomin' charm, wot? [*Venomously.*] Well, you'll need all the bloody charms you 'as before long, s' 'elp me!

JONES [*Judicially*]: Oh, I'se good for six months yit 'fore dey gits sick o' my game. Den, when I sees trouble comin', I makes my getaway.

SMITHERS: Ho! You got it all planned, ain't yer?

JONES: I ain't no fool. I knows dis Emperor's time is sho't. Dat why I make hay when de sun shine. Was you thinkin' I'se aimin' to hold down dis job for life? No, suh! What good is gittin' money if you stays back in dis raggedy country? I wants action when I spends. And when I sees dese niggers gittin' up deir nerve to tu'n me out, and I'se got all de money in sight, I resigns on de spot and beats it quick.

SMITHERS: Where to?

JONES: None o' yo' business.

SMITHERS: Not back to the bloody States, I'll lay my oath.

JONES [*Suspiciously*]: Why don't I? [*Then with an easy laugh*] You mean 'count of dat story 'bout me breakin' from jail back dere? Dat's all talk.

SMITHERS [*Skeptically*]: Ho, yes!

JONES [*Sharply*]: You ain't 'sinuatin' I'se a liar, is you?

SMITHERS [*Hastily*]: No, Gawd strike me! I was only thinkin' o' the bloody lies you told the blacks 'ere about killin' white men in the States.

JONES [*Angered*]: How come dey're lies?

SMITHERS: You'd 'ave been in jail if you 'ad, wouldn't yer then? [*With venom*] And from what I've 'eard, it ain't 'ealthy for a black to kill a white man in the States. They burns 'em in oil, don't they?

JONES [*With cool deadliness*]: You mean lynchin' 'd scare me? Well, I tells you, Smithers, maybe I does kill one white man back dere. Maybe I does. And maybe I kills another right heah 'fore long if he don't look out.

SMITHERS [*Trying to force a laugh*]: I was on'y spoofin' yer. Can't yer take a joke? And you was just sayin' you'd never been in jail.

JONES [*In the same tone—slightly boastful*]: Maybe I goes to jail dere for gettin' in an argument wid razors ovah a crap game. Maybe I gits twenty years when dat colored man die. Maybe I gits in 'nother argument wid de prison guard was overseer ovah us when we're wukin' de roads. Maybe he hits me wid a whip and I splits his head wid a shovel and runs away and files de chain off my leg and gits away safe. Maybe I does all dat an' maybe I don't. It's a story I tells you so's you knows I'se de kind of man dat if you evah repeats one word of it, I ends yo' stealin' on dis yearth mighty damn quick!

SMITHERS [*Terrified*]: Think I'd peach on yer? Not me! Ain't I always been yer friend?

JONES [*Suddenly relaxing*]: Sho' you has—and you better be.

SMITHERS [*Recovering his composure—and with it his malice*]: And just to show yer I'm yer friend, I'll tell yer that bit o' news I was goin' to.

JONES: Go ahead! Shoot de piece. Must be bad news from de happy way you look.

SMITHERS [*Warningly*]: Maybe it's gettin' time for you to

resign—with that bloomin' silver bullet, wot? [*He finishes with a mocking grin.*]

JONES [*Puzzled*]: What's dat you say? Talk plain.

SMITHERS: Ain't noticed any of the guards or servants about the place today, I 'aven't.

JONES [*Carelessly*]: Dey're all out in de garden sleepin' under de trees. When I sleeps, dey sneaks a sleep, too, and I pretends I never suspicions it. All I got to do is to ring de bell and dey come flyin', makin' a bluff dey was wukin' all de time.

SMITHERS [*In the same mocking tone*]: Ring the bell now an' you'll bloody well see what I means.

JONES [*Startled to alertness, but preserving the same careless tone*]: Sho' I rings. [*He reaches below the throne and pulls out a big, common dinner bell which is painted the same vivid scarlet as the throne. He rings this vigorously—then stops to listen. Then he goes to both doors, rings again, and looks out.*]

SMITHERS [*Watching him with malicious satisfaction, after a pause—mockingly*]: The bloody ship is sinkin' an' the bleedin' rats 'as slung their 'ooks.

JONES [*In a sudden fit of anger flings the bell clattering into a corner*]: Low-flung, woods' niggers! [*Then catching SMITHERS' eye on him, he controls himself and suddenly bursts into a low chuckling laugh.*] Reckon I overplays my hand dis once! A man can't take de pot on a bob-tailed flush all de time. Was I sayin' I'd sit in six months mo'? Well, I'se changed my mind den. I cashes in and resigns de job of Emperor right dis minute.

SMITHERS [*With real admiration*]: Blimey, but you're a cool bird, and no mistake.

JONES: No use'n fussin'. When I knows de game's up I kisses it good-bye widout no long waits. Dey've all run off to de hills, ain't dey?

SMITHERS: Yes—every bleedin' man jack of 'em.

JONES: Den de revolution is at de post. And de Emperor better git his feet smokin' up de trail. [*He starts for the door in rear.*]

SMITHERS: Goin' out to look for your 'orse? Yer won't find any. They steals the 'orses first thing. Mine was gone when I went for 'im this mornin'. That's wot first give me a suspicion of wot was up.

JONES [*Alarmed for a second, scratches his head, then philosophically*]: Well, den I hoofs it. Feet, do yo' duty! [*He pulls out a gold watch and looks at it.*] Three-thuty. Sundown's at six-thuty or dereabouts. [*Puts his watch back—with cool confidence.*] I got plenty o' time to make it easy.

SMITHERS: Don't be so bloomin' sure of it. They'll be after you 'ot and 'eavy. Ole Lem is at the bottom o' this business an' 'e 'ates you like 'ell. 'E'd rather do for you than eat 'is dinner, 'e would!

JONES [*Scornfully*]: Dat fool no-count nigger! Does you think I'se scared o' him? I stands him on his thick head more'n once befo' dis, and I does it again if he come in my way . . . [*Fiercely.*] And dis time I leave him a dead nigger fo' sho'!

SMITHERS: You'll 'ave to cut through the big forest—an' these blacks 'ere can sniff and follow a trail in the dark like 'ounds. You'd 'ave to 'ustle to get through that forest in twelve hours even if you knew all the bloomin' trails like a native.

JONES [*With indignant scorn*]: Look-a-heah, white man! Does you think I'se a natural bo'n fool? Give me credit fo' havin' some sense, fo' Lawd's sake! Don't you s'pose I'se looked ahead and made sho' of all de chances? I'se gone out in dat big forest, pretendin' to hunt, so many times dat I knows it high an' low like a book. I could go through on dem trails wid my eyes shut. [*With great contempt.*] Think dese ign'rent bush niggers dat ain't got brains enuff to know deir own names even can catch Brutus Jones? Huh, I s'pects not! Not on yo' life! Why, man, de white men went after me wid bloodhounds where I come from an' I jes' laughs at 'em. It's a shame to fool dese black trash around heah, dey're so easy. You watch me, man! I'll make dem look sick, I will. I'll be 'cross de plain to de edge of de forest by time dark comes. Once in de woods in de night, dey got a swell chance o' findin' dis baby! Dawn tomorrow I'll be out at de oder side and on de coast whar dat French gunboat is stayin'. She picks me up, take me to Martinique when she go dar, and dere I is safe wid a mighty big bankroll in my jeans. It's easy as rollin' off a log.

SMITHERS [*Maliciously*]: But s'posin' somethin' 'appens wrong an' they do nab yer?

JONES [*Decisively*]: Dey don't—dat's de answer.

SMITHERS: But, just for argyment's sake—what'd you do?

JONES [*Frowning*]: I'se got five lead bullets in dis gun good enuff fo' common bush niggers—and after dat I got de silver bullet left to cheat 'em out o' gittin' me.

SMITHERS [*Jeeringly*]: Ho, I was fergettin' that silver bullet. You'll bump yourself orf in style, won't yer? Blimey!

JONES [*Gloomily*]: You kin bet yo whole roll on one thing, white man. Dis baby plays out his string to de end and when he quits, he quits wid a bang de way he ought. Silver bullet ain't none too good for him when he go, dat's a fac'! [*Then shaking off his nervousness—with a confident laugh.*] Sho'! What is I talkin' about? Ain't come to dat yit and I never will—not wid trash niggers like dese yere. [*Boastfully.*] Silver bullet bring me luck anyway. I kin outguess, outrun, outfight, an' outplay de whole lot o' dem all ovah de board any time o' de day er night! You watch me! [*From the distant hills comes the faint, steady thump of a tom-tom, low and vibrating. It starts at a rate exactly corresponding to normal pulse beat—72 to the minute —and continues at a gradually accelerating rate from this point uninterruptedly to the very end of the play.*]

[JONES *starts at the sound. A strange look of apprehension creeps into his face for a moment as he listens. Then he asks, with an attempt to regain his most casual manner.*] What's dat drum beatin' fo'?

SMITHERS [*With a mean grin*]: For you. That means the bleedin' ceremony 'as started. I've 'eard it before and I knows.

JONES: Cer'mony? What cer'mony?

SMITHERS: The blacks is 'oldin' a bloody meetin', 'avin' a war dance, gettin' their courage worked up b'fore they starts after you.

JONES: Let dem! Dey'll sho' need it!

SMITHERS: And they're there 'oldin' their 'eathen religious service—makin' no end of devil spells and charms to 'elp 'em against your silver bullet. [*He guffaws loudly.*] Blimey, but they're balmy as 'ell!

JONES [*A tiny bit awed and shaken in spite of himself*]: Huh! Takes more'n dat to scare dis chicken!

SMITHERS [*Scenting the other's feeling—maliciously*]: Ter-night when it's pitch black in the forest, they'll 'ave their pet devils and ghosts 'oundin' after you. You'll find yer bloody 'air 'll be standin' on end before termorrow mornin'. [*Seriously.*]

It's a bleedin' queer place, that stinkin' forest, even in daylight. Yer don't know what might 'appen in there, it's that rotten still. Always sends the cold shivers down my back minute I gets in it.

JONES [*With a contemptuous sniff*]: I ain't no chicken-liver like you is. Trees an' me, we'se friends, and dar's a full moon comin' bring me light. And let dem po' niggers make all de fool spells dey'se a min' to. Does yo' s'pect I'se silly enuff to b'lieve in ghosts an' ha'nts an' all dat ole woman's talk? G'long, white man! You ain't talkin' to me. [*With a chuckle.*] Doesn't you know dey's got to do wid a man was member in good standin' o' de Baptist Church? Sho' I was dat when I was porter on de Pullmans, befo' I gits into my little trouble. Let dem try deir heathen tricks. De Baptist Church done pertect me and land dem all in hell. [*Then with more confident satisfaction.*] And I'se got little silver bullet o' my own, don't forgit.

SMITHERS: Ho! You 'aven't give much 'eed to your Baptist Church since you been down 'ere. I've 'eard myself you 'ad turned yer coat an' was takin' up with their blarsted witch-doctors, or whatever the 'ell yer calls the swine.

JONES [*Vehemently*]: I pretends to! Sho' I pretends! Dat's part o' my game from de fust. If I finds out dem niggers believes dat black is white, den I yells it out louder 'n deir loudest. It don't git me nothin' to do missionary work for de Baptist Church. I'se after de coin, an' I lays my Jesus on de shelf for de time bein'. [*Stops abruptly to look at his watch—alertly.*] But I ain't got de time to waste no more fool talk wid you. I'se gwine away from heah dis secon'. [*He reaches in under the throne and pulls out an expensive Panama hat with a bright multi-colored band and sets it jauntily on his head.*] So long, white man! [*With a grin.*] See you in jail sometime, maybe!

SMITHERS: Not me, you won't. Well, I wouldn't be in yer bloody boots for no bloomin' money, but 'ere's wishin' yer luck just the same.

JONES [*Contemptuously*]: You're de frightenedest man evah I see! I tells you I'se safe's 'f I was in New York City. It takes dem niggers from now to dark to git up de nerve to start somethin'. By dat time, I'se got a head start dey never kotch up wid.

SMITHERS [*Maliciously*]: Give my regards to any ghosts yer meets up with.

JONES [*Grinning*]: If dat ghost got money, I'll tell him never ha'nt you less'n he wants to lose it.

SMITHERS [*Flattered*]: Garn! [*Then curiously.*] Ain't yer takin' no luggage with yer?

JONES: I travels light when I wants to move fast. And I got tinned grub buried on de edge o' de forest. [*Boastfully.*] Now say dat I don't look ahead an' use my brains! [*With a wide, liberal gesture.*] I will all dat's left in de palace to you—and you better grab all you kin sneak away wid befo' dey gits here.

SMITHERS [*Gratefully*]: Righto—and thanks ter yer. [*As JONES walks toward the door in rear—cautioningly.*] Say! Look 'ere, you ain't goin' out that way, are yer?

JONES: Does you think I'd slink out de back door like a common nigger? I'se Emperor yit, ain't I? And de Emperor Jones leaves de way he comes, and dat black trash don't dare stop him—not yit, leastways. [*He stops for a moment in the doorway, listening to the far-off but insistent beat of the tom-tom.*] Listen to dat roll-call, will you? Must be mighty big drum carry dat far. [*Then with a laugh.*] Well, if dey ain't no whole brass band to see me off, I sho' got de drum part of it. So long, white man. [*He puts his hands in his pockets and with studied carelessness, whistling a tune, he saunters out of the doorway and off to the left.*]

SMITHERS [*Looks after him with a puzzled admiration*]: 'E's got 'is bloomin' nerve with 'im, s'elp me! [*Then angrily.*] Ho— the bleedin' nigger—puttin' on 'is bloody airs! I 'opes they nabs 'im an' gives 'im what's what! [*Then putting business before the pleasure of this thought, looking around him with cupidity.*] A bloke ought to find a 'ole lot in this palace that'd go for a bit of cash. Let's take a look, 'Arry, me lad. [*He starts for the doorway on right as*

[*The Curtain Falls.*]

SCENE TWO

SCENE—*Nightfall. The end of the plain where the Great Forest begins. The foreground is sandy, level ground dotted by*

*a few stones and clumps of stunted bushes cowering close
against the earth to escape the buffeting of the trade wind.
In the rear the forest is a wall of darkness dividing the world.
Only when the eye becomes accustomed to the gloom can the
outlines of separate trunks of the nearest trees be made out,
enormous pillars of deeper blackness. A somber monotone
of wind lost in the leaves moans in the air. Yet this sound
serves but to intensify the impression of the forest's relentless
immobility, to form a background throwing into relief its
brooding, implacable silence.*

[JONES *enters from the left, walking rapidly. He stops
as he nears the edge of the forest, looks around him quickly,
peering into the dark as if searching for some familiar land-
mark. Then, apparently satisfied that he is where he ought
to be, he throws himself on the ground, dog-tired.*]

Well, heah I is. In de nick o' time, too! Little mo' an' it'd
be blacker'n de ace of spades heahabouts. [*He pulls a bandana
handkerchief from his hip pocket and mops off his perspiring
face.*] Sho'! Gimme air! I'se tuckered out sho' nuff. Dat soft
Emperor job ain't no trainin' fo' a long hike ovah dat plain in
de brilin' sun. [*Then with a chuckle.*] Cheah up, nigger, de
worst is yet to come. [*He lifts his head and stares at the forest.
His chuckle peters out abruptly. In a tone of awe.*] My goodness, look at dem woods, will you? Dat no-count Smithers said
dey'd be black an' he sho' called de turn. [*Turning away from
them quickly and looking down at his feet, he snatches at a
chance to change the subject—solicitously.*] Feet, you is holdin'
up yo' end fine an' I sutinly hopes you ain't blisterin' none. It's
time you git a rest. [*He takes off his shoes, his eyes studiously
avoiding the forest. He feels of the soles of his feet gingerly.*]
You is still in de pink—on'y a little mite feverish. Cool yo'selfs.
Remember you done got a long journey yit befo' you. [*He sits
in a weary attitude, listening to the rhythmic beating of the
tom-tom. He grumbles in a loud tone to cover up a growing
uneasiness.*] Bush niggers! Wonder dey wouldn' git sick o'
beatin' dat drum. Sound louder, seem like. I wonder if dey's
startin' after me? [*He scrambles to his feet, looking back
across the plain.*] Couldn't see dem now, nohow, if dey was
hundred feet away. [*Then shaking himself like a wet dog to*

get rid of these depressing thoughts.] Sho', dey's miles an' miles behind. What you gittin' fidgety about? [*But he sits down and begins to lace up his shoes in great haste, all the time muttering reassuringly.*] You know what? Yo' belly is empty, dat's what's de matter wid you. Come time to eat! Wid nothin' but wind on yo' stumach, o' course you feels jiggedy. Well, we eats right heah an' now soon's I gits dese pesky shoes laced up! [*He finishes lacing up his shoes.*] Dere! Now le's see. [*Gets on his hands and knees and searches the ground around him with his eyes.*] White stone, white stone, where is you? [*He sees the first white stone and crawls to it—with satisfaction.*] Heah you is! I knowed dis was de right place. Box of grub, come to me. [*He turns over the stone and feels in under it—in a tone of dismay.*] Ain't heah! Gorry, is I in de right place or isn't I? Dere's 'nother stone. Guess dat's it. [*He scrambles to the next stone and turns it over.*] Ain't heah, neither! Grub, whar is you? Ain't heah. Gorry, has I got to go hungry into dem woods—all de night? [*While he is talking he scrambles from one stone to another, turning them over in frantic haste. Finally, he jumps to his feet excitedly.*] Is I lost de place? Must have! But how dat happen when I was followin' de trail across de plain in broad daylight? [*Almost plaintively.*] I'se hungry, I is! I gotta git my feed. Whar's my strength gonna come from if I doesn't? Gorry, I gotta find dat grub high an' low somehow! Why it come dark so quick like dat? Can't see nothin'. [*He scratches a match on his trousers and peers about him. The rate of the beat of the far-off tom-tom increases perceptibly as he does so. He mutters in a bewildered voice.*] How come all dese white stones come heah when I only remembers one? [*Suddenly, with a frightened gasp, he flings the match on the ground and stamps on it.*] Nigger, is you gone crazy mad? Is you lightin' matches to show dem whar you is? Fo' Lawd's sake, use yo' haid. Gorry, I'se got to be careful! [*He stares at the plain behind him apprehensively, his hand on his revolver.*] But how come all dese white stones? And whar's dat tin box o' grub I had all wrapped up in oil cloth?

[*While his back is turned, the* LITTLE FORMLESS FEARS *creep out from the deeper blackness of the forest. They are black, shapeless, only their glittering little eyes can be seen. If they have any describable form at all it is that of a grubworm about the size of a creeping child. They move noiselessly, but with deliberate, painful effort, striving to raise themselves on end, failing and sinking prone again.* JONES *turns about to face the forest. He stares up at the tops of the trees, seeking vainly to discover his whereabouts by their conformation.*]

Can't tell nothin' from dem trees! Gorry, nothin' 'round heah look like I evah seed it befo'. I'se done lost de place sho' 'nuff! [*With mournful foreboding.*] It's mighty queer! It's mighty queer! [*With sudden forced defiance—in an angry tone.*] Woods, is you tryin' to put somethin' ovah on me?

[*From the formless creatures on the ground in front of him comes a tiny gale of low mocking laughter like a rustling of leaves. They squirm upward toward him in twisted attitudes.* JONES *looks down, leaps backward with a yell of terror, yanking out his revolver as he does so—in a quavering voice.*] What's dat? Who's dar? What is you? Git away from me befo' I shoots you up! You don't? . . .

[*He fires. There is a flash, a loud report, then silence broken only by the far-off, quickened throb of the tom-tom. The formless creatures have scurried back into the forest.* JONES *remains fixed in his position, listening intently. The sound of the shot, the reassuring feel of the revolver in his hand, have somewhat restored his shaken nerve. He addresses himself with renewed confidence.*]

Dey're gone. Dat shot fix 'em. Dey was only little animals—little wild pigs, I reckon. Dey've maybe rooted out yo' grub an' eat it. Sho', you fool nigger, what you think dey is—ha'nts? [*Excitedly.*] Gorry, you give de game away when you fire dat shot. Dem niggers heah dat fo' su'tin! Time you beat it in de woods widout no long waits. [*He starts for the forest—hesitates before the plunge—then urging himself in with manful resolution.*] Git in, nigger! What you skeered at? Ain't nothin' dere but de trees! Git in! [*He plunges boldly into the forest.*]

SCENE THREE

SCENE—*Nine o'clock. In the forest. The moon has just risen. Its beams, drifting through the canopy of leaves, make a barely perceptible, suffused, eerie glow. A dense low wall of underbrush and creepers is in the nearer foreground, fencing in a small triangular clearing. Beyond this is the massed blackness of the forest like an encompassing barrier. A path is dimly discerned leading down to the clearing from left, rear, and winding away from it again toward the right. As the scene opens nothing can be distinctly made out. Except for the beating of the tom-tom, which is a trifle louder and quicker than in the previous scene, there is silence, broken every few seconds by a queer, clicking sound. Then gradually the figure of the negro, JEFF, can be discerned crouching on his haunches at the rear of the triangle. He is middle-aged, thin, brown in color, is dressed in a Pullman porter's uniform, cap, etc. He is throwing a pair of dice on the ground before him, picking them up, shaking them, casting them out with the regular, rigid, mechanical movements of an automaton. The heavy, plodding footsteps of someone approaching along the trail from the left are heard and JONES' voice, pitched in a slightly higher key and strained in a cheering effort to overcome its own tremors.*

De moon's rizen. Does you heah dat, nigger? You gits more light from dis out. No mo' buttin' yo' fool head agin' de trunks an' scratchin' de hide off yo' legs in de bushes. Now you sees whar yo'se gwine. So cheer up! From now on you has a snap. [*He steps just to the rear of the triangular clearing and mops off his face on his sleeve. He has lost his Panama hat. His face is scratched, his brilliant uniform shows several large rents.*] What time's it gittin' to be, I wonder? I dassent light no match to find out. Phoo'. It's wa'm an' dat's a fac'! [*Wearily.*] How long I been makin' tracks in dese woods? Must be hours an' hours. Seems like fo'evah! Yit can't be, when de moon's jes' riz. Dis am a long night fo' yo', yo' Majesty! [*With a mournful chuckle.*] Majesty! Der ain't much majesty 'bout dis baby now. [*With attempted cheerfulness.*] Never min'. It's all part o' de game. Dis night come to an end like everything else. And when you gits dar safe and has dat bankroll in yo' hands you laughs at all dis. [*He starts to whistle but checks himself abruptly.*] What yo' whistlin' for, you po' dope! Want all de worl' to heah you? [*He stops talking to listen.*] Heah dat ole drum! Sho' gits nearer from de sound. Dey're packin' it along wid 'em.

Time fo' me to move. [*He takes a step forward, then stops—worriedly.*] What's dat odder queer clickety sound I heah? Dere it is! Sound close! Sound like—sound like—Fo' God sake, sound like some nigger was shootin' crap! [*Frightenedly.*] I better beat it quick when I gits dem notions. [*He walks quickly into the clear space—then stands transfixed as he sees* JEFF—*in a terrified gasp.*] Who dar? Who dat? Is dat you, Jeff? [*Starting toward the other, forgetful for a moment of his surroundings and really believing it is a living man that he sees—in a tone of happy relief.*] Jeff! I'se sho' mighty glad to see you! Dey tol' me you done died from dat razor cut I gives you. [*Stopping suddenly, bewilderedly.*] But how you come to be heah, nigger? [*He stares fascinatedly at the other who continues his mechanical play with the dice.* JONES' *eyes begin to roll wildly. He stutters.*] Ain't you gwine—look up—can't you speak to me? Is you—is you—a ha'nt? [*He jerks out his revolver in a frenzy of terrified rage.*] Nigger, I kills you dead once. Has I got to kill you again? You take it den. [*He fires. When the smoke clears away* JEFF *has disappeared.* JONES *stands trembling—then with a certain reassurance.*] He's gone, anyway. Ha'nt or no ha'nt, dat shot fix him. [*The beat of the far-off tom-tom is perceptibly louder and more rapid.* JONES *becomes conscious of it—with a start, looking back over his shoulder.*] Dey's gittin' near! Dey's comin' fast! And heah I is shootin' shots to let 'em know jes' whar I is. Oh, Gorry, I'se got to run. [*Forgetting the path he plunges wildly into the underbrush in the rear and disappears in the shadow.*]

SCENE FOUR

SCENE—*Eleven o'clock. In the forest. A wide dirt road runs diagonally from right, front, to left, rear. Rising sheer on both sides the forest walls it in. The moon is now up. Under its light the road glimmers ghastly and unreal. It is as if the forest had stood aside momentarily to let the road pass through and accomplish its veiled purpose. This done, the forest will fold in upon itself again and the road will be no more.* JONES *stumbles in from the forest on the right. His uniform is ragged and torn. He looks about him with numbed surprise when he sees the road, his eyes blinking in the bright*

*moonlight. He flops down exhaustedly and pants heavily for
a while. Then with sudden anger.*

I'm meltin' wid heat! Runnin' an' runnin' an' runnin'! Damn
dis heah coat! Like a strait-jacket! [*He tears off his coat and
flings it away from him, revealing himself stripped to the
waist.*] Dere! Dat's better! Now I kin breathe! [*Looking down
at his feet, the spurs catch his eye.*] And to hell wid dese high-
fangled spurs. Dey're what's been a-trippin' me up an' breakin'
my neck. [*He unstraps them and flings them away dis-
gustedly.*] Dere! I gits rid o' dem frippety Emperor trappin's
an' I travels lighter. Lawd! I'se tired! [*After a pause, listening to the insistent beat of the tom-tom in the distance.*] I
must 'a put some distance between myself an' dem—runnin'
like dat—and yit—dat damn drum sound jes' de same—nearer,
even. Well, I guess I a'most holds my lead anyhow. Dey won't
never catch up. [*With a sigh.*] If on'y my fool legs stands up.
Oh, I'se sorry I evah went in for dis. Dat Emperor job is sho'
hard to shake. [*He looks around him suspiciously.*] How'd dis
road evah git heah? Good level road, too. I never remembers
seein' it befo'. [*Shaking his head apprehensively.*] Dese woods
is sho' full o' de queerest things at night. [*With a sudden
terror.*] Lawd God, don't let me see no more o' dem ha'nts!
Dey gits my goat! [*Then trying to talk himself into confidence.*]
Ha'nts! You fool nigger, dey ain't no such things! Don't de
Baptist parson tell you dat many time? Is you civilized, or is
you like dese ign'rent black niggers heah? Sho'! Dat was all
in yo' own head. Wasn't nothin' dere. Wasn't no Jeff! Know
what? You jus' get seein' dem things 'cause yo' belly's empty
and you's sick wid hunger inside. Hunger 'fects yo' head and
yo' eyes. Any fool know dat. [*Then pleading fervently.*] But
bless God, I don't come across no more o' dem, whatever dey
is! [*Then cautiously.*] Rest! Don't talk! Rest! You needs it.
Den you gits on yo' way again. [*Looking at the moon.*] Night's
half gone a'most. You hits de coast in de mawning! Den you'se
all safe.

[*From the right forward a small gang of Negroes enter. They
are dressed in striped convict suits, their heads are shaven, one
leg drags limpingly, shackled to a heavy ball and chain. Some
carry picks, the others shovels. They are followed by a white*

man dressed in the uniform of a prison guard. A Winchester rifle is slung across his shoulders and he carries a heavy whip. At a signal from the GUARD *they stop on the road opposite where* JONES *is sitting.* JONES, *who has been staring up at the sky, unmindful of their noiseless approach, suddenly looks down and sees them. His eyes pop out, he tries to get to his feet and fly, but sinks back, too numbed by fright to move. His voice catches in a choking prayer.*]

Lawd Jesus!

[*The* PRISON GUARD *cracks his whip—noiselessly—and at that signal all the convicts start to work on the road. They swing their picks, they shovel, but not a sound comes from their labor. Their movements, like those of* JEFF *in the preceding scene, are those of automatons,—rigid, slow, and mechanical. The* PRISON GUARD *points sternly at* JONES *with his whip, motions him to take his place among the other shovelers.* JONES *gets to his feet in a hypnotized stupor. He mumbles subserviently.*]

Yes, suh! Yes, suh! I'se comin'.

[*As he shuffles, dragging one foot, over to his place, he curses under his breath with rage and hatred.*]

God damn yo' soul, I gits even wid you yit, sometime.

[*As if there were a shovel in his hands he goes through weary, mechanical gestures of digging up dirt, and throwing it to the roadside. Suddenly the* GUARD *approaches him angrily, threateningly. He raises his whip and lashes* JONES *viciously across the shoulders with it.* JONES *winces with pain and cowers abjectly. The* GUARD *turns his back on him and walks away contemptuously. Instantly* JONES *straightens up. With arms upraised as if his shovel were a club in his hands he springs murderously at the unsuspecting* GUARD. *In the act of crashing down his shovel on the white man's skull,* JONES *suddenly becomes aware that his hands are empty. He cries despairingly.*]

Whar's my shovel? Gimme my shovel till I splits his damn head! [*Appealing to his fellow convicts.*] Gimme a shovel, one o' you, fo' God's sake!

[*They stand fixed in motionless attitudes, their eyes on the ground. The* GUARD *seems to wait expectantly, his back turned to the attacker.* JONES *bellows with baffled, terrified rage, tugging frantically at his revolver.*]

I kills you, you white debil, if it's de last thing I evah does! Ghost or debil, I kill you again!

[*He frees the revolver and fires point blank at the* GUARD'S *back. Instantly the walls of the forest close in from both sides, the road and the figures of the convict gang are blotted out in an enshrouding darkness. The only sounds are a crashing in the underbrush as* JONES *leaps away in mad flight and the throbbing of the tom-tom, still far distant, but increased in volume of sound and rapidity of beat.*]

SCENE FIVE

SCENE—*One o'clock. A large circular clearing, enclosed by the serried ranks of gigantic trunks of tall trees whose tops are lost to view. In the center is a big dead stump worn by time into a curious resemblance to an auction block. The moon floods the clearing with a clear light.* JONES *forces his way in through the forest on the left. He looks wildly about the clearing with hunted, fearful glances. His pants are in tatters, his shoes cut and misshapen, flapping about his feet. He slinks cautiously to the stump in the center and sits down in a tense position, ready for instant flight. Then he holds his head in his hands and rocks back and forth, moaning to himself miserably.*

Oh Lawd, Lawd! Oh Lawd, Lawd! [*Suddenly he throws himself on his knees and raises his clasped hands to the sky—in a voice of agonized pleading.*] Lawd Jesus, heah my prayer! I'se a po' sinner, a po' sinner! I knows I done wrong, I knows it! When I cotches Jeff cheatin' wid loaded dice my anger overcomes me and I kills him dead! Lawd, I done wrong! When dat guard hits me wid de whip, my anger overcomes me, and I kills him dead. Lawd, I done wrong! And down heah whar dese fool bush niggers raises me up to de seat o' de mighty, I steals all I could grab. Lawd, I done wrong! I knows it! I'se sorry! Forgive me, Lawd! Forgive dis po' sinner! [*Then beseeching terrifiedly.*] And keep dem away, Lawd! Keep dem away from me! And stop dat drum soundin' in my ears! Dat begin to sound ha'nted, too. [*He gets to his feet, evidently slightly reassured*

by his prayer—with attempted confidence.] De Lawd'll preserve me from dem ha'nts after dis. [*Sits down on the stump
again.*] I ain't skeered o' real men. Let dem come. But dem
odders . . . [*He shudders—then looks down at his feet, working his toes inside the shoes—with a groan.*] Oh, my po' feet!
Dem shoes ain't no use no more 'ceptin' to hurt. I'se better off
widout dem. [*He unlaces them and pulls them off—holds the
wrecks of the shoes in his hands and regards them mournfully.*]
You was real, A-one patin' leather, too. Look at you now. Emperor, you'se gittin' mighty low!

[*He sits dejectedly and remains with bowed shoulders, staring down at the shoes in his hands as if reluctant to throw them
away. While his attention is thus occupied, a crowd of figures
silently enter the clearing from all sides. All are dressed in
Southern costumes of the period of the fifties of the last century. There are middle-aged men who are evidently well-to-do
planters. There is one spruce, authoritative individual—the*
AUCTIONEER. *There is a crowd of curious spectators, chiefly
young belles and dandies who have come to the slave-market
for diversion. All exchange courtly greetings in dumb show and
chat silently together. There is something stiff, rigid, unreal,
marionettish about their movements. They group themselves
about the stump. Finally a batch of slaves are led in from the
left by an attendant—three men of different ages, two women,
one with a baby in her arms, nursing. They are placed to the
left of the stump, beside* JONES.

*The white planters look them over appraisingly as if they
were cattle, and exchange judgments on each. The dandies point
with their fingers and make witty remarks. The belles titter
bewitchingly. All this in silence save for the ominous throb of
the tom-tom. The* AUCTIONEER *holds up his hand, taking his
place at the stump. The group strain forward attentively. He
touches* JONES *on the shoulder peremptorily, motioning for him
to stand on the stump—the auction block.*

JONES *looks up, sees the figures on all sides, looks wildly for
some opening to escape, sees none, screams and leaps madly
to the top of the stump to get as far away from them as possible. He stands there, cowering, paralyzed with horror. The*
AUCTIONEER *begins his silent spiel. He points to* JONES, *appeals*

to the planters to see for themselves. Here is a good field hand, sound in wind and limb as they can see. Very strong still in spite of his being middle-aged. Look at that back. Look at those shoulders. Look at the muscles in his arms and his sturdy legs. Capable of any amount of hard labor. Moreover, of a good disposition, intelligent and tractable. Will any gentleman start the bidding? The PLANTERS *raise their fingers, make their bids. They are apparently all eager to possess* JONES. *The bidding is lively, the crowd interested. While this has been going on,* JONES *has been seized by the courage of desperation. He dares to look down and around him. Over his face abject terror gives way to mystification, to gradual realization—stutteringly.*]

What you all doin', white folks? What's all dis? What you all lookin' at me fo'? What you doin' wid me, anyhow? [*Suddenly convulsed with raging hatred and fear.*] Is dis a auction? Is you sellin' me like dey uster befo' de war? [*Jerking out his revolver just as the* AUCTIONEER *knocks him down to one of the planters—glaring from him to the purchaser.*] And *you* sells me? And *you* buys me? I shows you I'se a free nigger, damn yo' souls! [*He fires at the* AUCTIONEER *and at the* PLANTER *with such rapidity that the two shots are almost simultaneous. As if this were a signal the walls of the forest fold in. Only blackness remains and silence broken by* JONES *as he rushes off, crying with fear—and by the quickened, ever louder beat of the tom-tom.*]

SCENE SIX

SCENE—*Three o'clock. A cleared space in the forest. The limbs of the trees meet over it forming a low ceiling about five feet from the ground. The interlocked ropes of creepers reaching upward to entwine the tree trunks give an arched appearance to the sides. The space thus enclosed is like the dark, noisome hold of some ancient vessel. The moonlight is almost completely shut out and only a vague, wan light filters through. There is the noise of someone approaching from the left, stumbling and crawling through the undergrowth.* JONES' *voice is heard between chattering moans.*

Oh, Lawd, what I gwine do now? Ain't got no bullet left on'y de silver one. If mo' o' dem ha'nts come after me, how I gwine skeer dem away? Oh, Lawd, on'y de silver one left— an' I gotta save dat fo' luck. If I shoots dat one I'm a goner sho'! Lawd, it's black heah! Whar's de moon? Oh, Lawd, don't dis night evah come to an end? [*By the sounds, he is feeling his way cautiously forward.*] Dere! Dis feels like a clear space. I gotta lie down an' rest. I don't care if dem niggers does cotch me. I gotta rest.

[*He is well forward now where his figure can be dimly made out. His pants have been so torn away that what is left of them is no better than a breech cloth. He flings himself full length, face downward on the ground, panting with exhaustion. Gradually it seems to grow lighter in the enclosed space and two rows of seated figures can be seen behind* JONES. *They are sitting in crumpled, despairing attitudes, hunched, facing one another with their backs touching the forest walls as if they were shackled to them. All are Negroes, naked save for loin cloths. At first they are silent and motionless. Then they begin to sway slowly forward toward each other and back again in unison, as if they were laxly letting themselves follow the long roll of a ship at sea. At the same time, a low, melancholy murmur rises among them, increasing gradually by rhythmic degrees which seem to be directed and controlled by the throb of the tom-tom in the distance, to a long, tremulous wail of despair that reaches a certain pitch, unbearably acute, then falls by slow gradations of tone into silence and is taken up again.* JONES *starts, looks up, sees the figures, and throws himself down again to shut out the sight. A shudder of terror shakes his whole body as the wail rises up about him again. But the next time, his voice, as if under some uncanny compulsion, starts with the others. As their chorus lifts he rises to a sitting posture similar to the others, swaying back and forth. His voice reaches the highest pitch of sorrow, of desolation. The light fades out, the other voices cease, and only darkness is left.* JONES *can be heard scrambling to his feet and running off, his voice sinking down the scale and receding as he moves farther and farther away in the forest. The tom-tom beats louder, quicker, with a more insistent, triumphant pulsation.*]

SCENE SEVEN

SCENE—*Five o'clock. The foot of a gigantic tree by the edge of a great river. A rough structure of boulders, like an altar, is by the tree. The raised river bank is in the nearer background. Beyond this the surface of the river spreads out, brilliant and unruffled in the moonlight, blotted out and merged into a veil of bluish mist in the distance.* JONES' *voice is heard from the left rising and falling in the long, despairing wail of the chained slaves, to the rhythmic beat of the tom-tom. As his voice sinks into silence, he enters the open space. The expression of his face is fixed and stony, his eyes have an obsessed glare, he moves with a strange deliberation like a sleepwalker or one in a trance. He looks around at the tree, the rough stone altar, the moonlit surface of the river beyond, and passes his hand over his head with a vague gesture of puzzled bewilderment. Then, as if in obedience to some obscure impulse, he sinks into a kneeling, devotional posture before the altar. Then he seems to come to himself partly, to have an uncertain realization of what he is doing, for he straightens up and stares about him horrifiedly—in an incoherent mumble.*

What—what is I doin'? What is—dis place? Seems like— seems like I know dat tree—an' dem stones—an' de river. I remember—seems like I been heah befo'. [*Tremblingly.*] Oh, Gorry, I'se skeered in dis place! I'se skeered! Oh, Lawd, pertect dis sinner!

[*Crawling away from the altar, he cowers close to the ground, his face hidden, his shoulders heaving with sobs of hysterical fright. From behind the trunk of the tree, as if he had sprung out of it, the figure of the* CONGO WITCH-DOCTOR *appears. He is wizened and old, naked except for the fur of some small animal tied about his waist, its bushy tail hanging down in front. His body is stained all over a bright red. Antelope horns are on each side of his head, branching upward. In one hand he carries a bone rattle, in the other a charm stick with a bunch of white cockatoo feathers tied to the end. A great number of glass beads*

*and bone ornaments are about his neck, ears, wrists, and ankles.
He struts noiselessly with a queer prancing step to a position in
the clear ground between* JONES *and the altar. Then with a
preliminary, summoning stamp of his foot on the earth, he
begins to dance and to chant. As if in response to his summons
the beating of the tom-tom grows to a fierce, exultant boom
whose throbs seem to fill the air with vibrating rhythm.* JONES
*looks up, starts to spring to his feet, reaches a half-kneeling,
half-squatting position and remains rigidly fixed there, paralyzed with awed fascination by this new apparition. The
*WITCH-DOCTOR *sways, stamping with his foot, his bone rattle
clicking the time. His voice rises and falls in a weird, monot-
onous croon, without articulate word divisions. Gradually his
dance becomes clearly one of a narrative in pantomime, his
croon is an incantation, a charm to allay the fierceness of some
implacable deity demanding sacrifice. He flees, he is pursued
by devils, he hides, he flees again. Ever wilder and wilder becomes his flight, nearer and nearer draws the pursuing evil,
more and more the spirit of terror gains possession of him. His
croon, rising to intensity, is punctuated by shrill cries.* JONES
*has become completely hypnotized. His voice joins in the in-
cantation, in the cries, he beats time with his hands and sways
his body to and fro from the waist. The whole spirit and meaning of the dance has entered into him, has become his spirit.
Finally the theme of the pantomime halts on a howl of despair,
and is taken up again in a note of savage hope. There is a sal-
vation. The forces of evil demand sacrifice. They must be ap-
peased. The* WITCH-DOCTOR *points with his wand to the sacred
tree, to the river beyond, to the altar, and finally to* JONES
with a ferocious command. JONES *seems to sense the meaning of
this. It is he who must offer himself for sacrifice. He beats his
forehead abjectly to the ground, moaning hysterically.]*

Mercy, Oh Lawd! Mercy! Mercy on dis po' sinner.

[The WITCH-DOCTOR *springs to the river bank. He stretches
out his arms and calls to some god within its depths. Then he
starts backward slowly, his arms remaining out. A huge head
of a crocodile appears over the bank and its eyes, glittering
greenly, fasten upon* JONES. *He stares into them fascinatedly.
The* WITCH-DOCTOR *prances up to him, touches him with his
wand, motions with hideous command toward the waiting mon-*

ster. JONES *squirms on his belly nearer and nearer, moaning continually.*]

Mercy, Lawd! Mercy!

[*The crocodile heaves more of his enormous bulk onto the land.* JONES *squirms toward him. The* WITCH-DOCTOR'S *voice shrills out in furious exultation, the tom-tom beats madly.* JONES *cries out in a fierce, exhausted spasm of anguished pleading.*]

Lawd, save me! Lawd Jesus, heah my prayer!

[*Immediately, in answer to his prayer, comes the thought of the one bullet left him. He snatches at his hip, shouting defiantly.*]

De silver bullet! You don't git me yit!

[*He fires at the green eyes in front of him. The head of the crocodile sinks back behind the river bank, the* WITCH-DOCTOR *springs behind the sacred tree and disappears.* JONES *lies with his face to the ground, his arms outstretched, whimpering with fear as the throb of the tom-tom fills the silence about him with a somber pulsation, a baffled but revengeful power.*]

SCENE EIGHT

SCENE—*Dawn. Same as Scene Two, the dividing line of forest and plain. The nearest tree trunks are dimly revealed but the forest behind them is still a mass of glooming shadows. The tom-tom seems on the very spot, so loud and continuously vibrating are its beats.* LEM *enters from the left, followed by a small squad of his soldiers, and by the Cockney trader,* SMITHERS. LEM *is a heavy-set, ape-faced old savage of the extreme African type, dressed only in a loin cloth. A revolver and cartridge belt are about his waist. His soldiers are in different degrees of rag-concealed nakedness. All wear broad palm-leaf hats. Each one carries a rifle.* SMITHERS *is the same as in Scene One. One of the soldiers, evidently a tracker, is peering about keenly on the ground. He grunts and points to the spot where* JONES *entered the forest.* LEM *and* SMITHERS *come to look.*

SMITHERS [*After a glance, turns away in disgust*]: That's where 'e went in right enough. Much good it'll do yer. 'E's miles orf by this an' safe to the Coast, damn 'is 'ide! I tole yer yer'd lose 'im, didn't I?—wastin' the 'ole bloomin' night beatin' yer bloody drum and castin' yer silly spells! Gawd blimey, wot a pack!

LEM [*Gutturally*]: We cotch him. You see. [*He makes a motion to his soldiers who squat down on their haunches in a semicircle.*]

SMITHERS [*Exasperatedly*]: Well, ain't yer goin' in an' 'unt 'im in the woods? What the 'ell's the good of waitin'?

LEM [*Imperturbably—squatting down himself*]: We cotch him.

SMITHERS [*Turning away from him contemptuously*]: Aw! Garn! 'E's a better man than the lot o' you put together. I 'ates the sight o' 'im but I'll say that for 'im. [*A sound of snapping twigs comes from the forest. The soldiers jump to their feet, cocking their rifles alertly.* LEM *remains sitting with an imperturbable expression, but listening intently. The sound from the woods is repeated.* LEM *makes a quick signal with his hand. His followers creep quickly but noiselessly into the forest, scattering so that each enters at a different spot.*]

SMITHERS [*In the silence that follows—in a contemptuous whisper*]: You ain't thinkin' that would be 'im, I 'ope?

LEM [*Calmly*]: We cotch him.

SMITHERS: Blarsted fat 'eads! [*Then after a second's thought—wonderingly.*] Still an' all, it might 'appen. If 'e lost 'is bloody way in these stinkin' woods 'e'd likely turn in a circle without 'is knowin' it. They all does.

LEM [*Peremptorily*]: Sssh! [*The reports of several rifles sound from the forest, followed a second later by savage, exultant yells. The beating of the tom-tom abruptly ceases.* LEM *looks up at the white man with a grin of satisfaction.*] We cotch him. Him dead.

SMITHERS [*With a snarl*]: 'Ow d'yer know it's 'im an' 'ow d'yer know 'e's dead?

LEM: My mens dey got 'um silver bullets. Dey kill him shore.

SMITHERS [*Astonished*]: They got silver bullets?

LEM: Lead bullet no kill him. He got um strong charm. I cook um money, make um silver bullet, make um strong charm, too.

SMITHERS [*Light breaking upon him*]: So that's wot you was up to all night, wot? You was scared to put after 'im till you'd moulded silver bullets, eh?

LEM [*Simply stating a fact*]: Yes. Him got strong charm. Lead no good.

SMITHERS [*Slapping his thigh and guffawing*]: Haw-haw! If yer don't beat all 'ell! [*Then recovering himself—scornfully.*] I'll bet yer it ain't 'im they shot at all, yer bleedin' looney!

LEM [*Calmly*]: Dey come bring him now. [*The soldiers come out of the forest, carrying* JONES' *limp body. There is a little reddish-purple hole under his left breast. He is dead. They carry him to* LEM, *who examines his body with great satisfaction.* SMITHERS *leans over his shoulder—in a tone of frightened awe.*] Well, they did for yer right enough, Jonsey, me lad! Dead as a 'erring! [*Mockingly.*] Where's yer 'igh an' mighty airs now, yer bloomin' Majesty? [*Then with a grin.*] Silver bullets! Gawd blimey, but yer died in the 'eighth o' style, any'ow! [LEM *makes a motion to the soldiers to carry the body out left.* SMITHERS *speaks to him sneeringly.*]

SMITHERS: And I s'pose you think it's yer bleedin' charms and yer silly beatin' the drum that made 'im run in a circle when 'e'd lost 'imself, don't yer? [*But* LEM *makes no reply, does not seem to hear the question, walks out left after his men.* SMITHERS *looks after him with contemptuous scorn.*] Stupid as 'ogs, the lot of 'em! Blarsted niggers!

[*Curtain Falls.*]

Maxwell Anderson

WINTERSET

CHARACTERS

TROCK	JUDGE GAUNT
SHADOW	CARR
LUCIA	MIO
PINY	HERMAN
MIRIAMNE	A SAILOR
GARTH	STREET URCHIN
ESDRAS	POLICEMAN
1ST GIRL	RADICAL
2ND GIRL	SERGEANT
THE HOBO	URCHINS

TWO YOUNG MEN IN SERGE

ACT ONE

SCENE I

SCENE—*The scene is the bank of a river under a bridgehead.
A gigantic span starts from the rear of the stage and appears
to lift over the heads of the audience and out to the left. At
the right rear is a wall of solid supporting masonry. To the
left an apartment building abuts against the bridge and forms
the left wall of the stage with a dark basement window and
a door in the brick wall. To the right, and in the foreground,
an outcropping of original rock makes a barricade behind
which one may enter through a cleft. To the rear, against the
masonry, two sheds have been built by waifs and strays for
shelter. The riverbank, in the foreground, is black rock worn
smooth by years of trampling. There is room for exit and
entrance to the left around the apartment house, also around
the rock to the right. A single street lamp is seen at the left
—and a glimmer of apartment lights in the background beyond. It is an early, dark, December morning.*

TWO YOUNG MEN IN SERGE *lean against the masonry,
matching bills.* TROCK ESTRELLA *and* SHADOW *come in from
the left.*

TROCK: Go back and watch the car.
   [*The* TWO YOUNG MEN IN SERGE *go out.* TROCK *walks to the
   corner and looks toward the city.*]
   You roost of punks and gulls! Sleep, sleep it off,
   whatever you had last night, get down in warm,
   one big ham-fat against another—sleep,
   cling, sleep and rot! Rot out your pasty guts
   with diddling, you had no brain to begin. If you had
   there'd be no need for us to sleep on iron
   who had too much brains for you.
SHADOW: Now look, Trock, look,
   what would the warden say to talk like that?

35

TROCK: May they die as I die!
By God, what life they've left me
they shall keep me well! I'll have that out of them—
these pismires that walk like men!

SHADOW: Because, look, chief,
it's all against science and penology
for you to get out and begin to cuss that way
before your prison vittles are out of you. Hell,
you're supposed to leave the pen full of high thought,
kind of noble-like, loving toward all mankind,
ready to kiss their feet—or whatever parts
they stick out toward you. Look at me!

TROCK: I see you.
And even you may not live as long as you think.
You think too many things are funny. Well, laugh.
But it's not so funny.

SHADOW: Come on, Trock, you know me.
Anything you say goes, but give me leave
to kid a little.

TROCK: Then laugh at somebody else!
It's a lot safer! They've soaked me once too often
in that vat of poisoned hell they keep upstate
to soak men in, and I'm rotten inside, I'm all
one liquid puke inside where I had lungs
once, like yourself! And now they want to get me
and stir me in again—and that'd kill me—
and that's fine for them. But before that happens to me
a lot of these healthy boys'll know what it's like
when you try to breathe and have no place to put air—
they'll learn it from me!

SHADOW: They've got nothing on you, chief.

TROCK: I don't know yet. That's what I'm here to find out.
If they've got what they might have
it's not a year this time—
no, nor ten. It's screwed down under a lid.—
I can die quick enough, without help.

SHADOW: You're the skinny kind
that lives forever.

TROCK: He gave me a half a year,
the doc at the gate.

SHADOW: Jesus.

TROCK: Six months I get,
and the rest's dirt, six feet.

[LUCIA, *the street piano man, comes in right from behind
the rock and goes to the shed where he keeps his piano.* PINY,
the apple-woman, follows and stands in the entrance. LUCIA
speaks to ESTRELLA, *who still stands facing* SHADOW.]

LUCIA: Morning.

[TROCK *and* SHADOW *go out round the apartment house
without speaking.*]

PINY: Now what would you call them?

LUCIA: Maybe someting da river washed up.

PINY: Nothing ever washed him—that black one.

LUCIA: Maybe not, maybe so. More like his pa and ma raise-a
heem in da cellar.

[*He wheels out the piano.*]

PINY: He certainly gave me a turn.

[*She lays a hand on the rock.*]

LUCIA: You don' live-a right, ol' gal. Take heem easy. Look on
da bright-a side. Never say-a die. Me, every day in every
way I getta be da regular heller.

[*He starts out.*]

Curtain

SCENE II

SCENE—*A cellar apartment under the apartment building,
floored with cement and roofed with huge boa constrictor
pipes that run slantwise from left to right, dwarfing the room.
An outside door opens to the left and a door at the right
rear leads to the interior of the place. A low squat window
to the left. A table at the rear and a few chairs and books
make up the furniture.* GARTH, *son of* ESDRAS, *sits alone, holding a violin upside down to inspect a crack at its base. He
lays the bow on the floor and runs his fingers over the joint.*
MIRIAMNE *enters from the rear, a girl of fifteen.* GARTH *looks
up, then down again.*

MIRIAMNE: Garth—

GARTH: The glue lets go. It's the steam, I guess.

It splits the hair on your head.

MIRIAMNE: It can't be mended?

GARTH: I can't mend it.
No doubt there are fellows somewhere
who'd mend it for a dollar—and glad to do it.
That is if I had a dollar.—Got a dollar?
No, I thought not.

MIRIAMNE: Garth, you've sat at home here
three days now. You haven't gone out at all.
Something frightens you.

GARTH: Yes?

MIRIAMNE: And father's frightened.
He reads without knowing where. When a shadow falls
across the page he waits for a blow to follow
after the shadow. Then in a little while
he puts his book down softly and goes out
to see who passed.

GARTH: A bill collector, maybe.
We haven't paid the rent.

MIRIAMNE: No.

GARTH: You're a bright girl, sis.—
You see too much. You run along and cook.
Why don't you go to school?

MIRIAMNE: I don't like school.
They whisper behind my back.

GARTH: Yes? About what?

MIRIAMNE: What did the lawyer mean
that wrote to you?

GARTH [*Rising*]: What lawyer?

MIRIAMNE: I found a letter
on the floor of your room. He said, "Don't get me wrong,
but stay in out of the rain the next few days,
just for instance."

GARTH: I thought I burned that letter.

MIRIAMNE: Afterward you did. And then what was printed
about the Estrella gang—you hid it from me,
you and father. What is it—about this murder—?

GARTH: Will you shut up, you fool!

MIRIAMNE: But if you know
why don't you tell them, Garth?

If it's true—what they say—
you knew all the time Romagna wasn't guilty,
and could have said so—

GARTH: Everybody knew
Romagna wasn't guilty! But they weren't listening
to evidence in his favor. They didn't want it.
They don't want it now.

MIRIAMNE: But was that why
they never called on you?—

GARTH: So far as I know
they never'd heard of me—and I can assure you
I knew nothing about it—

MIRIAMNE: But something's wrong—
and it worries father—

GARTH: What could be wrong?

MIRIAMNE: I don't know.

[*A pause.*]

GARTH: And I don't know. You're a good kid, Miriamne,
but you see too many movies. I wasn't mixed up
in any murder, and I don't mean to be.
If I had a dollar to get my fiddle fixed
and another to hire a hall, by God I'd fiddle
some of the prodigies back into Sunday school
where they belong, but I won't get either, and so
I sit here and bite my nails—but if you hoped
I had some criminal romantic past
you'll have to look again!

MIRIAMNE: Oh, Garth, forgive me—
But I want you to be so far above such things
nothing could frighten you. When you seem to shrink
and be afraid, and you're the brother I love,
I want to run there and cry, if there's any question
they care to ask, you'll be quick and glad to answer,
for there's nothing to conceal!

GARTH: And that's all true—

MIRIAMNE: But then I remember—
how you dim the lights—
and we go early to bed—and speak in whispers—
and I could think there's a death somewhere behind us—
an evil death—

GARTH [*Hearing a step*]: Now for God's sake, be quiet!
  [ESDRAS, *an old rabbi with a kindly face, enters from the
  outside. He is hurried and troubled.*]
ESDRAS: I wish to speak alone with someone here if I may have
  this room. Miriamne—
MIRIAMNE [*Turning to go*]: Yes, father.
  [*The outer door is suddenly thrown open.* TROCK *appears.*]
TROCK [*After a pause*]: You'll excuse me for not knocking.
  [SHADOW *follows* TROCK *in.*]
  Sometimes it's best to come in quiet. Sometimes
  it's a good way to go out. Garth's home, I see.
  He might not have been here if I made a point
  of knocking at doors.
GARTH: How are you, Trock?
TROCK: I guess
  you can see how I am.
  [*To* MIRIAMNE.] Stay here. Stay where you are.
  We'd like to make your acquaintance.
  —If you want the facts
  I'm no better than usual, thanks. Not enough sun,
  my physician tells me. Too much close confinement.
  A lack of exercise and an overplus
  of beans in the diet. You've done well, no doubt?
GARTH: I don't know what makes you think so.
TROCK: Who's the family?
GARTH: My father and my sister.
TROCK: Happy to meet you.
  Step inside a minute. The boy and I
  have something to talk about.
ESDRAS: No, no—he's said nothing—
  nothing, sir, nothing!
TROCK: When I say go out, you go—
ESDRAS [*Pointing to the door*]: Miriamne—
GARTH: Go on out, both of you!
ESDRAS: Oh, sir—I'm old—
  old and unhappy—
GARTH: Go on!
  [MIRIAMNE *and* ESDRAS *go inside.*]
TROCK: And if you listen
  I'll riddle that door!

[SHADOW *shuts the door behind them and stands against it*]
I just got out, you see,
and I pay my first call on you.

GARTH: Maybe you think
I'm not in the same jam you are.

TROCK: That's what I do think.
Who started looking this up?

GARTH: I wish I knew,
and I wish he was in hell! Some damned professor
with nothing else to do. If you saw his stuff
you know as much as I do.

TROCK: It wasn't you
turning state's evidence?

GARTH: Hell, Trock, use your brain!
The case was closed. They burned Romagna for it
and that finished it. Why should I look for trouble
and maybe get burned myself?

TROCK: Boy, I don't know,
but I just thought I'd find out.

GARTH: I'm going straight, Trock.
I can play this thing, and I'm trying to make a living.
I haven't talked and nobody's talked to me.
Christ—it's the last thing I'd want!

TROCK: Your old man knows.

GARTH: That's where I got the money that last time
when you needed it. He had a little saved up,
but I had to tell him to get it. He's as safe
as Shadow there.

TROCK [*Looking at* SHADOW]: There could be people safer
than that son-of-a-bitch.

SHADOW: Who?

TROCK: You'd be safer dead
along with some other gorillas.

SHADOW: It's beginning to look
as if you'd feel safer with everybody dead,
the whole goddamn world.

TROCK: I would. These Jesus-bitten
professors! Looking up their half-ass cases!
We've got enough without that.

GARTH: There's no evidence
to reopen the thing.

TROCK: And suppose they called on you
and asked you to testify?

GARTH: Why then I'd tell 'em
that all I know is what I read in the papers.
And I'd stick to that.

TROCK: How much does your sister know?

GARTH: I'm honest with you, Trock. She read my name
in the professor's pamphlet, and she was scared
the way anybody would be. She got nothing
from me, and anyway she'd go to the chair
herself before she'd send me there.

TROCK: Like hell.

GARTH: Besides, who wants to go to trial again
except the radicals?—You and I won't spill
and unless we did there's nothing to take to court
as far as I know. Let the radicals go on howling
about getting a dirty deal. They always howl
and nobody gives a damn. This professor's red—
everybody knows it.

TROCK: You're forgetting the judge.
Where's the damn judge?

GARTH: What judge?

TROCK: Read the morning papers.
It says Judge Gaunt's gone off his nut. He's got
that damn trial on his mind, and been going round
proving to everybody he was right all the time
and the radicals were guilty—stopping people
in the street to prove it—and now he's nuts entirely
and nobody knows where he is.

GARTH: Why don't they know?

TROCK: Because he's on the loose somewhere! They've got
the police of three cities looking for him.

GARTH: Judge Gaunt?

TROCK: Yes. Judge Gaunt.

SHADOW: Why should that worry you?
He's crazy, ain't he? And even if he wasn't
he's arguing on your side. You're jittery, chief.
God, all the judges are looney. You've got the jitters,

and you'll damn well give yourself away some time
peeing yourself in public.

[TROCK *half turns toward* SHADOW *in anger.*]
Don't jump the gun now,
I've got pockets in my clothes, too.

[*His hand is in his coat pocket.*]

TROCK: All right. Take it easy.

[*He takes his hand from his pocket, and* SHADOW *does the
same.*]

[*To* GARTH.] Maybe you're lying to me and maybe you're
not. Stay at home a few days.

GARTH: Sure thing. Why not?

TROCK: And when I say stay home I mean stay home.
If I have to go looking for you you'll stay a long time
wherever I find you.

[*To* SHADOW.] Come on. We'll get out of here.

[*To* GARTH.] Be seeing you.

[SHADOW *and* TROCK *go out. After a pause* GARTH *walks
over to his chair and picks up the violin. Then he puts it
down and goes to the inside door, which he opens.*]

GARTH: He's gone.

[MIRIAMNE *enters,* ESDRAS *behind her.*]

MIRIAMNE [*Going up to* GARTH]: Let's not stay here.

[*She puts her hands on his arms.*]
I thought he'd come for something—horrible.
Is he coming back?

GARTH: I don't know.

MIRIAMNE: Who is he, Garth?

GARTH: He'd kill me if I told you who he is,
that is, if he knew.

MIRIAMNE: Then don't say it—

GARTH: Yes, and I'll say it! I was with a gang one time
that robbed a pay roll. I saw a murder done,
and Trock Estrella did it. If that got out
I'd go to the chair and so would he—that's why
he was here today—

MIRIAMNE: But that's not true—

ESDRAS: He says it
to frighten you, child.

GARTH: Oh, no I don't! I say it

because I've held it in too long! I'm damned
if I sit here forever, and look at the door,
waiting for Trock with his sub-machine gun, waiting
for police with a warrant!—I say I'm damned, and I am,
no matter what I do! These piddling scales
on a violin—first position, third, fifth,
arpeggios in E—and what I'm thinking
is Romagna dead for the murder—dead while I sat here
dying inside—dead for the thing Trock did
while I looked on—and I could have saved him, yes—
but I sat here and let him die instead of me
because I wanted to live! Well, it's no life,
and it doesn't matter who I tell, because
I mean to get it over!

MIRIAMNE: Garth, it's not true!

GARTH: I'd take some scum down with me if I died—
that'd be one good deed—

ESDRAS: Son, son, you're mad—
someone will hear—

GARTH: Then let them hear! I've lived
with ghosts too long, and lied too long. Goddamn you
if you keep me from the truth!—
[*He turns away.*]
Oh, goddamn the world!
I don't want to die!
[*He throws himself down.*]

ESDRAS: I should have known.
I thought you hard and sullen,
Garth, my son. And you were a child, and hurt
with a wound that might be healed.
—All men have crimes,
and most of them are hidden, and many are heavy
as yours must be to you.
[GARTH *sobs.*]
They walk the streets
to buy and sell, but a spreading crimson stain
tinges the inner vestments, touches flesh,
and burns the quick. You're not alone.

GARTH: I'm alone
in this.

ESDRAS: Yes, if you hold with the world that only
those who die suddenly should be revenged.
But those whose hearts are cancered, drop by drop
in small ways, little by little, till they've borne
all they can bear, and die—these deaths will go
unpunished now as always. When we're young
we have faith in what is seen, but when we're old
we know that what is seen is traced in air
and built on water. There's no guilt under heaven,
just as there's no heaven, till men believe it—
no earth, till men have seen it, and have a word
to say this is the earth.

GARTH: Well, I say there's an earth,
and I say I'm guilty on it, guilty as hell.

ESDRAS: Yet till it's known you bear no guilt at all—
unless you wish. The days go by like film,
like a long written scroll, a figured veil
unrolling out of darkness into fire
and utterly consumed. And on this veil,
running in sounds and symbols of men's minds
reflected back, life flickers and is shadow
going toward flame. Only what men can see
exists in that shadow. Why must you rise and cry out:
That was I, there in the raveled tapestry,
there, in that pistol flash, when the man was killed.
I was there, and was one, and am bloodstained!
Let the wind
and fire take that hour to ashes out of time
and out of mind! This thing that men call justice,
this blind snake that strikes men down in the dark,
mindless with fury, keep your hand back from it,
pass by in silence—let it be forgotten, forgotten!—
Oh, my son, my son—have pity!

MIRIAMNE: But if it was true
and someone died—then it was more than shadow—
and it doesn't blow away—

GARTH: Well, it was true.

ESDRAS: Say it if you must. If you have heart to die,
say it, and let them take what's left—there was little
to keep, even before—

GARTH: Oh, I'm a coward—
  I always was. I'll be quiet and live. I'll live
  even if I have to crawl. I know.
  [*He gets up and goes into the inner room.*]
MIRIAMNE: Is it better
  to tell a lie and live?
ESDRAS: Yes, child. It's better.
MIRIAMNE: But if I had to do it—
  I think I'd die.
ESDRAS: Yes, child. Because you're young.
MIRIAMNE: Is that the only reason?
ESDRAS: The only reason.

Curtain

SCENE III

SCENE—*Under the bridge, evening of the same day. When the
curtain rises* MIRIAMNE *is sitting alone on the ledge at the
rear of the apartment house. A spray of light falls on her
from a street lamp above. She shivers a little in her thin coat,
but sits still as if heedless of the weather. Through the rocks
on the other side a* TRAMP *comes down to the riverbank, hunt-
ing a place to sleep. He goes softly to the apple-woman's hut
and looks in, then turns away, evidently not daring to pre-
empt it. He looks at* MIRIAMNE *doubtfully. The door of the
street piano man is shut. The vagabond passes it and
picks carefully among some rags and shavings to the right.*
MIRIAMNE *looks up and sees him but makes no sign. She
looks down again, and the man curls himself up in a make-
shift bed in the corner, pulling a piece of sacking over his
shoulders.* TWO GIRLS *come in from round the apartment
house.*

1ST GIRL: Honest, I never heard of anything so romantic. Because you never liked him.
2ND GIRL: I certainly never did.
1ST GIRL: You've got to tell me how it happened. You've got to.
2ND GIRL: I couldn't. As long as I live I couldn't. Honest, it
  was terrible. It was terrible.

1ST GIRL: What was so terrible?

2ND GIRL: The way it happened.

1ST GIRL: Oh, please—not to a soul, never.

2ND GIRL: Well, you know how I hated him because he had such a big mouth. So he reached over and grabbed me, and I began all falling to pieces inside, the way you do—and I said, "Oh no you don't mister," and started screaming and kicked a hole through the windshield and lost a shoe, and he let go and was cursing and growling because he borrowed the car and didn't have money to pay for the windshield, and he started to cry, and I got so sorry for him I let him, and now he wants to marry me.

1ST GIRL: Honest, i never heard of anything so romantic!

[*She sees the sleeping* TRAMP.]

My God, what you won't see!

[*They give the* TRAMP *a wide berth, and go out right. The* TRAMP *sits up looking about him.* JUDGE GAUNT, *an elderly, quiet man, well-dressed but in clothes that have seen some weather, comes in uncertainly from the left. He holds a small clipping in his hand and goes up to the* HOBO.]

GAUNT [*Tentatively*]: Your pardon, sir. Your pardon, but perhaps you can tell me the name of this street.

HOBO: Huh?

GAUNT: The name of this street?

HOBO: This ain't no street.

GAUNT: There, where the street lamps are.

HOBO: That's the alley.

GAUNT: Thank you. It has a name, no doubt?

HOBO: That's the alley.

GAUNT: I see. I won't trouble you. You wonder why I ask, I daresay.—I'm a stranger. Why do you look at me? [*He steps back.*] I—I'm not the man you think. You've mistaken me, sir.

HOBO: Huh?

GAUNT: Perhaps misled by a resemblance. But you're mistaken —I had an errand in this city. It's only by accident that I'm here—

HOBO [*Muttering*]: You go to hell.

GAUNT [*Going nearer to him, bending over him*]: Yet why should I deceive you? Before God, I held the proofs in my hands. I hold them still. I tell you the defense was cunning beyond belief, and unscrupulous in its use of propaganda—they gagged at nothing—not even— [*He rises.*]

No, no—I'm sorry—this will hardly interest you. I'm sorry. I have an errand.

[*He looks toward the street.* ESDRAS *enters from the basement and goes to* MIRIAMNE. *The* JUDGE *steps back into the shadows.*]

ESDRAS: Come in, my daughter. You'll be cold here.

MIRIAMNE: After a while.

ESDRAS: You'll be cold. There's a storm coming.

MIRIAMNE: I didn't want him to see me crying. That was all.

ESDRAS: I know.

MIRIAMNE: I'll come soon.

[ESDRAS *turns reluctantly and goes out the way he came.* MIRIAMNE *rises to go in, pausing to dry her eyes.* MIO *and* CARR, *road boys of seventeen or so, come round the apartment house. The* JUDGE *has disappeared.*]

CARR: Thought you said you were never coming East again.

MIO: Yeah, but—I heard something changed my mind.

CARR: Same old business?

MIO: Yes. Just as soon not talk about it.

CARR: Where did you go from Portland?

MIO: Fishing—I went fishing. God's truth.

CARR: Right after I left?

MIO: Fell in with a fisherman's family on the coast and went after the beautiful mackerel fish that swim in the beautiful sea. Family of Greeks—Aristides Marinos was his lovely name. He sang while he fished. Made the pea-green Pacific ring with his bastard Greek chanties. Then I went to Hollywood High School for a while.

CARR: I'll bet that's a seat of learning.

MIO: It's the hind end of all wisdom. They kicked me out after a time.

CARR: For cause?

MIO: Because I had no permanent address, you see. That means nobody's paying school taxes for you, so out you go. [*To* MIRIAMNE.] What's the matter, kid?

MIRIAMNE: Nothing. [*She looks up at him, and they pause for a moment.*] Nothing.

MIO: I'm sorry.

MIRIAMNE: It's all right. [*She withdraws her eyes from his and goes out past him. He turns and looks after her.*]

CARR: Control your chivalry.

MIO: A pretty kid.

CARR: A baby.

MIO: Wait for me.

CARR: Be a long wait? [MIO *steps swiftly out after* MIRIAMNE, *then returns.*] Yeah?

MIO: She's gone.

CARR: Think of that.

MIO: No, but I mean—vanished. Presto—into nothing—prodigioso.

CARR: Damn good thing, if you ask me. The homely ones are bad enough, but the lookers are fatal.

MIO: You exaggerate, Carr.

CARR: I doubt it.

MIO: Well, let her go. This riverbank's loaded with typhus rats, too. Might as well die one death as another.

CARR: They say chronic alcoholism is nice but expensive. You can always starve to death.

MIO: Not always. I tried it. After the second day I walked thirty miles to Niagara Falls and made a tour of the plant to get the sample of shredded wheat biscuit on the way out.

CARR: Last time I saw you you couldn't think of anything you wanted to do except curse God and pass out. Still feeling low?

MIO: Not much different. [*He turns away, then comes back.*] Talk about the lost generation, I'm the only one fits that title. When the State executes your father, and your mother dies of grief, and you know damn well he was innocent, and the authorities of your home town politely inform you they'd consider it a favor if you lived somewhere else—that cuts you off from the world—with a meat ax.

CARR: They asked you to move?

MIO: It came to that.

CARR: God, that was white of them.

MIO: It probably gave them a headache just to see me after all that agitation. They knew as well as I did my father never staged a holdup. Anyway, I've got a new interest in life now.

CARR: Yes—I saw her.

MIO: I don't mean the skirt.—No, I got wind of something, out West, some college professor investigating the trial and turning up new evidence. Couldn't find anything he'd written out there, so I beat it East and arrived on this blessed island just in time to find the bums holing up in the public library for the winter. I know now what the unemployed have been doing since the depression started. They've been catching up on their reading in the main reference room. Man, what a stench! Maybe I stank, too, but a hobo has the stench of ten because his shoes are poor.

CARR: Tennyson.

MIO: Right. Jeez, I'm glad we met up again! Never knew anybody else that could track me through the driven snow of Victorian literature.

CARR: Now you're cribbing from some half-forgotten criticism of Ben Jonson's Roman plagiarisms.

MIO: Where did you get your education, sap?

CARR: Not in the public library, sap. My father kept a newsstand.

MIO: Well, you're right again. [*There is a faint rumble of thunder.*] What's that? Winter thunder?

CARR: Or Mister God, beating on His little tocsin. Maybe announcing the advent of a new social order.

MIO: Or maybe it's going to rain coffee and doughnuts.

CARR: Or maybe it's going to rain.

MIO: Seems more likely. [*Lowering his voice.*] Anyhow, I found Professor Hobhouse's discussion of the Romagna case. I think he has something. It occurred to me I might follow it up by doing a little sleuthing on my own account.

CARR: Yes?

MIO: I have done a little. And it leads me to somewhere in that tenement house that backs up against the bridge. That's how I happen to be here.

CARR: They'll never let you get anywhere with it, Mio. I told you that before.

MIO: I know you did.

CARR: The State can't afford to admit it was wrong, you see. Not when there's been that much of a row kicked up over it. So for all practical purposes the State was right and your father robbed the pay roll.

MIO: There's still such a thing as evidence.

CARR: It's something you can buy. In fact, at the moment I
don't think of anything you can't buy, including life, honor,
virtue, glory, public office, conjugal affection, and all kinds
of justice, from the traffic court to the immortal nine. Go
out and make yourself a pot of money and you can buy
all the justice you want. Convictions obtained, convictions
averted. Lowest rates in years.

MIO: I know all that.

CARR: Sure.

MIO: This thing didn't happen to you.
They've left you your name
and whatever place you can take. For my heritage
they've left me one thing only, and that's to be
my father's voice crying up out of the earth
and quicklime where they stuck him. Electrocution
doesn't kill, you know. They eviscerate them
with a turn of the knife in the dissecting room.
The blood spurts out. The man was alive. Then into
the lime pit, leave no trace. Make it short shrift
and chemical dissolution. That's what they thought
of the man that was my father. Then my mother—
I tell you these county burials are swift
and cheap and run for profit! Out of the house
and into the ground, you wife of a dead dog. Wait,
here's some Romagna spawn left.
Something crawls here—
something they called a son. Why couldn't he die
along with his mother? Well, ease him out of town,
ease him out, boys, and see you're not too gentle.
He might come back. And, by their own living Jesus,
I will go back, and hang the carrion
around their necks that made it!
Maybe I can sleep then
Or even live.

CARR: You have to try it?

MIO: Yes.
Yes. It won't let me alone. I've tried to live
and forget it—but I was birthmarked with hot iron
into the entrails. I've got to find out who did it

and make them see it till it scalds their eyes
and make them admit it till their tongues are blistered
with saying how black they lied!

[HERMAN, *a gawky shoe salesman, enters from the left.*]

HERMAN: Hello. Did you see a couple of girls go this way?

CARR: Couple of girls? Did we see a couple of girls?

MIO: No.

CARR: No. No girls.

[HERMAN *hesitates, then goes out right.* LUCIA *comes in from the left, trundling his piano.* PINY *follows him, weeping.*]

PINY: They've got no right to do it—

LUCIA: All right, hell what, no matter, I got to put him away, I got to put him away, that's what the hell!

[TWO STREET URCHINS *follow him in.*]

PINY: They want everybody on the relief rolls and nobody making a living?

LUCIA: The cops, they do what the big boss says. The big boss, that's the mayor, he says he heard it once too often, the sextette—

PINY: They want graft, that's all. It's a new way to get graft—

LUCIA: Oh, no, no, no! He's a good man, the mayor. He's just don't care for music, that's all.

PINY: Why shouldn't you make a living on the street? The National Biscuit Company ropes off Eighth Avenue—and does the mayor do anything? No, the police hit you over the head if you try to go through!

LUCIA: You got the big dough, you get the pull, fine. No big dough, no pull, what the hell, get off the city property! Tomorrow I start cooking chestnuts . . . [*He strokes the piano fondly. The* TWO GIRLS *and* HERMAN *come back from the right.*] She's a good little machine, this baby. Cost plenty —and two new records I only played twice. See, this one. [*He starts turning the crank, talking while he plays.*] Two weeks since they play this one in a picture house. [*A* SAILOR *wanders in from the left. One of the* STREET URCHINS *begins suddenly to dance a wild rumba, the others watch.*] Good boy—see, it's a lulu—it itches in the feet!

[HERMAN, *standing with his girl, tosses the boy a penny. He bows and goes on dancing; the other* URCHIN *joins him. The* SAILOR *tosses a coin.*]

SAILOR: Go it, Cuba! Go it!

[LUCIA *turns the crank, beaming.*]

2ND GIRL: Oh, Herman! [*She throws her arms around* HERMAN *and they dance.*]

URCHIN: Hey, pipe the professionals!

1ST GIRL: Do your glide, Shirley! Do your glide!

LUCIA: Maybe we can't play in front, maybe we can play behind! [*The* HOBO *gets up from his nest and comes over to watch. A* YOUNG RADICAL *wanders in.*] Maybe you don't know, folks! Tonight we play good-by to the piano! Good-by forever! No more piano on the streets! No more music! No more money for the music man! Last time, folks! Good-by to the piano—good-by forever! [MIRIAMNE *comes out the rear door of the apartment and stands watching. The* SAILOR *goes over to the* 1ST GIRL *and they dance together.*] Maybe you don't know, folks! Tomorrow will be sad as hell, tonight we dance! Tomorrow no more Verdi, no more rumba, no more good time! Tonight we play good-by to the piano, good-by forever! [*The* RADICAL *edges up to* MIRIAMNE, *and asks her to dance. She shakes her head and he goes to* PINY, *who dances with him. The* HOBO *begins to do a few lonely curvets on the side above.*] Hoy! Hoy! Pick 'em up and take 'em around! Use the head, use the feet! Last time forever!

[*He begins to sing to the air.*]

MIO: Wait for me, will you?

CARR: Now's your chance.

[MIO *goes over to* MIRIAMNE *and holds out a hand, smiling. She stands for a moment uncertain, then dances with him.* ESDRAS *comes out to watch.* JUDGE GAUNT *comes in from the left. There is a rumble of thunder.*]

LUCIA: Hoy! Hoy! Maybe it rains tonight, maybe it snows tomorrow! Tonight we dance good-by.

[*He sings the air lustily. A* POLICEMAN *comes in from the left and looks on.* TWO OR THREE PEDESTRIANS *follow him.*]

POLICE: Hey you!

[LUCIA *goes on singing.*]

Hey, you!

LUCIA [*Still playing*]: What you want?

POLICE: Sign off!

LUCIA: What you mean? I get off the street!

POLICE: Sign off!

LUCIA [*Still playing*]: What you mean?

[*The* POLICEMAN *walks over to him.* LUCIA *stops playing and the* DANCERS *pause.*]

POLICE: Cut it.

LUCIA: Is this a street?

POLICE: I say cut it out.

[*The* HOBO *goes back to his nest and sits in it, watching.*]

LUCIA: It's the last time. We dance good-by to the piano.

POLICE: You'll dance good-by to something else if I catch you cranking that thing again.

LUCIA: All right.

PINY: I'll bet you don't say that to the National Biscuit Company!

POLICE: Lady, you've been selling apples on my beat for some time now, and I said nothing about it—

PINY: Selling apples is allowed—

POLICE: You watch yourself—[*He takes a short walk around the place and comes upon the* HOBO.] What are you doing here? [*The* HOBO *opens his mouth, points to it, and shakes his head.*] Oh, you are, are you? [*He comes back to* LUCIA.] So you trundle your so-called musical instrument to wherever you keep it, and don't let me hear it again.

[*The* RADICAL *leaps on the base of the rock at right. The* 1ST GIRL *turns away from the* SAILOR *toward the* 2ND GIRL *and* HERMAN.]

SAILOR: Hey, captain, what's the matter with the music?

POLICE: Not a thing, admiral.

SAILOR: Well, we had a little party going here—

POLICE: I'll say you did.

2ND GIRL: Please, officer, we want to dance.

POLICE: Go ahead. Dance.

2ND GIRL: But we want music!

POLICE [*Turning to go*]: Sorry. Can't help you.

RADICAL: And there you see it, the perfect example of capitalistic oppression! In a land where music should be free as air and the arts should be encouraged, a uniformed minion of the rich, a guardian myrmidon of the Park Avenue pleasure hunters, steps in and puts a limit on the innocent enjoyments of the poor! We don't go to theaters! Why not? We

can't afford it! We don't go to night clubs, where women
dance naked and the music drips from saxophones and leaks
out of Rudy Vallee—we can't afford that either!—But we
might at least dance on the riverbank to the strains of a
barrel organ—

[GARTH *comes out of the apartment and listens.*]

POLICE: It's against the law!

RADICAL: What law? I challenge you to tell me what law of
God or man—what ordinance—is violated by this spontane-
ous diversion? None! I say none! An official whim of the
masters who should be our servants!—

POLICE: Get down! Get down and shut up!

RADICAL: By what law, by what ordinance do you order me to
be quiet?

POLICE: Speaking without a flag. You know it.

RADICAL [*Pulling out a small American flag*]: There's my flag!
There's the flag of this United States which used to guarantee
the rights of man—the rights of man now violated by every
third statute of the commonweal—

POLICE: Don't try to pull tricks on me! I've seen you before!
You're not making any speech, and you're climbing down—

GAUNT [*Who has come quietly forward*]: One moment, officer.
There is some difference of opinion even on the bench as to the
elasticity of police power when applied in minor emergencies
to preserve civil order. But the weight of authority would
certainly favor the defendant in any equable court, and he
would be upheld in his demand to be heard.

POLICE: Who are you?

GAUNT: Sir, I am not accustomed to answer that question.

POLICE: I don't know you.

GAUNT: I am a judge of some standing, not in your city but in
another with similar statutes. You are aware, of course, that
the bill of rights is not to be set aside lightly by the officers
of any municipality—

POLICE [*Looking over* GAUNT'S *somewhat bedraggled costume*]:
Maybe they understand you better in the town you come
from, but I don't get your drift.—[*To the* RADICAL.] I don't
want any trouble, but if you ask for it you'll get plenty.
Get down!

RADICAL: I'm not asking for trouble, but I'm staying right here.
[*The* POLICEMAN *moves toward him.*]

GAUNT [*Taking the* POLICEMAN'S *arm, but shaken off roughly*]:
I ask this for yourself, truly, not for the dignity of the law
nor the maintenance of precedent. Be gentle with them when
their threats are childish—be tolerant while you can—for
your least harsh word will return on you in the night—
return in a storm of cries!—[*He takes the* POLICEMAN'S *arm
again.*] Whatever they may have said or done, let them dis-
perse in peace! It is better that they go softly, lest when they
are dead you see their eyes pleading, and their outstretched
hands touch you, fingering cold on your heart!—I have
been harsher than you. I have sent men down that long
corridor into blinding light and blind darkness! [*He suddenly
draws himself erect and speaks defiantly.*] And it was well
that I did so! I have been an upright judge! They are all
liars! Liars!

POLICE [*Shaking* GAUNT *off so that he falls*]: Why, you fool.
you're crazy!

GAUNT: Yes, and there are liars on the force! They came to me
with their shifty lies! [*He catches at the* POLICEMAN, *who
pushes him away with his foot.*]

POLICE: You think I've got nothing better to do than listen
to a crazy fool?

1ST GIRL: Shame, shame!

POLICE: What have I got to be ashamed of? And what's going on
here, anyway? Where in hell did you all come from?

RADICAL: Tread on him! That's right! Tread down the poor and
the innocent!

[*There is a protesting murmur in the crowd.*]

SAILOR [*Moving in a little*]: Say, big boy, you don't have to
step on the guy.

POLICE [*Facing them, stepping back*]: What's the matter with
you? I haven't stepped on anybody!

MIO [*At the right, across from the* POLICEMAN]: Listen now,
fellows, give the badge a chance.
He's doing his job, what he gets paid to do,
the same as any of you. They're all picked men,
these metropolitan police, hand-picked
for loyalty and a fine upstanding pair

of shoulders on their legs—it's not so easy
to represent the law. Think what he does
for all of us, stamping out crime!
Do you want to be robbed and murdered in your beds?

SAILOR: What's eating you?

RADICAL: He must be a capitalist.

MIO: They pluck them fresh
from Ireland, and a paucity of headpiece
is a prime prerequisite. You from Ireland, buddy?

POLICE [*Surly*]: Where are you from?

MIO: Buddy, I tell you flat
I wish I was from Ireland, and could boast
some Tammany connections. There's only one drawback
about working on the force. It infects the brain,
it eats the cerebrum. There've been cases known,
fine specimens of manhood, too, where autopsies,
conducted in approved scientific fashion,
revealed conditions quite incredible
in policemen's upper layers. In some, a trace,
in others, when they've swung a stick too long,
there was nothing there!—but nothing! Oh, my friends,
this fine athletic figure of a man
that stands so grim before us, what will they find
when they saw his skull for the last inspection?
I fear me a little puffball dust will blow away
rejoining earth, our mother—and this same dust,
this smoke, this ash on the wind, will represent
all he had left to think with!

HOBO: Hooray!

[*The* POLICEMAN *turns on his heel and looks hard at the*
HOBO, *who slinks away.*]

POLICE: Oh, yeah?

MIO: My theme
gives ears to the deaf and voice to the dumb! But now
forgive me if I say you were most unkind
in troubling the officer. He's a simple man
of simple tastes, and easily confused
when faced with complex issues. He may reflect
on returning home, that is, so far as he
is capable of reflection, and conclude

that he was kidded out of his uniform pants,
and in his fury when this dawns on him
may smack his wife down!

POLICE: That'll be about enough from you, too, professor!

MIO: May I say that I think you have managed this whole
situation rather badly, from the beginning?—

POLICE: You may not!

[TROCK *slips in from the background. The* TWO YOUNG
MEN IN SERGE *come with him.*]

MIO: Oh, but your pardon, sir! It's apparent to the least com-
petent among us that you should have gone about your task
more subtly—the glove of velvet, the hand of iron, and all
that sort of thing—

POLICE: Shut that hole in your face!

MIO: Sir, for that remark I shall be satisfied with nothing less
than an unconditional apology! I have an old score to settle
with policemen, brother, because they're fools and fatheads,
and you're one of the most fatuous fatheads that ever walked
his feet flat collecting graft! Tell that to your sergeant back
in the booby hatch.

POLICE: Oh, you want an apology, do you? You'll get an apology
out of the other side of your mouth! [*He steps toward* MIO.
CARR *suddenly stands in his path.*] Get out of my way! [*He
pauses and looks round him; the crowd looks less and less
friendly. He lays a hand on his gun and backs to a position
where there is nobody behind him.*] Get out of here, all of
you! Get out! What are you trying to do—start a riot?

MIO: There now, that's better! That's in the best police tradition. Incite a riot yourself and then accuse the crowd.

POLICE: It won't be pleasant if I decide to let somebody have
it! Get out!

[*The onlookers begin to melt away. The* SAILOR *goes out
left with the* GIRLS *and* HERMAN. CARR *and* MIO *go out
right,* CARR *whistling "The Star Spangled Banner." The* HOBO
follows them. The RADICAL *walks past with his head in the air.*
PINY *and* LUCIA *leave the piano where it stands and slip away
to the left. At the end the* POLICEMAN *is left standing in the
center, the* JUDGE *near him.* ESDRAS *stands in the doorway.*
MIRIAMNE *is left sitting half in shadow and unseen by*
ESDRAS.]

GAUNT [*To the* POLICEMAN]: Yes, but should a man die, should
it be necessary that one man die for the good of many, make
not yourself the instrument of death, lest you sleep to wake
sobbing! Nay, it avails nothing that you are the law—this
delicate ganglion that is the brain, it will not bear these
things—!

[*The* POLICEMAN *gives the* JUDGE *the once-over, shrugs,
decides to leave him there and starts out left.* GARTH *goes to
his father—a fine sleet begins to fall through the street lights.*
TROCK *is still visible.*]

GARTH: Get him in here, quick.

ESDRAS: Who, son?

GARTH: The Judge, damn him!

ESDRAS: Is it Judge Gaunt?

GARTH: Who did you think it was? He's crazy as a bedbug and
telling the world. Get him inside! [*He looks round.*]

ESDRAS [*Going up to* GAUNT]: Will you come in, sir?

GAUNT: You will understand, sir. We old men know how softly
we must proceed with these things.

ESDRAS: Yes, surely, sir.

GAUNT: It was always my practice—always. They will tell you
that of me where I am known. Yet even I am not free of
regret—even I. Would you believe it?

ESDRAS: I believe we are none of us free of regret.

GAUNT: None of us? I would it were true. I would I thought it
were true.

ESDRAS: Shall we go in, sir? This is sleet that's falling.

GAUNT: Yes. Let us go in.

[ESDRAS, GAUNT, *and* GARTH *enter the basement and shut
the door.* TROCK *goes out with his men. After a pause* MIO
*comes back from the right, alone. He stands at a little dis-
tance from* MIRIAMNE.]

MIO: Looks like rain.

[*She is silent.*]

You live around here?

[*She nods gravely.*]

I guess

you thought I meant it—about waiting here to meet me.

[*She nods again.*]

I'd forgotten about it till I got that winter

across the face. You'd better go inside.
I'm not your kind. I'm nobody's kind but my own.
I'm waiting for this to blow over.
[*She rises.*]
I lied. I meant it—
I meant it when I said it—but there's too much black
whirling inside me—for any girl to know.
So go on in. You're somebody's angel child
and they're waiting for you.

MIRIAMNE: Yes. I'll go.
[*She turns.*]

MIO: And tell them
when you get inside where it's warm,
and you love each other,
and mother comes to kiss her darling, tell them
to hang on to it while they can, believe while they can
it's a warm safe world, and Jesus finds his lambs
and carries them in his bosom.—I've seen some lambs
that Jesus missed. If they ever want the truth
tell them that nothing's guaranteed in this climate
except it gets cold in winter, nor on this earth
except you die sometime.
[*He turns away.*]

MIRIAMNE: I have no mother.
And my people are Jews.

MIO: Then you know something about it.

MIRIAMNE: Yes.

MIO: Do you have enough to eat?

MIRIAMNE: Not always.

MIO: What do you believe in?

MIRIAMNE: Nothing.

MIO: Why?

MIRIAMNE: How can one?

MIO: It's easy if you're a fool. You see the words
in books. Honor, it says there, chivalry, freedom,
heroism, enduring love—and these
are words on paper. It's something to have them there.
You'll get them nowhere else.

MIRIAMNE: What hurts you?

MIO: Just that.
  You'll get them nowhere else.
MIRIAMNE: Why should you want them?
MIO: I'm alone, that's why. You see those lights,
  along the river, cutting across the rain—?
  those are the hearths of Brooklyn, and up this way
  the love nests of Manhattan—they turn their points
  like knives against me—outcast of the world,
  snake in the streets. I don't want a handout.
  I sleep and eat.
MIRIAMNE: Do you want me to go with you?
MIO: Where?
MIRIAMNE: Where you go.
  [*A pause. He goes nearer to her.*]
MIO: Why, you goddamned little fool—
  what made you say that?
MIRIAMNE: I don't know.
MIO: If you have a home
  stay in it. I ask for nothing. I've schooled myself
  to ask for nothing, and take what I can get,
  and get along. If I fell for you, that's my lookout,
  and I'll starve it down.
MIRIAMNE: Wherever you go, I'd go.
MIO: What do you know about loving?
  How could you know?
  Have you ever had a man?
MIRIAMNE [*After a slight pause*]: No. But I know.
  Tell me your name.
MIO: Mio. What's yours?
MIRIAMNE: Miriamne.
MIO: There's no such name.
MIRIAMNE: But there's no such name as Mio!
  M.I.O. It's no name.
MIO: It's for Bartolomeo.
MIRIAMNE: My mother's name was Miriam,
  so they called me Miriamne.
MIO: Meaning little Miriam?
MIRIAMNE: Yes.
MIO: So now little Miriamne will go in
  and take up quietly where she dropped them all

her small housewifely cares.—When I first saw you,
not a half-hour ago, I heard myself saying,
this is the face that launches ships for me—
and if I owned a dream—yes, half a dream—
we'd share it. But I have no dream. This earth
came tumbling down from chaos, fire and rock,
and bred up worms, blind worms that sting each other
here in the dark. These blind worms of the earth
took out my father—and killed him, and set a sign
on me—the heir of the serpent—and he was a man
such as men might be if the gods were men—
but they killed him—
as they'll kill all others like him
till the sun cools down to the stabler molecules,
yes, till men spin their tent-worm webs to the stars
and what they think is done, even in the thinking,
and they are the gods, and immortal, and constellations
turn for them all like mill wheels—still as they are
they will be, worms and blind. Enduring love,
oh gods and worms, what mockery!—And yet
I have blood enough in my veins. It goes like music,
singing, because you're here. My body turns
as if you were the sun, and warm. This men called love
in happier times, before the Freudians taught us
to blame it on the glands. Only go in
before you breathe too much of my atmosphere
and catch death from me.

MIRIAMNE: I will take my hands
and weave them to a little house, and there
you shall keep a dream—

MIO: God knows I could use a dream
and even a house.

MIRIAMNE: You're laughing at me, Mio!

MIO: The worms are laughing.
I tell you there's death about me
and you're a child! And I'm alone and half mad
with hate and longing. I shall let you love me
and love you in return, and then, why then
God knows what happens!

MIRIAMNE: Something most unpleasant?

MIO: Love in a boxcar—love among the children.
I've seen too much of it. Are we to live
in this same house you make with your two hands
mystically, out of air?

MIRIAMNE: No roof, no mortgage!
Well, I shall marry a baker out in Flatbush,
it gives hot bread in the morning! Oh, Mio, Mio,
in all the unwanted places and waste lands
that roll up into the darkness out of sun
and into sun out of dark, there should be one empty
for you and me.

MIO: No.

MIRIAMNE: Then go now and leave me.
I'm only a girl you saw in the tenements,
and there's been nothing said.

MIO: Miriamne.

[*She takes a step toward him.*]

MIRIAMNE: Yes.

[*He kisses her lips lightly.*]

MIO: Why, girl, the transfiguration on the mount
was nothing to your face. It lights from within—
a white chalice holding fire, a flower in flame,
this is your face.

MIRIAMNE: And you shall drink the flame
and never lessen it. And round your head
the aureole shall burn that burns there now,
forever. This I can give you. And so forever
the Freudians are wrong.

MIO: They're well-forgotten
at any rate.

MIRIAMNE: Why did you speak to me
when you first saw me?

MIO: I knew then.

MIRIAMNE: And I came back
because I must see you again. And we danced together
and my heart hurt me. Never, never, never,
though they should bind me down and tear out my eyes,
would I ever hurt you now. Take me with you, Mio,
let them look for us, whoever there is to look,
but we'll be away.

[MIO *turns away toward the tenement.*]

MIO: When I was four years old
we climbed through an iron gate, my mother and I,
to see my father in prison. He stood in the death cell
and put his hand through the bars and said, My Mio,
I have only this to leave you, that I love you,
and will love you after I die. Love me then, Mio,
when this hard thing comes on you, that you must live
a man despised for your father. That night the guards,
walking in floodlights brighter than high noon,
led him between them with his trousers slit
and a shaven head for the cathodes. This sleet and rain
that I feel cold here on my face and hands
will find him under thirteen years of clay
in prison ground. Lie still and rest, my father,
for I have not forgotten. When I forget
may I lie blind as you. No other love,
time passing, nor the spaced light-years of suns
shall blur your voice, or tempt me from the path
that clears your name—
till I have these rats in my grip
or sleep deep where you sleep.
[*To* MIRIAMNE.] I have no house,
nor home, nor love of life, nor fear of death,
nor care for what I eat, or who I sleep with,
or what color of calcimine the government
will wash itself this year or next to lure
the sheep and feed the wolves. Love somewhere else,
and get your children in some other image
more acceptable to the State! This face of mine
is stamped for sewage!
[*She steps back, surmising.*]

MIRIAMNE: Mio—

MIO: My road is cut
in rock, and leads to one end. If I hurt you, I'm sorry.
One gets over hurts.

MIRIAMNE: What was his name—
your father's name?

MIO: Bartolomeo Romagna.
I'm not ashamed of it.

MIRIAMNE: Why are you here?

MIO: For the reason
I've never had a home. Because I'm a cry
out of a shallow grave, and all roads are mine
that might revenge him!

MIRIAMNE: But Mio—why here—why here?

MIO: I can't tell you that.

MIRIAMNE: No—but—there's someone
lives here—lives not far—and you mean to see him—
you mean to ask him—
[*She pauses.*]

MIO: Who told you that?

MIRIAMNE: His name
is Garth—Garth Esdras—

MIO [*After a pause, coming nearer*]: Who are you, then?
You seem
to know a good deal about me.—Were you sent
to say this?

MIRIAMNE: You said there was death about you! Yes,
but nearer than you think! Let it be as it is—
let it all be as it is, never see this place
nor think of it—forget the streets you came
when you're away and safe! Go before you're seen
or spoken to!

MIO: Will you tell me why?

MIRIAMNE: As I love you
I can't tell you—and I can never see you—

MIO: I walk where I please—

MIRIAMNE: Do you think it's easy for me
to send you away?
[*She steps back as if to go.*]

MIO: Where will I find you then
if I should want to see you?

MIRIAMNE: Never—I tell you
I'd bring you death! Even now. Listen!
[SHADOW *and* TROCK *enter between the bridge and the
tenement house.* MIRIAMNE *pulls* MIO *back into the shadow
of the rock to avoid being seen.*]

TROCK: Why, fine.

SHADOW: You watch it now—just for the record, Trock—

you're going to thank me for staying away from it
and keeping you out. I've seen men get that way,
thinking they had to plug a couple of guys
and then a few more to cover it up, and then
maybe a dozen more. You can't own all
and territory adjacent, and you can't
slough all the witnesses, because every man
you put away has friends—

TROCK: I said all right.
I said fine.

SHADOW: They're going to find this judge,
and if they find him dead it's just too bad,
and I don't want to know anything about it—
and you don't either.

TROCK: You all through?

SHADOW: Why sure.

TROCK: All right.
We're through too, you know.

SHADOW: Yeah?
[*He becomes wary.*]

TROCK: Yeah, we're through.

SHADOW: I've heard that said before, and afterwards
somebody died.
[TROCK *is silent.*]
Is that what you mean?

TROCK: You can go.
I don't want to see you.

SHADOW: Sure, I'll go.
Maybe you won't mind if I just find out
what you've got on you. Before I turn my back
I'd like to know.
[*Silently and expertly he touches* TROCK'S *pockets, extract-
ing a gun.*]
Not that I'd distrust you,
but you know how it is.
[*He pockets the gun.*]
So long, Trock.

TROCK: So long.

SHADOW: I won't talk.
You can be sure of that.

TROCK: I know you won't.

> [SHADOW *turns and goes out right, past the rock and along the bank. As he goes the* TWO YOUNG MEN IN SERGE *enter from the left and walk slowly after* SHADOW. *They look toward* TROCK *as they enter and he motions with his thumb in the direction taken by* SHADOW. *They follow* SHADOW *out without haste.* TROCK *watches them disappear, then slips out the way he came.* MIO *comes a step forward, looking after the two men. Two or three shots are heard, then silence.* MIO *starts to run after* SHADOW.]

MIRIAMNE: Mio!

MIO: What do you know about this?

MIRIAMNE: The other way,

> Mio—quick!

> [CARR *slips in from the right, in haste.*]

CARR: Look, somebody's just been shot.

> He fell in the river. The guys that did the shooting
> ran up the bank.

MIO: Come on.

> [MIO *and* CARR *run out right.* MIRIAMNE *watches uncertainly, then slowly turns and walks to the rear door of the tenement. She stands there a moment, looking after* MIO, *then goes in, closing the door.* CARR *and* MIO *return.*]

CARR: There's a rip tide past the point. You'd never find him.

MIO: No.

CARR: You know a man really ought to carry insurance living around here.—God, it's easy, putting a fellow away. I never saw it done before.

MIO [*Looking at the place where* MIRIAMNE *stood*]: They have it all worked out.

CARR: What are you doing now?

MIO: I have a little business to transact in this neighborhood.

CARR: You'd better forget it.

MIO: No.

CARR: Need any help?

MIO: Well, if I did I'd ask you first. But I don't see how it would do any good. So you keep out of it and take care of yourself.

CARR: So long, then.

MIO: So long, Carr.

CARR [*Looking downstream*]: He was drifting face up. Must be halfway to the island the way the tide runs.

[*He shivers.*]

God, it's cold here. Well—

[*He goes out to the left.* MIO *sits on the edge of the rock.* LUCIA *comes stealthily back from between the bridge and the tenement, goes to the street piano and wheels it away.* PINY *comes in. They take a look at* MIO, *but say nothing.* LUCIA *goes into his shelter and* PINY *into hers.* MIO *rises, looks up at the tenement, and goes out to the left.*]

Curtain

ACT TWO

SCENE—*The basement as in Scene II of Act One. The same evening.* ESDRAS *sits at the table reading,* MIRIAMNE *is seated at the left, listening and intent. The door of the inner room is half-open and* GARTH'S *violin is heard. He is playing the theme from the third movement of Beethoven's Archduke Trio.* ESDRAS *looks up.*

ESDRAS: I remember when I came to the end
of all the Talmud said, and the commentaries,
then I was fifty years old—and it was time
to ask what I had learned. I asked this question
and gave myself the answer. In all the Talmud
there was nothing to find but the names of things,
set down that we might call them by those names
and walk without fear among things known. Since then
I have had twenty years to read on and on
and end with Ecclesiastes. Names of names,
evanid days, evanid nights and days
and words that shift their meaning. Space is time,
that which was is now—the men of tomorrow
live, and this is their yesterday. All things

that were and are and will be, have their being
then and now and to come. If this means little
when you are young, remember it. It will return
to mean more when you are old.

MIRIAMNE: I'm sorry—I
was listening for something.

ESDRAS: It doesn't matter.
It's a useless wisdom. It's all I have,
but useless. It may be there is no time,
but we grow old. Do you know his name?

MIRIAMNE: Whose name?

ESDRAS: Why, when we're young and listen for a step
the step should have a name—

[MIRIAMNE, *not hearing, rises and goes to the window.*
GARTH *enters from within, carrying his violin and carefully
closing the door.*]

GARTH [*As* ESDRAS *looks at him*]: Asleep.

ESDRAS: He may
sleep on through the whole night—then in the morning
we can let them know.

GARTH: We'd be wiser to say nothing—
let him find his own way back.

ESDRAS: How did he come here?

GARTH: He's not too crazy for that. If he wakes again
we'll keep him quiet and shift him off tomorrow.
Somebody'd pick him up.

ESDRAS: How have I come
to this sunken end of a street, at a life's end—?

GARTH: It was cheaper here—not to be transcendental—
So—we say nothing?

ESDRAS: Nothing.

MIRIAMNE: Garth, there's no place
in this whole city—not one—
where you wouldn't be safer
than here—tonight—or tomorrow.

GARTH [*Bitterly*]: Well, that may be.
What of it?

MIRIAMNE: If you slipped away and took
a place somewhere where Trock couldn't find you—

GARTH: Yes—

using what for money? and why do you think
I've sat here so far—because I love my home
so much? No, but if I stepped round the corner
it'd be my last corner and my last step.

MIRIAMNE: And yet—
if you're here—they'll find you here—
Trock will come again—
and there's woise to follow—

GARTH: Do you want to get me killed?

MIRIAMNE: No.

GARTH: There's no way out of it. We'll wait
and take what they send us.

ESDRAS: Hush! You'll wake him.

GARTH: I've done it.
I hear him stirring now.

[*They wait quietly.* JUDGE GAUNT *opens the door and enters.*]

GAUNT [*In the doorway*]: I beg your pardon—
no, no, be seated—keep your place—I've made
your evening difficult enough, I fear;
and I must thank you doubly for your kindness,
for I've been ill—I know it.

ESDRAS: You're better, sir?

GAUNT: Quite recovered, thank you. Able, I hope,
to manage nicely now. You'll be rewarded
for your hospitality—though at this moment
[*He smiles.*]
I'm low in funds.
[*He inspects his billfold.*]
Sir, my embarrassment
is great indeed—and more than monetary,
for I must own my recollection's vague
of how I came here—how we came together—
and what we may have said. My name is Gaunt,
Judge Gaunt, a name long known in the criminal courts,
and not unhonored there.

ESDRAS: My name is Esdras—
and this is Garth, my son. And Miriamne,
the daughter of my old age.

GAUNT: I'm glad to meet you.
Esdras. Garth Esdras.

[*He passes a hand over his eyes.*]
It's not a usual name.
Of late it's been connected with a case—
a case I knew. But this is hardly the man.
Though it's not a usual name.
[*They are silent.*]
Sir, how I came here,
as I have said, I don't well know. Such things
are sometimes not quite accident.

ESDRAS: We found you
outside our door and brought you in.

GAUNT: The brain
can be overworked, and weary, even when the man
would swear to his good health. Sir, on my word
I don't know why I came here, nor how, nor when,
nor what would explain it. Shall we say the machine
begins to wear? I felt no twinge of it.—
You will imagine how much more than galling
I feel it, to ask my way home—and where I am—
but I do ask you that.

ESDRAS: This is New York City—
or part of it.

GAUNT: Not the best part, I presume?
[*He smiles grimly.*]
No, not the best.

ESDRAS: Not typical, no.

GAUNT: And you—[*To* GARTH.]
you are Garth Esdras?

GARTH: That's my name.

GAUNT: Well, sir,
[*To* ESDRAS.] I shall lie under the deepest obligation
if you will set an old man on his path,
for I lack the homing instinct, if the truth
were known. North, east, and south mean nothing to me
here in this room.

ESDRAS: I can put you on your way.

GARTH: Only you'd be wiser to wait a while—
if I'm any judge.—

GAUNT: It happens I'm the judge—

[*With stiff humor.*] in more ways than one. You'll forgive me
  if I say
I find this place and my predicament
somewhat distasteful.
[*He looks round him.*]

GARTH: I don't doubt you do;
but you're better off here.

GAUNT: Nor will you find it wise
to cross my word as lightly as you seem
inclined to do. You've seen me ill and shaken—
and you presume on that.

GARTH: Have it your way.

GAUNT: Doubtless what information is required
we'll find nearby.

ESDRAS: Yes, sir—the terminal,—
if you could walk so far.

GAUNT: I've done some walking—
to look at my shoes.
[*He looks down, then puts out a hand to steady himself.*]
That—that was why I came—
never mind—it was there—and it's gone.
[*To* GARTH.] Professor Hobhouse—
that's the name—he wrote some trash about you
and printed it in a broadside.
—Since I'm here I can tell you
it's a pure fabrication—lacking facts
and legal import. Senseless and impudent,
written with bias—with malicious intent
to undermine the public confidence
in justice and the courts. I knew it then—
all he brings out about this testimony
you might have given. It's true I could have called you,
but the case was clear—Romagna was known guilty,
and there was nothing to add. If I've endured
some hours of torture over their attacks
upon my probity—and in this torture
have wandered from my place, wandered perhaps
in mind and body—and found my way to face you—
why, yes, it is so—I know it—I beg of you
say nothing. It's not easy to give up

a fair name after a full half century
of service to a State. It may well rock
the surest reason. Therefore I ask of you
say nothing of this visit.

GARTH: I'll say nothing.

ESDRAS: Nor any of us.

GAUNT: Why, no—for you'd lose, too.
You'd have nothing to gain.

ESDRAS: Indeed we know it.

GAUNT: I'll remember you kindly. When I've returned,
there may be some mystery made of where I was—
we'll leave it a mystery?

GARTH: Anything you say.

GAUNT: Why, now I go with much more peace of mind—if I can
call you friends.

ESDRAS: We shall be grateful
for silence on your part, Your Honor.

GAUNT: Sir—
if there were any just end to be served
by speaking out, I'd speak! There is none. No—
bear that in mind!

ESDRAS: We will, Your Honor.

GAUNT: Then—
I'm in some haste. If you can be my guide,
we'll set out now.

ESDRAS: Yes, surely.

[*There is a knock at the door. The four look at each other
with some apprehension.* MIRIAMNE *rises.*]
I'll answer it.

MIRIAMNE: Yes.

[*She goes into the inner room and closes the door.* ESDRAS
*goes to the outer door. The knock is repeated. He opens the
door.* MIO *is there.*]

ESDRAS: Yes, sir.

MIO: May I come in?

ESDRAS: Will you state your business, sir?
It's late—and I'm not at liberty—

MIO: Why, I might say
that I was trying to earn my tuition fees
by peddling magazines. I could say that,

or collecting old newspapers—paying cash—
highest rates—no questions asked—
[*He looks round sharply.*]

GARTH: We've nothing to sell.
　　What do you want?

MIO: Your pardon, gentlemen.
　　My business is not of an ordinary kind,
　　and I felt the need of this slight introduction
　　while I might get my bearings. Your name is Esdras,
　　or they told me so outside.

GARTH: What do you want?

MIO: Is that the name?

GARTH: Yes.

MIO: I'll be quick and brief.
　　I'm the son of a man who died many years ago
　　for a pay roll robbery in New England. You
　　should be Garth Esdras, by what I've heard. You have
　　some knowledge of the crime, if one can believe
　　what he reads in the public prints, and it might be
　　that your testimony, if given, would clear my father
　　of any share in the murder. You may not care
　　whether he was guilty or not. You may not know.
　　But I do care—and care deeply, and I've come
　　to ask you face to face.

GARTH: To ask me what?

MIO: What do you know of it?

ESDRAS: This man Romagna,
　　did he have a son?

MIO: Yes, sir, this man Romagna,
　　as you choose to call him, had a son, and I
　　am that son, and proud.

ESDRAS: Forgive me.

MIO: Had you known him,
　　and heard him speak, you'd know why I'm proud, and why
　　he was no malefactor.

ESDRAS: I quite believe you.
　　If my son can help he will. But at this moment,
　　as I told you—could you, I wonder, come tomorrow,
　　at your own hour?

MIO: Yes.

ESDRAS: By coincidence
 we too of late have had this thing in mind—
 there have been comments printed, and much discussion
 which we could hardly avoid.
MIO: Could you tell me then
 in a word?—What you know—
 is it for him or against him?—
 that's all I need.
ESDRAS: My son knows nothing.
GARTH: No.
 The picture-papers lash themselves to a fury
 over any rumor—make them up when they're short
 of bedroom slops.—This is what happened. I
 had known a few members of a gang one time
 up there—and after the murder they picked me up
 because I looked like someone that was seen
 in what they called the murder car. They held me
 a little while, but they couldn't identify me
 for the most excellent reason I wasn't there
 when the thing occurred. A dozen years later now
 a professor comes across this, and sees red
 and asks why I wasn't called on as a witness
 and yips so loud they syndicate his picture
 in all the rotos. That's all I know about it.
 I wish I could tell you more.
ESDRAS: Let me say too
 that I have read some words your father said,
 and you were a son fortunate in your father,
 whatever the verdict of the world.
MIO: There are few
 who think so, but it's true, and I thank you. Then—
 that's the whole story?
GARTH: All I know of it.
MIO: They cover their tracks well, the inner ring
 that distributes murder. I came three thousand miles
 to this dead end.
ESDRAS: If he was innocent
 and you know him so, believe it, and let the others
 believe as they like.
MIO: Will you tell me how a man's

to live, and face his life, if he can't believe
that truth's like a fire,
and will burn through and be seen
though it takes all the years there are?
While I stand up and have breath in my lungs
I shall be one flame of that fire;
it's all the life I have.

ESDRAS: Then you must live so.
One must live as he can.

MIO: It's the only way
of life my father left me.

ESDRAS: Yes? Yet it's true
the ground we walk on is impacted down
and hard with blood and bones of those who died
unjustly. There's not one title to land or life,
even your own, but was built on rape and murder,
back a few years. It would take a fire indeed
to burn out all this error.

MIO: Then let it burn down,
all of it!

ESDRAS: We ask a great deal of the world
at first—then less—and then less.
We ask for truth
and justice. But this truth's a thing unknown
in the lightest, smallest matter—and as for justice,
who has once seen it done? You loved your father,
and I could have loved him, for every word he spoke
in his trial was sweet and tolerant, but the weight
of what men are and have rests heavy on
the graves of those who lost. They'll not rise again,
and their causes lie there with them.

GAUNT: If you mean to say
that Bartolomeo Romagna was innocent,
you are wrong. He was guilty.
There may have been injustice
from time to time, by regrettable chance, in our courts,
but not in that case, I assure you.

MIO: Oh, you assure me!
You lie in your scrag teeth, whoever you are!
My father was murdered!

GAUNT: Romagna was found guilty
    by all due process of law, and given his chance
    to prove his innocence.

MIO: What chance? When a court
    panders to mob hysterics, and the jury
    comes in loaded to soak an anarchist
    and a foreigner, it may be due process of law
    but it's also murder!

GAUNT: He should have thought of that
    before he spilled blood.

MIO: He?

GAUNT: Sir, I know too well
    that he was guilty.

MIO: Who are you? How do you know?
    I've searched the records through, the trial and what
    came after, and in all that million words
    I found not one unbiased argument
    to fix the crime on him.

GAUNT: And you yourself,
    were you unprejudiced?

MIO: Who are you?

ESDRAS: Sir,
    this gentleman is here, as you are here,
    to ask my son, as you have asked, what ground
    there might be for this talk of new evidence
    in your father's case. We gave him the same answer
    we've given you.

MIO: I'm sorry. I'd supposed
    his cause forgotten except by myself. There's still
    a defense committee then?

GAUNT: There may be. I
    am not connected with it.

ESDRAS: He is my guest,
    and asks to remain unknown.

MIO [*After a pause, looking at* GAUNT]: The judge at the trial
    was younger, but he had your face. Can it be
    that you're the man?—Yes—Yes.—The jury charge—
    I sat there as a child and heard your voice,
    and watched that Brahminical mouth. I knew even then
    you meant no good to him. And now you're here

to winnow out truth and justice—the fountainhead
of the lies that slew him! Are you Judge Gaunt?

GAUNT: I am.

MIO: Then tell me what damnation to what inferno
would fit the toad that sat in robes and lied
when he gave the charge, and knew he lied! Judge that,
and then go to your place in that hell!

GAUNT: I know and have known
what bitterness can rise against a court
when it must say, putting aside all weakness,
that a man's to die. I can forgive you that,
for you are your father's son, and you think of him
as a son thinks of his father. Certain laws
seem cruel in their operation; it's necessary
that we be cruel to uphold them. This cruelty
is kindness to those I serve.

MIO: I don't doubt that.
I know who it is you serve.

GAUNT: Would I have chosen
to rack myself with other men's despairs,
stop my ears, harden my heart, and listen only
to the voice of law and light, if I had hoped
some private gain for serving? In all my years
on the bench of a long-established commonwealth
not once has my decision been in question
save in this case. Not once before or since.
For hope of heaven or place on earth, or power
or gold, no man has had my voice, nor will
while I still keep the trust that's laid on me
to sentence and define.

MIO: Then why are you here?

GAUNT: My record's clean. I've kept it so. But suppose
with the best intent, among the myriad tongues
that come to testify, I had missed my way
and followed a perjured tale to a lethal end
till a man was forsworn to death? Could I rest or sleep
while there was doubt of this,
even while there was question in a layman's mind?
For always, night and day,
there lies on my brain like a weight, the admonition:

see truly, let nothing sway you; among all functions
there's but one godlike, to judge. Then see to it
you judge as a god would judge, with clarity,
with truth, with what mercy is found consonant
with order and law. Without law men are beasts,
and it's a judge's task to lift and hold them
above themselves. Let a judge be once mistaken
or step aside for a friend, and a gap is made
in the dikes that hold back anarchy and chaos,
and leave men bond but free.

MIO: Then the gap's been made,
and you made it.

GAUNT: I feared that too. May you be a judge
sometime, and know in what fear,
through what nights long
in fear, I scanned and verified and compared
the transcripts of the trial.

MIO: Without prejudice,
no doubt. It was never in your mind to prove
that you'd been right.

GAUNT: And conscious of that, too—
that that might be my purpose—watchful of that,
and jealous as his own lawyer of the rights
that should hedge the defendant!
And still I found no error,
shook not one staple of the bolts that linked
the doer to the deed! Still following on
from step to step, I watched all modern comment,
and saw it centered finally on one fact—
Garth Esdras was not called. This is Garth Esdras,
and you have heard him. Would his deposition
have justified a new trial?

MIO: No. It would not.

GAUNT: And there I come, myself. If the man were still
in his cell, and waiting, I'd have no faint excuse
for another hearing.

MIO: I've told you that I read
the trial from beginning to end. Every word you spoke
was balanced carefully to keep the letter
of the law and still convict—convict, by Christ,

if it tore the seven veils! You stand here now
running cascades of casuistry, to prove
to yourself and me that no judge of rank and breeding
could burn a man out of hate! But that's what you did
under all your varnish!

GAUNT: I've sought for evidence,
and you have sought. Have you found it? Can you cite
one fresh word in defense?

MIO: The trial itself
was shot full of legerdemain, prearranged to lead
the jury astray—

GAUNT: Could you prove that?

MIO: Yes!

GAUNT: And if
the jury were led astray, remember it's
the jury, by our Anglo-Saxon custom,
that finds for guilt or innocence. The judge
is powerless in that matter.

MIO: Not you! Your charge
misled the jury more than the evidence,
accepted every biased meaning, distilled
the poison for them!

GAUNT: But if that were so
I'd be the first, I swear it, to step down
among all men, and hold out both my hands
for manacles—yes, publish it in the streets,
that all I've held most sacred was defiled
by my own act. A judge's brain becomes
a delicate instrument to weigh men's lives
for good and ill—too delicate to bear
much tampering. If he should push aside
the weights and throw the beam, and say, this once
the man is guilty, and I will have it so
though his mouth cry out from the ground,
and all the world
revoke my word, he'd have a short way to go
to madness. I think you'd find him in the squares,
stopping the passers-by with arguments,—
see, I was right, the man was guilty there—
this was brought in against him, this—and this—

and I was left no choice! It's no light thing
when a long life's been dedicate to one end
to wrench the mind awry!

MIO: By your own thesis
you should be mad, and no doubt you are.

GAUNT: But my madness
is only this—that I would fain look back
on a life well-spent—without one stain—one breath
of stain to flaw the glass—not in men's minds
nor in my own. I take my God as witness
I meant to earn that clearness, and believe
that I have earned it. Yet my name is clouded
with the blackest, fiercest scandal of our age
that's touched a judge. What I can do to wipe
that smutch from my fame I will. I think you know
how deeply I've been hated, for no cause
that I can find there. Can it not be—and I ask this
quite honestly—that the great injustice lies
on your side and not mine? Time and time again
men have come before me perfect in their lives,
loved by all who knew them, loved at home,
gentle, not vicious, yet caught so ripe red-handed
in some dark violence there was no denying
where the onus lay.

MIO: That was not so with my father!

GAUNT: And yet it seemed so to me. To other men
who sat in judgment on him. Can you be sure—
I ask this in humility—that you,
who were touched closest by the tragedy,
may not have lost perspective—may have brooded
day and night on one theme—till your eyes are tranced
and show you one side only?

MIO: I see well enough.

GAUNT: And would that not be part of the malady—
to look quite steadily at the drift of things
but see there what you wish—not what is there—
not what another man to whom the story
was fresh would say is there?

MIO: You think I'm crazy.
Is that what you meant to say?

GAUNT: I've seen it happen
 with the best and wisest men. I but ask the question.
 I can't speak for you. Is it not true wherever
 you walk, through the little town where you knew him well,
 or flying from it, inland or by the sea,
 still walking at your side, and sleeping only
 when you too sleep, a shadow not your own
 follows, pleading and holding out its hands
 to be delivered from shame?

MIO: How you know that
 by God I don't know.

GAUNT: Because one specter haunted you and me—
 and haunts you still, but for me it's laid to rest
 now that my mind is satisfied. He died
 justly and not by error.
 [*A pause.*]

MIO [*Stepping forward*]: Do you care to know
 you've come so near to death it's miracle
 that pulse still beats in your splotchy throat?
 Do you know
 there's murder in me?

GAUNT: There was murder in your sire,
 and it's to be expected! I say he died
 justly, and he deserved it!

MIO: Yes, you'd like too well
 to have me kill you! That would prove your case
 and clear your name, and dip my father's name
 in stench forever! You'll not get that from me!
 Go home and die in bed, get it under cover,
 your lux-et-lex putrefaction of the right thing,
 you man that walks like a god!

GAUNT: Have I made you angry
 by coming too near the truth?

MIO: This sets him up,
 this venomous slug, this sets him up in a gown,
 deciding who's to walk above the earth
 and who's to lie beneath! And giving reasons!
 The cobra giving reasons; I'm a god,
 by Buddha, holy and worshipful my fang,
 and can I sink it in!

[He pauses, turns as if to go, then sits.]
This is no good.
This won't help much.
[The JUDGE *and* ESDRAS *look at each other.]*
GAUNT: We should be going.
ESDRAS: Yes.
[They prepare to go.]
I'll lend you my coat.
GAUNT *[Looking at it with distaste]*: No, keep it. A little rain
shouldn't matter to me.
ESDRAS: It freezes as it falls,
and you've a long way to go.
GAUNT: I'll manage, thank you.
*[*GAUNT *and* ESDRAS *go out,* ESDRAS *obsequious, closing the
door.]*
GARTH *[Looking at* MIO's *back]*: Well?
MIO *[Not moving]*: Let me sit here a moment.
*[*GARTH *shrugs his shoulders and goes toward the inner door.*
MIRIAMNE *opens it and comes out.* GARTH *looks at her, then
at* MIO, *then lays his fingers on his lips. She nods.* GARTH *goes
out.* MIRIAMNE *sits and watches* MIO. *After a little he turns
and sees her.]*
How did you come here?
MIRIAMNE: I live here.
MIO: Here?
MIRIAMNE: My name is Esdras. Garth
is my brother. The walls are thin.
I heard what was said.
MIO *[Stirring wearily]*: I'm going. This is no place for me.
MIRIAMNE: What place
would be better?
MIO: None. Only it's better to go.
Just to go.
*[She comes over to him, puts her arm round him and kisses
his forehead.]*
MIRIAMNE: Mio.
MIO: What do you want?
Your kisses burn me—and your arms. Don't offer
what I'm never to have! I can have nothing. They say
they'll cross the void sometime to the other planets

and men will breathe in that air.
Well, I could breathe there,
but not here now. Not on this ball of mud.
I don't want it.
MIRIAMNE: They can take away so little
with all their words. For you're a king among them.
I heard you, and loved your voice.
MIO: I thought I'd fallen
so low there was no further, and now a pit
opens beneath. It was bad enough that he
should have died innocent, but if he were guilty—
then what's my life—what have I left to do—?
The son of a felon—and what they spat on me
was earned—and I'm drenched with the stuff.
Here on my hands
and cheeks, their spittle hanging! I liked my hands
because they were like his. I tell you I've lived
by his innocence, lived to see it flash
and blind them all—
MIRIAMNE: Never believe them, Mio,
never.
[*She looks toward the inner door.*]
MIO: But it was truth I wanted, truth—
not the lies you'd tell yourself, or tell a woman,
or a woman tells you! The judge with his cobra mouth
may have spat truth—and I may be mad! For me—
your hands are too clean to touch me. I'm to have
the scraps from hotel kitchens—and instead of love
those mottled bodies that hitch themselves through alleys
to sell for dimes or nickels. Go, keep yourself chaste
for the baker bridegroom—baker and son of a baker,
let him get his baker's dozen on you!
MIRIAMNE: No—
say once you love me—say it once; I'll never
ask to hear it twice, nor for any kindness,
and you shall take all I have!
[GARTH *opens the inner door and comes out.*]
GARTH: I interrupt
a love scene, I believe. We can do without
your adolescent mawkishness.

[*To* MIRIAMNE.] You're a child.
You'll both remember that.

MIRIAMNE: I've said nothing to harm you—
and will say nothing.

GARTH: You're my sister, though,
and I take a certain interest in you. Where
have you two met?

MIRIAMNE: We danced together.

GARTH: Then
the dance is over, I think.

MIRIAMNE: I've always loved you
and tried to help you, Garth. And you've been kind.
Don't spoil it now.

GARTH: Spoil it how?

MIRIAMNE: Because I love him.
I didn't know it would happen. We danced together.
And the world's all changed. I see you through a mist,
and our father, too. If you brought this to nothing
I'd want to die.

GARTH [*To* MIO]: You'd better go.

MIO: Yes, I know.
[*He rises. There is a trembling knock at the door.* MIRI-
AMNE *goes to it. The* HOBO *is there shivering.*]

HOBO: Miss, could I sleep under the pipes tonight, miss?
Could I, please?

MIRIAMNE: I think—not tonight.

HOBO: There won't be any more nights—
if I don't get warm, miss.

MIRIAMNE: Come in.
[*The* HOBO *comes in, looks round deprecatingly, then goes
to a corner beneath a huge heating pipe, which he crawls
under as if he'd been there before.*]

HOBO: Yes, miss, thank you.

GARTH: Must we put up with that?

MIRIAMNE: Father let him sleep there—
last winter.

GARTH: Yes, God, yes.

MIO: Well, good night.

MIRIAMNE: Where will you go?

MIO: Yes, where? As if it mattered.

GARTH: Oh, sleep here, too.
We'll have a row of you under the pipes.

MIO: No, thanks.

MIRIAMNE: Mio, I've saved a little money. It's only
some pennies, but you must take it.

[*She shakes some coins out of a box into her hand.*]

MIO: No, thanks.

MIRIAMNE: And I love you.
You've never said you love me.

MIO: Why wouldn't I love you
when you're clean and sweet,
and I've seen nothing sweet or clean
this last ten years? I love you. I leave you that
for what good it may do you. It's none to me.

MIRIAMNE: Then kiss me.

MIO [*Looking at* GARTH]: With that scowling over us? No.
When it rains, some spring
on the planet Mercury, where the spring comes often,
I'll meet you there, let's say. We'll wait for that.
It may be some time till then.

[*The outside door opens and* ESDRAS *enters with* JUDGE
GAUNT, *then, after a slight interval,* TROCK *follows.* TROCK
surveys the interior and its occupants one by one, carefully.]

TROCK: I wouldn't want to cause you inconvenience,
any of you, and especially the Judge.
I think you know that. You've all got things to do—
trains to catch, and so on. But trains can wait.
Hell, nearly anything can wait, you'll find,
only I can't. I'm the only one that can't
because I've got no time. Who's all this here?
Who's that?

[*He points to the* HOBO.]

ESDRAS: He's a poor half-wit, sir,
that sometimes sleeps there.

TROCK: Come out. I say come out,
whoever you are.

[*The* HOBO *stirs and looks up.*]

Yes, I mean you. Come out.

[*The* HOBO *emerges.*]

What's your name?

HOBO: They mostly call me Oke.

TROCK: What do you know?

HOBO: No, sir.

TROCK: Where are you from?

HOBO: I got a piece of bread.

[*He brings it out, trembling.*]

TROCK: Get back in there!

[*The* HOBO *crawls back into his corner.*]

Maybe you want to know why I'm doing this.

Well, I've been robbed, that's why—

robbed five or six times;

the police can't find a thing—so I'm out for myself—

if you want to know.

[*To* MIO.] Who are you?

MIO: Oh, I'm a half-wit,

came in here by mistake. The difference is

I've got no piece of bread.

TROCK: What's your name?

MIO: My name?

Theophrastus Such. That's respectable.

You'll find it all the way from here to the coast

on the best police blotters.

Only the truth is we're a little touched in the head,

Oke and me. You'd better ask somebody else.

TROCK: Who is he?

ESDRAS: His name's Romagna. He's the son.

TROCK: Then what's he doing here? You said you were on the level.

GARTH: He just walked in. On account of the stuff in the papers. We didn't ask him.

TROCK: God, we are a gathering. Now if we had Shadow we'd be all here, huh? Only I guess we won't see Shadow. No, that's too much to ask.

MIO: Who's Shadow?

TROCK: Now you're putting questions. Shadow was just nobody, you see. He blew away. It might happen to anyone.

[*He looks at* GARTH.]

Yes, anyone at all.

MIO: Why do you keep your hand in your pocket, friend?

TROCK: Because I'm cold, punk. Because I've been outside and

it's cold as the tomb of Christ. [*To* GARTH.] Listen, there's
a car waiting up at the street to take the Judge home. We'll
take him to the car.

GARTH: That's not necessary.

ESDRAS: No.

TROCK: I say it is, see? You wouldn't want to let the Judge
walk, would you? The Judge is going to ride where he's going,
with a couple of chauffeurs, and everything done in style.
Don't you worry about the Judge. He'll be taken care of.
For good.

GARTH: I want no hand in it.

TROCK: Anything happens to me happens to you too, musician.

GARTH: I know that.

TROCK: Keep your mouth out of it then. And you'd better keep
the punk here tonight, just for luck.

> [*He turns toward the door. There is a brilliant lightning
> flash through the windows, followed slowly by dying thunder.
> TROCK opens the door. The rain begins to pour in sheets.*]

Jesus, somebody tipped it over again!

> [*A cough racks him.*]

Wait till it's over. It takes ten days off me every time I step
into it.

> [*He closes the door.*]

Sit down and wait.

> [*Lightning flashes again. The thunder is fainter.* ESDRAS,
> GARTH, *and the* JUDGE *sit down.*]

GAUNT: We were born too early. Even you who are young
are not of the elect. In a hundred years
man will put his finger on life itself, and then
he will live as long as he likes. For you and me
we shall die soon—one day, one year more or less,
when or where, it's no matter. It's what we call
an indeterminate sentence. I'm hungry.

> [GARTH *looks at* MIRIAMNE.]

MIRIAMNE: There was nothing left
tonight.

HOBO: I've got a piece of bread.

> [*He breaks his bread in two and hands half to the* JUDGE.]

GAUNT: I thank you, sir.

> [*He eats.*]

This is not good bread.

[*He rises.*]

Sir, I am used
to other company. Not better, perhaps, but their clothes
were different. These are what it's the fashion to call
the underprivileged.

TROCK: Oh, hell!

[*He turns toward the door.*]

MIO [*To* TROCK]: It would seem that you and the Judge know
each other.

[TROCK *faces him.*]

TROCK: I've been around.

MIO: Maybe you've met before.

TROCK: Maybe we have.

MIO: Will you tell me where?

TROCK: How long do you want to live?

MIO: How long? Oh, I've got big ideas about that.

TROCK: I thought so. Well, so far I've got nothing against you
but your name, see? You keep it that way.

[*He opens the door. The rain still falls in torrents. He
closes the door. As he turns from it, it opens again, and*
SHADOW, *white, bloodstained and dripping, stands in the doorway.* GARTH *rises.* TROCK *turns.*]

GAUNT [*To the* HOBO]: Yet if one were careful of his health,
ate sparingly, drank not at all, used himself wisely, it might
be that even an old man could live to touch immortality. They
may come on the secret sooner than we dare hope. You see?
It does no harm to try.

TROCK [*Backing away from* SHADOW]: By God, he's out of his
grave!

SHADOW [*Leaning against the doorway, holding a gun in his
hands*]: Keep your hands where they belong, Trock.
You know me.

TROCK: Don't! Don't! I had nothing to do with it!

[*He backs to the opposite wall.*]

SHADOW: You said the doctor gave you six months to live—
well, I don't give you that much. That's what you had, six
months, and so you start bumping off your friends to make
sure of your damn six months. I got it from you.
I know where I got it.

Because I wouldn't give it to the Judge.
So he wouldn't talk.
TROCK: Honest to God—
SHADOW: What God?
  The one that let you put three holes in me
  when I was your friend? Well, He let me get up again
  and walk till I could find you. That's as far as I get,
  but I got there, by God! And I can hear you
  even if I can't see!
  [*He takes a staggering step forward.*]
  A man needs blood
  to keep going.—I got this far.—And now I can't see!
  It runs out too fast—too fast—
  when you've got three slugs
  clean through you.
  Show me where he is, you fools! He's here!
  I got here!
  [*He drops the gun.*]
  Help me! Help me! Oh, God! Oh, God!
  I'm going to die! Where does a man lie down?
  I want to lie down!
    [MIRIAMNE *starts toward* SHADOW. GARTH *and* ESDRAS *help
    him into the next room,* MIRIAMNE *following.* TROCK *squats
    in his corner, breathing hard, looking at the door.* MIO *stands,
    watching* TROCK. GARTH *returns, wiping his hand with a hand-
    kerchief.* MIO *picks up and pockets the gun.* MIRIAMNE *comes
    back and leans against the door jamb.*]
GAUNT: You will hear it said that an old man makes a good
  judge, being calm, clear-eyed, without passion. But this is
  not true. Only the young love truth and justice. The old are
  savage, wary, violent, swayed by maniac desires, cynical of
  friendship or love, open to bribery and the temptations of
  lust, corrupt and dastardly to the heart. I know these old
  men. What have they left to believe, what have they left to
  lose? Whorers of daughters, lickers of girls' shoes, contrivers
  of nastiness in the night, purveyors of perversion, worshipers
  of possession! Death is the only radical. He comes late, but
  he comes at last to put away the old men and give the young
  their places. It was time.
  [*He leers.*]

Here's one I heard yesterday:
Marmaduke behind the barn
  got his sister in a fix;
he says damn instead of darn;
ain't he cute? He's only six!

HOBO: He, he, he!

GAUNT: And the hoot owl hoots all night,
  and the cuckoo cooks all day,
and what with a minimum grace of God
  we pass the time away.

HOBO: He, he, he—I got ya!

[*He makes a sign with his thumb.*]

GAUNT [*Sings*]:
  And he led her all around
  and he laid her on the ground
  and he ruffled up the feathers of her
    cuckoo's nest!

HOBO: Ho, ho, ho!

GAUNT: I am not taken with the way you laugh. You should
  cultivate restraint.

[ESDRAS *reënters.*]

TROCK: Shut the door.

ESDRAS: He won't come back again.

TROCK: I want the door shut! He was dead, I tell you!

[ESDRAS *closes the door.*]

  And Romagna was dead, too, once! Can't they keep a man
  under ground?

MIO: No. No more! They don't stay under ground any more,
  and they don't stay under water! Why did you have him
  killed?

TROCK: Stay away from me! I know you!

MIO: Who am I, then?

TROCK: I know you, damn you! Your name's Romagna!

MIO: Yes! And Romagna was dead, too, and Shadow was dead,
  but the time's come when you can't keep them down, these
  dead men! They won't stay down! They come in with their
  heads shot off and their entrails dragging! Hundreds of them!
  One by one—all you ever had killed! Watch the door! See!
  —It moves!

TROCK [*Looking, fascinated, at the door*]: Let me out of here!
[*He tries to rise.*]

MIO [*The gun in his hand*]: Oh, no! You'll sit there and wait
for them! One by one they'll come through that door, pulling
their heads out of the gunny sacks where you tied them—
glauming over you with their rotten hands! They'll see without eyes and crawl over you—Shadow and the paymaster
and all the rest of them—putrescent bones without eyes!
Now! Look! Look! For I'm first among them!

TROCK: I've done for better men than you! And I'll do for you!

GAUNT [*Rapping on the table*]: Order, gentlemen, order! The
witness will remember that a certain decorum is essential in
the courtroom!

MIO: By God, he'll answer me!

GAUNT [*Thundering*]: Silence! Silence! Let me remind you of
courtesy toward the witness! What case is this you try?

MIO: The case of the state against Bartolomeo Romagna for the
murder of the paymaster!

GAUNT: Sir, that was disposed of long ago!

MIO: Never disposed of, never, not while I live!

GAUNT: Then we'll have done with it now! I deny the appeal!
I have denied the appeal before and I do so again!

HOBO: He, he!—He thinks he's in the moving pictures!
[*A flash of lightning.*]

GAUNT: Who set that flash! Bailiff, clear the court! This is not
Flemington, gentlemen! We are not conducting this case to
make a journalistic holiday!
[*The thunder rumbles faintly.* GARTH *opens the outside
door and faces a solid wall of rain.*]
Stop that man! He's one of the defendants!
[GARTH *closes the door.*]

MIO: Then put him on the stand!

GARTH: What do you think you're doing?

MIO: Have you any objection?

GAUNT: The objection is not sustained. We will hear the new
evidence. Call your witness.

MIO: Garth Esdras!

GAUNT: He will take the stand!

GARTH: If you want me to say what I said before I'll say it!

MIO: Call Trock Estrella then!

GAUNT: Trock Estrella to the stand!

TROCK: No, by God!

MIO: Call Shadow, then! He'll talk! You thought he was dead,
 but he'll get up again and talk!

TROCK [*Screaming*]: What do you want of me?

MIO: You killed the paymaster! You!

TROCK: You lie! It was Shadow killed him!

MIO: And now I know! Now I know!

GAUNT: Again I remind you of courtesy toward the witness!

MIO: I know them now!
 Let me remind you of courtesy toward the dead!
 He says that Shadow killed him! If Shadow were here
 he'd say it was Trock! There were three men involved
 in the new version of the crime for which
 my father died! Shadow and Trock Estrella
 as principals in the murder—Garth as witness!—
 Why are they here together?—and you—the Judge—
 why are you here? Why, because you were all afraid
 and you drew together out of that fear to arrange
 a story you could tell! And Trock killed Shadow
 and meant to kill the Judge out of that same fear—
 to keep them quiet! This is the thing I've hunted
 over the earth to find out, and I'd be blind
 indeed if I missed it now!
 [*To* GAUNT.] You heard what he said:
 It was Shadow killed him! Now let the night conspire
 with the sperm of hell! It's plain beyond denial
 even to this fox of justice—and all his words
 are curses on the wind! You lied! You lied!
 You knew this too!

GAUNT [*Low*]: Let me go. Let me go!

MIO: Then why
 did you let my father die?

GAUNT: Suppose it known,
 but there are things a judge must not believe
 though they should head and fester underneath
 and press in on his brain. Justice once rendered
 in a clear burst of anger, righteously,
 upon a very common laborer,
 confessed an anarchist, the verdict found

and the precise machinery of law
invoked to know him guilty—think what furor
would rock the state if the court then flatly said;
all this was lies—must be reversed? It's better,
as any judge can tell you, in such cases,
holding the common good to be worth more
than small injustice, to let the record stand,
let one man die. For justice, in the main,
is governed by opinion. Communities
will have what they will have, and it's quite as well,
after all, to be rid of anarchists. Our rights
as citizens can be maintained as rights
only while we are held to be the peers
of those who live about us. A vendor of fish
is not protected as a man might be
who kept a market. I own I've sometimes wished
this was not so, but it is. The man you defend
was unfortunate—and his misfortune bore
almost as heavily on me.—I'm broken—
broken across. You're much too young to know
how bitter it is when a worn connection chars
and you can't remember—can't remember.
[*He steps forward.*]
You
will not repeat this? It will go no further?
MIO: No.
No further than the moon takes the tides—no further
than the news went when he died—
when you found him guilty
and they flashed that round the earth. Wherever men
still breathe and think, and know what's done to them
by the powers above, they'll know. That's all I ask.
That'll be enough.
[TROCK *has risen and looks darkly at* MIO.]
GAUNT: Thank you. For I've said some things
a judge should never say.
TROCK: Go right on talking.
Both of you. It won't get far, I guess.
MIO: Oh, you'll see to that?
TROCK: I'll see to it. Me and some others.

Maybe I lost my grip there just for a minute.
That's all right.
MIO: Then see to it! Let it rain!
What can you do to me now when the night's on fire
with this thing I know? Now I could almost wish
there was a god somewhere—I could almost think
there was a god—and he somehow brought me here
and set you down before me here in the rain
where I could wring this out of you! For it's said,
and I've heard it, and I'm free! He was as I thought him,
true and noble and upright, even when he went
to a death contrived because he was as he was
and not your kind! Let it rain! Let the night speak fire
and the city go out with the tide, for he was a man
and I know you now, and I have my day!

[*There is a heavy knock at the outside door.* MIRIAMNE
opens it, at a glance from GARTH. *The* POLICEMAN *is there in
oilskins.*]

POLICE: Evening.
[*He steps in, followed by a* SERGEANT, *similarly dressed.*]
We're looking for someone
might be here. Seen an old man around
acting a little off?
[*To* ESDRAS.] You know the one
I mean. You saw him out there. Jeez! You've got
a funny crowd here!
[*He looks round. The* HOBO *shrinks into his corner.*]
That's the one I saw.
What do you think?
SERGEANT: That's him. You mean to say
you didn't know him by his pictures?
[*He goes to* GAUNT.]
Come on, old man.
You're going home.
GAUNT: Yes, sir. I've lost my way.
I think I've lost my way.
SERGEANT: I'll say you have.
About three hundred miles. Now don't you worry.
We'll get you back.

GAUNT: I'm a person of some rank
in my own city.
SERGEANT: We know that. One look at you
and we'd know that.
GAUNT: Yes, sir.
POLICE: If it isn't Trock!
Trock Estrella. How are you, Trock?
TROCK: Pretty good,
Thanks.
POLICE: Got out yesterday again, I hear?
TROCK: That's right.
SERGEANT: Hi'ye, Trock?
TROCK: O.K.
SERGEANT: You know we got orders
to watch you pretty close. Be good now, baby,
or back you go. Don't try to pull anything,
not in my district.
TROCK: No, sir.
SERGEANT: No bumping off.
If you want my advice quit carrying a gun.
Try earning your living for once.
TROCK: Yeah.
SERGEANT: That's an idea.
Because if we find any stiffs on the riverbank
we'll know who to look for.
MIO: Then look in the other room!
I accuse that man of murder! Trock Estrella!
He's a murderer!
POLICE: Hello. I remember you.
SERGEANT: Well, what murder?
MIO: It was Trock Estrella
that robbed the pay roll thirteen years ago
and did the killing my father died for! You know
the Romagna case! Romagna was innocent,
and Trock Estrella guilty!
SERGEANT [*Disgusted*]: Oh, what the hell!
That's old stuff—the Romagna case.
POLICE: Hey, Sarge!
[*The* SERGEANT *and* POLICEMAN *come closer together.*]
The boy's a professional kidder. He took me over

about half an hour ago. He kids the police
and then ducks out!

SERGEANT: Oh, yeah?

MIO: I'm not kidding now.
You'll find a dead man there in the next room
and Estrella killed him!

SERGEANT: Thirteen years ago?
And nobody smelled him yet?

MIO [*Pointing*]: I accuse this man
of two murders! He killed the paymaster long ago
and had Shadow killed tonight. Look, look for yourself!
He's there all right!

POLICE: Look, boy. You stood out there
and put the booby sign on the dumb police
because they're fresh out of Ireland. Don't try it twice.

SERGEANT [*To* GARTH]: Any corpses here?

GARTH: Not that I know of.

SERGEANT: I thought so.
[MIO *looks at* MIRIAMNE.]
[*To* MIO.] Think up a better one.

MIO: Have I got to drag him
out here where you can see him?
[*He goes toward the inner door.*]
Can't you scent a murder
when it's under your nose? Look in!

MIRIAMNE: No, no—there's no one—there's no one there!

SERGEANT [*Looking at* MIRIAMNE]: Take a look inside.

POLICE: Yes, sir.
[*He goes into the inside room. The* SERGEANT *goes up to
the door. The* POLICEMAN *returns.*]
He's kidding, Sarge. If there's a cadaver
in here I don't see it.

MIO: You're blind then!
[*He goes into the room, the* SERGEANT *following him.*]

SERGEANT: What do you mean?
[*He comes out,* MIO *following him.*]
When you make a charge of murder it's better to have
the corpus delicti, son. You're the kind puts in
fire alarms to see the engine!

MIO: By God, he was there!
  He went in there to die.
SERGEANT: I'll bet he did.
  And I'm Haile Selassie's aunt! What's your name?
MIO: Romagna.
  [*To* GARTH.] What have you done with him?
GARTH: I don't know what you mean.
SERGEANT [*To* GARTH]: What's he talking about?
GARTH: I wish I could tell you.
  I don't know.
SERGEANT: He must have seen something.
POLICE: He's got
  the Romagna case on the brain. You watch yourself,
  chump, or you'll get run in.
MIO: Then they're in it together!
  All of them!
  [*To* MIRIAMNE.] Yes, and you!
GARTH: He's nuts, I say.
MIRIAMNE [*Gently*]: You have dreamed something—isn't it
    true?
  You've dreamed—
  But truly, there was no one—
  [MIO *looks at her comprehendingly*.]
MIO: You want me to say it.
  [*He pauses.*]
  Yes, by God, I was dreaming.
SERGEANT [*To* POLICEMAN]: I guess you're right.
  We'd better be going. Haven't you got a coat?
GAUNT: No, sir.
SERGEANT: I guess I'll have to lend you mine.
  [*He puts his oilskins on* GAUNT.]
  Come on, now. It's getting late.
  [GAUNT, *the* POLICEMAN, *and the* SERGEANT *go out.*]
TROCK: They're welcome to him.
  His fuse is damp. Where is that walking fool
  with the three slugs in him?
ESDRAS: He fell in the hall beyond
  and we left him there.
TROCK: That's lucky for some of us. Is he out this time
  or is he still butting around?

ESDRAS: He's dead.

TROCK: That's perfect.

[*To* MIO.] Don't try using your firearms, amigo baby,
the Sarge is outside.

[*He turns to go.*]
Better ship that carrion
back in the river! The one that walks when he's dead;
maybe he'll walk the distance for you.

GARTH: Coming back?

TROCK: Well, if I come back,
you'll see me. If I don't, you won't. Let the punk
go far as he likes. Turn him loose and let him go.
And may you all rot in hell.

[*He pulls his coat around him and goes to the left.* MIRI-
AMNE *climbs up to look out a window.*]

MIRIAMNE: He's climbing up to the street,
along the bridgehead.

[*She turns.*]
Quick, Mio! It's safe now! Quick!

GARTH: Let him do as he likes.

MIRIAMNE: What do you mean? Garth! He means to kill him!
You know that!

GARTH: I've no doubt Master Romagna
can run his own campaign.

MIRIAMNE: But he'll be killed!

MIO: Why did you lie about Shadow?

[*There is a pause.* GARTH *shrugs, walks across the room,
and sits.*]
You were one of the gang!

GARTH: I can take a death if I have to! Go tell your story, only
watch your step, for I warn you, Trock's out gunning and
you may not walk very far. Oh, I could defend it but it's
hardly worth-while.
If they get Trock they get me too.
Go tell them. You owe me nothing.

ESDRAS: This Trock you saw,
no one defends him. He's earned his death so often
there's nobody to regret it. But his crime,
his same crime that has dogged you, dogged us down
from what little we had, to live here among the drains

where the water bugs break out like a scrofula
on what we eat—and if there's lower to go
we'll go there when you've told your story. And more
that I haven't heart to speak—

MIO [*To* GARTH]: My father died
in your place. And you could have saved him!
You were one of the gang!

GARTH: Why, there you are.
You certainly owe me nothing.

MIRIAMNE [*Moaning*]: I want to die.
I want to go away.

MIO: Yes, and you lied!
And trapped me into it!

MIRIAMNE: But Mio, he's my brother.
I couldn't give them my brother.

MIO: No. You couldn't.
You were quite right. The gods were damned ironic
tonight, and they've worked it out.

ESDRAS: What will be changed
if it comes to trial again? More blood poured out
to a mythical justice, but your father lying still
where he lies now.

MIO: The bright, ironical gods!
What fun they have in heaven! When a man prays hard
for any gift, they give it, and then one more
to boot that makes it useless.
[*To* MIRIAMNE.] You might have picked
some other stranger to dance with!

MIRIAMNE: I know.

MIO: Or chosen
some other evening to sit outside in the rain.
But no, it had to be this. All my life long
I've wanted only one thing, to say to the world
and prove it: the man you killed was clean and true
and full of love as the twelve-year-old that stood
and taught in the temple. I can say that now
and give my proofs—and now you stick a girl's face
between me and the rites I've sworn the dead
shall have of me! You ask too much! Your brother
can take his chance! He was ready enough to let

an innocent man take certainty for him
to pay for the years he's had. That parts us, then,
but we're parted anyway, by the same dark wind
that blew us together. I shall say what I have to say.
[*He steps back.*]
And I'm not welcome here.
MIRIAMNE: But don't go now! You've stayed
  too long! He'll be waiting!
MIO: Well, is this any safer?
  Let the winds blow, the four winds of the world,
  and take us to the four winds.
  [*The three are silent before him. He turns and goes out.*]

Curtain

ACT THREE

SCENE—*The riverbank outside the tenement, a little before the
close of the previous act. The rain still falls through the street
lamps. The* TWO YOUNG MEN IN SERGE *are leaning against the
masonry in a ray of light, concentrating on a game of chance.
Each holds in his hand a packet of ten or fifteen crisp bills.
They compare the numbers on the top notes and immediately
a bill changes hands. This goes on with varying fortune until
the tide begins to run toward the* 1ST GUNMAN, *who has ac-
cumulated nearly the whole supply. They play on in complete silence, evidently not wishing to make any noise. Occa-
sionally they raise their heads slightly to look carefully about.
Luck begins to favor the* 2ND GUNMAN, *and the notes come
his way. Neither evinces the slightest interest in how the
game goes. They merely play on, bored, half absorbed. There
is a slight noise at the tenement door. They put the bills
away and watch.* TROCK *comes out, pulls the door shut and
comes over to them. He says a few words too low to be heard,
and without changing expression the* YOUNG MEN *saunter
toward the right.* TROCK *goes out to the left, and the* 2ND

PLAYER, *catching that out of the corner of his eye, lingers in
a glimmer of light to go on with the game. The* 1ST, *with an
eye on the tenement door, begins to play without ado, and
the bills again shift back and forth, then concentrate in the
hands of the* 1ST GUNMAN. *The* 2ND *shrugs his shoulders,
searches his pockets, finds one bill, and playing with it begins to win heavily. They hear the door opening, and putting
the notes away, slip out in front of the rock.* MIO *emerges,
closes the door, looks round him, and walks to the left. Near
the corner of the tenement he pauses, reaches out his hand to
try the rain, looks up toward the street, and stands uncertainly a moment. He returns and leans against the tenement
wall.* MIRIAMNE *comes out.* MIO *continues to look off into
space as if unaware of her. She looks away.*

MIO: This rather takes one off his high horse.—What I mean,
tough weather for a hegira. You see, this is my sleeping suit,
and if I get it wet—basta!
MIRIAMNE: If you could only hide here.
MIO: Hide?
MIRIAMNE: Lucia would take you in. The street piano man.
MIO: At the moment I'm afflicted with claustrophobia. I prefer
to die in the open, seeking air.
MIRIAMNE: But you could stay there till daylight.
MIO: You're concerned about me.
MIRIAMNE: Shall I ask him?
MIO: No. On the other hand, there's a certain reason in your
concern. I looked up the street and our old friend Trock
hunches patiently under the warehouse eaves.
MIRIAMNE: I was sure of that.
MIO: And here I am, a young man on a cold night, waiting the
end of the rain. Being read my lesson by a boy, a blind boy—
you know the one I mean. Knee-deep in the salt marsh,
Miriamne, bitten from within, fought.
MIRIAMNE: Wouldn't it be better if you came back in the house?
MIO: You forget my claustrophobia.
MIRIAMNE: Let me walk with you, then. Please. If I stay beside
you he wouldn't dare.
MIO: And then again he might.—We don't speak the same lan-
guage, Miriamne.

MIRIAMNE: I betrayed you. Forgive me.

MIO: I wish I knew this region. There's probably a path along the bank.

MIRIAMNE: Yes. Shadow went that way.

MIO: That's true, too. So here I am, a young man on a wet night, and blind in my weather eye. Stay and talk to me.

MIRIAMNE: If it happens—it's my fault.

MIO: Not at all, sweet. You warned me to keep away. But I would have it. Now I have to find a way out. It's like a chess game. If you think long enough there's always a way out.— For one or the other.—I wonder why white always wins and black always loses in the problems. White to move and mate in three moves. But what if white were to lose—ah, what then? Why, in that case, obviously black would be white and white would be black.—As it often is.—As we often are.— Might makes white. Losers turn black. Do you think I'd have time to draw a gun?

MIRIAMNE: No.

MIO: I'm a fair shot. Also I'm fair game.

[*The door of the tenement opens and* GARTH *comes out to look about quickly. Seeing only* MIO *and* MIRIAMNE *he goes in and comes out again almost immediately carrying one end of a door on which a body lies covered with a cloth. The* HOBO *carries the other end. They go out to the right with their burden.*]

This is the burial of Shadow, then;
feet first he dips, and leaves the haunts of men.
Let us make mourn for Shadow, wetly lying,
in elegiac stanzas and sweet crying.
Be gentle with him, little cold waves and fishes;
nibble him not, respect his skin and tissues—

MIRIAMNE: Must you say such things?

MIO: My dear, some requiem is fitting over the dead, even for Shadow. But the last rhyme was bad.
Whittle him not, respect his dying wishes.
That's better. And then to conclude:
His aromatic virtues, slowly rising
will circumnamb the isle, beyond disguising.
He clung to life beyond the wont of men.
Time and his silence drink us all. Amen.

How I hate these identicals. The French allow them, but
the French have no principles anyway. You know, Miriamne,
there's really nothing mysterious about human life. It's purely
mechanical, like an electric appliance. Stop the engine that
runs the generator and the current's broken. When we think
the brain gives off a small electric discharge—quite measur-
able, and constant within limits. But that's not what makes
your hair stand up when frightened.

MIRIAMNE: I think it's a mystery.

MIO: Human life? We'll have to wear veils if we're to keep it
a mystery much longer. Now if Shadow and I were made up
into sausages we'd probably make very good sausages.

MIRIAMNE: Don't—

MIO: I'm sorry. I speak from a high place, far off, long ago,
looking down. The cortège returns.

[GARTH *and the* HOBO *return, carrying the door, the cloth
lying loosely over it.*]

I hope you placed an obol in his mouth to pay the ferryman?
Even among the Greeks a little money was prerequisite to
Elysium.

[GARTH *and the* HOBO *go inside, silent.*]

No? It's grim to think of Shadow lingering among lesser
shades on the hither side. For lack of a small gratuity.

[ESDRAS *comes out the open door and closes it behind him.*]

ESDRAS: You must wait here, Mio, or go inside. I know
you don't trust me, and I haven't earned your trust.
You're young enough to seek truth—
and there is no truth;
and I know that—
but I shall call the police and see that you
get safely off.

MIO: It's a little late for that.

ESDRAS: I shall try.

MIO: And your terms? For I daresay you make terms?

ESDRAS: No.

MIO: Then let me remind you what will happen.
The police will ask some questions.
When they're answered
they'll ask more, and before they're done with it
your son will be implicated.

ESDRAS: Must he be?

MIO: I shall not keep quiet.

[*A pause.*]

ESDRAS: Still, I'll go.

MIO: I don't ask help, remember. I make no truce.
  He's not on my conscience, and I'm not on yours.

ESDRAS: But you
  could make it easier, so easily.
  He's my only son. Let him live.

MIO: His chance of survival's
  better than mine, I'd say.

ESDRAS: I'll go.

MIO: I don't urge it.

ESDRAS: No. I put my son's life in your hands.
  When you're gone,
  that may come to your mind.

MIO: Don't count on it.

ESDRAS: Oh,
  I count on nothing.

    [*He turns to go.* MIRIAMNE *runs over to him and silently
    kisses his hands.*]

  Not mine, not mine, my daughter!
  They're guilty hands.

  [*He goes out left.* GARTH'S *violin is heard within.*]

MIO: There was a war in heaven
  once, all the angels on one side, and all
  the devils on the other, and since that time
  disputes have raged among the learned, concerning
  whether the demons won, or the angels. Maybe
  the angels won, after all.

MIRIAMNE: And again, perhaps
  there are no demons or angels.

MIO: Oh, there are none.
  But I could love your father.

MIRIAMNE: I love him. You see,
  he's afraid because he's old. The less one has
  to lose the more he's afraid.

MIO: Suppose one had
  only a short stub end of life, or held
  a flashlight with the batteries run down

till the bulb was dim, and knew that he could live
while the glow lasted. Or suppose one knew
that while he stood in a little shelter of time
under a bridgehead, say, he could live, and then,
from then on, nothing. Then to lie and turn
with the earth and sun, and regard them not in the least
when the bulb was extinguished or he stepped beyond
his circle into the cold? How would he live
that last dim quarter-hour, before he went,
minus all recollection, to grow in grass
between cobblestones?

MIRIAMNE: Let me put my arms round you, Mio.
Then if anything comes, it's for me, too.
[*She puts both arms round him.*]

MIO: Only suppose
this circle's charmed! To be safe until he steps
from this lighted space into dark! Time pauses here
and high eternity grows in one quarter-hour
in which to live.

MIRIAMNE: Let me see if anyone's there—
there in the shadows.
[*She looks toward the right.*]

MIO: It might blast our eternity—
blow it to bits. No, don't go. This is forever,
here where we stand. And I ask you, Miriamne,
how does one spend a forever?

MIRIAMNE: You're frightened?

MIO: Yes.
So much that time stands still.

MIRIAMNE: Why didn't I speak—
tell them—when the officers were here? I failed you
in that one moment!

MIO: His life for mine? Oh, no.
I wouldn't want it, and you couldn't give it.
And if I should go on living we're cut apart
by that brother of yours.

MIRIAMNE: Are we?

MIO: Well, think about it.
A body lies between us, buried in quicklime.

Your allegiance is on the other side of that grave
and not to me.

MIRIAMNE: No, Mio! Mio, I love you!

MIO: I love you, too, but in case my life went on
beyond that barrier of dark—then Garth
would run his risk of dying.

MIRIAMNE: He's punished, Mio.
His life's been torment to him. Let him go,
for my sake, Mio.

MIO: I wish I could. I wish
I'd never seen him—or you. I've steeped too long
in this thing. It's in my teeth and bones. I can't
let go or forget. And I'll not add my lie
to the lies that cumber his ground. We live our days
in a storm of lies that drifts the truth too deep
for path or shovel; but I've set my foot on a truth
for once, and I'll trail it down!

[*A silence.* MIRIAMNE *looks out to the right.*]

MIRIAMNE: There's someone there—
I heard—

[CARR *comes in from the right.*]

MIO: It's Carr.

CARR: That's right. No doubt about it.
Excuse me.

MIO: Glad to see you. This is Miriamne.
Carr's a friend of mine.

CARR: You're better employed
than when I saw you last.

MIO: Bow to the gentleman,
Miriamne. That's meant for you.

MIRIAMNE: Thank you, I'm sure.
Should I leave you, Mio? You want to talk?

MIO: Oh, no,
we've done our talking.

MIRIAMNE: But—

CARR: I'm the one's out of place—
I wandered back because I got worried about you,
that's the truth.—Oh—those two fellows with the hats
down this way, you know, the ones that ran

after we heard the shooting—they're back again,
lingering or malingering down the bank,
revisiting the crime, I guess. They may
mean well.

MIO: I'll try to avoid them.

CARR: I didn't care
for the way they looked at me.—No luck, I suppose,
with that case history? The investigation
you had on hand?

MIO: I can't say. By the way,
the stiff that fell in the water and we saw swirling
down the eddy, he came trudging up, later on,
long enough to tell his name. His name was Shadow,
but he's back in the water now. It's all in an evening.
These things happen here.

CARR: Good God!

MIO: I know.
I wouldn't believe it if you told it.

CARR: But—
the man was alive?

MIO: Oh, not for long! He's dunked
for good this time. That's all that's happened.

CARR: Well,
if you don't need me—

MIRIAMNE: You had a message to send—
have you forgotten—?

MIO: I?—Yes, I had a message—
but I won't send it—not now.

MIRIAMNE: Then I will—!

MIO: No.
Let it go the way it is! It's all arranged
another way. You've been a good scout, Carr,
the best I ever knew on the road.

CARR: That sounds
like making your will.

MIO: Not yet, but when I do
I've thought of something to leave you. It's the view
of Mount Rainier from the Seattle jail,
snow over cloud. And the rusty chain in my pocket

from a pair of handcuffs my father wore. That's all
the worldly goods I'm seized of.

CARR: Look, Mio—hell—
if you're in trouble—

MIO: I'm not. Not at all. I have
a genius that attends me where I go,
and guards me now. I'm fine.

CARR: Well, that's good news.
He'll have his work cut out.

MIO: Oh, he's a genius.

CARR: I'll see you then.
I'll be at the Grand Street place. I'm lucky tonight,
and I can pay. I could even pay for two.

MIO: Thanks, I may take you up.

CARR: Good night.

MIO: Right, Carr.

CARR [*To* MIRIAMNE]: Good night.

MIRIAMNE [*After a pause*]: Good night.
    [CARR *goes out to the left.*]
Why did you do that? He's your genius, Mio,
and you let him go.

MIO: I couldn't help it.

MIRIAMNE: Call him.
Run after him and call him!

MIO: I tried to say it
and it strangled in my throat. I might have known
you'd win in the end.

MIRIAMNE: Is it for me?

MIO: For you?
It stuck in my throat, that's all I know.

MIRIAMNE: Oh, Mio,
I never asked for that! I only hoped
Garth could go clear.

MIO: Well, now he will.

MIRIAMNE: But you—
It was your chance!

MIO: I've lost
my taste for revenge if it falls on you. Oh, God,
deliver me from the body of this death

I've dragged behind me all these years! Miriamne!
Miriamne!

MIRIAMNE: Yes!

MIO: Miriamne, if you love me
teach me a treason to what I am, and have been,
till I learn to live like a man! I think I'm waking
from a long trauma of hate and fear and death
that's hemmed me from my birth—and glimpse a life
to be lived in hope—but it's young in me yet, I can't
get free, or forgive! But teach me how to live
and forget to hate!

MIRIAMNE: He would have forgiven.

MIO: He?

MIRIAMNE: Your father.
[*A pause.*]

MIO: Yes.
[*Another pause.*]
You'll think it strange, but I've never
remembered that.

MIRIAMNE: How can I help you?

MIO: You have.

MIRIAMNE: If I were a little older—if I knew
the things to say! I can only put out my hands
and give you back the faith you bring to me
by being what you are. Because to me
you are all hope and beauty and brightness drawn
across what's black and mean!

MIO: He'd have forgiven—
Then there's no more to say—I've groped long enough
through this everglades of old revenges—here
the road ends.—Miriamne, Miriamne,
the iron I wore so long—it's eaten through
and fallen from me. Let me have your arms.
They'll say we're children—Well—the world's made up
of children.

MIRIAMNE: Yes.

MIO: But it's too late for me.

MIRIAMNE: No.
[*She goes into his arms, and they kiss for the first time.*]
Then we'll meet again?

MIO: Yes.

MIRIAMNE: Where?

MIO: I'll write—
or send Carr to you.

MIRIAMNE: You won't forget?

MIO: Forget?
Whatever streets I walk, you'll walk them, too,
from now on, and whatever roof or stars
I have to house me, you shall share my roof
and stars and morning. I shall not forget.

MIRIAMNE: God keep you!

MIO: And keep you. And this to remember!
if I should die, Miriamne, this half hour
is our eternity. I came here seeking
light in darkness, running from the dawn,
and stumbled on a morning.

[*One of the* TWO YOUNG MEN IN SERGE *strolls in casually
from the right, looks up and down without expression, then,
seemingly having forgotten something, retraces his steps and
goes out.* ESDRAS *comes in slowly from the left. He has lost
his hat, and his face is bleeding from a slight cut on the temple. He stands abjectly near the tenement.*]

MIRIAMNE: Father—what is it?

[*She goes toward* ESDRAS.]

ESDRAS: Let me alone.

[*He goes nearer to* MIO.]
He wouldn't let me pass.
The street's so icy up along the bridge
I had to crawl on my knees—he kicked me back
three times—and then he held me there—I swear
what I could do I did! I swear to you
I'd save you if I could.

MIO: What makes you think
that I need saving?

ESDRAS: Child, save yourself if you can!
He's waiting for you.

MIO: Well, we knew that before.

ESDRAS: He won't wait much longer. He'll come here—
he told me so. Those damned six months of his—

he wants them all—and you're to die—you'd spread
his guilt—I had to listen to it—

MIO: Wait—

[*He walks forward and looks casually to the right, then
returns.*]

There must be some way up through the house and out
across the roof—

ESDRAS: He's watching that. But come in—
and let me look.—

MIO: I'll stay here, thanks. Once in
and I'm a rat in a deadfall—I'll stay here—
look for me if you don't mind.

ESDRAS: Then watch for me—
I'll be on the roof—

[*He goes in hurriedly.*]

MIO [*Looking up*]: Now all you silent powers
that make the sleet and dark, and never yet
have spoken, give us a sign, let the throw be ours
this once, on this longest night, when the winter sets
his foot on the threshold leading up to spring
and enters with remembered cold—let fall
some mercy with the rain. We are two lovers
here in your night, and we wish to live.

MIRIAMNE: Oh, Mio—
if you pray that way, nothing good will come!
You're bitter, Mio.

MIO: How many floors has this building?

MIRIAMNE: Five or six. It's not as high as the bridge.

MIO: No, I thought not. How many pomegranate seeds
did you eat, Persephone?

MIRIAMNE: Oh, darling, darling,
if you die, don't die alone.

MIO: I'm afraid I'm damned
to hell, and you're not damned at all. Good God,
how long he takes to climb!

MIRIAMNE: The stairs are steep.

[*A slight pause.*]

MIO: I'll follow him.

MIRIAMNE: He's there—at the window—now.
He waves you to go back, not to go in.

Mio, see, that path between the rocks—
they're not watching that—they're out at the river—
I can see them there—they can't watch both—
it leads to a street above.

MIO: I'll try it, then.
Kiss me. You'll hear. But if you never hear—
then I'm the king of hell, Persephone,
and I'll expect you.

MIRIAMNE: Oh, lover, keep safe.

MIO: Good-by.

*[He slips out quickly between the rocks. There is a quick
machine gun rat-tat. The violin stops.* MIRIAMNE *runs toward
the path.* MIO *comes back slowly, a hand pressed under his
heart.]*

It seems you were mistaken.

MIRIAMNE: Oh, God, forgive me!

[She puts an arm round him. He sinks to his knees.]

Where is it, Mio? Let me help you in! Quick, quick,
let me help you!

MIO: I hadn't thought to choose—this—ground—
but it will do.

[He slips down.]

MIRIAMNE: Oh, God, forgive me!

MIO: Yes?
The king of hell was not forgiven then,
Dis is his name, and Hades is his home—
and he goes alone—

MIRIAMNE: Why does he bleed so? Mio, if you go
I shall go with you.

MIO: It's better to stay alive.
I wanted to stay alive—because of you—
I leave you that—and what he said to me dying:
I love you, and will love you after I die.
Tomorrow, I shall still love you, as I've loved
the stars I'll never see, and all the mornings
that might have been yours and mine. Oh, Miriamne,
you taught me this.

MIRIAMNE: If only I'd never seen you
then you could live—

MIO: That's blasphemy—Oh, God,

there might have been some easier way of it.
You didn't want me to die, did you, Miriamne—?
You didn't send me away—?

MIRIAMNE: Oh, never, never—

MIO: Forgive me—kiss me—I've got blood on your lips—
I'm sorry—it doesn't matter—I'm sorry—

[ESDRAS *and* GARTH *come out.*]

MIRIAMNE: Mio—
I'd have gone to die myself—you must hear this, Mio,
I'd have died to help you—you must listen, sweet,
you must hear it—

[*She rises.*]

I can die, too, see! You! There!
You in the shadows!—You killed him to silence him!

[*She walks toward the path.*]

But I'm not silenced! All that he knew I know,
and I'll tell it tonight! Tonight—
tell it and scream it
through all the streets—that Trock's a murderer
and he hired you for this murder!
Your work's not done—
and you won't live long! Do you hear?
You're murderers, and I know who you are!

[*The machine gun speaks again. She sinks to her knees.*
GARTH *runs to her.*]

GARTH: You little fool!

[*He tries to lift her.*]

MIRIAMNE: Don't touch me!

[*She crawls toward* MIO.]

Look, Mio! They killed me, too. Oh, you can believe me
now, Mio. You can believe I wouldn't hurt you,
because I'm dying! Why doesn't he answer me?
Oh, now he'll never know!

[*She sinks down, her hand over her mouth, choking.* GARTH
kneels beside her, then rises, shuddering. The HOBO *comes
out.* LUCIA *and* PINY *look out.*]

ESDRAS: It lacked only this.

GARTH: Yes.

[ESDRAS *bends over* MIRIAMNE, *then rises slowly.*]

Why was the bastard born? Why did he come here?

ESDRAS: Miriamne—Miriamne—yes, and Mio,
  one breath shall call you now—forgive us both—
  forgive the ancient evil of the earth
  that brought you here—
GARTH: Why must she be a fool?
ESDRAS: Well, they were wiser than you and I. To die
  when you are young and untouched, that's beggary
  to a miser of years, but the devils locked in synod
  shake and are daunted when men set their lives
  at hazard for the heart's love, and lose. And these,
  who were yet children, will weigh more than all
  a city's elders when the experiment
  is reckoned up in the end. Oh, Miriamne,
  and Mio—Mio, my son—know this where you lie,
  this is the glory of earthborn men and women,
  not to cringe, never to yield, but standing,
  take defeat implacable and defiant,
  die unsubmitting. I wish that I'd died so,
  long ago; before you're old you'll wish
  that you had died as they have. On this star,
  in this hard star-adventure, knowing not
  what the fires mean to right and left, nor whether
  a meaning was intended or presumed,
  man can stand up, and look out blind, and say:
  in all these turning lights I find no clue,
  only a masterless night, and in my blood
  no certain answer, yet is my mind my own,
  yet is my heart a cry toward something dim
  in distance, which is higher than I am
  and makes me emperor of the endless dark
  even in seeking! What odds and ends of life
  men may live otherwise, let them live, and then
  go out, as I shall go, and you. Our part
  is only to bury them. Come, take her up.
  They must not lie here.

  [LUCIA *and* PINY *come near to help.* ESDRAS *and* GARTH
  stoop to carry MIRIAMNE.]

Curtain

George S. Kaufman
and
Moss Hart

THE MAN WHO CAME TO DINNER

TO

ALEXANDER WOOLLCOTT

*For reasons that are
nobody's business*

THE AUTHORS

CHARACTERS

MRS. ERNEST W. STANLEY

MISS PREEN

RICHARD STANLEY

JUNE STANLEY

JOHN

SARAH

MRS. DEXTER

MRS. MCCUTCHEON

MR. STANLEY

MAGGIE CUTLER

DR. BRADLEY

SHERIDAN WHITESIDE

HARRIET STANLEY

BERT JEFFERSON

PROFESSOR METZ

THE LUNCHEON GUESTS

MR. BAKER

EXPRESSMAN

LORRAINE SHELDON

SANDY

BEVERLY CARLTON

WESTCOTT

RADIO TECHNICIANS

SIX YOUNG BOYS

BANJO

TWO DEPUTIES

A PLAINCLOTHES MAN

SCENES

The scene is the home of Mr. and Mrs. Stanley, in a small own in Ohio.

ACT ONE

Scene I—A December morning
Scene II—About a week later

ACT TWO

Another week has passed
Christmas Eve

ACT THREE

Christmas morning

ACT ONE

SCENE I

SCENE—*The curtain rises on the attractive living room in the home of* MR. *and* MRS. ERNEST W. STANLEY, *in a small town in Ohio. The* STANLEYS *are obviously people of means. The room is large, comfortable, tastefully furnished. Double doors lead into a library; there is a glimpse of a dining room at the rear, and we see the first half dozen steps of a handsome curved staircase. At the other side, bay windows, the entrance hall, the outer door.*

MRS. STANLEY *is hovering nervously near the library doors, which are tightly closed. She advances a step or two, retreats, advances again and this time musters up enough courage to listen at the door. Suddenly the doors are opened and she has to leap back.*

A NURSE *in full uniform emerges—scurries, rather, out of the room.*

An angry voice from within speeds her on her way: "Great dribbling cow!"

MRS. STANLEY [*Eagerly*]: How is he? Is he coming out?

[*But the* NURSE *has already disappeared into the dining room.*]

[*Simultaneously the doorbell rings—at the same time a young lad of twenty-one,* RICHARD STANLEY, *is descending the stairs.*]

RICHARD: I'll go, Mother.

[JOHN, *a white-coated servant, comes hurrying in from the dining room and starts up the stairs, two at a time.*]

MRS. STANLEY: What's the matter? What is it?

JOHN: They want pillows. [*And he is out of sight.*]

[*Meanwhile the* NURSE *is returning to the sick room. The voice is heard again as she opens the doors. "Don't call your-*

self a doctor in my presence! You're a quack if I ever saw one!"]

[RICHARD *returns from the hall, carrying two huge packages and a sheaf of cablegrams.*]

RICHARD: Four more cablegrams and more packages. . . . Dad is going crazy upstairs, with that bell ringing all the time.

[*Meanwhile* JUNE, *the daughter of the house, has come down the stairs. An attractive girl of twenty. At the same time the telephone is ringing.*]

MRS. STANLEY: Oh, dear! . . . June, will you go? . . . What did you say, Richard?

RICHARD [*Examining the packages*]: One's from New York and one from San Francisco.

MRS. STANLEY: There was something from Alaska early this morning.

JUNE [*At the telephone*]: Yes? . . . Yes, that's right.

MRS. STANLEY: Who is it?

[*Before* JUNE *can answer, the double doors are opened again and the* NURSE *appears. The voice calls after her: "Doesn't that bird-brain of yours ever function?"*]

THE NURSE: I—I'll get them right away. . . . He wants some Players Club cigarettes.

MRS. STANLEY: Players Club?

RICHARD: They have 'em at Kitchener's. I'll run down and get 'em.

[*He is off.*]

JUNE [*Still at the phone*]: Hello. . . . Yes, I'm waiting.

MRS. STANLEY: Tell me, Miss Preen, is he—are they bringing him out soon?

MISS PREEN [*Wearily*]: We're getting him out of bed now. He'll be out very soon . . . Oh, thank you. [*This last is to* JOHN, *who has descended the stairs with three or four pillows.*]

MRS. STANLEY: Oh, I'm so glad. He must be very happy.

[*And again we hear the invalid's voice as* MISS PREEN *passes into the room. "Trapped like a rat in this hell-hole! Take your fish-hooks off me!"*]

JUNE [*At the phone*]: Hello. . . . Yes, he's here, but he can't come to the phone right now . . . London? [*She covers the transmitter with her hand.*] It's London calling Mr. Whiteside.

MRS. STANLEY: London? My, my!

JUNE: Two o'clock? Yes, I think he could talk then. All right. [*She hangs up.*] Well, who do you think that was? Mr. H. G. Wells.

MRS. STANLEY [*Wild-eyed*]: H. G. Wells? On our telephone? [*The doorbell again.*]

JUNE: I'll go. This is certainly a busy house.

[*In the meantime* SARAH, *the cook, has come from the dining room with a pitcher of orange juice.*]

MRS. STANLEY [*As* SARAH *knocks on the double doors*]: Oh, that's fine, Sarah. Is it fresh?

SARAH: Yes, ma'am.

[*The doors are opened;* SARAH *hands the orange juice to the nurse. The voice roars once more: "You have the touch of a sex-starved cobra!"*]

SARAH [*Beaming*]: His voice is just the same as on the radio.

[*She disappears into the dining room as* JUNE *returns from the entrance hall, ushering in two friends of her mother's,* MRS. DEXTER *and* MRS. MCCUTCHEON. *One is carrying a flowering plant, partially wrapped; the other is holding, with some care, what turns out to be a jar of calf's-foot jelly.*]

THE LADIES: Good morning!

MRS. STANLEY: Girls, what do you think? He's getting up and coming out today!

MRS. MCCUTCHEON: You don't mean it!

MRS. DEXTER: Can we stay and see him?

MRS. STANLEY: Why, of course—he'd love it. Girls, do you know what just happened?

JUNE [*Departing*]: I'll be upstairs, Mother, if you want me.

MRS. STANLEY: What? . . . Oh, yes. June, tell your father he'd better come down, will you? Mr. Whiteside is coming out.

MRS. DEXTER: Is he really coming out today? I brought him a plant— Do you think it's all right if I give it to him?

MRS. STANLEY: Why, I think that would be lovely.

MRS. MCCUTCHEON: And some calf's-foot jelly.

MRS. STANLEY: Why, how nice! Who do you think was on the phone just now? H. G. Wells, from London. And look at those cablegrams. He's had calls and messages from all over this country and Europe. The New York *Times,* and Radio City Music Hall—I don't know why *they* called—and Felix Frankfurter, and Dr. Dafoe, the Mount Wilson Observatory—I just can't tell you what's been going on.

MRS. DEXTER: There's a big piece about it in this week's *Time*. Did you see it? [*Drawing it out of her bag.*]

MRS. STANLEY: No—really?

MRS. MCCUTCHEON: Your name's in it too, Daisy. It tells all about the whole thing. Listen: "Portly Sheridan Whiteside, critic, lecturer, wit, radio orator, intimate friend of the great and near great, last week found his celebrated wit no weapon with which to combat a fractured hip. The Falstaffian Mr. Whiteside, trekking across the country on one of his annual lecture tours, met his Waterloo in the shape of a small piece of ice on the doorstep of Mr. and Mrs. Ernest W. Stanley, of Mesalia, Ohio. Result: Cancelled lectures and disappointment to thousands of adoring clubwomen in Omaha, Denver, and points west. Further result: The idol of the air waves rests until further notice in home of surprised Mr. and Mrs. Stanley. Possibility: Christmas may be postponed this year." What's *that* mean?

MRS. STANLEY: Why, what do you think of that?

[*She takes the magazine; reads.*]

"A small piece of ice on the doorstep of Mr. and Mrs. Ernest"— think of it!

MRS. MCCUTCHEON: Of course if it were *my* house, Daisy, I'd have a bronze plate put on the step, right where he fell.

MRS. STANLEY: Well, of course I felt terrible about it. He just never goes to dinner anywhere, and he finally agreed to come here, and then *this* had to happen. Poor Mr. Whiteside! But it's going to be so wonderful having him with us, even for a little while. Just think of it! We'll sit around in the evening and discuss books and plays, all the great people he's known. And he'll talk in that wonderful way of his. He may even read *Good-bye, Mr. Chips* to us.

[MR. STANLEY, *solid, substantial—the American business man—is descending the stairs.*]

STANLEY: Daisy, I can't wait any longer. If—ah, good morning, ladies.

MRS. STANLEY: Ernest, he's coming out any minute, and H. G. Wells telephoned from London, and we're in *Time*. Look!

STANLEY [*Taking the magazine*]: I don't like this kind of

publicity at all, Daisy. When do you suppose he's going to leave?

MRS. STANLEY: Well, he's only getting up this morning—after all, he's had quite a shock, and he's been in bed for two full weeks. He'll certainly have to rest a few days, Ernest.

STANLEY: Well, I'm sure it's a great honor, his being in the house, but it *is* a little upsetting—phone going all the time, bells ringing, messenger boys running in and out—

[*Out of the sick room comes a businesslike-looking young woman about thirty. Her name is* MARGARET CUTLER—MAGGIE *to her friends.*]

MAGGIE: Pardon me, Mrs. Stanley—have the cigarettes come yet?

MRS. STANLEY: They're on the way, Miss Cutler. My son went for them.

MAGGIE: Thank you.

MRS. STANLEY: Ah—this is Miss Cutler, Mr. Whiteside's secretary. [*An exchange of "How do you do's?"*]

MAGGIE: May I move this chair?

MRS. STANLEY [*All eagerness*]: You mean he's—coming out now?

MAGGIE [*Quietly*]: He is indeed.

MRS. STANLEY: Ernest, call June. June! June! Mr. Whiteside is coming out!

[JOHN, *visible in the dining room, summons* SARAH *to attend the excitement.* "Sarah! Sarah!"]

[SARAH *and* JOHN *appear in the dining-room entrance,* JUNE *on the stairs.* MRS. STANLEY *and the two other ladies are keenly expectant; even* MR. STANLEY *is on the qui vive.*]

[*The double doors are opened once more, and* DR. BRADLEY *appears, bag in hand. He has taken a good deal of punishment, and speaks with a rather false heartiness.*]

DR. BRADLEY: Well, here we are, merry and bright. Good morning, good morning. Bring our little patient out, Miss Preen.

[*A moment's pause, and then a wheelchair is rolled through the door. It is full of pillows, blankets, and* SHERIDAN WHITESIDE. SHERIDAN WHITESIDE *is indeed portly and Falstaffian. He is wearing an elaborate velvet smoking jacket and a very loud tie, and he looks like every caricature ever drawn of him.*]

[*There is a hush as the wheelchair rolls into the room. Welcoming smiles break over every face. The chair comes to a halt;* MR. WHITESIDE *looks slowly around, into each and every beaming face. His fingers drum for a moment on the arm of the chair. He looks slowly around once more. And then he speaks.*]

WHITESIDE [*Quietly, to* MAGGIE]: I may vomit.

MRS. STANLEY [*With a nervous little laugh*]: Good morning, Mr. Whiteside. I'm Mrs. Ernest Stanley—remember? And this is Mr. Stanley.

STANLEY: How do you do, Mr. Whiteside? I hope that you are better.

WHITESIDE: Thank you. I am suing you for a hundred and fifty thousand dollars.

STANLEY: How's that? What?

WHITESIDE: I said I am suing you for a hundred and fifty thousand dollars.

MRS. STANLEY: You mean—because you fell on our steps, Mr. Whiteside?

WHITESIDE: Samuel J. Liebowitz will explain it to you in court. . . . Who are those two harpies standing there like the kiss of death?

[MRS. MCCUTCHEON, *with a little gasp, drops the calf's-foot jelly. It smashes on the floor.*]

MRS. MCCUTCHEON: Oh, dear! My calf's-foot jelly.

WHITESIDE: Made from your own foot, I have no doubt. And now, Mrs. Stanley, I have a few small matters to take up with you. Since this corner druggist at my elbow tells me that I shall be confined in this mouldy mortuary for at least another ten days, due entirely to your stupidity and negligence, I shall have to carry on my activities as best I can. I shall require the exclusive use of this room, as well as that drafty sewer which you call the library. I want no one to come in or out while I am in this room.

STANLEY: What do you mean, sir?

MRS. STANLEY [*Stunned*]: But we have to go up the stairs to get to our rooms, Mr. Whiteside.

WHITESIDE: Isn't there a back entrance?

MRS. STANLEY: Why—yes.

WHITESIDE: Then use that. I shall also require a room for

my secretary, Miss Cutler. I shall have a great many incoming and outgoing calls, so please use the telephone as little as possible. I sleep until noon and require quiet through the house until that hour. There will be five for lunch today. Where is the cook?

STANLEY: Mr. Whiteside, if I may interrupt for a moment—

WHITESIDE: You may not, sir. . . . Will you take your clammy hand off my chair? [*This last to the nurse.*] . . . And now will you all leave quietly, or must I ask Miss Cutler to pass among you with a baseball bat?

[MRS. DEXTER *and* MRS. MCCUTCHEON *are beating a hasty retreat, their gifts still in hand.*]

MRS. MCCUTCHEON: Well—good-bye, Daisy. We'll call you— Oh, no, we mustn't use the phone. Well—we'll see you. [*And they are gone.*]

STANLEY [*Boldly*]: Now look here, Mr. Whiteside—

WHITESIDE: There is nothing to discuss, sir. Considering the damage I have suffered at your hands, I am asking very little. Good day.

STANLEY [*Controlling himself*]: I'll call you from the office later, Daisy.

WHITESIDE: Not on this phone, please.

[STANLEY *gives him a look, but goes.*]

WHITESIDE: Here is the menu for lunch. [*He extends a slip of paper to* MRS. STANLEY.]

MRS. STANLEY: But—I've already ordered lunch.

WHITESIDE: It will be sent up to you on a tray. I am using the dining room for my guests. . . . Where are those cigarettes?

MRS. STANLEY: Why—my son went for them. I don't know why he—here, Sarah. [*She hands* SARAH *the luncheon slip.*] I'll—have mine upstairs on a tray. [SARAH *and* JOHN *depart.*]

WHITESIDE [*To* JUNE, *who has been posed on the landing during all this*]: Young lady, will you either go up those stairs or come down them? I cannot stand indecision.

[JUNE *is about to speak, decides against it, and ascends the stairs with a good deal of spirit.*]

[MRS. STANLEY *is hovering uncertainly on the steps as* RICHARD *returns with the cigarettes.*]

RICHARD: Oh, good morning. I'm sorry I was so long—I had to go to three different stores.

WHITESIDE: How did you travel? By ox-cart?

[RICHARD *is considerably taken aback. His eyes go to his mother, who motions to him to come up the stairs. They disappear together, their eyes unsteadily on* WHITESIDE.]

WHITESIDE: Is there a man in the world who suffers as I do from the gross inadequacies of the human race! [*To the* NURSE, *who is fussing around the chair again.*] Take those canal boats away from me! [*She obeys, hastily.*] Go in and read the life of Florence Nightingale and learn how unfitted you are for your chosen profession. [MISS PREEN *glares at him, but goes.*]

DR. BRADLEY [*Heartily*]: Well, I think I can safely leave you in Miss Cutler's capable hands. Shall I look in again this afternoon?

WHITESIDE: If you do, I shall spit right in your eye.

DR. BRADLEY: What a sense of humor you writers have! By the way, it isn't really worth mentioning, but—I've been doing a little writing myself. About my medical experiences.

WHITESIDE [*Quietly*]: Am I to be spared nothing?

DR. BRADLEY: Would it be too much to ask you to—glance over it while you're here?

WHITESIDE [*Eyes half closed, as though the pain were too exquisite to bear*]: Trapped.

DR. BRADLEY [*Delving into his bag*]: I just happen to have a copy with me. [*He brings out a tremendous manuscript.*] "Forty Years an Ohio Doctor. The Story of a Humble Practitioner."

WHITESIDE: I shall drop everything.

DR. BRADLEY: Much obliged, and I hope you like it. Well, see you on the morrow. Keep that hip quiet and don't forget those little pills. [*He goes.*]

WHITESIDE [*Handing the manuscript to* MAGGIE]: Maggie, will you take *Forty Years Below the Navel* or whatever it's called?

MAGGIE [*Surveying him*]: I must say you have certainly behaved with all of your accustomed grace and charm.

WHITESIDE: Look here, Puss—I am in no mood to discuss my behavior, good or bad.

MAGGIE: These people have done everything in their power to make you comfortable. And they happen, God knows why, to look upon you with a certain wonder and admiration.

WHITESIDE: If they had looked a little more carefully at their doorstep I would not be troubling them now. I did not wish to cross their cheerless threshold. I was hounded and badgered into it. I now find myself, after two weeks of racking pain, accused of behaving without charm. What would you have me do? Kiss them?

MAGGIE [*Giving up*]: Very well, Sherry. After ten years I should have known better than to try to do anything about your manners. But when I finally give up this job I may write a book about it all. *Cavalcade of Insult,* or *Through the Years with Prince Charming.*

WHITESIDE: Listen, Repulsive, you are tied to me with an umbilical cord made of piano wire. And now if we may dismiss the subject of my charm, for which, incidentally, I receive fifteen hundred dollars per appearance, possibly we can go to work . . . Oh, no, we can't. Yes?

[*This last is addressed to a wraithlike lady of uncertain years, who has more or less floated into the room. She is carrying a large spray of holly, and her whole manner suggests something not quite of this world.*]

· THE LADY [*Her voice seems to float, too*]: My name is Harriet Stanley. I know you are Sheridan Whiteside. I saw this holly, framed green against the pine trees. I remembered what you had written, about *Tess* and *Jude the Obscure*. It was the nicest present I could bring you. [*She places the holly in his lap, and drifts out of the room again.*]

WHITESIDE [*His eyes following her*]: For God's sake, what was that?

MAGGIE: That was Mr. Stanley's sister, Harriet. I've talked to her a few times—she's quite strange.

WHITESIDE: Strange? She's right out of *The Hound of the Baskervilles*. . . . You know, I've seen that face before somewhere.

· MAGGIE: Nonsense. You couldn't have.

WHITESIDE [*Dismissing it*]: Oh, well! Let's get down to work. [*He hands her the armful of holly.*] Here! Press this in the doctor's book. [*He picks up the first of a pile of papers.*] If young men keep asking me how to become dramatic critics— [*He tears up the letter and drops the pieces on the floor.*]

MAGGIE [*Who has picked up the little sheaf of messages from the table*]: Here are some telegrams.

WHITESIDE [*A letter in his hand*]: What date is this?

MAGGIE: December tenth.

WHITESIDE: Send a wire to Columbia Broadcasting. "You can schedule my Christmas Eve broadcast from the New York studio, as I shall return East instead of proceeding to Hollywood. Stop. For special New Year's Eve broadcast will have as my guests Jascha Heifetz, Katharine Cornell, Schiaparelli, the Lunts, and Dr. Alexis Carrel, with Anthony Eden on short wave from England. Whiteside."

MAGGIE: Are you sure you'll be all right by Christmas, Sherry?

WHITESIDE: Of course I will. Send a cable to Sacha Guitry: "Will be in Paris June ninth. Dinner seven-thirty. Whiteside." . . . Wire to *Harper's Magazine:* "Do not worry, Stinky. Copy will arrive. Whiteside." . . . Send a cable to the Maharajah of Jehraput, Bombay: "Dear Boo-Boo: Schedule changed. Can you meet me Calcutta July twelfth? Dinner eight-thirty. Whiteside." . . . Arturo Toscanini. Where *is* he?

MAGGIE: I'll find him.

WHITESIDE: "Counting on you January 4th Metropolitan Opera House my annual benefit Home for Paroled Convicts. As you know this is a very worthy cause and close to my heart. Tibbett, Rethberg, Martinelli and Flagstad have promised me personally to appear. Will you have quiet supper with me and Ethel Barrymore afterwards? Whiteside." [*The telephone rings.*] If that's for Mrs. Stanley tell them she's too drunk to talk.

MAGGIE: Hello . . . Hollywood?

WHITESIDE: If it's Goldwyn, hang up.

MAGGIE: Hello . . . Banjo! [*Her face lights up.*]

WHITESIDE: Banjo! Give me that phone!

MAGGIE: Banjo, you old so-and-so! How are you, darling?

WHITESIDE: Come on—give me that!

MAGGIE: Shut up, Sherry! . . . Are you coming East, Banjo? I miss you . . . No, we're not going to Hollywood . . . Oh, he's going to live.

WHITESIDE: Stop driveling and give me the phone.

MAGGIE: In fact, he's screaming at me now. Here he is.

WHITESIDE [*Taking the phone*]: How are you, you fawn's

behind? And what are you giving me for Christmas? [*He roars with laughter at* BANJO's *answer.*] What news, Banjo, my boy? How's the picture coming? . . . How are Wacko and Sloppo? . . . No, no, I'm all right. . . . Yes, I'm in very good hands. Dr. Crippen is taking care of me. . . . What about you? Having any fun? . . . Playing any cribbage? . . . What? [*Again he laughs loudly.*] . . . Well, don't take all his money—leave a little bit for me . . . You're what? . . . Having your portrait painted? By whom? Milt Gross? . . . No, I'm going back to New York from here. I'll be there for twelve days, and then I go to Dartmouth for the Drama Festival. You wouldn't understand . . . Well, I can't waste my time talking to Hollywood riffraff. Kiss Louella Parsons for me. Good-bye. [*He hangs up and turns to* MAGGIE.] He took fourteen hundred dollars from Sam Goldwyn at cribbage last night, and Sam said, "Banjo, I will never play garbage with you again."

MAGGIE: What's all this about his having his portrait painted?

WHITESIDE: Mm. Salvador Dali. That's all that face of his needs— a surrealist to paint it. . . . Now what do *you* want, Miss Bed Pan?

[*This is addressed to the* NURSE, *who has returned somewhat apprehensively to the room.*]

MISS PREEN: It's—it's your pills. One every—forty-five minutes. [*She drops them into his lap and hurries out of the room.*]

WHITESIDE: Now where were we?

MAGGIE [*The messages in her hand*]: Here's a cable from that dear friend of yours, Lorraine Sheldon.

WHITESIDE: Let me see it.

MAGGIE [*Reading the message in a tone that gives* MISS SHELDON *none the better of it*]: "Sherry, my poor sweet lamb, have been in Scotland on a shooting party with Lord and Lady Cunard and only just heard of your poor hip." [MAGGIE *gives a faint raspberry, then reads on.*] "Am down here in Surrey with Lord Bottomley. Sailing Wednesday on the *Normandie* and cannot wait to see my poor sweet Sherry. Your blossom girl, Lorraine." . . . In the words of the master, I may vomit.

WHITESIDE: Don't be bitter, Puss, just because Lorraine is more beautiful than you are.

MAGGIE: Lorraine Sheldon is a very fair example of that small but vicious circle you move in.

WHITESIDE: Pure sex jealousy if ever I saw it . . . Give me the rest of those.

MAGGIE [*Mumbling to herself*]: Lorraine Sheldon . . . Lord Bottomley . . . My Aunt Fanny.

WHITESIDE [*Who has opened the next message*]: Ah! It's from Destiny's Tot.

MAGGIE [*Peering over his shoulder*]: England's little Rover Boy?

WHITESIDE: Um-hm. [*He reads.*] "Treacle Face, what is this I hear about a hip fractured in some bordello brawl? Does this mean our Hollywood Christmas party is off? Finished the new play in Pago-Pago and it's superb. Myself and a ukulele leave Honolulu tomorrow, in that order. By the way, the Sultan of Zanzibar wants to meet Ginger Rogers. Let's face it. Oscar Wilde."

MAGGIE: He does travel, doesn't he? You know, it'd be nice if the world went around Beverly Carlton for a change.

WHITESIDE: Hollywood next week—why couldn't he stop over on his way to New York? Send him a cable: "Beverly Carlton, Royal Hawaiian Hotel, Honolulu—" [*The doorbell rings.* MR. WHITESIDE *is properly annoyed.*] If these people intend to have their friends using the front door—

MAGGIE: What do you want them to use—a rope ladder?

WHITESIDE: I will not have a lot of mildewed pus-bags rushing in and out of this house—

[*He stops as the voice of* JOHN *is heard at the front door.* "Oh, good morning, Mr. Jefferson." *The answering voice of* MR. JEFFERSON *is not quite audible.*]

WHITESIDE [*Roaring*]: There's nobody home! The Stanleys have been arrested for counterfeiting! Go away!

[*But the visitor, meanwhile, has already appeared in the archway.* MR. JEFFERSON *is an interesting-looking young man in his early thirties.*]

JEFFERSON: Good morning, Mr. Whiteside. I'm Jefferson, of the Mesalia *Journal.*

WHITESIDE [*Sotto voce, to* MAGGIE]: Get rid of him.

MAGGIE [*Brusquely*]: I'm sorry—Mr. Whiteside is seeing no one.

JEFFERSON: Really?

MAGGIE: So will you please excuse us? Good day.

JEFFERSON [*Not giving up*]: Mr. Whiteside seems to be sitting up and taking notice.

MAGGIE: I'm afraid he isn't taking notice of the Mesalia *Journal*. Do you mind?

JEFFERSON: You know, if I'm going to be insulted I'd like it to be by Mr. Whiteside himself. I never did like road companies.

WHITESIDE [*Looking around, interested*]: Mm. Touché if I ever heard one. And in Mesalia too, Maggie dear.

MAGGIE [*Still on the job*]: Will you please leave?

JEFFERSON [*Ignoring her*]: How about an interview, Mr. Whiteside?

WHITESIDE: I never give them. Go away.

JEFFERSON: Mr. Whiteside, if I don't get this interview, I lose my job.

WHITESIDE: That would be quite all right with me.

JEFFERSON: Now you don't mean that, Mr. Whiteside. You used to be a newspaper man yourself. You know what editors are like. Well, mine's the toughest one that ever lived.

WHITESIDE: You won't get around me that way. If you don't like him, get off the paper.

JEFFERSON: Yes, but I happen to think it's a good paper. William Allen White could have got out of Emporia, but he didn't.

WHITESIDE: You have the effrontery, in my presence, to compare yourself with William Allen White?

JEFFERSON: Only in the sense that William Allen White stayed in Emporia, and I want to stay here and say what I want to say.

WHITESIDE: Such as what?

JEFFERSON: Well, I can't put it into words, Mr. Whiteside— it'd sound like an awful lot of hooey. But the *Journal* was my father's paper. It's kind of a sentimental point with me, the paper. I'd like to carry on where he left off.

WHITESIDE: Ah—just a minute. Then this terrifying editor, this dread journalistic Apocalypse is—you?

JEFFERSON: Ah—yes, in a word. [WHITESIDE *chuckles with appreciation.*]

MAGGIE [*Annoyed*]: In the future, Sherry, I wish you would let me know when you don't want to talk to people. I'll usher them right in. [*She goes into the library.*]

WHITESIDE: Young man, that kind of journalistic trick went out with Richard Harding Davis . . . Come over here. I suppose you've written that novel?

JEFFERSON: No, I've written that play.

WHITESIDE: Well, I don't want to read it. But you can send me your paper—I'll take a year's subscription. Do you write the editorials, too?

JEFFERSON: Every one of them.

WHITESIDE: I know just what they're like. Ah, me! I'm afraid you're that noble young newspaper man—crusading, idealistic, dull. [*He looks him up and down.*] Very good casting, too.

JEFFERSON: You're not bad casting yourself, Mr. Whiteside.

WHITESIDE: We won't discuss it. . . . Do these old eyes see a box of goodies over there? Hand them to me on your way out.

JEFFERSON [*As he passes over the candy*]: The trouble is, Mr. Whiteside, that your being in this town comes under the heading of news. Practically the biggest news since the Armistice.

WHITESIDE [*Examining the candy*]: Mm. Pecan butternut fudge.

[MISS PREEN, *on her way to the kitchen from the library, stops short as she sees* MR. WHITESIDE *with a piece of candy in his hand.*]

MISS PREEN: Oh, my! You mustn't eat candy, Mr. Whiteside. It's very bad for you.

WHITESIDE [*Turning*]: My great-aunt Jennifer ate a whole box of candy every day of her life. She lived to be a hundred and two, and when she had been dead three days she looked better than you do now. [*He swings blandly back to his visitor.*] What were you saying, old fellow?

JEFFERSON [*As* MISS PREEN *makes a hasty exit*]: I can at least report to my readers that chivalry is not yet dead.

WHITESIDE: We won't discuss it. . . . Well, now that you have won me with your pretty ways, what do you want?

JEFFERSON: Well, how about a brief talk on famous murders? You're an authority on murder as a fine art.

WHITESIDE: My dear boy, when I talk about murder I get paid for it. I have made more money out of the Snyder-Gray case than the lawyers did. So don't expect to get it for nothing.

JEFFERSON: Well, then, what do you think of Mesalia, how long are you going to be here, where are you going, things like that?

WHITESIDE: Very well. (a) Mesalia is a town of irresistible charm, (b) I cannot wait to get out of it, and (c) I am going from here to Crockfield, for my semi-annual visit to the Crockfield Home for Paroled Convicts, for which I have raised over half a million dollars in the last five years. From there I go to New York. . . . Have you ever been to Crockfield, Jefferson?

JEFFERSON: No, I haven't. I always meant to.

WHITESIDE: As a newspaper man you ought to go, instead of wasting your time with me. It's only about seventy-five miles from here. Did you ever hear how Crockfield started?

JEFFERSON: No, I didn't.

WHITESIDE: Ah! Sit down, Jefferson. It is one of the most endearing and touching stories of our generation. One misty St. Valentine's Eve—the year was 1901—a little old lady who had given her name to an era, Victoria, lay dying in Windsor Castle. Maude Adams had not yet caused every young heart to swell as she tripped across the stage as Peter Pan; Irving Berlin had not yet written the first note of a ragtime rigadoon that was to set the nation's feet a-tapping, and Elias P. Crockfield was just emerging from the State penitentiary. Destitute, embittered, cruel of heart, he wandered, on this St. Valentine's Eve, into a little church. But there was no godliness in his heart that night, no prayer upon his lips. In the faltering twilight, Elias P. Crockfield made his way toward the poor box. With callous fingers he ripped open this poignant testimony of a simple people's faith. Greedily he clutched at the few pitiful coins within. And then a child's wavering treble broke the twilight stillness. "Please, Mr. Man," said a little girl's voice, "won't you be my Valentine?" Elias P. Crockfield turned. There stood before him a bewitching little creature of five, her yellow curls cascading over her shoulders like a golden Niagara, in her tiny outstretched hand a humble valentine. In that one crystal moment a sealed door opened in the heart of Elias P. Crockfield, and in his mind was born an idea. Twenty-five years later three thousand ruddy-cheeked convicts were gamboling on the broad lawns of Crockfield Home, frolicking in the cool depths of its swimming pool, broadcasting with their own symphony orchestra from their own radio station. Elias P. Crockfield has long since gone to his Maker, but the little girl of the golden curls, now grown to lovely womanhood, is known as the Angel of Crockfield, for she is the wife of the warden, and in the main hall of Crockfield, between a Rembrandt and an El Greco, there hangs, in a simple little frame, a humble valentine.

MAGGIE [*Who has emerged from the library in time to hear the finish of this*]: And in the men's washroom, every Christmas Eve, the ghost of Elias P. Crockfield appears in one of the booths . . . Will you sign these, please?

[*The doorbell is heard.*]

WHITESIDE: This aging ingénue, Mr. Jefferson, I retain in my employ only because she is the sole support of her two-headed brother.

JEFFERSON: I understand. . . . Well, thank you very much, Mr. Whiteside—you've been very kind. By the way, I'm a cribbage player, if you need one while you're here.

WHITESIDE: Fine. How much can you afford to lose?

JEFFERSON: I usually win.

WHITESIDE: We won't discuss that. Come back at eight-thirty. We'll play three-handed with Elsie Dinsmore . . . Metz!

[JOHN, *who has answered the doorbell, has ushered in a strange-looking little man in his fifties. His hair runs all over his head and his clothes are too big for him.*]

WHITESIDE: Metz, you incredible beetle-hound! What are you doing here?

METZ [*With a mild Teutonic accent*]: I explain, Sherry. First I kiss my little Maggie.

MAGGIE [*Embracing him*]: Metz darling, what a wonderful surprise!

WHITESIDE: The enchanted Metz! Why aren't you at the university? . . . Jefferson, you are standing in the presence of one of the great men of our time. When you write that inevitable autobiography, be sure to record the day that you met Professor Adolph Metz, the world's greatest authority on insect life. Metz, stop looking at me adoringly and tell me why you're here.

METZ: You are sick, Sherry, so I come to cheer you.

MAGGIE: Metz, you tore yourself away from your little insects and came here? Sherry, you don't deserve it.

WHITESIDE: How are all your little darlings, Metz? Jefferson, would you believe that eight volumes could be written on the mating instinct of the female white ant? He did it.

METZ: Seven on the female, Sherry. One on the male.

WHITESIDE: Lived for two years in a cave with nothing but plant lice. He rates three pages in the *Encyclopaedia Britannica*. Don't you, my little hookworm?

METZ: Please, Sherry, you embarrass me. Look—I have brought you a present to while away the hours. [*He motions to* JOHN, *who comes forward bearing a great box, wrapped in brown paper. He unwraps it as he speaks.*]

METZ: I said to my students: "Boys and girls, I want to give a present to my sick friend, Sheridan Whiteside." So you know what we did? We made for you a community of *Periplaneta Americana,* commonly known as the American cockroach. Behold, Sherry! [*He strips off the paper.*] Roach City! Inside here are ten thousand cockroaches.

JOHN: Ten thousand— [*Heading for the kitchen in great excitement.*] Sarah! Sarah!

METZ: Here in Roach City they play, they make love, they mate, they die. See—here is the graveyard. They even bury their own dead.

MAGGIE: I'm glad of that, or I'd have to do it.

WHITESIDE [*Glaring at her*]: Ssh!

METZ: You can watch them, Sherry, while they live out their whole lives. It is fascinating. Look! Here is where they store their grain, here is the commissary of the aristocracy, here is the maternity hospital.

WHITESIDE: Magnificent! This is my next piece for the London *Mercury*.

METZ: With these earphones, Sherry, you listen to the mating calls. There are microphones down inside. Listen! [*He puts the earphones over* WHITESIDE'S *head.*]

WHITESIDE [*Listening, rapt*]: Mm. How long has this been going on?

[MRS. STANLEY *starts timorously to descend the stairs. She tiptoes as far as the landing, then pauses as she sees the group below.*]

[*Meanwhile* PROF. METZ, *his mind ever on his work, has moved in the direction of the dining room.*]

METZ [*Suddenly his face lights up*]: Aha! *Periplaneta Americana!* There are cockroaches in this house!

MRS. STANLEY [*Shocked into speech*]: I beg your pardon! [*The doorbell rings.*] Mr. Whiteside, I don't know who this man is, but I will not stand here and—

WHITESIDE: Then go upstairs. These are probably my luncheon guests. Metz, you're staying for the day, of course? Jefferson, stay for lunch? Maggie, tell 'em there'll be two more. Ah, come right in, Baker. Good morning, gentlemen. [*The gentlemen addressed are three in number—two white, one black. They are convicts, and they look the part. Prison gray, handcuffed together.* BAKER, *in uniform, is a prison guard. He carries a rifle.*] Jefferson, here are the fruits of that humble valentine. These men, now serving the final months of their prison terms, have chosen to enter the ivy-covered walls of Crockfield. They have come here today to learn from me a little of its tradition . . . Gentlemen, I envy you your great adventure.

JOHN [*In the dining-room doorway*]: Lunch is ready, Mr. Whiteside.

WHITESIDE: Good! Let's go right in. [*To one of the convicts, as they pass.*] You're Michaelson, aren't you? Butcher-shop murders?

MICHAELSON: Yes, sir.

WHITESIDE: Thought I recognized you. . . . After you, Baker. . . . The other fellow, Jefferson— [*He lowers his tone.*] —is Henderson, the hatchet fiend. Always did it in a bathtub —remember? [*His voice rises as he wheels himself into the dining room.*] We're having chicken livers Tetrazzini, and Cherries Jubilee for dessert. I hope every little tummy is a-flutter with gastric juices. Serve the white wine with the fish, John, and close the doors. I don't want a lot of people prying on their betters.

[*The doors close. Only* MRS. STANLEY *is left outside. She collapses quietly into a chair.*]

The Curtain Falls

SCENE II

SCENE—*Late afternoon, a week later. Only a single lamp is lit. The room, in the week that has passed, has taken on something of the character of its occupant. Books and papers everywhere. Stacks of books on the tables, some of them just half out of their cardboard boxes. Half a dozen or so volumes, which apparently have not appealed to the Master, have been thrown onto the floor. A litter of crumpled papers around the* WHITESIDE *wheelchair; an empty candy box has slid off his lap. An old pair of pants have been tossed over one chair, a seedy bathrobe over another. A handsome Chinese vase has been moved out of its accustomed spot and is doing duty as an ash receiver.*

MR. WHITESIDE *is in his wheelchair, asleep. Roach City is on a stand beside him, the earphones, over his head. He has apparently dozed off while listening to the mating calls of* Periplaneta Americana.

For a moment only his rhythmic breathing is heard. Then MISS PREEN *enters from the library. She brings some medicine —a glass filled with a murky mixture. She pauses when she sees that he is asleep, then, after a good deal of hesitation, gently touches him on the shoulder. He stirs a little; she musters up her courage and touches him again.*

WHITESIDE [*Slowly opening his eyes*]: I was dreaming of Lillian Russell, and I wake to find *you*.

MISS PREEN: Your—your medicine, Mr. Whiteside.

WHITESIDE [*Taking the glass*]: What time is it?

MISS PREEN: About half-past six.

WHITESIDE: Where is Miss Cutler?

MISS PREEN: She went out.

WHITESIDE: Out?

MISS PREEN: With Mr. Jefferson. [*She goes into the library.*] [JOHN, *meanwhile, has entered from the dining room.*]

JOHN: All right if I turn the lights up, Mr. Whiteside?

WHITESIDE: Yes. Go right ahead, John.

JOHN: And Sarah has something for you, Mr. Whiteside. Made it special.

WHITESIDE: She has? Where is she? My Soufflé Queen!

SARAH [*Proudly entering with a tray on which reposes her latest delicacy*]: Here I am, Mr. Whiteside.

WHITESIDE: She walks in beauty like the night, and in those deft hands there is the art of Michelangelo. Let me taste the new creation. [*With one hand he pours the medicine into the Chinese vase, then swallows at a gulp one of* SARAH'S *not so little cakes. An ecstatic expression comes over his face.*] Poetry! Sheer poetry!

SARAH [*Beaming*]: I put a touch of absinthe in the dough. Do you like it?

WHITESIDE [*Rapturously*]: Ambrosia!

SARAH: And I got you your terrapin Maryland for dinner.

WHITESIDE: I have known but three great cooks in my time. The Khedive of Egypt had one, my great-aunt Jennifer another, and the third, Sarah, is you.

SARAH: Oh, Mr. Whiteside!

WHITESIDE [*Lowering his voice*]: How would you like to come to New York and work for me? You and John.

SARAH: Why, Mr. Whiteside!

JOHN: Sarah! . . . It would be wonderful, Mr. Whiteside, but what would we say to Mr. and Mrs. Stanley?

WHITESIDE: Just "good-bye."

SARAH: But—but they'd be awfully mad, wouldn't they? They've been very kind to us.

WHITESIDE [*Lightly*]: Well, if they ever come to New York we can have them for dinner, if I'm not in town. Now run along and think it over. This is our little secret—just between us. And put plenty of sherry in that terrapin . . . Miss Preen! [SARAH *and* JOHN *withdraw in considerable excitement.* WHITESIDE *raises his voice to a roar.*] Miss Preen!

MISS PREEN [*Appearing, breathless*]: Yes? Yes?

WHITESIDE: What have you *got* in there, anyway? A sailor?

MISS PREEN: I was—just washing my hands.

WHITESIDE: What time did Miss Cutler go out?

MISS PREEN: A couple of hours ago.

WHITESIDE: Mr. Jefferson called for her?

MISS PREEN: Yes, sir.

WHITESIDE [*Impatiently*]: All right, all right. Go back to your sex life.

[MISS PREEN *goes.* WHITESIDE *tries to settle down to his book, but his mind is plainly troubled. He shifts a little, looks anxiously toward the outer door.*]

[HARRIET STANLEY *comes softly down the steps. She seems delighted to find* MR. WHITESIDE *alone.*]

HARRIET [*Opening an album that she has brought with her*]: Dear Mr. Whiteside, may I show you a few mementoes of the past? I somehow feel that you would love them as I do.

WHITESIDE: I'd be delighted. [*Observing her.*] Miss Stanley, haven't we met somewhere before?

HARRIET: Oh, no. I would have remembered. It would have been one of my cherished memories—like these. [*She spreads the portfolio before him.*] Look! Here I am with my first sweetheart, under our lovely beechwood tree. I was eight and he was ten. I have never forgotten him. What happy times we had! What— [*She stops short as she hears footsteps on the stairway.*] There's someone coming! I'll come back! . . . [*She gathers up her album and vanishes into the dining room.*]

[WHITESIDE *looks after her, puzzled.*]

[*It is* MR. STANLEY *who comes down the stairs. He is carrying a slip of paper in his hand, and he is obviously at the boiling point.*]

[*A few steps behind comes* MRS. STANLEY, *apprehensive and nervous.*]

MRS. STANLEY: Now, Ernest, please—

STANLEY: Be quiet, Daisy. . . . Mr. Whiteside, I want to talk to you. I don't care whether you're busy or not. I have stood all that I'm going to stand.

WHITESIDE: Indeed?

STANLEY: This is the last straw. I have just received a bill from the telephone company for seven hundred and eighty-four dollars. [*He reads from the slip in his hand.*] Oklahoma City, Calcutta, Hollywood, Paris, Brussels, Rome, New York, New York, New York, New York, New York, New York— [*His voice trails off in an endless succession of New Yorks.*] Now I realize, Mr. Whiteside, that you are a distinguished man of letters—

MRS. STANLEY: Yes, of course. We both do.

STANLEY: Please . . . But in the past week we have not been able to call our souls our own. We have not had a meal in the dining room *once*. I have to tiptoe out of the house in the mornings.

MRS. STANLEY: Now, Ernest—

STANLEY [*Waving her away*]: I come home to find convicts sitting at my dinner table—butcher-shop murderers. A man putting cockroaches in the kitchen.

MRS. STANLEY: They just escaped, Ernest.

STANLEY: That's not the point. I don't like coming home to find twenty-two Chinese students using my bathroom. I tell you I won't stand for it, no matter *who* you are.

WHITESIDE: Have you quite finished?

STANLEY: No, I have not. I go down into the cellar this morning and trip over that octopus that William Beebe sent you. I tell you I won't stand it. Mr. Whiteside, I want you to leave this house as soon as you can and go to a hotel. . . . Stop pawing me, Daisy. . . . That's all I've got to say, Mr. White-side.

WHITESIDE: And quite enough, I should say. May I remind you again, Mr. Stanley, that I am not a willing guest in this house? I am informed by my doctor that I must remain quiet for another ten days, at which time I shall get out of here so fast that the wind will knock you over, I hope. If, however, you insist on my leaving before that, thereby causing me to suffer a relapse, I shall sue you for every additional day that I am held inactive, which will amount, I assure you, to a tidy sum.

STANLEY [*To his wife*]: This is outrageous. Do we have to—

WHITESIDE: As for the details of your petty complaints, those twenty-two Chinese students came straight from the White House, where I assure you they used the bathroom too.

MRS. STANLEY: Mr. Whiteside, my husband didn't mean—

STANLEY: Yes, I did. I meant every word of it.

WHITESIDE: There is only one point that you make in which I see some slight justice. I do not expect you to pay for my telephone calls, and I shall see to it that restitution is made. Can you provide me with the exact amount?

STANLEY: I certainly can, and I certainly will.

WHITESIDE: Good. I shall instruct my lawyers to deduct it from the hundred and fifty thousand dollars that I am suing you for.

[MR. STANLEY *starts to speak, but simply chokes with rage. Furious, he storms up the steps again,* MRS. STANLEY *following.*]

WHITESIDE: [*Calling after him*]: And I'll thank you not to trip over that octopus, which is very sensitive.

[*Left alone,* MR. WHITESIDE *enjoys his triumph for a moment, then his mind jumps to more important matters. He looks at his watch, considers a second, then wheels himself over to the telephone.*]

WHITESIDE: Give me the Mesalia *Journal,* please. [*He peers at Roach City while waiting.*] Hello, *Journal*? . . . Is Mr. Jefferson there? . . . When do you expect him? . . . No. No message. [*He hangs up, drums impatiently on the arm of his chair. Then he turns sharply at the sound of the outer door opening. But it is the younger Stanleys,* RICHARD *and* JUNE, *who enter. They are in winter togs, with ice skates under their arms. In addition,* RICHARD *has a camera slung over his shoulder.*]

[*Their attitudes change as they see that* WHITESIDE *is in the room. They slide toward the stairs, obviously trying to be as unobtrusive as possible.*]

WHITESIDE: Come here, you two. . . . Come on, come on. I'm not going to bite you. . . . Now look here. I am by nature a gracious and charming person. If I err at all it is on the side of kindness and amiability. I have been observing you two for this past week, and you seem to me to be extremely likeable young people. I am afraid that when we first met I was definitely unpleasant to you. For that I am sorry, and I wish that in the future you would not treat me like something out of Edgar Allan Poe. How do you like my new tie?

JUNE: Thank you, Mr. Whiteside. This makes things much pleasanter. And I think the tie is very pretty.

RICHARD: Well, now that we're on speaking terms, Mr. Whiteside, I don't mind telling you that I have been admiring all your ties.

WHITESIDE: Do you like this one?

RICHARD: I certainly do.

WHITESIDE: It's yours. [*He takes it off and tosses it to him.*] Really, this curious legend that I am a difficult person is pure fabrication. . . . Ice-skating, eh? Ah, me! I used to cut figure eights myself, arm in arm with Betsy Ross, waving the flag behind us.

JUNE: It was wonderful on the ice today. Miss Cutler and Mr. Jefferson were there.

WHITESIDE: Maggie? Skating?

RICHARD: Yes, and she's good, too. I got a marvelous picture of her.

WHITESIDE: Were they still there when you left?

RICHARD: I think so. Say, Mr. Whiteside, mind if I take a picture of you? I'd love to have one.

WHITESIDE: Very well. Do you want my profile? [*He indicates his stomach.*]

JUNE: [*Starting up the stairs*]: I'm afraid you're done for, Mr. Whiteside. My brother is a camera fiend.

RICHARD [*Clicking his camera*]: Thank you, Mr. Whiteside. I got a great one. [*He and* JUNE *go up the stairs as* MAGGIE *enters from the hallway. They call a "Hello, Miss Cutler!" as they disappear.*]

MAGGIE: Hello, there. . . . Good evening, Sherry. Really Sherry, you've got this room looking like an old parrot-cage. . . . Did you nap while I was out? [WHITESIDE *merely glowers at her.*] What's the matter, dear? Cat run away with your tongue? [*She is on her knees, gathering up debris.*]

WHITESIDE [*Furious*]: Don't look up at me with those great cow-eyes, you sex-ridden hag. Where have you been all afternoon? Alley-catting around with Bert Jefferson?

MAGGIE [*Her face aglow*]: Sherry—Bert read his play to me this afternoon. It's superb. It isn't just that play written by a newspaper man. It's superb. I want you to read it *tonight*. [*She puts it in his lap.*] It just cries out for Cornell. If you like it, will you send it to her, Sherry? And will you read it tonight?

WHITESIDE: No, I will not read it tonight or any other time. And while we're on the subject of Mr. Jefferson, you might ask him if he wouldn't like to pay your salary, since he takes up all your time.

MAGGIE: Oh, come now, Sherry. It isn't as bad as that.

WHITESIDE: I have not even been able to reach you, not knowing what haylofts you frequent.

MAGGIE: Oh, stop behaving like a spoiled child, Sherry.

WHITESIDE: Don't take that patronizing tone with me, you flea-bitten Cleopatra. I am sick and tired of your sneaking out like some lovesick high-school girl every time my back is turned.

MAGGIE: Well, Sherry— [*She pulls together the library doors and faces* WHITESIDE.]—I'm afraid you've hit the nail on the head. [*With a little flourish, she removes her hat.*]

WHITESIDE: Stop acting like Zasu Pitts and explain yourself.

MAGGIE: I'll make it quick, Sherry. I'm in love.

WHITESIDE: Nonsense. This is merely delayed puberty.

MAGGIE: No, Sherry, I'm afraid this is it. You're going to lose a very excellent secretary.

WHITESIDE: You are out of your mind.

MAGGIE: Yes, I think I am, a little. But I'm a girl who's waited a long time for this to happen, and now it has. Mr. Jefferson doesn't know it yet, but I'm going to try my darnedest to marry him.

WHITESIDE [*As she pauses*]: Is that all?

MAGGIE: Yes, except that—well—I suppose this is what might be called my resignation—as soon as you've got someone else.

WHITESIDE [*There is a slight pause*]: Now listen to me, Maggie. We have been together for a long time. You are indispensable to me, but I think I am unselfish enough not to let that stand in the way where your happiness is concerned. Because, whether you know it or not, I have a deep affection for you.

MAGGIE: I know that, Sherry.

WHITESIDE: That being the case, I will not stand by and allow you to make a fool of yourself.

MAGGIE: I'm not, Sherry.

WHITESIDE: You are, my dear. You are behaving like a Booth Tarkington heroine. It's—it's incredible. I cannot believe that a girl who for the past ten years has had the great of the world served up on a platter before her—I cannot believe that it is anything but a kind of temporary insanity when you are swept off your feet in seven days by a second-rate, small-town newspaper man.

MAGGIE: Sherry, I can't explain what's happened. I can only tell you that it's so. It's hard for me to believe too, Sherry. Here I am, a hard-bitten old cynic, behaving like *True Story*

Magazine, and liking it. Discovering the moon, and ice-skating —I keep laughing to myself all the time, but there it is. What can I do about it, Sherry? I'm in love.

WHITESIDE [*With sudden decision*]: We're leaving here tomorrow. Hip or no hip, we're leaving here tomorrow. I don't care if I fracture the other one. Get me a train schedule and start packing. *I'*ll pull you out of this, Miss Stardust. *I'*ll get the ants out of those moonlit pants.

MAGGIE: It's no good, Sherry. I'd be back on the next streamlined train.

WHITESIDE: It's completely unbelievable. Can you see yourself, the wife of the editor of the Mesalia *Journal,* having an evening at home for Mr. and Mrs. Stanley, Mr. and Mrs. Poop-Face, and the members of the Book-of-the-Month Club?

MAGGIE: Sherry, I've had ten years of the great figures of our time, and don't think I'm not grateful to you for it. I've loved every minute of it. They've been wonderful years, Sherry. Gay and stimulating—why, I don't think anyone has ever had the fun we've had. But a girl can't laugh all the time, Sherry. There comes a time when she wants—Bert Jefferson. You don't know Bert, Sherry. He's gentle, and he's unassuming, and—well, I love him, that's all.

WHITESIDE: I see. Well, I remain completely unconvinced. You are drugging yourself into this Joan Crawford fantasy, and before you become completely anesthetized I shall do everything in my power to bring you to your senses.

MAGGIE [*Wheeling on him*]: Now listen to me, Whiteside. I know you. Lay off. I know what a devil you can be. I've seen you do it to other people, but don't you dare to do it to me. Don't drug *yourself* into the idea that all you're thinking of is my happiness. You're thinking of yourself a little bit, too, and all those months of breaking in somebody new. I've seen you in a passion before when your life has been disrupted, and you couldn't dine in Calcutta on July twelfth with Boo-Boo. Well, that's too bad, but there it is. I'm going to marry Bert if he'll have me, and don't you dare try any of your tricks. I'm on to every one of them. So lay off. That's my message to *you,* Big Lord Fauntleroy. [*And she is up the stairs.*]

[*Left stewing in his own juice,* MR. WHITESIDE *is in a per-*

fect fury. He bangs the arm of his chair, then slaps at the manuscript in his lap. As he does so, the dawn of an idea comes into his mind. He sits perfectly still for a moment, thinking it over. Then, with a slow smile, he takes the manuscript out of its envelope.

He looks at the title page, ruffles through the script, then stops and thinks again. His face breaks out into one great smile. Then he quickly wheels himself over to the table and hunts hurriedly through a pile of old cablegrams and letters, until he finds the one he wants. With this in his hand, he takes up the telephone receiver.]

WHITESIDE [*In a lowered voice*]: Long distance, please. I want to put in a trans-Atlantic call. [*He looks at the cablegram again for confirmation.*] Hello. Trans-Atlantic operator? . . . This is Mesalia one four two. I want to talk to Miss Lorraine Sheldon—S-h-e-l-d-o-n. She's on the *Normandie*. It sailed from Southampton day before yesterday. . . . Will it take long? . . . All right. My name is Whiteside. . . . Thank you. [*He hangs up as the doorbell rings. He goes back to the manuscript again and looks through it.* JOHN *then ushers in* DR. BRADLEY.]

DR. BRADLEY [*Hearty, as usual*]: Well, well! Good evening, Mr. Whiteside!

WHITESIDE: Come back tomorrow—I'm busy.

DR. BRADLEY [*Turning cute*]: Now what would be the best news that I could possibly bring you?

WHITESIDE: You have hydrophobia.

DR. BRADLEY [*Laughing it off*]: No, no. . . . Mr. Whiteside, you are a well man. You can get up and walk *now*. You can leave here tomorrow.

WHITESIDE: What do you mean?

DR. BRADLEY: Well, sir! I looked at those X-rays again this morning, and do you know what? I had been looking at the wrong X-rays. I had been looking at old Mrs. Moffat's X-rays. You are perfectly, absolutely well!

WHITESIDE: Lower your voice, will you?

DR. BRADLEY: What's the matter? Aren't you pleased?

WHITESIDE: Delighted. . . . Naturally. . . . Ah—this is a very unexpected bit of news, however. It comes at a very curious moment. [*He is thinking fast; suddenly he gets an idea. He clears his throat and looks around apprehensively.*] Dr. Bradley, I—ah—I have some good news for you, too. I have been reading your book—ah—*Forty Years*—what is it?

DR. BRADLEY [*Eagerly*]: *An Ohio Doctor*—yes?

WHITESIDE: I consider it extremely close to being one of the great literary contributions of our time.

DR. BRADLEY: Mr. Whiteside!

WHITESIDE: So strongly do I feel about it, Dr. Bradley, that I have a proposition to make to you. Just here and there the book is a little uneven, a little rough. What I would like to do is to stay here in Mesalia and work with you on it.

DR. BRADLEY [*All choked up*]: Mr. Whiteside, I would be so terribly honored—

WHITESIDE: Yes. But there is just one difficulty. You see, if my lecture bureau and my radio sponsors were to learn that I am well, they would insist on my fulfilling my contracts, and I would be forced to leave Mesalia. Therefore, we must not tell anyone—not anyone at all—that I am well.

DR. BRADLEY: I see. I see.

WHITESIDE: Not even Miss Cutler, you understand.

DR. BRADLEY: No, I won't. Not a soul. Not even my wife.

WHITESIDE: That's fine.

DR. BRADLEY: When do we start work—tonight? I've got just one patient that's dying and then I'll be perfectly free.

[*The phone rings.*]

WHITESIDE [*Waving him away*]: Ah—tomorrow morning. This is a private call—would you forgive me? . . . Hello. . . . Yes, I'm on. [*He turns again to the* DOCTOR.] Tomorrow morning.

DR. BRADLEY: Tomorrow morning it is. Good night. You've made me very proud, Mr. Whiteside. [*He goes.*]

WHITESIDE: [*Again on the phone*]: Yes, yes, this is Mr. Whiteside on the phone. Put them through. . . . Hello. Is this my Blossom Girl? How are you, my lovely? . . . No, no, I'm all right. . . . Yes, still out here. . . . Lorraine dear, when do you land in New York? . . . Tuesday? That's fine. . . . Now listen closely, my pet. I've great news for you. I've discovered a wonderful play with an enchanting part in it for you. Cornell would give her eye teeth to play it, but I think I can get it for you. . . . Now wait, wait. Let me tell you. The author is a young newspaper man in this town. Of course he wants Cornell, but if you jump on a train and get right out here, I think you could swing it, if you play your cards right. . . . No, he's young, and very attractive, and just your dish, my dear. It just takes a little doing, and you're the girl that can do it. Isn't that exciting, my pet? . . . Yes. . . . Yes, that's right. . . . And look. Don't send me any messages. Just get on a train and arrive. . . . Oh, no, don't thank me, my darling. It's perfectly all right. Have a nice trip and hurry out here. Good-bye, my blossom. [*He hangs up and looks guiltily around. Then he straightens up and gleefully rubs his hands together.*]

[MISS PREEN *enters, medicine in hand, and frightened, as usual.*]

WHITESIDE [*Jovial as hell*]: Hello, Miss Preen. My, you're looking radiant this evening.

MISS PREEN [*Staggered*]: What?

WHITESIDE: Nothing. Nothing at all. Just said you are ravishing. [*He takes the medicine from her and swallows it at one gulp.* MISS PREEN, *still staggered, retreats into the library, just as* MAGGIE *comes down the stairs. She is dressed for the street.*]

MAGGIE [*Pausing on the landing*]: Sherry, I'm sorry for what I said before. I'm afraid I was a little unjust.

WHITESIDE [*All nobility*]: That's all right, Maggie dear. We all lose our tempers now and then.

MAGGIE: I promised to have dinner with Bert and go to a movie, but we'll come back and play cribbage with you instead.

WHITESIDE: Fine.

MAGGIE: See you soon, Sherry dear. [*She kisses him lightly on the forehead and goes on her way.*]

[WHITESIDE *looks after her until he hears the doors close. Then his face lights up again and he bursts happily into song as he wheels himself into the library.*]

WHITESIDE:

"I'se des a 'ittle wabbit in the sunshine,
I'se des a 'ittle wabbit in the wain—"

Curtain

ACT TWO

SCENE—*A week later, late afternoon.*

The room is now dominated by a large Christmas tree, set in the curve of the staircase, and hung with the customary Christmas ornaments.

SARAH *and* JOHN *are passing in and out of the library, bringing forth huge packages which they are placing under the tree.* MAGGIE *sits at a little table at one side, going through a pile of correspondence.*

JOHN: Well, I guess that's all there are, Miss Cutler. They're all under the tree.

MAGGIE: Thank you, John.

SARAH: My, I never saw anyone get so many Christmas presents. I can hardly wait to see what's in 'em.

JOHN: When'll Mr. Whiteside open them, Miss Cutler?

MAGGIE: Well, John, you see Christmas is Mr. Whiteside's personal property. He invented it and it belongs to him. First thing tomorrow morning, Mr. Whiteside will open each and every present, and there will be the damnedest fuss you ever saw.

SARAH [*Bending over the packages*]: My, look who he's got presents from! Shirley Temple, William Lyon Phelps, Billy Rose, Ethel Waters, Somerset Maugham—I can hardly wait for tonight.

[*The doorbell rings.* JOHN *departs for the door.*]

SARAH: My, it certainly is wonderful. And Mr. Whiteside's tree is so beautiful, too. Mr. and Mrs. Stanley had to put theirs in their bedroom, you know. They can hardly undress at night.

[*It is* BERT JEFFERSON *who enters.*]

BERT: Hello, Maggie. Merry Christmas, Sarah.

SARAH: Merry Christmas, Mr. Jefferson. [*She and* JOHN *disappear into the dining room.*]

BERT [*Observing the pile of packages under the tree*]: Say, business is good, isn't it? My, what a little quiet blackmail and a weekly radio hour can get you. What did his sponsors give him?

MAGGIE: They gave him a full year's supply of their product, Cream of Mush.

BERT: Well, he'll give it right back to them over the air.

MAGGIE: Wait until you hear tonight's broadcast, old fellow. It's so sticky I haven't been able to get it off my fingers since I copied it.

BERT: I'll bet . . . Look, I'll come clean. Under the influence of God knows what I have just bought you a Christmas present.

MAGGIE [*Surprised*]: Why, Mr. Jefferson, sir.

BERT: Only I'd like you to see it before I throw away my hard-earned money. Can you run downtown with me and take a look at it?

MAGGIE: Bert, this is very sweet of you. I'm quite touched. What is it? I can't wait.

BERT: A two years' subscription to *Screen Romances*. . . . Listen, do you think I'm going to tell you? Come down and see.

MAGGIE [*She calls into the library*]: Sherry! Sherry, I'm going out for a few minutes. With Horace Greeley. I won't be long. [*She goes into the hallway for her coat and hat.*]

BERT [*Raising his voice*]: Noel, Noel, Mr. W.! How about some cribbage after your broadcast tonight?

[*The* WHITESIDE *wheelchair is rolling into the room.*]

WHITESIDE: No, I will not play cribbage with you, Klondike Harry. You have been swindling the be-jesus out of me for two weeks. . . . Where are you off to now, Madame Butterfly?

MAGGIE: I'm being given a Christmas present. Anything you want done downtown?

WHITESIDE: 'Es. B'ing baby a lollipop. . . . What are *you* giving me for Christmas, Jefferson? I have enriched your feeble life beyond your capacity to repay me.

BERT: Yes, that's what I figured, so I'm not giving you anything.

WHITESIDE: I see. Well, I was giving you my old truss, but now I shan't. . . . Maggie, what time are those radio men coming?

MAGGIE: About six-thirty—I'll be here. You've got to cut, Sherry. You're four minutes over. Oh, by the way, there was a wire from Beverly. It's there somewhere. He doesn't know what train he can get out of Chicago, but he'll be here some time this evening.

WHITESIDE: Good! Is he staying overnight?

MAGGIE: No, he has to get right out again. He's sailing Friday on the *Queen Mary*.

BERT: Think I could peek in at the window and get a look at him? Beverly Carlton used to be one of my heroes.

WHITESIDE: Used to be, you ink-stained hack? Beverly Carlton is the greatest single talent in the English theatre today. Take this illiterate numbskull out of my sight, Maggie, and don't bring him back.

BERT: Yes, Mr. Whiteside, sir. I won't come back until Beverly Carlton gets here.

MAGGIE [*As they go on their way*]: Where are we going, Bert? I want to know what you've bought me—I'm like a ten-year-old kid.

BERT [*Laughing a little*]: You know, you look like a ten-year-old kid right now, Maggie, at that. [*They are out of earshot by this time.*]

[WHITESIDE *looks after them intently, listens until the door closes. He considers for a second, then wheels himself over to the telephone.*]

WHITESIDE [*On the phone*]: Will you give me the Mansion House, please? . . . No, I don't know the number. . . . Hello? Mansion House? . . . Tell me, has a Miss Lorraine Sheldon arrived yet? . . . Yes, that's right—Miss Lorraine Sheldon. From New York. . . . She hasn't, eh? Thank you. [*He hangs up, drums with his fingers on the chair arm, looks at his watch. He slaps his knees impatiently, stretches. Then, vexed at his self-imposed imprisonment, he looks cautiously around the room, peers up the stairs. Then, slowly, he gets out of his chair; standing beside it, he indulges in a few mild calisthenics, looking cautiously around all the while.*]

[*Then the sound of the library doors being opened sends him scurrying back to his chair. It is* MISS PREEN *who emerges.*]

WHITESIDE [*Annoyed*]: What do you want, coming in like that? Why don't you knock before you come into a room?

MISS PREEN: But—I wasn't coming in. I was coming out.

WHITESIDE: Miss Preen, you are obviously *in* this room. That is true, isn't it?

MISS PREEN: Yes, it is, but—

WHITESIDE: Therefore you came in. Hereafter, please knock.

[*Before* MISS PREEN *can reply, however,* JOHN *enters from the dining room.*]

JOHN [*En route to the front door*]: There're some express-men here with a crate, Mr. Whiteside. I told them to come around the front.

WHITESIDE: Thank you, John. . . . Don't stand there, Miss Preen. You look like a frozen custard. Go away.

MISS PREEN [*Controlling herself as best as she can*]: Yes, sir. [*She goes.*]

[*At the same time two* EXPRESSMEN, *carrying a crate, enter from the front door.*]

JOHN: Bring it right in here. Careful there—don't scrape the wall. Why, it's some kind of animals.

EXPRESSMAN: I'll say it's animals. We had to feed 'em at seven o'clock this morning.

WHITESIDE: Bring it over here, John. Who's it from?

JOHN [*Reading from the top of the crate as they set it down*]: Admiral Richard E. Byrd. Say!

WHITESIDE [*Peering through the slats*]: Why, they're penguins. Two—three—four penguins. Hello, my pretties.

EXPRESSMAN: Directions for feeding are right on top. These two slats are open.

JOHN [*Reading*]: "To be fed only whale blubber, eels and cracked lobster."

EXPRESSMAN: They got Coca-Cola this morning. And liked it. [*They go.*]

WHITESIDE [*Peering through the slats again*]: Hello, hello, hello. You know, they make the most entrancing companions, John. Admiral Byrd has one that goes on all his lecture tours. I want these put right in the library with me. Take 'em right in.

JOHN [*Picking up the crate*]: Yes, sir.

WHITESIDE: Better tell Sarah to order a couple of dozen lobsters. I don't suppose there's any whale blubber in Mesalia.

[*At which point* DR. BRADLEY *obligingly enters from the hall.* MR. WHITESIDE *is equal to the occasion.*]

WHITESIDE [*With just the merest glance at the* DOCTOR]: Oh, yes, there is.

DR. BRADLEY: The door was open, so I— Good afternoon, Mr. Whiteside. And Merry Christmas.

WHITESIDE: Merry Christmas, Merry Christmas. Do you happen to know if eels are in season, Doctor?

DR. BRADLEY: How's that?

WHITESIDE: Never mind. I was a fool to ask you.

[JOHN *returns from the library, carefully closing the doors.*]

JOHN: I opened those two slats a little, Mr. Whiteside—they seemed so crowded in there.

WHITESIDE: Thank you, John. [JOHN *goes on his way.*] On your way downtown, Doctor, will you send these air mail? Miss Cutler forgot them. [*He hands him a few letters.*] Good-bye. Sorry you dropped in just now. I have to do my Yogi exercises. [*He folds his arms, leans back and closes his eyes.*]

DR. BRADLEY: But, Mr. Whiteside, it's been a week now. My book, you know—when are we going to start work on the book? [WHITESIDE, *his eyes still closed, places his fingers to his lips, for absolute silence.*] I was hoping that today you'd be— [*He stops short as* MISS PREEN *returns from the dining room.*] Good afternoon, Miss Preen.

MISS PREEN: Good afternoon, Dr. Bradley. [*She opens the doors to enter the library, then freezes in her tracks. She closes the doors again and turns to the* DOCTOR, *glassy-eyed. She raises a trembling hand to her forehead.*] Doctor, perhaps I'm—not well, but—when I opened the doors just now I thought I saw a penguin with a thermometer in its mouth.

WHITESIDE: What's this? Have those penguins got out of their crate?

MISS PREEN: Oh, thank God. I thought perhaps the strain had been too much.

DR. BRADLEY [*Incredulous*]: Penguins?

WHITESIDE: Yes. Doctor, will you go in and capture them, please, and put them back in the crate? There're four of them.

DR. BRADLEY [*Somewhat staggered*]: Very well. Do you suppose that later on, Mr. Whiteside, we might—

WHITESIDE: We'll see, we'll see. First catch the penguins. And, Miss Preen, will you amuse them, please, until I come in?

MISS PREEN [*Swallowing hard*]: Yes, sir.

[*Meanwhile* JOHN *has descended the stairs.*]

JOHN: The Christmas tree just fell on Mr. Stanley. He's got a big bump on his forehead.

WHITESIDE [*Brightly*]: Why, isn't that too bad? . . . Go ahead, Doctor. Go on, Miss Preen.

[RICHARD *pops in from the hallway.*]

RICHARD: Hello, Mr. Whiteside.

WHITESIDE: Hello, Dickie, my boy.

DR. BRADLEY [*Still lingering*]: Mr. Whiteside, will you have some time later?

WHITESIDE [*Impatient*]: I don't know, Doctor. I'm busy now.

DR. BRADLEY: Well, suppose I wait a little while? I'll—I'll wait a little while. [*He goes into the library.*]

WHITESIDE: Dr. Bradley is the greatest living argument for mercy killings. . . . Well, Dickie, would you like a candid camera shot of my left nostril this evening?

RICHARD: I'm sort of stocked up on those. Have you got a minute to look at some new ones I've taken?

WHITESIDE: I certainly have. . . . Why, these are splendid, Richard. There's real artistry in them—they're as good as anything by Margaret Bourke-White. I like all the things you've shown me. This is the essence of photographic journalism.

RICHARD: Say, I didn't know they were as good as that. I just like to take pictures, that's all.

WHITESIDE: Richard, I've been meaning to talk to you about this. You're not just a kid fooling with a camera any more. These are good. This is what you ought to do. You ought to get out of here and do some of the things you were telling me about. Just get on a boat and get off wherever it stops. Galveston, Mexico, Singapore—work your way through and just take pictures—everything.

RICHARD: Say, wouldn't I like to, though! It's what I've been dreaming of for years. If I could do that I'd be the happiest guy in the world.

WHITESIDE: Well, why can't you do it? If I were your age, I'd do it like a shot.

RICHARD: Well, you know why. Dad.

WHITESIDE: Richard, do you really want to do this more than anything else in the world?

RICHARD: I certainly do.

WHITESIDE: Then do it.

[JUNE *comes quietly in from the dining room. Obviously there is something on her mind.*]

JUNE: Hello, Dick. Good afternoon, Mr. Whiteside.

WHITESIDE: Hello, my lovely. . . . So I'm afraid it's up to *you*, Richard.

RICHARD: I guess it is. Well, thank you, Mr. Whiteside. You've been swell and I'll never forget it.

WHITESIDE: Righto, Richard.

RICHARD: June, are you coming upstairs?

JUNE: Ah—in a few minutes, Richard.

RICHARD: Well—knock on my door, will you? I want to talk to you.

JUNE: Yes, I will.

[RICHARD *disappears up the stairs.*]

WHITESIDE [*Brightly opening his book*]: June, my lamb, you were too young to know about the Elwell murder, weren't you? Completely fascinating. I have about five favorite murders, and the Elwell case is one of them. Would you like to hear about it?

JUNE: Well, Mr. Whiteside, I wanted to talk to you. Would you mind, for a few minutes? It's important.

WHITESIDE: Why, certainly, my dear. I take it this is all about your young Lothario at the factory?

JUNE: Yes. I just can't seem to make Father understand. It's like talking to a blank wall. He won't meet him—he won't even talk about it. What are we going to do, Mr. Whiteside? Sandy and I love each other. I don't know where to turn.

WHITESIDE: My dear, I'd like to meet this young man. I'd like to see him for myself.

JUNE: Would you, Mr. Whiteside? Would you meet him? He's—he's outside now. He's in the kitchen.

WHITESIDE: Good! Bring him in.

JUNE [*Hesitating*]: Mr. Whiteside, he's—he's a very sensitive boy. You will be nice to him, won't you?

WHITESIDE: God damn it, June, when will you learn that I am *always* kind and courteous! Bring this idiot in!

JUNE [*Calling through the dining room in a low voice*]: Sandy. . . . Sandy. . . . [*She stands aside as a young man enters. Twenty-three or -four, keen-looking, neatly but simply dressed.*] Here he is, Mr. Whiteside. This is Sandy.

SANDY: How do you do, sir?

WHITESIDE: How do you do? Young man, I've been hearing a good deal about you from June this past week. It seems, if I have been correctly informed, that you two babes in the woods have quietly gone out of your minds.

JUNE: There's another name for it. It's called love.

WHITESIDE: Well, you've come to the right place. Dr. Sheridan Whiteside, Broken Hearts Mended, Brakes Relined, Hamburgers. Go right ahead.

SANDY: Well, if June has told you anything at all, Mr. Whiteside, you know the jam we're in. You see, I work for the union, Mr. Whiteside. I'm an organizer. I've been organizing the men in Mr. Stanley's factory, and Mr. Stanley's pretty sore about it.

WHITESIDE: I'll bet.

SANDY: Did June tell you that?

WHITESIDE: Yes, she did.

SANDY: Well, that being the case, Mr. Whiteside, I don't think I have the right to try to influence June. If she marries me it means a definite break with her family, and I don't like to bring that about. But Mr. Stanley's so stubborn about it, so arbitrary. You know, this is not something I've done just to spite him. We fell in love with each other. But Mr. Stanley behaves as though it were all a big plot—John L. Lewis sent me here just to marry his daughter.

JUNE: He's tried to fire Sandy twice, out at the factory, but he couldn't on account of the Wagner Act, thank God!

SANDY: Yes, he thinks I wrote that, too.

JUNE: If he'd only let me talk to him. If he'd let Sandy talk to him.

SANDY: Well, we've gone over all that, June. Anyway, this morning I got word I'm needed in Chicago. I may have to go on to Frisco from there. So you see the jam we're in.

JUNE: Sandy's leaving tonight, Mr. Whiteside. He'll probably be gone a year. We've simply got to decide. *Now.*

WHITESIDE: My dear, this is absurdly simple. It's no problem at all. Now to my jaundiced eye— [*The telephone rings.*] Oh-h! Hello. . . . Yes. . . . This is Whiteside. . . . Excuse me—it's a trans-Atlantic call. . . . Yes? . . . Yes, I'm on. Who's calling me? [*His tone suddenly becomes one of keen delight.*] All right—put her through. [*He turns to the young pair.*] It's Gertrude Stein, in Paris. . . . Hello. . . . Hello, Gertie! How's my little nightingale? . . . Yes, I hoped you would. How'd you know I was here? . . . I see. Well, it's wonderful of you to call. . . . Yes. Yes, I'm listening. Ten seconds more? [*A quick aside to the others.*] It'll be Christmas in Paris in ten seconds, and every year—yes? . . . Yes, Gertie, I hear them. It's wonderful. As though they were right outside. . . . June! [*He holds the receiver out to* JUNE *for a second.*] Thank you, my dear, and a very Merry Christmas to *you*. Don't forget we're dining on June tenth. . . . Pourquoi ne pas se réunir chez vous après? Tachez d'avoir Picasso, Matisse, Cocteau. Je serai seulement là pour quelques jours et je veux voir tout-le-monde. N'est-ce pas? Ah! Bon! Au revoir—au revoir. [*He hangs up.*] You know what that was you listened to? The bells of Notre Dame.

JUNE: Not really.

WHITESIDE: Miss Stein calls me every Christmas, no matter where I am, so that I can hear them. Two years ago I was walking on the bottom of the ocean in a diving suit with William Beebe, but she got me. . . . Now, where were we? Oh, yes. . . . June, I like your young man. I have an unerring instinct about people—I've never been wrong. That's why I wanted to meet him. My feeling is that you two will be very happy together. Whatever his beliefs are, he's entitled to them, and you shouldn't let anything stand in your way. As I see it, it's no problem at all. Stripped of its externals, what does it come down to? Your father. The possibility of making him unhappy. Is that right?

JUNE: *Very* unhappy.

WHITESIDE: That isn't the point. Suppose your parents *are* unhappy—it's good for them. Develops their characters. Look at me. I left home at the age of four and haven't been back since. They hear me on the radio and that's enough for them.

SANDY: Then—your advice is to go ahead, Mr. Whiteside?

WHITESIDE: It is. Marry him tonight, June.

JUNE [*Almost afraid to make the leap*]: You—you mean that, Mr. Whiteside?

WHITESIDE [*Bellowing*]: No, I mean you should marry Senator Borah. If I didn't mean it I wouldn't say it. What do you want me to do—say it all over again? My own opinion is—

[*The voice of* MR. STANLEY *is heard at the head of the stairs.* "*Come on, Daisy—stop dawdling.*"]

[JUNE *quickly pushes her young man out of the room, as* MR. *and* MRS. STANLEY *descend the stairs.*]

STANLEY [*With deep sarcasm*]: Forgive us for trespassing, Mr. Whiteside.

WHITESIDE: Not at all, old fellow—not at all. It's Christmas, you know. Merry Christmas, Merry Christmas.

MRS. STANLEY [*Nervously*]: Ah—yes. Merry Christmas. . . . Would you like to come along with us, June? We're taking some presents over to the Dexters.

JUNE: No—no, thank you, Mother. I—I have to write some letters. [*She hurries up the stairs.*]

STANLEY [*Who has been donning his coat*]: Come along, Daisy. [*Turning, he reveals a great patch of court plaster on his head.*]

WHITESIDE [*Entirely too sweetly*]: Why, Mr. Stanley, what happened to your forehead? Did you have an accident?

STANLEY [*Just as sweetly*]: No, Mr. Whiteside. I'm taking boxing lessons. . . . Come, Daisy. [*They go.*]

[HARRIET, *who has been hovering at the head of the stairs, hurries down as the* STANLEYS *depart. She is carrying a little Christmas package.*]

HARRIET: Dear Mr. Whiteside, I've been trying all day to see you. To give you—*this.*

WHITESIDE: Why, Miss Stanley. A Christmas gift for me?

HARRIET: It's only a trifle, but I wanted you to have it. It's a picture of me as I used to be. It was taken on another Christmas Eve, many years ago. Don't open it till the stroke of midnight, will you? [*The doorbell rings.* HARRIET *looks apprehensively over her shoulder.*] Merry Christmas, dear Mr. Whiteside. Merry Christmas.

WHITESIDE: Merry Christmas to you, Miss Stanley, and thank you. [*She glides out of the room.*]

[*In the hallway, as* JOHN *opens the door, we hear a woman's voice, liquid and melting.* "*This is the Stanley residence, isn't it?*" "*Yes, it is.*" "*I've come to see Mr. Whiteside. Will you tell him Miss Sheldon is here?*"]

WHITESIDE: Lorraine! My Blossom Girl!

LORRAINE [*Coming into view*]: Sherry, my sweet!

[*And quite a view it is.* LORRAINE SHELDON *is known as the most chic actress on the New York or London stage, and justly so. She glitters as she walks. She is beautiful, and even, God save the word, glamorous. . . . Her rank as one of the Ten Best-Dressed Women of the World is richly deserved. She is, in short, a siren of no mean talents, and knows it.*]

LORRAINE [*Wasting no time*]: Oh, darling, look at that poor sweet tortured face! Let me kiss it! You poor darling, your eyes have a kind of gallant compassion. How drawn you are! Sherry, my sweet, I want to cry.

WHITESIDE: All right, all right. You've made a very nice entrance. Now relax, dear.

LORRAINE: But, Sherry, darling, I've been so worried. And now seeing you in that chair . . .

WHITESIDE: This chair fits my fanny as nothing else ever has. I feel better than I have in years, and my only concern is news of the outside world. So take that skunk off and tell me everything. How are you, my dear?

LORRAINE [*Removing a cascade of silver fox from her shoulders*]: Darling, I'm so relieved. You look perfectly wonderful —I never saw you look better. My dear, do I look a wreck? I just dashed through New York. Didn't do a thing about Christmas. Hattie Carnegie and had my hair done, and got right on the train. And the *Normandie* coming back was simply hectic. Fun, you know, but simply exhausting. Jock Whitney, and Cary Grant, and Dorothy di Frasso—it was *too* exhausting. And of course London before that was so magnificent, my dear —well, I simply never got to bed at all. Darling, I've so much to tell you I don't know where to start.

WHITESIDE: Well, start with the dirt first, dear—that's what I want to hear.

LORRAINE: Let me see. . . . Well, Sybil Cartwright got thrown right out of Ciro's—it was the night before I sailed. She was wearing one of those new cellophane dresses, and you could absolutely see Trafalgar Square. And, oh, yes—Sir Harry Montrose—the painter, *you* know—is suing his mother for disorderly conduct. It's just shocked *every*one. Oh, and before I forget—Anthony Eden told me he's going to be on your New Year's broadcast, and he gave me a message for you. He said for God's sake not to introduce him again as the English Grover Whalen.

WHITESIDE: Nonsense. . . . Now come, dear, what about *you?* What about your love life? I don't believe for one moment that you never got to bed at all, if you'll pardon the expression.

LORRAINE: Sherry dear, you're dreadful.

WHITESIDE: What about that splendid bit of English mutton, Lord Bottomley? Haven't you hooked him yet?

LORRAINE: Sherry, please. Cedric is a very dear friend of mine.

WHITESIDE: Now, Blossom Girl, this is Sherry. Don't try to pull the bed clothes over *my* eyes. Don't tell *me* you wouldn't like to be Lady Bottomley, with a hundred thousand pounds a year and twelve castles. By the way, has he had his teeth fixed yet? Every time I order Roquefort cheese I think of those teeth.

LORRAINE: Sherry, really! . . . Cedric may not be brilliant, but he's rather sweet, poor lamb, and he's very fond of me, and he does represent a kind of English way of living that I like. Surrey, and London for the season—shooting box in Scotland —that lovely old castle in Wales. You were there, Sherry—you know what I mean.

WHITESIDE: Mm. I do indeed.

LORRAINE: Well, really, Sherry, why not? If I can marry Cedric I don't know why I shouldn't. Shall I tell you something, Sherry? I think, from something he said just before I sailed, that he's finally coming around to it. It wasn't definite, mind you, but—don't be surprised if I *am* Lady Bottomley before very long.

WHITESIDE: Lady Bottomley! Won't Kansas City be surprised! However, I shall be a flower girl and give the groom an iron toothpick as a wedding present. Come ahead, my blossom —let's hear some more of your skullduggery.

[*The library doors are quietly opened at this point and the* DOCTOR'S *head appears.*]

DR. BRADLEY [*In a heavy whisper*]: Mr. Whiteside.

WHITESIDE: What? No, no—not now. I'm busy. [*The* DOCTOR *disappears.*]

LORRAINE: Who's that?

WHITESIDE: He's fixing the plumbing. . . . Now come on, come on—I want more news.

LORRAINE: But, Sherry, what about this play? After all, I've come all the way from New York—even on Christmas Eve—I've been so excited ever since your phone call. Where is it? When can I read it?

WHITESIDE: Well, here's the situation. This young author—his name is Bert Jefferson—brought me the play with the understanding that I send it to Kit Cornell. It's a magnificent part, and God knows I feel disloyal to Kit, but there you are. Now *I've* done *this* much—the rest is up to you. He's young and attractive—now, just how you'll go about persuading him, I'm sure you know more about that than I do.

LORRAINE: Darling, how can I ever thank you? Does he know I'm coming—Mr. Jefferson, I mean?

WHITESIDE: No, no. You're just out here visiting me. You'll meet him, and that's that. Get him to take you to dinner, and work around to the play.. Good God, I don't have to tell you how to do these things. How did you get all those other parts?

LORRAINE: Sherry! . . . Well, I'll go back to the hotel and get into something more attractive. I just dumped my bags and rushed right over here. Darling, you're wonderful. [*Lightly kissing him.*]

WHITESIDE: All right—run along and get into your working clothes. Then come right back here and spend Christmas Eve with Sherry and I'll have Mr. Jefferson on tap. By the way, I've got a little surprise for you. Who do you think's paying me a flying visit tonight? None other than your old friend and fellow actor, Beverly Carlton.

LORRAINE [*Not too delighted*]: Really? Beverly? I thought he was being glamorous again on a tramp steamer.

WHITESIDE: Come, come, dear—mustn't be bitter because he got better notices than you did.

LORRAINE: Don't be silly, Sherry. I never read notices. I simply wouldn't care to act with him again, that's all. He's not staying here, is he? I *hope* not!

WHITESIDE: Temper, temper, temper. No, he's not. . . . Where'd you get that diamond clip, dear? That's a new bit of loot, isn't it?

LORRAINE: Haven't you seen this before? Cedric gave it to me for his mother's birthday. . . . Look, darling, I've got a taxi outside. If I'm going to get back here—

[*At this point the voice of* MAGGIE *is heard in the hallway.*]

MAGGIE: Sherry, what do you think? I've just been given the most beautiful . . . [*She stops short and comes to a dead halt as she sees* LORRAINE.]

LORRAINE: Oh, hello, Maggie. I knew you must be around somewhere. How are you, my dear?

WHITESIDE: Santa's been at work, my pet. Blossom Girl just dropped in out of the blue and surprised us.

MAGGIE [*Quietly*]: Hello, Lorraine.

WHITESIDE [*As* JEFFERSON *appears*]: Who's that—Bert? This is Mr. Bert Jefferson, Lorraine. Young newspaper man. Miss Lorraine Sheldon.

BERT: How do you do, Miss Sheldon?

LORRAINE: How do you do? I didn't quite catch the name— Jefferson?

WHITESIDE [*Sweetly*]: That's right, Pet.

LORRAINE [*Full steam ahead*]: Why, Mr. Jefferson, you don't look like a newspaper man. You don't look like a newspaper man at all.

BERT: Really? I thought it was written all over me in neon lights.

LORRAINE: Oh, no, not at all. I should have said you were— oh, I don't know—an aviator or an explorer or something. They have that same kind of dash about them. I'm simply enchanted with your town, Mr. Jefferson. It gives one such a warm, gracious feeling. Tell me—have you lived here all your life?

BERT: Practically.

WHITESIDE: If you wish to hear the story of his life, Lorraine, kindly do so on your own time. Maggie and I have work to do. Get out of here, Jefferson. On your way, Blossom.

LORRAINE: He's the world's rudest man, isn't he? Can I drop you, Mr. Jefferson? I'm going down to the—Mansion House, I think it's called.

BERT: Thank you, but I've got my car. Suppose I drop you?

LORRAINE: Oh, would you? That'd be lovely—we'll send the taxi off. See you in a little while, Sherry. 'Bye, Maggie.

BERT: Good-bye, Miss C. [*He turns to* WHITESIDE.] I'm invited back for dinner, am I not?

WHITESIDE: Yes—yes, you are. At Christmas I always feed the needy. Now please stop oozing out—*get* out.

LORRAINE: Come on, Mr. Jefferson. I want to hear more about this charming little town. And I want to know a good deal about you, too.

[*And they are gone.*]

[*There is a slight but pregnant pause after they go.* MAGGIE *simply stands looking at* WHITESIDE, *waiting for what may come forth.*]

WHITESIDE [*As though nothing had happened*]: Now let's see, have you got a copy of that broadcast? How much did you say they wanted out—four minutes?

MAGGIE: That's right—four minutes. . . . She's looking very well, isn't she?

WHITESIDE [*Busy with his manuscript*]: What's that? Who?

MAGGIE: The Countess di Pushover. . . . Quite a surprise, wasn't it—her dropping in?

WHITESIDE: Yes—yes, it was. Now come on, Maggie, come on. Get to work.

MAGGIE: Why, she must have gone through New York like a dose of salts. How long's she going to stay?

WHITESIDE [*Completely absorbed*]: What? Oh, I don't know —a few days . . . [*He reads from his manuscript.*] "At this joyous season of the year, when in the hearts of men—" I can't cut that.

MAGGIE: Isn't it curious? There was Lorraine, snug as a bug in somebody's bed on the *Normandie*—

WHITESIDE [*So busy*]: "Ere the Yuletide season pass—"

MAGGIE [*Quietly taking the manuscript out of his hands*]: Now, Sherry dear, we will talk a bit.

WHITESIDE: Now look here, Maggie. Just because a friend of mine happens to come out to spend Christmas with me— [*The doorbell rings.*] I have a hunch that's Beverly. Maggie, see if it is. Go ahead—run! Run!

[MAGGIE *looks at him—right through him, in fact. Then she goes slowly toward the door.*]

[*We hear her voice at the door:* "Beverly!" *Then, in clipped English tones:* "Magpie! A large, moist, incestuous kiss for my Magpie!"]

WHITESIDE [*Roaring*]: Come in here, you Piccadilly pen-pusher, and gaze upon a soul in agony.

[BEVERLY CARLTON *enters, arm in arm with* MAGGIE. *Very confident, very British, very Beverly Carlton.*]

BEVERLY: Don't tell me how you are, Sherry dear. I want none of the tiresome details. I have only a little time, so the conversation will be entirely about *me*, and I shall love it. Shall I tell you how I glittered through the South Seas like a silver scimitar, or would you rather hear how I frolicked through Zambesia, raping the Major General's daughter and finishing a three-act play at the same time? . . . Magpie dear, you are the moonflower of my middle age, and I love you very much. Say something beautiful to me. Sherry dear, without going into mountainous waves of self-pity, how are you?

WHITESIDE: I'm fine, you presumptuous Cockney. . . . Now, how was the trip, wonderful?

BEVERLY: Fabulous. I did a fantastic amount of work. By the way, did I glimpse that little boudoir butterfly, La Sheldon, in a motor-car as I came up the driveway?

MAGGIE: You did indeed. She's paying us a Christmas visit.

BEVERLY: Dear girl! They do say she set fire to her mother, but I don't believe it. . . . Sherry, my evil one, not only have I written the finest comedy since Molière, but also the best revue since my last one and an operetta that frightens me—it's so good. I shall play it for eight weeks in London and six in New York—that's all. No matinees. Then I am off to the Grecian Islands. . . . Magpie, why don't you come along? Why don't you desert this cannon ball of fluff and come with me?

MAGGIE: Beverly dear, be careful. You're catching me at a good moment.

WHITESIDE [*Changing the subject*]: Tell me, did you have a good time in Hollywood? How long were you there?

BEVERLY: Three unbelievable days. I saw everyone from Adrian to Zanuck. They came, poor dears, as to a shrine. I was insufferably charming and ruthlessly firm in refusing seven million dollars for two minutes' work.

WHITESIDE: What about Banjo? Did you see my wonderful Banjo in Hollywood?

BEVERLY: I did. He gave a dinner for me. I arrived, in white tie and tails, to be met at the door by two bewigged flunkies, who quietly proceeded to take my trousers off. I was then ushered, in my lemon silk drawers, into a room full of Norma Shearer, Claudette Colbert, and Aldous Huxley, among others. Dear, sweet, incomparable Banjo.

WHITESIDE: I'll never forget that summer at Antibes, when Banjo put a microphone in Lorraine's mattress, and then played the record the next day at lunch.

BEVERLY: I remember it indeed. Lorraine left Antibes by the next boat.

MAGGIE [*Half to herself*]: I wish Banjo were here now.

BEVERLY: What's the matter, Magpie? Is Lorraine being her own sweet sick-making self?

MAGGIE: You wouldn't take her to the Grecian Islands with you, would you, Beverly? Just for me?

WHITESIDE: Now, now. Lorraine is a charming person who has gallantly given up her own Christmas to spend it with me.

BEVERLY: Oh, I knew I had a bit of dirt for us all to nibble on. [*He draws a letter out of his pocket.*]

[*Again the library doors are opened and the* DOCTOR'S *head comes through.*]

DR. BRADLEY: Mr. Whiteside.

WHITESIDE: No, no, not now. Go away.

[*The* DOCTOR *withdraws.*]

BEVERLY: Have you kidnapped someone, Sherry?

WHITESIDE: Yes, that was Charley Ross . . . Go ahead. Is this something juicy?

BEVERLY: Juicy as a pomegranate. It is the latest report from London on the winter maneuvers of Miss Lorraine Sheldon against the left flank—in fact, all flanks—of Lord Cedric Bottomley. Listen: "Lorraine has just left us in a cloud of Chanel Number Five. Since September, in her relentless pursuit of His Lordship, she has paused only to change girdles and check her oil. She has chased him, panting, from castle to castle, till he finally took refuge, for several week-ends, in the gentlemen's lavatory of the House of Lords. Practically no one is betting on the Derby this year; we are all making book on Lorraine. She is sailing tomorrow on the *Normandie,* but would return on the *Yankee Clipper* if Bottomley so much as belches in her direction." Have you ever met Lord Bottomley, Magpie dear? [*He goes immediately into an impersonation of His Lordship. Very British, very full of teeth, stuttering.*]

"No v-v-very good shooting today, blast it. Only s-s-six partridges, f-f-four grouse, and the D-D-Duke of Sutherland."

WHITESIDE [*Chuckling*]: My God, that's Bottomley to the very bottom.

BEVERLY [*Still in character*]: "R-r-ripping debate in the House today. Old Basil spoke for th-th-three hours. D-d-dropped dead at the end of it. Ripping."

MAGGIE: You're making it up, Beverly. No one sounds like that.

WHITESIDE: It's so good it's uncanny. . . . Damn it, Beverly, why must you race right out of here? I never see enough of you, you ungrateful moppet.

BEVERLY: Sherry darling, I can only tell you that my love for you is so great that I changed trains at Chicago to spend ten minutes with you and wish you a Merry Christmas. Merry Christmas, my lad. My little Magpie. [*A look at his watch.*] And now I have just time for one magnificent number, to give you a taste of how brilliant the whole thing is. It's the second number in the revue. [*He strikes a chord on the piano, but before he can go further the telephone rings.*]

WHITESIDE: Oh, damn! Get rid of them, Maggie.

MAGGIE: Hello . . . Oh, hello, Bert . . . Oh! Well, just a minute. . . . Beverly, would you talk to a newspaper man for just two minutes? I kind of promised him.

BEVERLY: Won't have time, Magpie, unless he's under the piano.

MAGGIE: Oh! [*Into the phone.*] Wait a minute. [*To* BEVERLY *again.*] Would you see him at the station, just for a minute before the train goes? [BEVERLY *nods.*] Bert, go to the station and wait for him. He'll be there in a few minutes. . . . 'Bye.

WHITESIDE: The stalls are impatient, Beverly. Let's have this second-rate masterpiece.

BEVERLY [*His fingers rippling over the keys*]: It's called: "What Am I to Do?"

> "Oft in the nightfall
> I think I might fall
> Down from my perilous height;

Deep in the heart of me,
Always a part of me,
    Quivering, shivering light.
Run, little lady,
Ere the shady
    Shafts of time
Barb you with their winged desire,
Singe you with their sultry fire.
    Softly a fluid
                Druid
                    Meets me,
Olden
    and golden
        the dawn that greets me;
Cherishing,
        Perishing.
Up to the stars
    I climb.

"What am I to do
    Toward ending this madness,
    This sadness,
That's rending me through?
The flowers of yesteryear
    Are haunting me,
    Taunting me,
Darling, for wanting you.
What am I to say
    To warnings of sorrow
    When morning's tomorrow
Greets the dew?
    Will I see the cosmic Ritz
    Shattered and scattered to bits?
What *not* am I to do?"

[*As he swings into the chorus for a second time the door
bell rings, and* JOHN *is glimpsed as he goes to the door.*]
[*It is a trio of* RADIO MEN *who appear in the doorway, their
arms filled with equipment for* MR. WHITESIDE'S *broadcast.*]
WHITESIDE: Oh, come in, Westcott. . . . Beverly, it's superb.

The best thing you've ever written. It'll be played by every ragtag orchestra from Salem to Singapore.

BEVERLY: Please! Let *me* say that . . . Ah, the air waves, eh? Well, I shan't have to hear you, thank God. I shall be on the train.

MAGGIE: Come on, Whiteside, say good-bye. Mr. Westcott, he's still four minutes over—you'll have to chisel it out.

WHITESIDE [*As* MAGGIE *starts to wheel him into the library*]: Stop this nonsense. Beverly, my lamb—

MAGGIE: You can kiss Beverly in London on July twelfth. [*Then to the technicians.*] The microphone set-up is right there, gentlemen, and you can connect up outside. John, show them where it is.

WHITESIDE: Maggie, what the hell are you—

BEVERLY [*Calling after the fast-disappearing* WHITESIDE]: Au revoir, Sherry. Merry Christmas. Magpie, come get a kiss.

MAGGIE [*Emerging from the library and closing the doors behind her*]: Beverly, I want one minute. I must have it. You'll make the train. The station's a minute and a half from here.

BEVERLY: Why, what's the matter, Magpie?

[*At which the library doors are opened and the* DOCTOR *emerges, rather apologetically. He is sped on his way by* MR. WHITESIDE'S *roaring voice—"Oh, get out of here!"*]

DR. BRADLEY: I'm—I'm just waiting in the kitchen until Mr. Whiteside is— Excuse me. [*He darts out through the dining room.*]

BEVERLY: Who *is* that man?

MAGGIE: Never mind . . . Beverly, I'm in great trouble.

BEVERLY: Why, Magpie dear, what's the matter?

MAGGIE: I've fallen in love. For the first time in my life. Beverly, I'm in love. I can't tell you about it—there isn't time. But Sherry is trying to break it up. In his own fiendish way he's doing everything he can to break it up.

BEVERLY: Why, the old devil! What's he doing?

MAGGIE: Lorraine. He's brought Lorraine here to smash it.

BEVERLY: Oh, it's somebody *here?* In this town?

MAGGIE [*Nodding*]: He's a newspaper man—the one you're going to see at the station—and he's written a play, and I know Sherry must be using that as bait. You know Lorraine—she'll eat him up alive. You've got to help me, Beverly.

BEVERLY: Of course I will, Magpie. What do you want me to do?

MAGGIE: I've got to get Lorraine out of here—the farther away the better—and you can do it for me.

BEVERLY: But how? How can I? I'm leaving.

[*The library doors are opened and* WESTCOTT, *the radio man, emerges.*]

WESTCOTT: Have you a carbon copy of the broadcast, Miss Cutler?

MAGGIE: It's on that table.

WESTCOTT: Thank you. One of those penguins ate the original.

[*The voice of* WHITESIDE *is now heard calling from his room.*]

WHITESIDE: Beverly, are you still there?

MAGGIE: No, he's gone, Sherry. [*She lowers her voice.*] Come out here.

[*Maneuvering him into the hall, we see her whisper to him; his head bobs up and down quickly in assent. Then he lets out a shriek of laughter.*]

BEVERLY: I'd love it. I'd absolutely love it. [MAGGIE *puts a quick finger to his lips, peers toward the* WHITESIDE *room. But* MR. WESTCOTT *has gone in; the doors are closed.*] It's simply enchanting, and bitches Sherry and Lorraine at the same time. It's pure heaven! I adore it, and I shall do it up brown. [*He embraces her.*]

MAGGIE: Darling, the first baby will be named Beverly. You're wonderful.

BEVERLY: Of course I am. Come to Chislewick for your honeymoon and I'll put you up. Good-bye, my lovely. I adore you. [*And he is gone.*]

[MAGGIE *comes back into the room, highly pleased with herself. She even sings a fragment of* BEVERLY'S *song. "What am I to do? Tra-la-la-la-la-la."*]

[JOHN, *entering from the dining room, breaks the song.*]

JOHN: Shall I straighten up the room for the broadcast, Miss Cutler?

MAGGIE: No, John, it isn't television, thank God. They only *hear* that liquid voice.

JOHN: He's really wonderful, isn't he? The things he finds time to do.

MAGGIE: Yes, he certainly sticks his nose into everything, John. [*She goes into the library.*]

[JOHN *is putting the room in order when suddenly* JUNE *comes quietly down the stairs. She is dressed for the street and is carrying a suitcase.*]

JOHN: Why, Miss June, are you going away?

JUNE: Why—no, John. No. I'm just— Mr. Whiteside is inside, I suppose?

JOHN: Yes, he's getting ready to go on the radio.

JUNE: Oh! Well, look, John—

[*And then* RICHARD *darts down the stairs. A light bag, two cameras slung over his shoulder.*]

RICHARD [*To* JUNE, *in a heavy whisper*]: Where's Mr. Whiteside? In there?

JUNE: Yes, he is.

RICHARD: Oh! Well, maybe we ought to—

[*The doorbell rings.* RICHARD *and* JUNE *exchange looks, then scurry out quickly through the dining room.*]

[JOHN *looks after them for a second, puzzled, then goes to the door.*]

[*It is* LORRAINE *who comes in, resplendent now in evening dress and wrap, straight from Paris. At the same time* MAGGIE *emerges from the library and* JOHN *goes on his way.*]

LORRAINE: Hello, dear. Where's Sherry?

MAGGIE: Inside, working—he's broadcasting very soon.

LORRAINE: Oh, of course—Christmas Eve. What a wonderful man Sheridan Whiteside is! You know, my dear, it must be such an utter joy to be secretary to somebody like Sherry.

MAGGIE: Yes, you meet such interesting people. . . . That's quite a gown, Lorraine. Going anywhere?

LORRAINE: This? Oh, I just threw on anything at all. Aren't you dressing for dinner?

MAGGIE: No, just what meets the eye. [*She has occasion to carry a few papers across the room at this point.* LORRAINE'S *eye watches her narrowly.*]

LORRAINE: Who does your hair, Maggie?

MAGGIE: A little French woman named Maggie Cutler comes in every morning.

LORRAINE: You know, every time I see you I keep thinking

your hair could be so lovely. I always want to get my hands on it.

MAGGIE [*Quietly*]: I've always wanted to get mine on yours, Lorraine.

LORRAINE [*Absently*]: What, dear?

[*One of the radio men drifts into the room, plugs into the control board, drifts out again.* LORRAINE'S *eyes follow him idly. Then she turns to* MAGGIE *again.*]

By the way, what time does Beverly get here? I'm not over-anxious to meet him.

MAGGIE: He's been and gone, Lorraine.

LORRAINE: Really? Well, I'm very glad. . . . Of course you're great friends, aren't you—you and Beverly?

MAGGIE: Yes, we are. I think he's a wonderful person.

LORRAINE: Oh, I suppose so. But when I finished acting with him I was a perfect wreck. All during that tender love scene that the critics thought was so magnificent he kept dropping peanut shells down my dress. I wouldn't act with him again if I were starving.

MAGGIE [*Casually*]: Tell me, Lorraine, have you found a new play yet?

LORRAINE [*At once on guard*]: No. No, I haven't. There was a pile of manuscripts waiting in New York for me, but I hurried right out here to Sherry.

MAGGIE: Yes, it was wonderful of you, Lorraine—to drop everything that way and rush to Sherry's wheelchair.

LORRAINE: Well, after all, Maggie dear, what else has one in this world but friends? . . . How long will Sherry be in there, I wonder?

MAGGIE: Not long. . . . Did you know that Mr. Jefferson has written quite a good play? The young man that drove you to the hotel.

LORRAINE: Really? No, I didn't. Isn't that interesting?

MAGGIE: Yes, isn't it?

[*There is a considerable pause. The ladies smile at each other.*]

LORRAINE [*Evading* MAGGIE'S *eyes*]: They've put a polish on my nails I simply loathe. I don't suppose Elizabeth Arden has a branch in this town.

MAGGIE [*Busy with her papers*]: Not if she has any sense.

LORRAINE: Oh, well, I'll just bear it, but it does depress me. [*She rises, wanders aimlessly for a moment, picks up a book from the table.*] Have you read this, Maggie? Everybody was reading it on the boat. I hear you simply can't put it down.

MAGGIE: *I* put it down—right there.

[LORRAINE *casually strikes a note or two on the piano.*]

[*The telephone rings.*]

MAGGIE [*Taking up the receiver a little too casually*]: Hello . . . Yes . . . Yes . . . Miss Lorraine Sheldon? Yes, she's here . . . There's a trans-Atlantic call coming through for you. Lorraine.

LORRAINE: Trans-Atlantic—for me? Here? Why, what in the world—

MAGGIE [*As she hands over the receiver*]: It's London.

LORRAINE: London? . . . Hello. [*Then in a louder tone.*] Hello . . . Cedric! Cedric, is this you? . . . Why, Cedric, you darling! Why, what a surprise! How'd you know I was here? . . . Darling, don't talk so fast and you won't stutter so . . . That's better . . . Yes, now I can hear you . . . Yes, very clearly. It's as though you were just around the corner. . . . I see . . . What? . . . Darling! Cedric, dearest, would you wait just one moment? [*She turns to* MAGGIE.] Maggie, would you mind? It's Lord Bottomley—a *very* personal call. Would you mind?

MAGGIE: Oh, not at all. [*She goes into the dining room; almost does a little waltz step as she goes.*]

LORRAINE: Yes, my dearest—now tell me . . . Cedric, please don't stutter so. Don't be nervous. [*She listens for a moment again.*] Oh, my darling. Oh, my sweet. You don't know how I've prayed for this, every night on the boat . . . Darling, yes! YES, a thousand times Yes! . . . I'll take a plane right out of here and catch the next boat. Oh, my sweet, we're going to be the happiest people in the world. I wish I were there now in your arms, Cedric . . . What? . . . Cedric, don't stutter so . . . Yes, and I love *you*, my darling—oh, so much! . . . Oh, my dear sweet. My darling, my darling. . . . Yes, yes! I will, I will, darling! I'll be thinking of you every moment . . . You've made me the happiest girl in the world . . . Good-bye, good-bye, darling. Good-bye. [*Bursting with her news, she throws open the library doors.*] Sherry, Sherry! Do you know what's happened? Cedric just called from London— He's asked me to marry him. Sherry, think of it! At last! I've got to get right out of here and catch the next boat. How far are we from Chicago? I can get a plane from there.

MAGGIE [*Emerging, mouse-like, from the dining room*]: May I come in?

LORRAINE: Maggie dear, can I get a plane out of here right away? Or I'll even take a train to Chicago and fly from there. I've simply got to get the next boat for England. When is it— do you know? Is there a newspaper here?

MAGGIE: The *Queen Mary* sails Friday. Why, what's all the excitement, Lorraine? What's happened?

LORRAINE: Maggie, the most wonderful thing in the world has happened. Lord Bottomley has asked me to marry him . . . Oh, Maggie! [*And in her exuberance she throws her arms around her.*]

MAGGIE: Really? Well, what do you know?

LORRAINE: Isn't it wonderful? I'm so excited I can hardly think. Maggie dear, you must help me get out of here.

MAGGIE: I'd be delighted to, Lorraine.

LORRAINE: Oh, thank you, thank you. Will you look things up right away?

MAGGIE: Yes, I've a time-table right here. And don't worry, because if there's no train I'll drive you to Toledo and you can catch the plane from there.

LORRAINE: Maggie darling, you're wonderful. . . . Sherry, what's the matter with you? You haven't said a word. You haven't even congratulated me.

WHITESIDE [*Who has been sitting through this like a thundercloud*]: Let me understand this, Lorraine. Am I to gather from your girlish squeals that you are about to toss your career into the ashcan?

LORRAINE: Oh, not at all. Of course I may not be able to play this season, but there'll be other seasons, Sherry.

WHITESIDE: I see. And everything goes into the ashcan with it— Is that right?

LORRAINE: But, Sherry, you couldn't expect me to—

WHITESIDE [*Icily*]: Don't explain, Lorraine. I understand only too well. And I also understand why Cornell remains the First Actress of our theatre.

MAGGIE [*Busy with her time-tables*]: Oh, this is wonderful!
We're in luck, Lorraine. You can get a plane out of Toledo at
ten-three. It takes about an hour to get there. Why, it all works
out wonderfully, doesn't it, Sherry?

WHITESIDE [*Through his teeth*]: Peachy!

LORRAINE [*Heading for the phone*]: Maggie, what's the number of that hotel I'm at? I've got to get my maid started packing.

MAGGIE: Mesalia three two.

LORRAINE [*Into the phone*]: Mesalia three two, please . . .
Let's see—I sail Friday, five-day boat, that means I ought to be
in London Wednesday night. . . . Hello. This is Miss Sheldon.
. . . That's right. Connect me with my maid.

MAGGIE [*At the window*]: Oh, look, Sherry, it's starting to
snow. Isn't that wonderful, Sherry? Oh, I never felt more like
Christmas in my life. Don't you, Sherry dear?

WHITESIDE: Shut your nasty little face!

LORRAINE [*On the phone*]: Cosette? . . . Now listen carefully, Cosette. Have you got a pencil? . . . We're leaving here
tonight by plane and sailing Friday on the *Queen Mary*. Start
packing immediately and I'll call for you in about an hour . . .
Yes, that's right . . . Now I want you to send these cables for
me . . . Ready? . . . The first one goes to Lord and Lady
Cunard—you'll find all these addresses in my little book. It's
in my dressing case. "Lord and Lady Cunard. My darlings.
Returning Friday *Queen Mary*. Cedric and I being married immediately on arrival. Wanted you to be the first to know. Love.
—Lorraine." . . . Now send the same message—what? . . .
Oh, thank you, Cosette. Thank you very much . . . Send
the same message to Lady Astor, Lord Beaverbrook, and the
Duchess of Sutherland . . . Got that? . . . And send a cable
to Molyneaux, in Paris. "Please meet me Claridge's Thursday of
next week with sketches of bridal gown and trousseau.—Lorraine Sheldon." And then send one to Monsieur Pierre Cartier,
Cartier's, Paris: "Can you bring over to London the triple string
of pearls I picked out in October? Cable me *Queen Mary*.—
Lorraine Sheldon." . . . Have you got all that straight, Cosette?
. . . That's fine. Now you'll have to rush, my dear—I'll be at
the hotel in about an hour, so be ready. . . . Good-bye. [*She
hangs up*.] Thank goodness for Cosette—I'd die without her

She's the most wonderful maid in the world. . . . Well! Life is really just full of surprises, isn't it? Who'd have thought an hour ago that I'd be on my way to London?

MAGGIE: An *hour* ago? No, I certainly wouldn't have thought it an hour ago.

WHITESIDE [*Beside himself with temper*]: Will you both stop this female drooling? I have a violent headache.

MAGGIE [*All solicitude*]: Oh, Sherry! Can I get you something?

LORRAINE: Look here, Sherry, I'm sorry if I've offended you, but after all my life is my own and I'm not going to— [*She stops as* BERT JEFFERSON *comes in from the outside.*]

BERT: Hello, everybody. Say, do you know it's snowing out? Going to have a real old-fashioned Christmas.

WHITESIDE: Why don't you telephone your scoop to the New York *Times?*

MAGGIE: Bert, Miss Sheldon has to catch a plane tonight, from Toledo. Can we drive her over, you and I?

BERT: Why, certainly. Sorry you have to go, Miss Sheldon. No bad news, I hope?

LORRAINE: Oh, on the contrary—very good news. Wonderful news.

MAGGIE: Yes, indeed—calls for a drink, I think. You're not being a very good host, Sherry. How about a bottle of champagne?

BERT: Oh, I can do better than that—let me mix you something. It's a Jefferson Special. Okay, Mr. Whiteside?

WHITESIDE: Yes, yes, yes, yes, yes. Mix anything. Only stop driveling.

BERT [*On his way to the dining room*]: Anybody admired my Christmas present yet, Maggie?

MAGGIE: Oh, dear, I forgot. [*She raises her arm, revealing a bracelet.*] Look, everybody! From Mr. Jefferson to me.

LORRAINE: Oh, it's charming. Let me see it. Oh! Why, it's inscribed, too. "To Maggie. Long may she wave. Bert." Maggie, it's a lovely Christmas present. Isn't it sweet, Sherry?

WHITESIDE [*Glowering*]: Ducky!

MAGGIE: I told you it was beautiful, Bert. See?

BERT: Well, shows what you get if you save your coupons.

LORRAINE [*Looking from* BERT *to* MAGGIE]: Well, what's going on between you two, anyhow? Maggie, are you hiding something from us?

WHITESIDE [*A hand to his head*]: Great God, will this drivel never stop? My head is bursting.

BERT: A Jefferson Special will cure anything. . . . By the way, I got a two-minute interview with Beverly Carlton at the station. You were right, Mr. Whiteside— He's quite something.

MAGGIE [*Uneasily*]: Go ahead, Bert—mix the drinks.

BERT: I was lucky to get even two minutes. He was in a telephone booth most of the time. Couldn't hear what he was saying, but from the faces he was making it looked like a scene from one of his plays.

MAGGIE [*Hiding her frenzy*]: Bert, mix those drinks, will you?

WHITESIDE [*Suddenly galvanized*]: Just a minute, if you please, Jefferson. Mr. Carlton was in a telephone booth at the station?

BERT: Certainly was—I thought he'd never come out. Kept talking and making the damnedest faces for about five minutes.

MAGGIE [*Tensely*]: Bert, for goodness sake, will you—

WHITESIDE [*Ever so sweetly*]: Bert, my boy, I have an idea I shall love the Jefferson Special. Make me a double one, will you? My headache has gone with the wind.

BERT: Okay. [*He goes.*]

[WHITESIDE, *his eyes gleaming, immediately whirls his wheelchair across the room to the telephone.*]

WHITESIDE [*A finger to his lips*]: Sssh! Philo Vance is now at work.

LORRAINE: What?

WHITESIDE: Sssh! [*He picks up the telephone. His voice is absolutely musical.*] Operator! Has there been a call from England over this telephone within the past half hour? . . . Yes, I'll wait.

LORRAINE: Sherry, what *is* all this?

WHITESIDE: What's that? There have been no calls from England for the past three days? Thank you . . . Now, will you repeat that, please? . . . Blossom Girl. [*He beckons to LORRAINE, then puts the receiver to her ear.*] Hear it, dear? [*Then again to the operator.*] Thank you, and a Merry Christmas. [*He hangs up.*] Yes, indeed, it seems we're going to have a real old-fashioned Christmas.

LORRAINE [*Stunned*]: Sherry, what is all this? What's going on? What does this mean?

WHITESIDE: My dear, you have just played the greatest love scene of your career with your old friend, Beverly Carlton.

LORRAINE: Why—why, that's not true. I was talking to Cedric. What do you mean?

WHITESIDE: I mean, my blossom, that that was Beverly you poured out your girlish heart to, not Lord Bottomley. Ah, me, who'd have thought five minutes ago that you would not be going to London!

LORRAINE: Sherry, stop it! What is this? I want this explained.

WHITESIDE: Explained? You heard the operator, my dear. All I can tell you is that Beverly was indulging in one of his famous bits of mimicry, that's all. You've heard him do Lord Bottomley before, haven't you?

LORRAINE [*As it dawns on her*]: Yes . . . Yes, of course . . . But—but why would he want to do such a thing! This is one of the most dreadful—oh, my God! Those cables! [*In one bound she is at the telephone.*] Give me the hotel—whatever it's called—I want the hotel—I'll pay him off for this if it's the last thing that I— Why, the cad! The absolute unutterable cad! The dirty rotten— Mansion House? Connect me with my maid . . . What? . . . Who the hell do you *think* it is? Miss Sheldon, of course . . . Oh, God! Those cables! If only Cosette hasn't— Cosette! Cosette! Did you send those cables? . . . Oh, God! Oh, God! . . . Now listen, Cosette, I want you to send another cable to every one of those people, and tell them somebody has been using my name, and to disregard anything and everything they hear from me—except this, of course . . . Don't ask questions—do as you're told . . . Don't argue with me, you French bitch—God damn it, do as you're told . . . And unpack—we're not going! [*She hangs up.*]

WHITESIDE: Now steady, my blossom. Take it easy.

LORRAINE [*In a white rage*]: What do you mean take it easy? Do you realize I'll be the laughingstock of England? Why, I won't dare show my face! I always knew Beverly Carlton was low, but not this low. Why? WHY? It isn't even funny. Why would he do it, that's what I'd like to know. Why would he do it! Why would anyone in the world want to play a silly trick like this? I can't understand it. Do you, Sherry? Do you, Maggie? You both saw him this afternoon. Why would he walk out of here, go right to a phone booth, and try to ship me over to England on a fool's errand! There must have been some reason—there must have. It doesn't make sense otherwise. Why would Beverly Carlton, or anybody else for that matter, want me to— [*She stops as a dim light begins to dawn.*] Oh! Oh! [*Her eye, which has been on* MAGGIE, *goes momentarily to the dining room, where* BERT *has disappeared. Then her gaze returns to* MAGGIE *again.*] I—I think I begin to—of course! Of course! That's it. Of course that's it. Yes, and that's a very charming bracelet that Mr. Jefferson gave you—isn't it, Maggie dear? Of course. It makes complete sense now. And to think that I nearly—well! Wild horses couldn't get me out of here *now*, Maggie. And if I were you I'd hang onto that bracelet, dear. It'll be something to remember him by!

[*Out of the library comes* MR. WESTCOTT, *his hands full of papers. At the same time the two technicians emerge from the dining room and go to the control board.*]

WESTCOTT [*His eyes on his watch*]: All right, Mr. Whiteside. Almost time. Here's your new copy. Hook her up, boys. Start testing.

WHITESIDE: How much time?

WESTCOTT [*Bringing him a microphone*]: Couple of minutes.

[*One of the radio technicians is talking into a microphone, testing:* "One, two, three, four, one, two, three, four. How are we coming in, New York? . . . A, B, C, A, B, C. Mary had a little lamb, Mary had a little lamb."]

[MR. *and* MRS. STANLEY, *having delivered their Christmas presents, enter from the hallway and start up the stairs.* MRS. STANLEY *looks hungrily at the radio goings-on, but* MR. STANLEY *delivers a stern* "Come, Daisy," *and she follows him up the stairs.*]

[*The voices of the technicians drone on:* "One, two, three, four, one, two, three, four. O.K., New York. Waiting." MR. WESTCOTT *stands with watch in hand.*]

[*From the dining room comes* BERT JEFFERSON, *a tray of drinks in hand.*]

BERT: Here comes the Jefferson Special . . . Oh! Have we time?

LORRAINE: Oh, I'm sure we have. Mr. Jefferson, I'm not leaving after all. My plans are changed.

BERT: Really? Oh, that's good.

LORRAINE: And I hear you've written a simply marvelous play, Mr. Jefferson. I want you to read it to me—tonight. Will you? We'll go back to the Mansion House right after dinner, and you'll read me your play.

BERT: Why—why, I should say so. I'd be delighted. . . . Maggie, did you hear that? Say! I'll bet *you* did this. You arranged the whole thing. Well, it's the finest Christmas present you could have given me.

[MAGGIE *looks at him for one anguished moment. Then, without a word, she dashes into the hall, grabs her coat and flings herself out of the house.*]

[BERT, *bewildered, stands looking after her.* MR. *and* MRS. STANLEY *come pellmell down the stairs. Each clutches a letter, and they are wild-eyed.*]

STANLEY: *Mr.* Whiteside! My son has run off on a freighter and my daughter is marrying an anarchist! They say *you* told them to do it!

MRS. STANLEY: My poor June! My poor Richard! This is the most awful—

WESTCOTT: Quiet! Quiet, please! We're going on the air.

STANLEY: How dare you! This is the most outrageous—

WESTCOTT [*Raising his voice*]: Please! *Please!* Quiet! We're going on the air.

[STANLEY *chokes and looks with fury.* MRS. STANLEY *is softly crying.*]

[*In this moment of stillness,* DR. BRADLEY *emerges from the dining room.*]

DR. BRADLEY: Oh! I see you're still busy.

STANLEY [*Bursting forth*]: Mr. Whiteside, you are the—

WESTCOTT [*Yelling*]: *Quiet!* For God's sake, quiet! QUIET! . . . All right, boys!

[*From the hallway come six* CHOIR BOYS, *dressed in their robes. They take their places by the microphone as the voice of the technician completes the hook-up.*]

TECHNICIAN: O.K., New York. [*He raises his arm, waiting to give the signal.* WESTCOTT *is watching him. There is a dead pause of about five seconds.* JOHN *and* SARAH *are on tiptoe in the dining room. Then the arm drops.*]

WESTCOTT [*Into the microphone*]: Good evening, everybody. Cream of Mush brings you Sheridan Whiteside.

[*The* LEADER *gestures to the* CHOIR BOYS, *and they raise their lovely voices in "Heilige Nacht." Another gesture from* WESTCOTT, *and* WHITESIDE *begins to speak, with the boys singing as a background.*]

WHITESIDE: This is Whiteside speaking. On this eve of eves, when my own heart is overflowing with peace and kindness, I think it is most fitting to tell once again the story of that still and lustrous night, nigh onto two thousand years ago, when first the star of Bethlehem was glimpsed in a wondrous sky . . .

[*The famous* WHITESIDE *voice goes out over the air to the listening millions as—*

The Curtain Falls

ACT THREE

SCENE—*Christmas morning.*

The bright December sunlight streams in through the window.

But the Christmas calm is quickly broken. From the library comes the roaring voice of MR. WHITESIDE. *"Miss Preen! Miss Preen!"*

MISS PREEN, *who is just coming through the dining room, rushes to open the library doors.*

MISS PREEN [*Nervously*]: Yes, sir. Yes, sir.

[MR. WHITESIDE, *in a mood, rolls himself into the room.*]

WHITESIDE: Where *do* you disappear to all the time, My Lady Nausea?

MISS PREEN [*Firmly*]: Mr. Whiteside, I can only be in one place at a time.

WHITESIDE: That's very fortunate for this community. . . . Go away, Miss Preen. You remind me of last week's laundry.

[MISS PREEN *goes indignantly into the library and slams the doors after her.*]

[JOHN *emerges from the dining room.*]

JOHN: Good morning, Mr. Whiteside. Merry Christmas.

WHITESIDE [*Testily*]: Merry Christmas, John. Merry Christmas.

JOHN: And Sarah and I want to thank you for the wonderful present.

WHITESIDE: That's quite all right, John.

JOHN: Are you ready for your breakfast, Mr. Whiteside?

WHITESIDE: No, I don't think I want any breakfast. . . . Has Miss Cutler come down yet?

JOHN: No, sir, not yet.

WHITESIDE: Is she in her room, do you know?

JOHN: Yes, sir, I think she is. Shall I call her?

WHITESIDE: No, no. That's all, John.

JOHN: Yes, sir.

[MAGGIE *comes down the stairs. She wears a traveling suit, and carries a bag.* WHITESIDE *waits for her to speak.*]

MAGGIE: I'm taking the one o'clock train, Sherry. I'm leaving.

WHITESIDE: You're doing nothing of the kind!

MAGGIE: Here are your keys—your driving license. The key to the safe-deposit vault is in the apartment in New York. I'll go in here now and clear things up. [*She opens the library doors.*]

WHITESIDE: Just a moment, Mrs. Siddons! Where *were* you until three o'clock this morning? I sat up half the night in this station wagon, worrying about you. You heard me calling to you when you came in. Why didn't you answer me?

MAGGIE: Look, Sherry, it's over, and you've won. I don't want to talk about it.

WHITESIDE: Oh, come, come, come, come, come. What are you trying to do—make me feel like a naughty, naughty boy? Honestly, Maggie, sometimes you can be very annoying.

MAGGIE [*Looking at him in wonder*]: You know, you're quite wonderful, Sherry, in a way. *You're* annoyed. I wish there was a laugh left in me. Shall I tell you something, Sherry? I think you are a selfish, petty egomaniac who would see his mother burned at the stake if that was the only way he could light his cigarette. I think you'd sacrifice your best friend without a moment's hesitation if he disturbed the sacred routine of your self-centered, paltry little life. I think you are incapable of any human emotion that goes higher up than your stomach, and I was the fool of the world for ever thinking I could trust you.

WHITESIDE [*Pretty indignant at this*]: Well, as long as I live, I shall never do anyone a good turn again. I won't ask you to apologize, Maggie, but six months from now you will be thanking me instead of berating me.

MAGGIE: In six months, Sherry, I expect to be so far away from you— [*She is halted by a loud voice from the hallway, as the door bangs. "Hello—hello—hello!" It is* BERT JEFFERSON *who enters, full of Christmas cheer.*]

BERT: Merry Christmas, everybody! Merry Christmas! I'm a little high, but I can explain everything. Hi, Maggie! Hi, Mr. Whiteside! Shake hands with a successful playwright. Maggie, why'd you run away last night? Where were you? Miss Sheldon thinks the play is wonderful. I read her the play and she thinks it's wonderful. Isn't that wonderful?

MAGGIE: Yes, that's fine, Bert.

BERT: Isn't that wonderful, Mr. Whiteside?

WHITESIDE: Jefferson, I think you ought to go home, don't you?

BERT: What? No—biggest day of my life. I know I'm a little drunk, but this is a big day. We've been sitting over in Billy's Tavern all night. Never realized it was daylight until it was daylight. . . . Listen, Maggie—Miss Sheldon says the play needs just a little bit of fixing—do it in three weeks. She's going to take me to a little place she's got in Lake Placid—just for three weeks. Going to work on the play together. Isn't it wonderful? Why don't you say something, Maggie?

WHITESIDE: Look, Bert, I suggest you tell us all about this later. Now, why don't you— [*He stops as* DR. BRADLEY *enters from the hallway.*]

DR. BRADLEY: Oh, excuse me! Merry Christmas, everybody. Merry Christmas.

BERT: God bless us all, and Tiny Tim.

DR. BRADLEY: Yes. . . . Mr. Whiteside, I thought perhaps if I came very early—

BERT: You know what, Doc? I'm going to Lake Placid for three weeks—isn't that wonderful? Ever hear of Lorraine Sheldon, the famous actress? Well, we're going to Lake Placid for three weeks.

WHITESIDE: Dr. Bradley, would you do me a favor? I think Mr. Jefferson would like some black coffee and a little breakfast. Would you take care of him, please?

DR. BRADLEY [*None too pleased*]: Yes, yes, of course.

BERT: Dr. Bradley, I'm going to buy breakfast for *you*—biggest breakfast you ever had.

DR. BRADLEY: Yes, yes. Come along, Jefferson.

BERT: You know what, Doctor? Let's climb down a couple of chimneys. I got a friend doesn't believe in Santa Claus—let's climb down his chimney and frighten the hell out of him. [*He goes out with the* DOCTOR.]

WHITESIDE [*In a burst of magnanimity*]: Now listen to me, Maggie. I am willing to forgive your tawdry outburst and talk about this calmly.

MAGGIE [*Now crying openly*]: I love him so terribly. Oh, Sherry, Sherry, why did you do it? Why did you do it? [*She goes stumblingly into the library.*]

[WHITESIDE, *left alone, looks at his watch; heaves a long sigh. Then* HARRIET *comes down the steps, dressed for the street.*]

HARRIET: Merry Christmas, Mr. Whiteside.

WHITESIDE: Oh! . . . Merry Christmas, Miss Stanley.

HARRIET [*Nervously*]: I'm afraid I shouldn't be seen talking to you, Mr. Whiteside—my brother is terribly angry. I just couldn't resist asking—did you like my Christmas present?

WHITESIDE: I'm very sorry, Miss Stanley—I haven't opened it. I haven't opened any of my presents yet.

HARRIET: Oh, dear. I was so anxious to—it's right here, Mr. Whiteside. [*She goes to the tree.*] Won't you open it now?

WHITESIDE [*As he undoes the string*]: I appreciate your thinking of me, Miss Stanley. This is very thoughtful of you. [*He takes out the gift.*] Why, it's lovely. I'm very fond of these old photographs. Thank you very much.

HARRIET: I was twenty-two when that was taken. That was my favorite dress. . . . Do you really like it?

WHITESIDE: I do indeed. When I get back to town I shall send *you* a little gift.

HARRIET: Will you? Oh, thank you, Mr. Whiteside. I shall treasure it. . . . Well, I shall be late for church. Good-bye. Good-bye.

WHITESIDE: Good-bye, Miss Stanley.

[*As she goes out the front door,* WHITESIDE'S *eyes return to the gift. He puzzles over it for a second, shakes his head. Mumbles to himself—"What is there about that woman?" Shakes his head again in perplexity.*]

[JOHN *comes from the dining room, en route to the second floor with* MRS. STANLEY'S *tray.*]

JOHN: Sarah's got a little surprise for you, Mr. Whiteside. She's just taking it out of the oven.

WHITESIDE: Thank you, John.

[JOHN *disappears up the stairs.*]

[*Then suddenly there is a great ringing of the doorbell. It stops for a second, then picks up violently again—rhythmically, this time. It continues until the door is opened.*]

WHITESIDE: Miss Preen! Miss Preen!

[MISS PREEN *comes hurrying from the library.*]

MISS PREEN: Yes, sir. Yes, sir.

WHITESIDE: Answer the door, will you? John is upstairs.

[MISS PREEN, *obviously annoyed, hurries to the door.*]

[*We hear her voice from the hallway: "Who is it?" An answering male voice: "Polly Adler's?" Then a little shriek from* MISS PREEN, *and in a moment we see the reason why. She is carried into the room in the arms of a pixie-like gentleman, who is kissing her over and over.*]

THE GENTLEMAN CARRYING MISS PREEN: I love you madly—madly! Did you hear what I said—madly! Kiss me! Again! Don't be afraid of my passion. Kiss me! I can feel the hot blood pounding through your varicose veins.

MISS PREEN [*Through all this*]: Put me down! Put me down, do you hear! Don't you dare kiss me! Who are you! Put me down or I'll scream. Mr. Whiteside! Mr. Whiteside!

WHITESIDE: Banjo! Banjo, for God's sake!

BANJO [*Quite calmly*]: Hello, Whiteside. Will you sign for this package, please?

WHITESIDE: Banjo, put that woman down. That is my nurse, you mental delinquent.

BANJO [*Putting* MISS PREEN *on her feet*]: Come to my room in half an hour and bring some rye bread. [*And for good measure he slaps* MISS PREEN *right on the fanny.*]

MISS PREEN [*Outraged*]: Really, Mr. Whiteside! [*She adjusts her clothes with a quick jerk or two and marches into the library.*]

BANJO: Whiteside, I'm here to spend Christmas with you. Give me a kiss! [*He starts to embrace him.*]

WHITESIDE: Get away from me, you reform-school fugitive. How did you get here anyway?

BANJO: Darryl Zanuck loaned me his reindeer. . . . Whiteside, we finished shooting the picture yesterday and I'm on my way to Nova Scotia. Flew here in twelve hours—borrowed an airplane from Howard Hughes. Whiteside, I brought you a wonderful Christmas present. [*He produces a little tissue-wrapped package.*] This brassière was once worn by Hedy Lamarr.

WHITESIDE: Listen, you idiot, how long can you stay?

BANJO: Just long enough to take a bath. I'm on my way to Nova Scotia. Where's Maggie?

WHITESIDE: Nova Scotia? What are you going to Nova Scotia for?

BANJO: I'm sick of Hollywood and there's a dame in New York I don't want to see. So I figured I'd go to Nova Scotia and get some good salmon. . . . Where the hell's Maggie? I want to see her. . . . What's the matter with you? Where is she?

WHITESIDE: Banjo, I'm glad you're here. I'm very annoyed at Maggie. Very!

BANJO: What's the matter? . . . [*To his considerable surprise, at this point, he sees* WHITESIDE *get up out of his chair and start to pace up and down the room.*] Say, what *is* this? I thought you couldn't walk.

WHITESIDE: Oh, I've been all right for weeks. That isn't the point. I'm furious at Maggie. She's turned on me like a viper. You know how fond I am of her. Well, after all these years she's repaying my affection by behaving like a fishwife.

BANJO: What are you talking about?

WHITESIDE: But I never believed for a moment she was really in love with him.

BANJO: In love with *who?* I just got here—remember.

WHITESIDE: Great God, I'm telling you, you Hollywood nitwit. A young newspaper man here in town.

BANJO [*Surprised and pleased*]: Maggie finally fell—well, what do you know? What kind of a guy is he?

WHITESIDE: Oh, shut up and listen, will you?

BANJO: Well, go on. What happened?

WHITESIDE: Well, Lorraine Sheldon happened to come out here and visit me.

BANJO: Old Hot-pants—here?

WHITESIDE: Now listen! He'd written a play—this young fellow. You can guess the rest. He's going away with Lorraine this afternoon. To "rewrite." So there you are. Maggie's in there now, crying her eyes out.

BANJO: Gee! . . . [*Thinking it over.*] Say, wait a minute. What do you mean Lorraine Sheldon *happened* to come out here? I smell a rat, Sherry—a rat with a beard.

[*And it might be well to add, at this point, that* MR. SHERIDAN WHITESIDE *wears a beard.*]

WHITESIDE: Well, all right, all right. But I did it for Maggie—because I thought it was the right thing for her.

BANJO: Oh, sure. You haven't thought of yourself in years. . . . Gee, poor kid. Can I go in and talk to her?

WHITESIDE: No—no. Leave her alone.

BANJO: Any way I could help, Sherry? Where's this guy live—this guy she likes? Can we get hold of him?

WHITESIDE: Now, wait a minute, Banjo. We don't want any phony warrants, or you pretending to be J. Edgar Hoover. I've been through all that with you before. [*He paces again.*] I got Lorraine out here and I've got to get her away.

BANJO: It's got to be good, Sherry. Lorraine's no dope. . . . Now, there must be *something* that would get her out of here like a bat out of hell. . . . Say! I think I've got it! That fellow she's so crazy about over in England—Lord Fanny or whatever it is. Bottomley—that's it!

WHITESIDE [*With a pained expression*]: No, Banjo. No.

BANJO: Wait a minute—you don't catch on. We send Lorraine a cablegram from Lord Bottomley—

WHITESIDE: I catch on, Banjo. Lorraine caught on, too. It's been tried.

BANJO: Oh! . . . I told you she was no dope. . . . [*Seeing* WHITESIDE'S *chair, he sits in it and leans back with a good deal of pleasure.*] Well, you've got a tough proposition on your hands.

WHITESIDE: The trouble is there's so damned little time. . . . Get out of my chair! [WHITESIDE *gets back into it.*] Lorraine's taking him away with her this afternoon. Oh, damn, damn, damn. There must be some way out. The trouble is I've done this job too well. Hell and damnation.

BANJO [*Pacing*]: Stuck, huh?

WHITESIDE: In the words of one of our greatest lyric poets, you said it.

BANJO: Yeh. . . . Gee, I'm hungry. We'll think of something, Sherry—you watch. We'll get Lorraine out of here if I have to do it one piece at a time.

[SARAH *enters from the dining room bearing a tray on which reposes the culinary surprise that* JOHN *has mentioned. She holds it behind her back.*]

SARAH: Merry Christmas, Mr. Whiteside. . . . Excuse me. [*This last is to* BANJO.] I've got something for you. . . .

[BANJO *blandly lifts the latest delicacy and proceeds to eat it as* SARAH *presents the empty plate to* WHITESIDE.]

SARAH [*Almost in tears*]: But, Mr. Whiteside, it was for you.

WHITESIDE: Never mind, Sarah. He's quite mad.

BANJO: Come, Petrouchka, we will dance in the snow until all St. Petersburg is aflame with jealousy. [*He clutches* SARAH *and waltzes her toward the kitchen, loudly humming the Merry Widow waltz.*]

SARAH [*As she is borne away*]: Mr. Whiteside! Mr. Whiteside!

WHITESIDE: Just give him some breakfast, Sarah. He's harmless.

[MR. WHITESIDE *barely has a moment in which to collect his thoughts before the library doors are opened and* MISS PREEN *emerges. It is* MISS PREEN *in street clothes this time, and with a suitcase in her hand.*]

[*She plants herself squarely in front of* WHITESIDE, *puts down her bag and starts drawing on a pair of gloves.*]

WHITESIDE: And just what does this mean?

MISS PREEN: It means, Mr. Whiteside, that I am leaving. My address is on the desk inside; you can send me a check.

WHITESIDE: You realize, Miss Preen, that this is completely unprofessional.

MISS PREEN: I do indeed. I am not only walking out on this case, Mr. Whiteside—I am leaving the nursing profession. I became a nurse because all my life, ever since I was a little girl, I was filled with the idea of serving a suffering humanity. After one month with you, Mr. Whiteside, I am going to work in a munitions factory. From now on anything that I can do to help exterminate the human race will fill me with the greatest of pleasure. If Florence Nightingale had ever nursed *you*, Mr. Whiteside, she would have married Jack the Ripper instead of founding the Red Cross. Good day. [*And she sails out.*]

[*Before* WHITESIDE *has time to digest this little bouquet,* MRS. STANLEY, *in a state of great fluttery excitement, rushes down the stairs.*]

MRS. STANLEY: Mr. Stanley is here with June. He's brought June back. Thank goodness, thank goodness. [*We hear her at the door.*] June, June, thank God you're back. You're not married, are you?

JUNE [*From the hallway*]: No, Mother, I'm not. And please don't be hysterical.

[MRS. STANLEY *comes into view, her arms around a rebellious* JUNE. *Behind them looms* MR. STANLEY, *every inch the stern father.*]

MRS. STANLEY: Oh, June, if it had been anyone but that awful boy. You know how your father and I felt. . . . Ernest, thank goodness you stopped it. How did you do it?

STANLEY: Never mind that, Daisy. Just take June upstairs. I have something to say to Mr. Whiteside.

MRS. STANLEY: What about Richard? Is there any news?

STANLEY: It's all right, Daisy—all under control. Just take June upstairs.

JUNE: Father, haven't we had enough melodrama? I don't have to be taken upstairs—I'll go upstairs. . . . Merry Christmas, Mr. Whiteside. It looks bad for John L. Lewis. Come on, Mother—lock me in my room.

MRS. STANLEY: Now, June, you'll feel much better after

you've had a hot bath, I know. Have you had anything to eat? [*She follows her daughter up the stairs.*]

[STANLEY *turns to* MR. WHITESIDE.]

STANLEY: I am pleased to inform you, sir, that your plans for my daughter seem to have gone a trifle awry. She is not, nor will she ever be, married to that labor agitator that you so kindly picked out for her. As for my son, he has been apprehended in Toledo, and will be brought back home within the hour. Not having your gift for invective, I cannot tell you what I think of your obnoxious interference in my affairs, but I have now arranged that you will interfere no longer. [*He turns toward the hallway.*] Come in, gentlemen. [*Two burly* MEN *come into view and stand in the archway.*] Mr. Whiteside, these gentlemen are deputy sheriffs. They have a warrant by which I am enabled to put you out of this house, and I need hardly add that it will be the greatest moment of my life. Mr. Whiteside— [*He looks at his watch.*]—I am giving you fifteen minutes in which to pack up and get out. If you are not gone in fifteen minutes, Mr. Whiteside, these gentlemen will forcibly eject you. [*He turns to the deputies.*] Thank you, gentlemen. Will you wait outside, please? [*The* TWO MEN *file out.*] Fifteen minutes, Mr. Whiteside—and that means bag, baggage, wheelchair, penguins, octopus and cockroaches. I am now going upstairs to smash our radio, so that not even accidentally will I ever hear your voice again.

WHITESIDE: Sure you don't want my autograph, old fellow?

STANLEY: Fifteen minutes, Mr. Whiteside. [*And he goes.*]

[BANJO, *still eating, returns from the kitchen.*]

BANJO: Well, Whiteside, I didn't get an idea. Any news from the front?

WHITESIDE: Yes. The enemy is at my rear, and nibbling.

BANJO: Where'd you say Maggie was? In there?

WHITESIDE: It's no use, Banjo. She's taking the one o'clock train out.

BANJO: No kidding? You didn't tell me that. You mean she's quitting you, after all these years? She's really leaving?

WHITESIDE: She is!

BANJO: That means you've only got till one o'clock to do something?

WHITESIDE: No, dear. I have exactly fifteen minutes—[*He*

looks at his watch.]—ah—fourteen minutes—in which to pull out of my hat the God-damnedest rabbit you have ever seen.

BANJO: What do you mean fifteen minutes?

WHITESIDE: In exactly fifteen minutes Baby's rosy little body is being tossed into the snow. My host has sworn out a warrant. I am being kicked out.

BANJO: What? I never heard of such a thing. What would he do a thing like that for?

WHITESIDE: Never mind, never mind. The point is, I have only fifteen minutes. Banjo dear, the master is growing a little desperate.

BANJO [*Paces a moment*]: What about laying your cards on the table with Lorraine?

WHITESIDE: Now, Banjo. You know Dream Girl as well as I do. What do *you* think?

BANJO: You're right. . . . Say! If I knew where she was I could get a car and run her over. It wouldn't hurt her much.

WHITESIDE [*Wearily*]: Banjo, for God's sake. Go in and talk to Maggie for a minute—right in there. I want to think.

BANJO: Could we get a doctor to say Lorraine has smallpox?

WHITESIDE: Please, Banjo. I've got to think.

BANJO [*Opening the library doors*]: Pardon me, miss, is this the Y.M.C.A.?

[*The doors close.*]

[WHITESIDE *is alone again. He leans back, concentrating intensely. He shakes his head as, one after another, he discards a couple of ideas.*]

[*We hear the outer door open and close, and from the hallway comes* RICHARD. *Immediately behind him is a stalwart-looking* MAN *with an air of authority.*]

THE MAN [*To* RICHARD, *as he indicates* WHITESIDE]: Is this your father?

RICHARD: No, you idiot. . . . Hello, Mr. Whiteside. I didn't get very far. Any suggestions?

WHITESIDE: I'm very sorry, Richard—very sorry indeed. I wish I were in position—

STANLEY [*Descending the stairs*]: Well, you're *not* in position. . . . Thank you very much, officer. Here's a little something for your trouble.

THE MAN: Thank you, sir. Good day. [*He goes.*]

STANLEY: Will you go upstairs please, Richard?

[RICHARD *hesitates for a second. Looks at his father, then at* WHITESIDE; *silently goes up the steps.*]

[MR. STANLEY *follows him, but pauses on the landing.*]

STANLEY: *Ten* minutes, Mr. Whiteside. [*And he goes.*]

[JOHN *enters from the dining room, bringing a glass of orange juice.*]

JOHN: Here you are, Mr. Whiteside. Feeling any better?

WHITESIDE: Superb. Any cyanide in this orange juice, John? [*The doorbell rings.*] Open the door, John. It's probably some mustard gas from an old friend.

JOHN [*En route to the door*]: Yes, sir. . . . Say, that crazy fellow made a great hit with Sarah. He wants to give her a screen test.

[*At the outer door we hear* LORRAINE'S *voice:* "Good morning! Is Mr. Whiteside up yet?" JOHN'S *answer:* "Yes, he is, Miss Sheldon—he's right here."]

[WHITESIDE *groans as he hears her voice.*]

LORRAINE [*Entering, in a very smart Christmas morning costume*]: Merry Christmas, darling! Merry Christmas! I've come to have Christmas breakfast with you, my dear. May I? [*She kisses him.*]

WHITESIDE [*Nothing matters any more*]: Of course, my sprite. John, a tray for Miss Sheldon—better make it one-minute eggs.

LORRAINE: Sherry, it's the most perfect Christmas morning—the snow is absolutely glistening. Too bad you can't get out.

WHITESIDE: Oh, I'll probably see a bit of it. . . . I hear you're off for Lake Placid, my blossom. What time are you going?

LORRAINE: Oh, Sherry, how did you know? Is Bert here?

WHITESIDE: No, he rolled in a little while ago. Worked rather fast, didn't you, dear?

LORRAINE: Darling, I was just swept off my feet by the play —it's fantastically good. Sherry, it's the kind of part that only comes along once in ten years. I'm so grateful to you, darling. Really, Sherry, sometimes I think that you're the only friend I have in the world.

WHITESIDE [*Dryly*]: Thank you, dear. What time did you say you were leaving—you and Jefferson?

LORRAINE: Oh, I don't know—I think it's four o'clock. You know, quite apart from anything else, Sherry, Bert is really a very attractive man. It makes it rather a pleasure, squaring accounts with little Miss Vitriol. In fact, it's all worked out beautifully. . . . Sherry lamb, I want to give you the most beautiful Christmas present you've ever had in your life. Now, what do you want? Anything! I'm so deliriously happy that— [*A bellowing laugh comes from the library. She stops, lips compressed.*] That sounds like Banjo. Is he here?

WHITESIDE: He is, my dear. Just the family circle gathering at Christmas. [*A look at his watch.*] My, how time flies when you're having fun.

[BANJO *emerges from the library.*]

BANJO: Why, hello, Sweetie Pants! How are you?

LORRAINE [*Not over-cordial*]: Very well, thank you. And you, Banjo?

BANJO: I'm fine, fine. How's the mattress business, Lorraine?

LORRAINE: *Very* funny. It's too bad, Banjo, that your pictures aren't as funny as you seem to think *you* are.

BANJO: You've got me there, mama. Say, you look in the pink, Lorraine. . . . Anything in the wind, Whiteside?

WHITESIDE: Not a glimmer.

BANJO: What time does the boat sail?

WHITESIDE: Ten minutes.

LORRAINE: What boat is this?

BANJO: The good ship Up the Creek. . . . Oh, well! You feel fine, huh, Lorraine?

LORRAINE: What? Yes, of course I do. . . . Where's that breakfast, Sherry?

[MAGGIE *emerges from the library, a sheaf of papers in her hand. She stops imperceptibly as she sees* LORRAINE.]

MAGGIE: I've listed everything except the New Year's Eve broadcast. Wasn't there a schedule on that?

WHITESIDE [*Uneasily*]: I think it's on the table there, some place.

MAGGIE: Thank you. [*She turns to the papers on the table.*]

LORRAINE [*Obviously for* MAGGIE'S *ears*]: New Year's Eve? Oh, Bert and I'll hear it in Lake Placid. You were at my cottage up there once, weren't you, Sherry? It's lovely, isn't it? Away from everything. Just snow and clear, cold nights. [*The doorbell rings.*] Oh, that's probably Bert. I told him to meet me here. [MAGGIE, *as though she had not heard a word, goes quietly into the library.* LORRAINE *relaxes.*] You know, I'm looking forward to Lake Placid. Bert's the kind of man who will do all winter sports beautifully.

BANJO [*Gently*]: Will he get time?

[*Voices are heard from the hallway. "Whiteside?" "Yes, sir." "American Express."* JOHN *backs into the room, obviously directing a major operation.*]

JOHN: All right—come ahead. Care now—careful—right in here. It's for you, Mr. Whiteside.

LORRAINE: Why, Sherry, what's this?

[*Into view come two* EXPRESSMEN, *groaning and grunting under the weight of nothing more or less than an Egyptian mummy case. It seems that* MR. WHITESIDE'S *friends are liable to think of anything.*]

EXPRESSMAN: Where do you want this put?

JOHN: Right there.

WHITESIDE: Dear God, if there was one thing I needed right now it was an Egyptian mummy.

BANJO [*Reading from a tag*]: "Merry Christmas from the Khedive of Egypt." What did you send *him?* Grant's Tomb?

[MR. STANLEY, *drawn by the voices of the* EXPRESSMEN, *has descended the stairs in time to witness this newest hue and cry.*]

STANLEY [*Surveying the scene*]: *Five* minutes, Mr. Whiteside! [*He indicates the mummy case.*] Including *that.* [*And up the stairs again.*]

LORRAINE: Why, what was all that about? Who is that man?

WHITESIDE: He announces the time every few minutes. I pay him a small sum.

LORRAINE: But what on earth for, Sherry?

WHITESIDE [*Violently*]: I lost my watch!

[*From the hallway a familiar figure peeps in.*]

DR. BRADLEY: Oh, excuse me, Mr. Whiteside. Are you busy?

WHITESIDE [*Closing his eyes*]: Good God!

DR. BRADLEY [*Coming into the room*]: I've written a new chapter on the left kidney. Suppose I— [*He smiles apologetically at* LORRAINE *and* BANJO.] Pardon me. [*Goes into the library.*]

LORRAINE: Is that the plumber again, Sherry? . . . Oh, dear, I wonder where Bert is. . . . Darling, you're not very Christmasy—you're usually bubbling over on Christmas morning. . . . *Who* sent this to you, Sherry—the Khedive of Egypt? You know, I think it's rather beautiful. I must go to Egypt some day—I really must. I know I'd love it. The first time I went to Pompeii I cried all night. All those people—all those lives. Where are they now? Sherry! Don't you ever think about that? I do. Here was a woman—like myself—a woman who once lived and loved, full of the same passions, fears, jealousies, hates. And what remains of any of it now? Just this, and nothing more. [*She opens the case, then, with a sudden impulse, steps into it and folds her arms, mummy-fashion.*] A span of four thousand years—a mere atom in the eternity of time—and here am I, another woman living out her life. I want to cry. [*She closes her eyes, and as she stands there, immobilized, the eyes of* BANJO *and* WHITESIDE *meet. The same idea has leaped into their minds.* BANJO, *rising slowly from the couch, starts to approach the mummy case, casually whistling "Dixie." But just before he reaches it* LORRAINE *steps blandly out.*]

LORRAINE: Oh, I mustn't talk this way today. It's Christmas, it's Christmas!

[BANJO *puts on a great act of unconcern.*]

WHITESIDE [*Rising to the occasion, and dripping pure charm*]: Lorraine dear, have you ever played Saint Joan?

LORRAINE: No, I haven't, Sherry. What makes you ask that?

WHITESIDE: There was something about your expression as you stood in that case—there was an absolute halo about you.

LORRAINE: Why, Sherry, how sweet!

WHITESIDE: It transcended any mortal expression I've ever seen. Step into it again, dear.

LORRAINE: Sherry, you're joshing me—aren't you?

WHITESIDE: My dear, I don't make light of these things. I was deeply moved. There was a strange beauty about you, Lorraine—pure da Vinci. Please do it again.

LORRAINE: Well, I don't know exactly what it was that I did, but I'll— [*She starts to step into the case again, then changes her mind.*] Oh, I feel too silly, Sherry.

[BANJO'S *eyes are fixed somewhere on the ceiling, but he is somewhat less innocent than he seems.*]

WHITESIDE [*Returning to the battle*]: Lorraine dear, in that single moment you approached the epitome of your art, and you should not be ashamed of it. You asked me a little while ago what I wanted for a Christmas present. All that I want, Lorraine, is the memory of you in that mummy case.

LORRAINE: Why, darling, I'm—all choked up. [*Crossing her arms, she takes a moment or two to throw herself in the mood, then steps reverently into the case.*] "Dust thou art, and dust to dust—"

[*Bang!* BANJO *has closed the case and fastened it.* WHITE-SIDE *leaps out of the chair.*]

WHITESIDE: Eureka!

BANJO: There's service for you!

WHITESIDE: Will she be all right in there?

BANJO: Sure—she can breathe easy. I'll let her out as soon as we get on the plane. . . . What are we going to do now? How do we get this out of here?

WHITESIDE: One thing at a time—that's the next step.

BANJO: Think fast, Captain. Think fast.

[*And* MAGGIE *enters from the library, papers in hand.* WHITESIDE *scrambles back into his chair;* BANJO *is again the little innocent.*]

MAGGIE: This is everything, Sherry—I'm leaving three carbons. Is there anything out here? [*She inspects a small basket fastened to his chair.*] What's in this basket?

WHITESIDE [*Eager to be rid of her*]: Nothing at all. Thank you, thank you.

MAGGIE: Shall I file these letters? Do you want this picture?

WHITESIDE: No—throw everything away. Wait—give me the picture. I want the picture.

MAGGIE: The only thing I haven't done is to put all your broadcasts in order. Do you want me to do that?

WHITESIDE [*A flash of recollection has come to him as he takes* HARRIET'S *photograph in his hand, but he contrives to smother his excitement*]: What? . . . Ah—do that, will you? Do it right away—it's very important. Right away, Maggie.

MAGGIE: I'll see you before I go, Banjo. [*She goes into the library again, closing the doors.*]

WHITESIDE [*Watching her out, then jumping up in great excitement*]: I've got it!

BANJO: What?

WHITESIDE: I knew I'd seen this face before! I knew it! Now I know how to get this out of here.

BANJO: What face? How?

[*And, at that instant,* MR. STANLEY *comes down the stairs, watch in hand.*]

STANLEY [*Vastly enjoying himself*]: The time is up, Mr. Whiteside. Fifteen minutes.

WHITESIDE: Ah, yes, Mr. Stanley. Fifteen minutes. But just one favor before I go. I would like you to summon those two officers and ask them to help this gentleman down to the airport with this mummy case. Would you be good enough to do that, Mr. Stanley?

STANLEY: I will do nothing of the kind.

WHITESIDE [*Ever so sweetly*]: Oh, I think you will, Mr. Stanley. Or shall I inform my radio audience, on my next broadcast, that your sister, Harriet Stanley, is none other than the famous Harriet Sedley, who murdered her mother and father with an axe twenty-five years ago in Gloucester, Massachusetts. . . . [*At which* MR. STANLEY *quietly collapses into a chair.*] Come, Mr. Stanley, it's a very small favor. Or would you rather have the good folk of Mesalia repeating at your very doorstep that once popular little jingle:

"Harriet Sedley took an axe
And gave her mother forty whacks,
And when the job was nicely done,
She gave her father forty-one."

Remember, Mr. Stanley, I too am giving up something. It would make a hell of a broadcast. . . . Well?

STANLEY [*Licked at last*]: Mr. Whiteside, you are the damnedest person I have ever met.

WHITESIDE: I often think so myself, old fellow. . . . Officers, will you come in here, please?

BANJO: Whiteside, you're a great man. [*He places a reverent kiss on the mummy case.*]

WHITESIDE [*As the* DEPUTIES *enter*]: Come right in, officers. Mr. Stanley would like you to help this gentleman down to the airport with this mummy case. He is sending it to a friend in Nova Scotia.

BANJO: Collect.

WHITESIDE: Right, Mr. Stanley?

STANLEY [*Weakly*]: Yes. . . . Yes.

WHITESIDE: Thank you, gentlemen—handle it carefully. . . . Banjo, my love, you're wonderful and I may write a book about you.

BANJO: Don't bother—I can't read. [*To* MAGGIE, *as she enters from library.*] Good-bye, Maggie—love conquers all. . . . Don't drop that case, boys—it contains an antique. [*And out he goes with the mummy case, to say nothing of* MISS LORRAINE SHELDON.]

MAGGIE [*Catching on to what has happened*]: Sherry! Sherry, was that—?

WHITESIDE: It was indeed. The field is clear and you have my blessing.

MAGGIE: Sherry! Sherry, you old reprobate!

WHITESIDE: Just send me a necktie some time. My hat and coat, Maggie, and also your railroad ticket. I am leaving for New York.

MAGGIE: You're leaving, Sherry?

WHITESIDE: Don't argue, Rat Girl— Do as you're told.

MAGGIE: Yes, Mr. Whiteside. [*She goes happily into the library, just as* BERT *returns.*]

BERT: Mr. Whiteside, I want to apologize for—

WHITESIDE: Don't give it a thought, Bert. There's been a slight change of plan. Miss Sheldon is off on a world cruise—I am taking your play to Katharine Cornell. Miss Cutler will explain everything. [MAGGIE *brings* WHITESIDE'S *coat, hat, cane.*] Oh, thank you, Maggie, my darling.

[*And just then the* DOCTOR *comes out of the library. Still trying.*]

DR. BRADLEY: Mr. Whiteside, are you very busy?

WHITESIDE: Ah, yes, Doctor. *Very* busy. But if you ever get to New York, Doctor, try and find me. [*He takes* MAGGIE *in his arms.*] Good-bye, my lamb. I love you very much.

MAGGIE: Sherry, you're wonderful.

WHITESIDE: Nonsense. . . . Good-bye, Jefferson. You'll never know the trouble you've caused.

BERT: Good-bye, Mr. Whiteside.

WHITESIDE: Good-bye, Mr. Stanley. I would like to hear, in the near future, that your daughter has married her young man

and that your son has been permitted to follow his own bent.
OR ELSE. . . . Merry Christmas, everybody! [*And out he
strolls.*]

 [*But the worst is yet to come. There is a loud crash on the
porch, followed by an anguished yell.* MAGGIE *gives a little
shriek and rushes out.* BERT *and the* DOCTOR *rush after her.
Down the stairs come* MRS. STANLEY, JUNE *and* RICHARD.
From the dining room JOHN *and* SARAH *come running.
"What's happened?" "What is it?"*]

 [*And then we see. Into view come* BERT *and the* DOCTOR,
carrying MR. WHITESIDE *between them. He is screaming his
head off.*]

WHITESIDE: Miss Preen! Miss Preen! I want Miss Preen
back! . . . Mr. Stanley, I am suing you for *three* hundred and
fifty thousand dollars!

 [MR. STANLEY *throws up his hands in despair.* MRS. STAN-
LEY *simply faints away.*]

Curtain

Lillian Hellman

THE LITTLE FOXES

*"Take us the foxes, the little foxes,
that spoil the vines; for our vines
have tender grapes."*

CHARACTERS

ADDIE

CAL

BIRDIE HUBBARD

OSCAR HUBBARD

LEO HUBBARD

REGINA GIDDENS

WILLIAM MARSHALL

BENJAMIN HUBBARD

ALEXANDRA GIDDENS

HORACE GIDDENS

The scene of the play is the living room of the Giddens house in a small town in the South.

ACT ONE: The Spring of 1900, evening.

ACT TWO: A week later, early morning.

ACT THREE: Two weeks later, late afternoon.

———

There has been no attempt to write Southern dialect. It is to be understood that the accents are Southern.

ACT ONE

SCENE—*The living room of the Giddens house, in a small town in the deep South, the Spring of 1900. Upstage is a staircase leading to the second story. Upstage, right, are double doors to the dining room. When these doors are open we see a section of the dining room and the furniture. Upstage, left, is an entrance hall with a coat-rack and umbrella stand. There are large lace-curtained windows on the left wall. The room is lit by a center gas chandelier and painted china oil lamps on the tables. Against the wall is a large piano. Downstage, right, are a high couch, a large table, several chairs. Against the left back wall are a table and several chairs. Near the window there are a smaller couch and tables. The room is good-looking, the furniture expensive; but it reflects no particular taste. Everything is of the best and that is all.*

AT RISE: ADDIE, *a tall, nice-looking Negro woman of about fifty-five, is closing the windows. From behind the closed dining-room doors there is the sound of voices. After a second,* CAL, *a middle-aged Negro, comes in from the entrance hall carrying a tray with glasses and a bottle of port.* ADDIE *crosses, takes the tray from him, puts it on table, begins to arrange it.*

ADDIE [*Pointing to the bottle*]: You gone stark out of your head?

CAL: No, smart lady, I ain't. Miss Regina told me to get out that bottle. [*Points to bottle.*] That very bottle for the mighty honored guest. When Miss Regina changes orders like that you can bet your dime she got her reason.

ADDIE [*Points to dining room*]: Go on. You'll be needed.

CAL: Miss Zan she had two helpings frozen fruit cream and she tell that honored guest, she tell him that you make the best frozen fruit cream in all the South.

ADDIE [*Smiles, pleased*]: Did she? Well, see that Belle saves a little for her. She like it right before she go to bed. Save a few little cakes, too, she like—

[*The dining-room doors are opened and quickly closed
again by* BIRDIE HUBBARD. BIRDIE *is a woman of about forty,
with a pretty, well-bred, faded face. Her movements are
usually nervous and timid, but now, as she comes running
into the room, she is gay and excited.* CAL *turns to* BIRDIE.]

BIRDIE: Oh, Cal. [*Closes door.*] I want you to get one of the
kitchen boys to run home for me. He's to look in my desk drawer
and— [*To* ADDIE.] My, Addie. What a good supper! Just as
good as good can be.

ADDIE: You look pretty this evening, Miss Birdie, and young.

BIRDIE [*Laughing*]: Me, young? [*Turns back to* CAL.]
Maybe you better find Simon and tell him to do it himself. He's
to look in my desk, the left drawer, and bring my music album
right away. Mr. Marshall is very anxious to see it because of his
father and the opera in Chicago. [*To* ADDIE.] Mr. Marshall is
such a polite man with his manners and very educated and cultured and I've told him all about how my mama and papa used
to go to Europe for the music— [*Laughs. To* ADDIE.] Imagine
going all the way to Europe just to listen to music. Wouldn't
that be nice, Addie? Just to sit there and listen and— [*Turns
and steps to* CAL.] *Left* drawer, Cal. Tell him that twice because
he forgets. And tell him not to let any of the things drop out of
the album and to bring it right in here when he comes back.

[*The dining-room doors are opened and quickly closed by*
OSCAR HUBBARD. *He is a man in his late forties.*]

CAL: Yes'm. But Simon he won't get it right. But I'll tell
him.

BIRDIE: Left drawer, Cal, and tell him to bring the blue book
and—

OSCAR [*Sharply*]: Birdie.

BIRDIE [*Turning nervously*]: Oh, Oscar. I was just sending
Simon for my music album.

OSCAR [*To* CAL]: Never mind about the album. Miss Birdie
has changed her mind.

BIRDIE: But, really, Oscar. Really I promised Mr. Marshall.
I—

[CAL *looks at them, exits.*]

OSCAR: Why do you leave the dinner table and go running
about like a child?

BIRDIE [*Trying to be gay*]: But, Oscar, Mr. Marshall said

most specially he *wanted* to see my album. I told him about the time Mama met Wagner, and Mrs. Wagner gave her the signed program and the big picture. Mr. Marshall wants to see that. Very, very much. We had such a nice talk and—

OSCAR [*Taking a step to her*]: You have been chattering to him like a magpie. You haven't let him be for a second. I can't think he came South to be bored with you.

BIRDIE [*Quickly, hurt*]: He wasn't bored. I don't believe he was bored. He's a very educated, cultured gentleman. [*Her voice rises.*] I just don't believe it. You always talk like that when I'm having a nice time.

OSCAR [*Turning to her, sharply*]: You have had too much wine. Get yourself in hand now.

BIRDIE [*Drawing back, about to cry, shrilly*]: What am I doing? I am not doing anything. What am I doing?

OSCAR [*Taking a step to her, tensely*]: I said get yourself in hand. Stop acting like a fool.

BIRDIE [*Turns to him, quietly*]: I don't believe he was bored. I just don't believe it. Some people like music and like to talk about it. That's all I was doing.

[LEO HUBBARD *comes hurrying through the dining-room door. He is a young man of twenty, with a weak kind of good looks.*]

LEO: Mama! Papa! They are coming in now.

OSCAR [*Softly*]: Sit down, Birdie. Sit down now. [BIRDIE *sits down, bows her head as if to hide her face.*]

[*The dining-room doors are opened by* CAL. *We see people beginning to rise from the table.* REGINA GIDDENS *comes in with* WILLIAM MARSHALL. REGINA *is a handsome woman of forty.* MARSHALL *is forty-five, pleasant-looking, self-possessed. Behind them comes* ALEXANDRA GIDDENS, *a very pretty, rather delicate-looking girl of seventeen. She is followed by* BENJA-MIN HUBBARD, *fifty-five, with a large jovial face and the light graceful movements that one often finds in large men.*]

REGINA: Mr. Marshall, I think you're trying to console me. Chicago may be the noisiest, dirtiest city in the world but I should still prefer it to the sound of our horses and the smell of our azaleas. I should like crowds of people, and theatres, and lovely women— *Very* lovely women, Mr. Marshall?

MARSHALL [*Crossing to sofa*]: In Chicago? Oh, I suppose so.

But I can tell you this: I've never dined there with three *such* lovely ladies.

[ADDIE *begins to pass the port.*]

BEN: Our Southern women are well favored.

LEO [*Laughs*]: But one must go to Mobile for the ladies, sir. Very elegant worldly ladies, too.

BEN [*Looks at him very deliberately*]: Worldly, eh? *Worldly,* did you say?

OSCAR [*Hastily, to* LEO]: Your uncle Ben means that worldliness is not a mark of beauty in any woman.

LEO [*Quickly*]: Of course, Uncle Ben. I didn't mean—

MARSHALL: Your port is excellent, Mrs. Giddens.

REGINA: Thank you, Mr. Marshall. We had been saving that bottle, hoping we could open it just for you.

ALEXANDRA [*As* ADDIE *comes to her with the tray*]: Oh. May I *really*, Addie?

ADDIE: Better ask Mama.

ALEXANDRA: May I, Mama?

REGINA [*Nods, smiles*]: In Mr. Marshall's honor.

ALEXANDRA [*Smiles*]: Mr. Marshall, this will be the first taste of port I've ever had.

[ADDIE *serves* LEO.]

MARSHALL: No one ever had their first taste of a better port. [*He lifts his glass in a toast; she lifts hers; they both drink.*] Well, I suppose it is all true, Mrs. Giddens.

REGINA: What is true?

MARSHALL: That you Southerners occupy a unique position in America. You live better than the rest of us, you eat better, you drink better. I wonder you find time, or want to find time, to do business.

BEN: A great many Southerners don't.

MARSHALL: Do all of you live here together?

REGINA: Here with me? [*Laughs.*] Oh, no. My brother Ben lives next door. My brother Oscar and his family live in the next square.

BEN: But we are a very close family. We've always *wanted* it that way.

MARSHALL: That is very pleasant. Keeping your family together to share each other's lives. My family moves around too much. My children seem never to come home. Away at school in the winter; in the summer, Europe with their mother—

REGINA [*Eagerly*]: Oh, yes. Even down here we read about Mrs. Marshall in the society pages.

MARSHALL: I dare say. She moves about a great deal. And all of you are part of the same business? Hubbard Sons?

BEN [*Motions to* OSCAR]: Oscar and me. [*Motions to* REGINA.] My sister's good husband is a banker.

MARSHALL [*Looks at* REGINA, *surprised*]: Oh.

REGINA: I am so sorry that my husband isn't here to meet you. He's been very ill. He is at Johns Hopkins. But he will be home soon. We think he is getting better now.

LEO: I work for Uncle Horace. [REGINA *looks at him.*] I mean I work for Uncle Horace at his bank. I keep an eye on things while he's away.

REGINA [*Smiles*]: Really, Leo?

BEN [*Looks at* LEO, *then to* MARSHALL]: Modesty in the young is as excellent as it is rare. [*Looks at* LEO *again.*]

OSCAR [*To* LEO]: Your uncle means that a young man should speak more modestly.

LEO [*Hastily, taking a step to* BEN]: Oh, I didn't mean, sir—

MARSHALL: Oh, Mrs. Hubbard. Where's that Wagner autograph you promised to let me see? My train will be leaving soon and—

BIRDIE: The autograph? Oh. Well. Really, Mr. Marshall, I didn't mean to chatter so about it. Really I— [*Nervously, looking at* OSCAR.] You must excuse me. I didn't get it because, well, because I had—I—I had a little headache and—

OSCAR: My wife is a miserable victim of headaches.

REGINA [*Quickly*]: Mr. Marshall said at supper that he would like you to play for him, Alexandra.

ALEXANDRA [*Who has been looking at* BIRDIE]: It's not I who play well, sir. It's my aunt. She plays just wonderfully. She's my teacher. [*Rises. Eagerly.*] May we play a duet? May we, Mama?

BIRDIE [*Taking* ALEXANDRA's *hand*]: Thank you, dear. But I have my headache now. I—

OSCAR [*Sharply*]: Don't be stubborn, Birdie. Mr. Marshall wants you to play.

MARSHALL: Indeed I do. If your headache isn't—

BIRDIE [*Hesitates, then gets up, pleased*]: But I'd like to, sir. Very much. [*She and* ALEXANDRA *go to the piano.*]

MARSHALL: It's very remarkable how you Southern aristocrats have kept together. Kept together and kept what belonged to you.

BEN: You misunderstand, sir. Southern aristocrats have *not* kept together and have *not* kept what belonged to them.

MARSHALL [*Laughs, indicates room*]: You don't call this keeping what belongs to you?

BEN: But we are not aristocrats. [*Points to* BIRDIE *at the piano.*] Our brother's wife is the only one of us who belongs to the Southern aristocracy.

[BIRDIE *looks towards* BEN.]

MARSHALL [*Smiles*]: My information is that you people have been here, and solidly here, for a long time.

OSCAR: And so we have. Since our great-grandfather.

BEN [*Smiles*]: Who was *not* an aristocrat, like Birdie's.

MARSHALL [*A little sharply*]: You make great distinctions.

BEN: Oh, they have been made for us. And maybe they are important distinctions. [*Leans forward, intimately.*] Now you take Birdie's family. When my great-grandfather came here they were the highest-tone plantation owners in this state.

LEO [*Steps to* MARSHALL. *Proudly*]: My mother's grandfather was *governor* of the state before the war.

OSCAR: They owned the plantation, Lionnet. You may have heard of it, sir?

MARSHALL [*Laughs*]: No, I've never heard of anything but brick houses on a lake, and cotton mills.

BEN: Lionnet in its day was the best cotton land in the South. It still brings us in a fair crop. [*Sits back.*] Ah, they were great days for those people—even when I can remember. They had the best of everything. [BIRDIE *turns to them.*] Cloth from Paris, trips to Europe, horses you can't raise any more, niggers to lift their fingers—

BIRDIE [*Suddenly*]: We were good to our people. Everybody knew that. We were better to them than—

[MARSHALL *looks up at* BIRDIE.]

REGINA: Why, Birdie. You aren't playing.

BEN: But when the war comes these fine gentlemen ride off and leave the cotton, *and* the women, to rot.

BIRDIE: My father was killed in the war. He was a fine soldier, Mr. Marshall. A fine man.

REGINA: Oh, certainly, Birdie. A famous soldier.

BEN [*To* BIRDIE]: But that isn't the tale I am telling Mr. Marshall. [*To* MARSHALL.] Well, sir, the war ends. [BIRDIE *goes back to piano.*] Lionnet is almost ruined, and the sons finish ruining it. And there were thousands like them. Why? [*Leans forward.*] Because the Southern aristocrat can adapt himself to nothing. Too high-tone to try.

MARSHALL: Sometimes it is difficult to learn new ways. [BIRDIE *and* ALEXANDRA *begin to play.* MARSHALL *leans forward, listening.*]

BEN: Perhaps, perhaps. [*He sees that* MARSHALL *is listening to the music. Irritated, he turns to* BIRDIE *and* ALEXANDRA *at the piano, then back to* MARSHALL.] You're right, Mr. Marshall. It is difficult to learn new ways. But maybe that's why it's profitable. *Our* grandfather and *our* father learned the new ways and learned how to make them pay. They work. [*Smiles nastily.*] *They* are in trade. Hubbard Sons, Merchandise. Others, Birdie's family, for example, look down on them. [*Settles back in chair.*] To make a long story short, Lionnet now belongs to *us.* [BIRDIE *stops playing.*] Twenty years ago we took over their land, their cotton, and their daughter.

[BIRDIE *rises and stands stiffly by the piano.* MARSHALL, *who has been watching her, rises.*]

MARSHALL: May I bring you a glass of port, Mrs. Hubbard?

BIRDIE [*Softly*]: No, thank you, sir. You are most polite.

REGINA [*Sharply, to* BEN]: You are boring Mr. Marshall with these ancient family tales.

BEN: I hope not. I hope not. I am trying to make an important point— [*Bows to* MARSHALL.] for our future business partner.

OSCAR [*To* MARSHALL]: My brother always says that it's folks like us who have struggled and fought to bring to our land some of the prosperity of your land.

BEN: Some people call that patriotism.

REGINA [*Laughs gaily*]: I hope you don't find my brothers

too obvious, Mr. Marshall. I'm afraid they mean that this is the time for the ladies to leave the gentlemen to talk business.

MARSHALL [*Hastily*]: Not at all. We settled everything this afternoon. [MARSHALL *looks at his watch.*] I have only a few minutes before I must leave for the train. [*Smiles at her.*] And I insist they be spent with you.

REGINA: *And* with another glass of port.

MARSHALL: Thank you.

BEN [*To* REGINA]: My sister is right. [*To* MARSHALL.] I am a plain man and I am trying to say a plain thing. A man ain't only in business for what he can get out of it. It's got to give him something here. [*Puts hand to his breast.*] That's every bit as true for the nigger picking cotton for a silver quarter, as it is for you and me. [REGINA *gives* MARSHALL *a glass of port.*] If it don't give him something here, then he don't pick the cotton right. Money isn't all. Not by three shots.

MARSHALL: Really? Well, I always thought it was a great deal.

REGINA: And so did I, Mr. Marshall.

MARSHALL [*Leans forward. Pleasantly, but with meaning*]: Now you don't have to convince me that you are the right people for the deal. I wouldn't be here if you hadn't convinced me six months ago. You want the mill here, and I want it here. It isn't my business to find out *why* you want it.

BEN: To bring the machine to the cotton, and not the cotton to the machine.

MARSHALL [*Amused*]: You have a turn for neat phrases, Hubbard. Well, however grand your reasons are, mine are simple: I want to make money and I believe I'll make it on you. [*As* BEN *starts to speak, he smiles.*] Mind you, I have no objections to more high-minded reasons. They are mighty valuable in business. It's fine to have partners who so closely follow the teachings of Christ. [*Gets up.*] And now I must leave for my train.

REGINA: I'm sorry you won't stay over with us, Mr. Marshall, but you'll come again. Any time you like.

BEN [*Motions to* LEO, *indicating the bottle*]: Fill them up, boy, fill them up. [LEO *moves around filling the glasses as* BEN *speaks.*] Down here, sir, we have a strange custom. We drink the *last* drink for a toast. That's to prove that the Southerner is always still on his feet for the last drink. [*Picks up his glass.*] It was Henry Frick, your Mr. Henry Frick, who said, "Railroads are the Rembrandts of investments." Well, *I* say, "Southern cotton mills *will be* the Rembrandts of investment." So I give you the firm of Hubbard Sons and Marshall, Cotton Mills, and to it a long and prosperous life.

[*They all pick up their glasses.* MARSHALL *looks at them, amused. Then he, too, lifts his glass, smiles.*]

OSCAR: The children will drive you to the depot. Leo! Alexandra! You will drive Mr. Marshall down.

LEO [*Eagerly, looks at* BEN *who nods*]: Yes, sir. [*To* MARSHALL.] Not often Uncle Ben lets *me* drive the horses. And a beautiful pair they are. [*Starts for hall.*] Come on, Zan.

ALEXANDRA: May I drive tonight, Uncle Ben, please? I'd like to and—

BEN [*Shakes his head, laughs*]: In your evening clothes? Oh, no, my dear.

ALEXANDRA: But Leo always— [*Stops, exits quickly.*]

REGINA: I don't like to say good-bye to you, Mr. Marshall.

MARSHALL: Then we won't say good-bye. You have promised that you would come and let me show you Chicago. Do I have to make you promise again?

REGINA [*Looks at him as he presses her hand*]: I promise again.

MARSHALL [*Touches her hand again, then moves to* BIRDIE]: Good-bye, Mrs. Hubbard.

BIRDIE [*Shyly, with sweetness and dignity*]: Good-bye, sir.

MARSHALL [*As he passes* REGINA]: Remember.

REGINA: I will.

OSCAR: We'll see you to the carriage.

[MARSHALL *exits, followed by* BEN *and* OSCAR. *For a second* REGINA *and* BIRDIE *stand looking after them. Then* REGINA *throws up her arms, laughs happily.*]

REGINA: And there, Birdie, goes the man who has opened the door to our future.

BIRDIE [*Surprised at the unaccustomed friendliness*]: What?

REGINA [*Turning to her*]: Our future. Yours and mine, Ben's and Oscar's, the children— [*Looks at* BIRDIE'S *puzzled face, laughs.*] Our future! [*Gaily.*] You were charming at supper, Birdie. Mr. Marshall certainly thought so.

BIRDIE [*Pleased*]: Why, Regina! Do you think he did?

REGINA: Can't you tell when you're being admired?

BIRDIE: Oscar said I bored Mr. Marshall. [*Then quietly.*] But he admired *you*. He told me so.

REGINA: What did he say?

BIRDIE: He said to me, "I hope your sister-in-law will come to Chicago. Chicago will be at her feet." He said the ladies would bow to your manners and the gentlemen to your looks.

REGINA: Did he? He seems a lonely man. Imagine being lonely with all that money. I don't think he likes his wife.

BIRDIE: Not like his wife? What a thing to say.

REGINA: She's away a great deal. He said that several times. And once he made fun of her being so social and high-tone. But that fits in all right. [*Sits back, arms on back of sofa, stretches.*] Her being social, I mean. She can introduce me. It won't take long with an introduction from her.

BIRDIE [*Bewildered*]: Introduce you? In Chicago? You mean you really might go? Oh, Regina, you can't leave here. What about Horace?

REGINA: Don't look so scared about everything, Birdie. I'm going to live in Chicago. I've always wanted to. And now there'll be plenty of money to go with.

BIRDIE: But Horace won't be able to move around. You know what the doctor wrote.

REGINA: There'll be millions, Birdie, millions. You know what I've always said when people told me we were rich? I said I think you should either be a nigger or a millionaire. In be-tween, like us, what for? [*Laughs. Looks at* BIRDIE.] But I'm not going away tomorrow, Birdie. There's plenty of time to worry about Horace when he comes home. If he ever decides to come home.

BIRDIE: Will we be going to Chicago? I mean, Oscar and Leo and me?

REGINA: You? I shouldn't think so. [*Laughs.*] Well, we must remember tonight. It's a very important night and we mustn't forget it. We shall plan all the things we'd like to have and then we'll really have them. Make a wish, Birdie, any wish. It's bound to come true now.

[BEN *and* OSCAR *enter.*]

BIRDIE [*Laughs*]: Well. Well, I don't know. Maybe. [REGINA *turns to look at* BEN.] Well, I guess I'd know right off what I wanted.

[OSCAR *stands by the upper window, waves to the departing carriage.*]

REGINA [*Looks up at* BEN, *smiles. He smiles back at her*]: Well, you did it.

BEN: Looks like it might be we did.

REGINA [*Springs up, laughs*]: Looks like it! Don't pretend. You're like a cat who's been licking the cream. [*Crosses to wine bottle.*] Now we must all have a drink to celebrate.

OSCAR: The children, Alexandra and Leo, make a very handsome couple, Regina. Marshall remarked himself what fine young folks they were. How well they looked together!

REGINA [*Sharply*]: Yes. You said that before, Oscar.

BEN: Yes, sir. It's beginning to look as if the deal's all set. I may not be a subtle man—but— [*Turns to them. After a second.*] Now somebody ask me how I know the deal is set.

OSCAR: What do you mean, Ben?

BEN: You remember I told him that down here we drink the *last* drink for a toast?

OSCAR [*Thoughtfully*]: Yes. I never heard that before.

BEN: Nobody's ever heard it before. God forgives those who invent what they need. I already had his signature. But we've all done business with men whose word over a glass is better than a bond. Anyway it don't hurt to have both.

OSCAR [*Turns to* REGINA]: You understand what Ben means?

REGINA [*Smiles*]: Yes, Oscar. I understand. I understood immediately.

BEN [*Looks at her admiringly*]: Did you, Regina? Well, when he lifted his glass to drink, I closed my eyes and saw the bricks going into place.

REGINA: And *I* saw a lot more than that.

BEN: Slowly, slowly. As yet we have only our hopes.

REGINA: Birdie and I have just been planning what we want. I know what I want. What will you want, Ben?

BEN: Caution. Don't count the chickens. [*Leans back, laughs.*] Well, God would allow us a little daydreaming. Good for the soul when you've worked hard enough to deserve it.

[*Pauses.*] I think I'll have a stable. For a long time I've had my good eyes on Carter's in Savannah. A rich man's pleasure, the sport of kings, why not the sport of Hubbards? Why not?

REGINA [*Smiles*]: Why not? What will you have, Oscar?

OSCAR: I don't know. [*Thoughtfully.*] The pleasure of seeing the bricks grow will be enough for me.

BEN: Oh, of course. Our *greatest* pleasure will be to see the bricks grow. But we are all entitled to a little side indulgence.

OSCAR: Yes, I suppose so. Well, then, I think we might take a few trips here and there, eh, Birdie?

BIRDIE [*Surprised at being consulted*]: Yes, Oscar. I'd like that.

OSCAR: We might even make a regular trip to Jekyll Island. I've heard the Cornelly place is for sale. We might think about buying it. Make a nice change. Do you good, Birdie, a change of climate. Fine shooting on Jekyll, the best.

BIRDIE: I'd like—

OSCAR [*Indulgently*]: What would you like?

BIRDIE: *Two* things. Two things I'd like most.

REGINA: Two! I should like a thousand. You are modest, Birdie.

BIRDIE [*Warmly, delighted with the unexpected interest*]: I should like to have Lionnet back. I know you own it now, but I'd like to see it fixed up again, the way Mama and Papa had it. Every year it used to get a nice coat of paint—Papa was very particular about the paint—and the lawn was so smooth all the way down to the river, with the trims of zinnias and red-feather plush. And the figs and blue little plums and the scuppernongs— [*Smiles. Turns to* REGINA.] The organ is still there and it wouldn't cost much to fix. We could have parties for Zan, the way Mama used to have for me.

BEN: That's a pretty picture, Birdie. Might be a most pleasant way to live. [*Dismissing* BIRDIE.] What do you want, Regina?

BIRDIE [*Very happily, not noticing that they are no longer listening to her*]: I could have a cutting garden. Just where Mama's used to be. Oh, I do think we could be happier there. Papa used to say that *nobody* had ever lost their temper at Lionnet, and *nobody* ever would. Papa would never let anybody be nasty-spoken or mean. No, sir. He just didn't like it.

BEN: What do you want, Regina?

REGINA: I'm going to Chicago. And when I'm settled there and know the right people and the right things to buy—because I certainly don't know—I shall go to Paris and buy them. [*Laughs.*] I'm going to leave you and Oscar to count the bricks.

BIRDIE: Oscar. Please let me have Lionnet back.

OSCAR [*To* REGINA]: You are serious about moving to Chicago?

BEN: She is going to see the great world and leave us in the little one. Well, we'll come and visit you and meet all the great and be proud to think you are our sister.

REGINA [*Gaily*]: Certainly. And you won't even have to learn to be subtle, Ben. Stay as you are. You will be rich and the rich don't have to be subtle.

OSCAR: But what about Alexandra? She's seventeen. Old enough to be thinking about marrying.

BIRDIE: And, Oscar, I have one more wish. Just one more wish.

OSCAR [*Turns*]: What is it, Birdie? What are you saying?

BIRDIE: I want you to stop shooting. I mean, so much. I don't like to see animals and birds killed just for the killing. You only throw them away—

BEN [*To* REGINA]: It'll take a great deal of money to live as you're planning, Regina.

REGINA: Certainly. But there'll be plenty of money. You have estimated the profits very high.

BEN: I have—

BIRDIE [OSCAR *is looking at her furiously*]: And you never let anybody else shoot, and the niggers need it so much to keep from starving. It's wicked to shoot food just because you like to shoot, when poor people need it so—

BEN [*Laughs*]: I have estimated the profits very high—for myself.

REGINA: What did you say?

BIRDIE: I've always wanted to speak about it, Oscar.

OSCAR [*Slowly, carefully*]: What are you chattering about?

BIRDIE [*Nervously*]: I was talking about Lionnet and—and about your shooting—

OSCAR: You are exciting yourself.

REGINA [*To* BEN]: I didn't hear you. There was so much talking.

OSCAR [*To* BIRDIE]: You have been acting very childish, very excited, all evening.

BIRDIE: Regina asked me what I'd like.

REGINA: What did you say, Ben?

BIRDIE: Now that we'll be so rich everybody was saying what they would like, so *I* said what *I* would like, too.

BEN: I said— [*He is interrupted by* OSCAR.]

OSCAR [*To* BIRDIE]: Very well. We've all heard you. That's enough now.

BEN: I am waiting. [*They stop.*] I am waiting for you to finish. You and Birdie. Four conversations are three too many. [BIRDIE *slowly sits down.* BEN *smiles, to* REGINA.] I said that I had, and I do, estimate the profits very high—for myself, and Oscar, of course.

REGINA [*Slowly*]: And what does that mean?

[BEN *shrugs, looks towards* OSCAR.]

OSCAR [*Looks at* BEN, *clears throat*]: Well, Regina, it's like this. For forty-nine per cent Marshall will put up four hundred thousand dollars. For fifty-one per cent— [*Smiles archly.*] a controlling interest, mind you, we will put up two hundred and twenty-five thousand dollars besides offering him certain benefits that our [*Looks at* BEN.] local position allows us to manage. Ben means that two hundred and twenty-five thousand dollars is a lot of money.

REGINA: I know the terms and I know it's a lot of money.

BEN [*Nodding*]: It is.

OSCAR: Ben means that we are ready with our two-thirds of the money. Your third, Horace's I mean, doesn't seem to be ready. [*Raises his hand as* REGINA *starts to speak.*] Ben has written to Horace, I have written, and you have written. He answers. But he never mentions this business. Yet we have explained it to him in great detail, and told him the urgency. Still he never mentions it. Ben has been very patient, Regina. Naturally, you are our sister and we want you to benefit from anything we do.

REGINA: And in addition to your concern for me, you do not want control to go out of the family. [*To* BEN.] That right, Ben?

BEN: That's cynical. [*Smiles.*] Cynicism is an unpleasant way of saying the truth.

OSCAR: No need to be cynical. We'd have no trouble raising the third share, the share that you want to take.

REGINA: I am sure you could get the third share, the share you were saving for me. But that would give you a strange partner. And strange partners sometimes want a great deal. [*Smiles unpleasantly.*] But perhaps it would be wise for you to find him.

OSCAR: Now, now. Nobody says we *want* to do that. We would like to have you in and you would like to come in.

REGINA: Yes. I certainly would.

BEN [*Laughs, puts up his hand*]: But we haven't heard from Horace.

REGINA: I've given my word that Horace will put up the money. That should be enough.

BEN: Oh, it was enough. I took your word. But I've got to have more than your word now. The contracts will be signed this week, and Marshall will want to see our money soon after. Regina, Horace has been in Baltimore for five months. I know that you've written him to come home, and that he hasn't come.

OSCAR: It's beginning to look as if he doesn't want to come home.

REGINA: Of course he wants to come home. You can't move around with heart trouble at any moment you choose. You know what doctors are like once they get their hands on a case like this—

OSCAR: They can't very well keep him from answering letters, can they? [REGINA *turns to* BEN.] They couldn't keep him from arranging for the money if he wanted to—

REGINA: Has it occurred to you that Horace is also a good business man?

BEN: Certainly. He is a shrewd trader. Always has been. The bank is proof of that.

REGINA: Then, possibly, he may be keeping silent because he doesn't think he is getting enough for his money. [*Looks at* OSCAR.] Seventy-five thousand he has to put up. That's a lot of money, too.

OSCAR: Nonsense. He knows a good thing when he hears it. He knows that we can make *twice* the profit on cotton goods manufactured *here* than can be made in the North.

BEN: That isn't what Regina means. [*Smiles.*] May I interpret you, Regina? [*To* OSCAR.] Regina is saying that Horace wants *more* than a third of our share.

OSCAR: But he's only putting up a third of the money. You put up a third and you get a third. What else *could* he expect?

REGINA: Well, *I* don't know. I don't know about these things. It would seem that if you put up a third you should only get a third. But then again, there's no law about it, is there? I should think that if you knew your money was very badly needed, well, you just might say, I want more, I want a bigger share. You boys have done that. I've heard you say so.

BEN [*After a pause, laughs*]: So you believe he has deliberately held out? For a larger share? [*Leaning forward.*] Well, I *don't* believe it. But I *do* believe that's what *you* want. Am I right, Regina?

REGINA: Oh, I shouldn't like to be too definite. But I *could* say that I wouldn't like to persuade Horace unless he did get a larger share. I must look after his interests. It seems only natural—

OSCAR: And where would the larger share come from?

REGINA: I don't know. That's not my business. [*Giggles.*] But perhaps it could come off your share, Oscar.

[REGINA *and* BEN *laugh.*]

OSCAR [*Rises and wheels furiously on both of them as they laugh*]: What kind of talk is this?

BEN: I haven't said a thing.

OSCAR [*To* REGINA]: *You* are talking very big tonight.

REGINA [*Stops laughing*]: Am I? Well, you should know me well enough to know that I wouldn't be asking for things I didn't think I could get. ·

OSCAR: Listen. I don't believe you can even get Horace to come home, much less get money from him or talk quite so big about what you want.

REGINA: Oh, I can get him home.

OSCAR: Then why haven't you?

REGINA: I thought I should fight his battles for him, before he came home. Horace is a very sick man. And even if *you* don't care how sick he is, I do.

BEN: Stop this foolish squabbling. How can you get him home?

REGINA: I will send Alexandra to Baltimore. She will ask him to come home. She will say that she *wants* him to come home, and that *I* want him to come home.

BIRDIE [*Suddenly*]: Well, of course she wants him here, but he's sick and maybe he's happy where he is.

REGINA [*Ignores* BIRDIE, *to* BEN]: You agree that he will come home if she asks him to, if she says that I miss him and want him—

BEN [*Looks at her, smiles*]: I admire you, Regina. And I agree. That's settled now and— [*Starts to rise.*]

REGINA [*Quickly*]: But before she brings him home, I want to know what he's going to get.

BEN: What do you want?

REGINA: Twice what you offered.

BEN: Well, you won't get it.

OSCAR [*To* REGINA]: I think you've gone crazy.

REGINA: I don't want to fight, Ben—

BEN: I don't either. You won't get it. There isn't any chance of that. [*Roguishly.*] You're holding us up, and that's not pretty, Regina, not pretty. [*Holds up his hand as he sees she is about to speak.*] But we need you, and I don't want to fight. Here's what I'll do: I'll give Horace forty per cent, instead of the thirty-three and a third he really should get. I'll do that, provided he is home and his money is up within two weeks. How's that?

REGINA: All right.

OSCAR: I've asked before: where is this extra share coming from?

BEN [*Pleasantly*]: From you. From your share.

OSCAR [*Furiously*]: From me, is it? That's just fine and dandy. That's my reward. For thirty-five years I've worked my hands to the bone for you. For thirty-five years I've done all the things you didn't want to do. And this is what I—

BEN [*Turns slowly to look at* OSCAR. OSCAR *breaks off*]: My, my. I am being attacked tonight on all sides. First by my sister, then by my brother. And I ain't a man who likes being attacked. I can't believe that God wants the strong to parade their strength, but I don't mind doing it if it's got to be done. [*Leans back in his chair.*] You ought to take these things better, Oscar. I've made you money in the past. I'm going to make you more money now. You'll be a very rich man. What's the difference to any of us if a little more goes here, a little less goes there—it's all in the family. And it will stay in the family. I'll never marry. [ADDIE *enters, begins to gather the glasses from the table.* OSCAR *turns to* BEN.] So my money will go to Alexandra and Leo. They may even marry some day and— [ADDIE *looks at* BEN.]

BIRDIE [*Rising*]: Marry—Zan and Leo—

OSCAR [*Carefully*]: That would make a great difference in my feelings. If they married.

BEN: Yes, that's what I mean. Of course it would make a difference.

OSCAR [*Carefully*]: Is that what *you* mean, Regina?

REGINA: Oh, it's too far away. We'll talk about it in a few years.

OSCAR: I want to talk about it now.

BEN [*Nods*]: Naturally.

REGINA: There's a lot of things to consider. They are first cousins, and—

OSCAR: That isn't unusual. Our grandmother and grandfather were first cousins.

REGINA [*Giggles*]: And look at us.

[BEN *giggles*.]

OSCAR [*Angrily*]: You're both being very gay with my money.

BEN [*Sighs*]: These quarrels. I dislike them so. [*Leans forward to* REGINA.] A marriage might be a very wise arrangement, for several reasons. And then, Oscar has given up something for you. You should try to manage something for him.

REGINA: I haven't said I was opposed to it. But Leo is a wild boy. There were those times when he took a little money from the bank and—

OSCAR: That's all past history—

REGINA: Oh, I know. And I know all young men are wild. I'm only mentioning it to show you that there are considerations—

BEN [*Irritated because she does not understand that he is trying to keep* OSCAR *quiet*]: All right, so there are. But please assure Oscar that you will think about it very seriously.

REGINA [*Smiles, nods*]: Very well. I assure Oscar that I will think about it seriously.

OSCAR [*Sharply*]: That is not an answer.

REGINA [*Rises*]: My, you're in a bad humor and you shall put me in one. I have said all that I am willing to say now. After all, Horace has to give his consent, too.

OSCAR: Horace will do what you tell him to.

REGINA: Yes, I think he will.

OSCAR: And I have your word that you will try to—

REGINA [*Patiently*]: Yes, Oscar. You have my word that I will think about it. Now do leave me alone.

[*There is the sound of the front door being closed.*]

BIRDIE: I—Alexandra is only seventeen. She—

REGINA [*Calling*]: Alexandra? Are you back?

ALEXANDRA: Yes, Mama.

LEO [*Comes into the room*]: Mr. Marshall got off safe and sound. Weren't those fine clothes he had? You can always spot clothes made in a good place. Looks like maybe they were done in England. Lots of men in the North send all the way to England for their stuff.

BEN [*To* LEO]: Were you careful driving the horses?

LEO: Oh, yes, sir. I was.

[ALEXANDRA *has come in on* BEN'S *question, hears the answer, looks angrily at* LEO.]

ALEXANDRA: It's a lovely night. You should have come, Aunt Birdie.

REGINA: Were you gracious to Mr. Marshall?

ALEXANDRA: I think so, Mama. I liked him.

REGINA: Good. And now I have great news for you. You are going to Baltimore in the morning to bring your father home.

ALEXANDRA [*Gasps, then delighted*]: Me? Papa said I should come? That must mean— [*Turns to* ADDIE.] Addie, he must be well. Think of it, he'll be back home again. We'll bring him home.

REGINA: You are going alone, Alexandra.

ADDIE [ALEXANDRA *has turned in surprise*]: Going alone? Going by herself? A child that age! Mr. Horace ain't going to like Zan traipsing up there by herself.

REGINA [*Sharply*]: Go upstairs and lay out Alexandra's things.

ADDIE: He'd expect me to be along—

REGINA: I'll be up in a few minutes to tell you what to pack.
[ADDIE *slowly begins to climb the steps. To* ALEXANDRA.] I
should think you'd like going alone. At your age it certainly
would have delighted me. You're a strange girl, Alexandra.
Addie has babied you so much.

ALEXANDRA: I only thought it would be more fun if Addie
and I went together.

BIRDIE [*Timidly*]: Maybe I could go with her, Regina. I'd
really like to.

REGINA: She is going alone. She is getting old enough to take
some responsibilities.

OSCAR: She'd better learn now. She's almost old enough to
get married. [*Jovially, to* LEO, *slapping him on shoulder.*] Eh,
son?

LEO: Huh?

OSCAR [*Annoyed with* LEO *for not understanding*]: Old
enough to get married, you're thinking, eh?

LEO: Oh, yes, sir. [*Feebly.*] Lots of girls get married at Zan's
age. Look at Mary Prester and Johanna and—

REGINA: Well, she's not getting married tomorrow. But she
is going to Baltimore tomorrow, so let's talk about that. [*To*
ALEXANDRA.] You'll be glad to have Papa home again.

ALEXANDRA: I wanted to go before, Mama. You remember
that. But you said *you* couldn't go, and that *I* couldn't go alone.

REGINA: I've changed my mind. [*Too casually.*] You're to
tell Papa how much you missed him, and that he must come
home now—for your sake. Tell him that you *need* him home.

ALEXANDRA: Need him home? I don't understand.

REGINA: There is nothing for you to understand. You are
simply to say what I have told you.

BIRDIE [*Rises*]: He may be too sick. She couldn't do that—

ALEXANDRA: Yes. He may be too sick to travel. I couldn't
make him think he had to come home for me, if he is too
sick to—

REGINA [*Looks at her, sharply, challengingly*]: You *couldn't*
do what I tell you to do, Alexandra?

ALEXANDRA [*Quietly*]: No. I couldn't. If I thought it would
hurt him.

REGINA [*After a second's silence, smiles pleasantly*]: But

you are doing this for Papa's own good. [*Takes* ALEXANDRA'S *hand.*] You must let me be the judge of his condition. It's the best possible cure for him to come home and be taken care of here. He mustn't stay there any longer and listen to those alarmist doctors. You are doing this entirely for his sake. Tell your papa that I want him to come home, that I miss him very much.

ALEXANDRA [*Slowly*]: Yes, Mama.

REGINA [*To the others. Rises*]: I must go and start getting Alexandra ready now. Why don't you all go home?

BEN [*Rises*]: I'll attend to the railroad ticket. One of the boys will bring it over. Good night, everybody. Have a nice trip, Alexandra. The food on the train is very good. The celery is so crisp. Have a good time and act like a little lady. [*Exits.*]

REGINA: Good night, Ben. Good night, Oscar— [*Playfully.*] Don't be so glum, Oscar. It makes you look as if you had chronic indigestion.

BIRDIE: Good night, Regina.

REGINA: Good night, Birdie. [*Exits upstairs.*]

OSCAR [*Starts for hall*]: Come along.

LEO [*To* ALEXANDRA]: Imagine your not wanting to go! What a little fool you are. Wish it were me. What I could do in a place like Baltimore!

ALEXANDRA [*Angrily, looking away from him*]: Mind your business. I can guess the kind of things *you* could do.

LEO [*Laughs*]: Oh, no, you couldn't. [*He exits.*]

REGINA [*Calling from the top of the stairs*]: Come on, Alexandra.

BIRDIE [*Quickly, softly*]: Zan.

ALEXANDRA: I don't understand about my going, Aunt Birdie. [*Shrugs.*] But anyway, Papa will be home again. [*Pats* BIRDIE's *arm.*] Don't worry about me. I can take care of myself. Really I can.

BIRDIE [*Shakes her head, softly*]: That's not what I'm worried about. Zan—

ALEXANDRA [*Comes close to her*]: What's the matter?

BIRDIE: It's about Leo—

ALEXANDRA [*Whispering*]: He beat the horses. That's why we were late getting back. We had to wait until they cooled off. He always beats the horses as if—

BIRDIE [*Whispering frantically, holding* ALEXANDRA'S *hands*]: He's my son. My own son. But you are more to me—more to me than my own child. I love you more than anybody else—

ALEXANDRA: Don't worry about the horses. I'm sorry I told you.

BIRDIE [*Her voice rising*]: *I am not worrying about the horses*. I am worrying about *you*. You are *not* going to marry Leo. I am not going to let them do that to you—

ALEXANDRA: Marry? To Leo? [*Laughs.*] I wouldn't marry, Aunt Birdie. I've never even thought about it—

BIRDIE: But they have thought about it. [*Wildly.*] Zan, I couldn't stand to think about such a thing. You and—

[OSCAR *has come into the doorway on* ALEXANDRA'S *speech. He is standing quietly, listening.*]

ALEXANDRA [*Laughs*]: But I'm not going to marry. And I'm certainly not going to marry Leo.

BIRDIE: Don't you understand? They'll make you. They'll make you—

ALEXANDRA [*Takes* BIRDIE'S *hands, quietly, firmly*]: That's foolish, Aunt Birdie. I'm grown now. Nobody can make me do anything.

BIRDIE: I just couldn't stand—

OSCAR [*Sharply*]: Birdie. [BIRDIE *looks up, draws quickly away from* ALEXANDRA. *She stands rigid, frightened. Quietly.*] Birdie, get your hat and coat.

ADDIE [*Calls from upstairs*]: Come on, baby. Your mama's waiting for you, and she ain't nobody to keep waiting.

ALEXANDRA: All right. [*Then softly, embracing* BIRDIE.] Good night, Aunt Birdie. [*As she passes* OSCAR.] Good night, Uncle Oscar. [BIRDIE *begins to move slowly towards the door as* ALEXANDRA *climbs the stairs.* ALEXANDRA *is almost out of view when* BIRDIE *reaches* OSCAR *in the doorway. As* BIRDIE *quickly attempts to pass him, he slaps her hard, across the face.* BIRDIE *cries out, puts her hand to her face. On the cry,* ALEXANDRA *turns, begins to run down the stairs.*] Aunt Birdie! What happened? What happened? I—

BIRDIE [*Softly, without turning*]: Nothing, darling. Nothing happened. [*Quickly, as if anxious to keep* ALEXANDRA *from coming close.*] Now go to bed. [OSCAR *exits.*] Nothing happened.

[*Turns to* ALEXANDRA *who is holding her hand.*] I only—I only twisted my ankle. [*She goes out.* ALEXANDRA *stands on the stairs looking after her as if she were puzzled and frightened.*]

Curtain

ACT TWO

SCENE—*Same as Act One. A week later, morning.*

AT RISE: *The light comes from the open shutter of the right window; the other shutters are tightly closed.* ADDIE *is standing at the window, looking out. Near the dining-room doors are brooms, mops, rags, etc. After a second,* OSCAR *comes into the entrance hall, looks in the room, shivers, decides not to take his hat and coat off, comes into the room. At the sound of the door,* ADDIE *turns to see who has come in.*

ADDIE [*Without interest*]: Oh, it's you, Mr. Oscar.

OSCAR: What is this? It's not night. What's the matter here? [*Shivers.*] Fine thing at this time of the morning. Blinds all closed. [ADDIE *begins to open shutters.*] Where's Miss Regina? It's cold in here.

ADDIE: Miss Regina ain't down yet.

OSCAR: She had any word?

ADDIE [*Wearily*]: No, sir.

OSCAR: Wouldn't you think a girl that age could get on a train at one place and have sense enough to get off at another?

ADDIE: Something must have happened. If Zan say she was coming last night, she's coming last night. Unless something happened. Sure fire disgrace to let a baby like that go all that way alone to bring home a sick man without—

OSCAR: You do a lot of judging around here, Addie, eh? Judging of your white folks, I mean.

ADDIE [*Looks at him, sighs*]: I'm tired. I been up all night watching for them.

REGINA [*Speaking from the upstairs hall*]: Who's downstairs, Addie? [*She appears in a dressing gown, peers down from the landing.* ADDIE *picks up broom, dustpan and brush and exits.*] Oh, it's you, Oscar. What are you doing here so early? I haven't been down yet. I'm not finished dressing.

OSCAR [*Speaking up to her*]: You had any word from them?

REGINA: No.

OSCAR: Then something certainly has happened. People don't just say they are arriving on Thursday night, and they haven't come by Friday morning.

REGINA: Oh, nothing has happened. Alexandra just hasn't got sense enough to send a message.

OSCAR: If nothing's happened, then why aren't they here?

REGINA: You asked me that ten times last night. My, you do fret so, Oscar. Anything might have happened. They may have missed connections in Atlanta, the train may have been delayed —oh, a hundred things could have kept them.

OSCAR: Where's Ben?

REGINA [*As she disappears upstairs*]: Where should he be? At home, probably. Really, Oscar, I don't tuck him in his bed and I don't take him out of it. Have some coffee and don't worry so much.

OSCAR: Have some coffee? There isn't any coffee. [*Looks at his watch, shakes his head. After a second* CAL *enters with a large silver tray, coffee urn, small cups, newspaper.*] Oh, there you are. Is everything in this fancy house always late?

CAL [*Looks at him surprised*]: You ain't out shooting this morning, Mr. Oscar?

OSCAR: First day I missed since I had my head cold. First day I missed in eight years.

CAL: Yes, sir. I bet you. Simon he say you had a mighty good day yesterday morning. That's what Simon say. [*Brings* OSCAR *coffee and newspaper.*]

OSCAR: Pretty good, pretty good.

CAL [*Laughs, slyly*]: Bet you got enough bobwhite and squirrel to give every nigger in town a Jesus-party. Most of 'em ain't had no meat since the cotton picking was over. Bet they'd give anything for a little piece of that meat—

OSCAR [*Turns his head to look at* CAL]: Cal, if I catch a

nigger in this town going shooting, you know what's going to happen.

[LEO *enters.*]

CAL [*Hastily*]: Yes, sir, Mr. Oscar. I didn't say nothing about nothing. It was Simon who told me and— Morning, Mr. Leo. You gentlemen having your breakfast with us here?

LEO: The boys in the bank don't know a thing. They haven't had any message.

[CAL *waits for an answer, gets none, shrugs, moves to door, exits.*]

OSCAR [*Peers at* LEO]: What you doing here, son?

LEO: You told me to find out if the boys at the bank had any message from Uncle Horace or Zan—

OSCAR: I told you if they had a message to bring it here. I told you that if they didn't have a message to stay at the bank and do your work.

LEO: Oh, I guess I misunderstood.

OSCAR: You didn't misunderstand. You just were looking for any excuse to take an hour off. [LEO *pours a cup of coffee.*] You got to stop that kind of thing. You got to start settling down. You going to be a married man one of these days.

LEO: Yes, sir.

OSCAR: You also got to stop with that woman in Mobile. [*As* LEO *is about to speak.*] You're young and I haven't got no objections to outside women. That is, I haven't got no objections so long as they don't interfere with serious things. Outside women are all right in their place, but *now* isn't their place. You got to realize that.

LEO [*Nods*]: Yes, sir. I'll tell her. She'll act all right about it.

OSCAR: Also, you got to start working harder at the bank. You got to convince your Uncle Horace you going to make a fit husband for Alexandra.

LEO: What do you think has happened to them? Supposed to be here last night— [*Laughs.*] Bet you Uncle Ben's mighty worried. Seventy-five thousand dollars worried.

OSCAR [*Smiles happily*]: Ought to be worried. Damn well ought to be. First he don't answer the letters, then he don't come home— [*Giggles.*]

LEO: What will happen if Uncle Horace don't come home or don't—

oscar: Or don't put up the money? Oh, we'll get it from outside. Easy enough.

leo [*Surprised*]: But *you* don't want outsiders.

oscar: What do I care who gets my share? I been shaved already. Serve Ben right if he had to give away some of his.

leo: Damn shame what they did to you.

oscar [*Looking up the stairs*]: Don't talk so loud. Don't you worry. When I die, you'll have as much as the rest. You might have yours *and* Alexandra's. I'm not so easily licked.

leo: I wasn't thinking of myself, Papa—

oscar: Well, you should be, you should be. It's every man's duty to think of himself.

leo: You think Uncle Horace don't want to go in on this?

oscar [*Giggles*]: That's my hunch. He hasn't showed any signs of loving it yet.

leo [*Laughs*]: But he hasn't listened to Aunt Regina yet, either. Oh, he'll go along. It's too good a thing. Why wouldn't he want to? He's got plenty and plenty to invest with. He don't even have to sell anything. Eighty-eight thousand worth of Union Pacific bonds sitting right in his safe deposit box. All he's got to do is open the box.

oscar [*After a pause. Looks at his watch*]: Mighty late breakfast in this fancy house. Yes, he's had those bonds for fifteen years. Bought them when they were low and just locked them up.

leo: Yeah. Just has to open the box and take them out. That's all. Easy as easy can be. [*Laughs.*] The things in that box! There's all those bonds, looking mighty fine. [oscar *slowly puts down his newspaper and turns to* leo.] Then right next to them is a baby shoe of Zan's and a cheap old cameo on a string, and, *and*—nobody'd believe this—a piece of an old violin. Not even a whole violin. Just a piece of an old thing, a piece of a violin.

oscar [*Very softly, as if he were trying to control his voice*]: A piece of a violin! What do you think of that!

leo: Yes, sirree. A lot of other crazy things, too. A poem, I guess it is, signed with his mother's name, and two old schoolbooks with notes and— [leo *catches* oscar's *look. His voice trails off. He turns his head away.*]

OSCAR [*Very softly*]: How do you know what's in the box, son?

LEO [*Stops, draws back, frightened, realizing what he has said*]: Oh, well. Well, er. Well, one of the boys, sir. It was one of the boys at the bank. He took old Manders' keys. It was Joe Horns. He just up and took Manders' keys and, and—well, took the box out. [*Quickly.*] Then they all asked me if I wanted to see, too. So I looked a little, I guess, but then I made them close up the box quick and I told them never—

OSCAR [*Looks at him*]: Joe Horns, you say? He opened it?

LEO: Yes, sir, yes, he did. My word of honor. [*Very nervously looking away.*] I suppose that don't excuse *me* for looking— [*Looking at* OSCAR.] but I did make him close it up and put the keys back in Manders' drawer—

OSCAR [*Leans forward, very softly*]: Tell me the truth, Leo. I am not going to be angry with you. Did you open the box yourself?

LEO: *No, sir, I didn't.* I told you I didn't. No, I—

OSCAR [*Irritated, patient*]: I am *not* going to be angry with you. [*Watching* LEO *carefully.*] Sometimes a young fellow deserves credit for looking round him to see what's going on. Sometimes that's a good sign in a fellow your age. [OSCAR *rises.*] Many great men have made their fortune with their eyes. Did you open the box?

LEO [*Very puzzled*]: No. I—

OSCAR [*Moves to* LEO]: Did you open the box? It may have been—well, it may have been a good thing if you had.

LEO [*After a long pause*]: I opened it.

OSCAR [*Quickly*]: Is that the truth? [LEO *nods.*] Does anybody else know that you opened it? Come, Leo, don't be afraid of speaking the truth to me.

LEO: No. Nobody knew. Nobody was in the bank when I did it. But—

OSCAR: Did your Uncle Horace ever know you opened it?

LEO [*Shakes his head*]: He only looks in it once every six months when he cuts the coupons, and sometimes Manders even does that for him. Uncle Horace don't even have the keys. Manders keeps them for him. Imagine not looking at all that. You can bet if I had the bonds, I'd watch 'em like—

OSCAR: If you had them. [LEO *watches him.*] *If* you had them. Then you could have a share in the mill, you and me. A fine, big share, too. [*Pauses, shrugs.*] Well, a man can't be shot for wanting to see his son get on in the world, can he, boy?

LEO [*Looks up, begins to understand*]: No, he can't. Natural enough. [*Laughs.*] But I haven't got the bonds and Uncle Horace has. And now he can just sit back and wait to be a millionaire.

OSCAR [*Innocently*]: You think your Uncle Horace likes you well enough to lend you the bonds if he decides not to use them himself?

LEO: Papa, it must be that you haven't had your breakfast! [*Laughs loudly.*] Lend me the bonds! My God—

OSCAR [*Disappointed*]: No, I suppose not. Just a fancy of mine. A loan for three months, maybe four, easy enough for us to pay it back then. Anyway, this is only April— [*Slowly counting the months on his fingers.*] and if he doesn't look at them until Fall, he wouldn't even miss them out of the box.

LEO: That's it. He wouldn't even miss them. Ah, well—

OSCAR: No, sir. Wouldn't even miss them. How could he miss them if he never looks at them? [*Sighs as* LEO *stares at him.*] Well, here we are sitting around waiting for him to come home and invest his money in something he hasn't lifted his hand to get. But I can't help thinking he's acting strange. You laugh when I say he could lend you the bonds if he's not going to use them himself. But would it hurt him?

LEO [*Slowly looking at* OSCAR]: No. No, it wouldn't.

OSCAR: People ought to help other people. But that's not always the way it happens. [BEN *enters, hangs his coat and hat in hall. Very carefully.*] And so sometimes you got to think of yourself. [*As* LEO *stares at him,* BEN *appears in the doorway.*] Morning, Ben.

BEN [*Coming in, carrying his newspaper*]: Fine sunny morning. Any news from the runaways?

REGINA [*On the staircase*]: There's no news or you would have heard it. Quite a convention so early in the morning, aren't you all? [*Goes to coffee urn.*]

OSCAR: You rising mighty late these days. Is that the way they do things in Chicago society?

BEN [*Looking at his paper*]: Old Carter died up in Senateville. Eighty-one is a good time for us all, eh? What do you think has really happened to Horace, Regina?

REGINA: Nothing.

BEN [*Too casually*]: You don't think maybe he never started from Baltimore and never intends to start?

REGINA [*Irritated*]: Of course they've started. Didn't I have a letter from Alexandra? What is so strange about people arriving late? He has that cousin in Savannah he's so fond of. He may have stopped to see him. They'll be along today some time, very flattered that you and Oscar are so worried about them.

BEN: I'm a natural worrier. Especially when I am getting ready to close a business deal and one of my partners remains silent *and* invisible.

REGINA [*Laughs*]: Oh, is that it? I thought you were worried about Horace's health.

OSCAR: Oh, that too. Who could help but worry? I'm worried. This is the first day I haven't shot since my head cold.

REGINA [*Starts towards dining room*]: Then you haven't had your breakfast. Come along. [OSCAR *and* LEO *follow her.*]

BEN: Regina. [*She turns at dining-room door.*] That cousin of Horace's has been dead for years and, in any case, the train does not go through Savannah.

REGINA [*Laughs, continues into dining room, seats herself*]: Did he die? You're always remembering about people dying. [BEN *rises.*] Now I intend to eat my breakfast in peace, and read my newspaper.

BEN [*Goes towards dining room as he talks*]: This is second breakfast for me. My first was bad. Celia ain't the cook she used to be. Too old to have taste any more. If she hadn't belonged to Mama, I'd send her off to the country.

[OSCAR *and* LEO *start to eat.* BEN *seats himself.*]

LEO: Uncle Horace will have some tales to tell, I bet. Baltimore is a lively town.

REGINA [*To* CAL]: The grits isn't hot enough. Take it back.

CAL: Oh, yes'm. [*Calling into kitchen as he exits.*] Grits didn't hold the heat. Grits didn't hold the heat.

LEO: When I was at school three of the boys and myself took a train once and went over to Baltimore. It was so big we thought we were in Europe. I was just a kid then—

REGINA: I find it very pleasant [ADDIE *enters.*] to have breakfast alone. I hate chattering before I've had something hot. [CAL *closes the dining-room doors.*] Do be still, Leo.

[ADDIE *comes into the room, begins gathering up the cups, carries them to the large tray. Outside there are the sounds of voices. Quickly* ADDIE *runs into the hall. A few seconds later she appears again in the doorway, her arm around the shoulders of* HORACE GIDDENS, *supporting him.* HORACE *is a tall man of about forty-five. He has been good looking, but now his face is tired and ill. He walks stiffly, as if it were an enormous effort, and carefully, as if he were unsure of his balance.* ADDIE *takes off his overcoat and hangs it on the hall tree. She then helps him to a chair.*]

HORACE: How are you, Addie? How have you been?

ADDIE: I'm all right, Mr. Horace. I've just been worried about you.

[ALEXANDRA *enters. She is flushed and excited, her hat awry, her face dirty. Her arms are full of packages, but she comes quickly to* ADDIE.]

ALEXANDRA: Now don't tell me how worried you were. We couldn't help it and there was no way to send a message.

ADDIE [*Begins to take packages from* ALEXANDRA]: Yes, sir, I was mighty worried.

ALEXANDRA: We had to stop in Mobile over night. Papa— [*Looks at him.*] Papa didn't feel well. The trip was too much for him, and I made him stop and rest— [*As* ADDIE *takes the last package.*] No, don't take that. That's father's medicine. I'll hold it. It mustn't break. Now, about the stuff outside. Papa must have his wheel chair. I'll get that and the valises—

ADDIE [*Very happy, holding* ALEXANDRA'S *arms*]: Since when you got to carry your own valises? Since when I ain't old enough to hold a bottle of medicine? [HORACE *coughs.*] You feel all right, Mr. Horace?

HORACE [*Nods*]: Glad to be sitting down.

ALEXANDRA [*Opening package of medicine*]: He doesn't feel all right. [ADDIE *looks at her, then at* HORACE.] He just says that. The trip was very hard on him, and now he must go right to bed.

ADDIE [*Looking at him carefully*]: Them fancy doctors, they give you help?

HORACE: They did their best.

ALEXANDRA [*Has become conscious of the voices in the dining room*]: I bet Mama was worried. I better tell her we're here now. [*She starts for door.*]

HORACE: Zan. [*She stops.*] Not for a minute, dear.

ALEXANDRA: Oh, Papa, you feel bad again. I knew you did. Do you want your medicine?

HORACE: No, I don't feel that way. I'm just tired, darling. Let me rest a little.

ALEXANDRA: Yes, but Mama will be mad if I don't tell her we're here.

ADDIE: They're all in there eating breakfast.

ALEXANDRA: Oh, are they all here? Why do they *always* have to be here? I was hoping Papa wouldn't have to see anybody, that it would be nice for him and quiet.

ADDIE: Then let your papa rest for a minute.

HORACE: Addie, I bet your coffee's as good as ever. They don't have such good coffee up North. [*Looks at the urn.*] Is it as good, Addie?

[ADDIE *starts for coffee urn.*]

ALEXANDRA: No. Dr. Reeves said not much coffee. Just now and then. I'm the nurse now, Addie.

ADDIE: You'd be a better one if you didn't look so dirty. Now go and take a bath, Miss Grown-up. Change your linens, get out a fresh dress and give your hair a good brushing—go on—

ALEXANDRA: Will you be all right, Papa?

ADDIE: Go on.

ALEXANDRA [*On stairs, talks as she goes up*]: The pills Papa must take once every four hours. And the bottle only when—only if he feels very bad. Now don't move until I come back and don't talk much and remember about his medicine, Addie—

ADDIE: Ring for Belle and have her help you and then I'll make you a fresh breakfast.

ALEXANDRA [*As she disappears*]: How's Aunt Birdie? Is she here?

ADDIE: It ain't right for you to have coffee? It will hurt you?

HORACE [*Slowly*]: Nothing can make much difference now. Get me a cup, Addie. [*She looks at him, crosses to urn, pours a cup.*] Funny. They can't make coffee up North. [ADDIE *brings him a cup.*] They don't like red pepper, either. [*He takes the cup and gulps it greedily.*] God, that's good. You remember how I used to drink it? Ten, twelve cups a day. So strong it had to stain the cup. [*Then slowly.*] Addie, before I see anybody else, I want to know why Zan came to fetch me home. She's tried to tell me, but she doesn't seem to know herself.

ADDIE [*Turns away*]: I don't know. All I know is big things are going on. Everybody going to be high-tone rich. Big rich. You too. All because smoke's going to start out of a building that ain't even up yet.

HORACE: I've heard about it.

ADDIE: And, er— [*Hesitates—steps to him.*] And—well, Zan, she going to marry Mr. Leo in a little while.

HORACE [*Looks at her, then very slowly*]: What are you talking about?

ADDIE: That's right. That's the talk, God help us.

HORACE [*Angrily*]: *What's* the talk?

ADDIE: I'm telling you. There's going to be a wedding— [*Angrily turns away.*] Over my dead body there is.

HORACE [*After a second, quietly*]: Go and tell them I'm home.

ADDIE [*Hesitates*]: Now you ain't to get excited. You're to be in your bed—

HORACE: Go on, Addie. Go and say I'm back. [ADDIE *opens dining-room doors. He rises with difficulty, stands stiff, as if he were in pain, facing the dining room.*]

ADDIE: Miss Regina. They're home. They got here—

REGINA: Horace! [REGINA *quickly rises, runs into the room. Warmly.*] Horace! You've finally arrived. [*As she kisses him, the others come forward, all talking together.*]

BEN [*In doorway, carrying a napkin*]: Well, sir, you had us all mighty worried. [*He steps forward. They shake hands.* ADDIE *exits.*]

OSCAR: You're a sight for sore eyes.

HORACE: Hello, Ben.

[LEO *enters, eating a biscuit.*]

OSCAR: And how you feel? Tip-top, I bet, because that's the way you're looking.

HORACE [*Coldly, irritated with* OSCAR's *lie*]: Hello, Oscar. Hello, Leo, how are you?

LEO [*Shaking hands*]: I'm fine, sir. But a lot better now that you're back.

REGINA: Now sit down. What did happen to you and where's Alexandra? I am so excited about seeing you that I almost forgot about her.

HORACE: I didn't feel good, a little weak, I guess, and we stopped over night to rest. Zan's upstairs washing off the train dirt.

REGINA: Oh, I am so sorry the trip was hard on you. I didn't think that—

HORACE: Well, it's just as if I had never been away. All of you here—

BEN: Waiting to welcome you home.

[BIRDIE *bursts in. She is wearing a flannel kimono and her face is flushed and excited.*]

BIRDIE [*Runs to him, kisses him*]: Horace!

HORACE [*Warmly pressing her arm*]: I was just wondering where you were, Birdie.

BIRDIE [*Excited*]: Oh, I would have been here. I didn't know you were back until Simon said he saw the buggy. [*She draws back to look at him. Her face sobers.*] Oh, you don't look well, Horace. No, you don't.

REGINA [*Laughs*]: Birdie, what a thing to say—

HORACE [*Looking at* OSCAR]: Oscar thinks I look very well.

OSCAR [*Annoyed. Turns on* LEO]: Don't stand there holding that biscuit in your hand.

LEO: Oh, well. I'll just finish my breakfast, Uncle Horace, and then I'll give you all the news about the bank— [*He exits into the dining room.*]

OSCAR: And what is that costume you have on?

BIRDIE [*Looking at* HORACE]: Now that you're home, you'll feel better. Plenty of good rest and we'll take such fine care of you. [*Stops.*] But where is Zan? I missed her so much.

OSCAR: I asked you what is that strange costume you're parading around in?

BIRDIE [*Nervously, backing towards stairs*]: Me? Oh! It's my wrapper. I was so excited about Horace I just rushed out of the house—

OSCAR: Did you come across the square dressed that way? My dear Birdie, I—

HORACE [*To* REGINA, *wearily*]: Yes, it's just like old times.

REGINA [*Quickly to* OSCAR]: Now, no fights. This is a holiday.

BIRDIE [*Runs quickly up the stairs*]: Zan! Zannie!

OSCAR: Birdie! [*She stops.*]

BIRDIE: Oh. Tell Zan I'll be back in a little while. [*Whispers.*] Sorry, Oscar. [*Exits.*]

REGINA [*To* OSCAR *and* BEN]: Why don't you go finish your breakfast and let Horace rest for a minute?

BEN [*Crossing to dining room with* OSCAR]: Never leave a meal unfinished. There are too many poor people who need the food. Mighty glad to see you home, Horace. Fine to have you back. Fine to have you back.

OSCAR [*To* LEO *as* BEN *closes dining-room doors*]: Your mother has gone crazy. Running around the streets like a woman—

[*The moment* REGINA *and* HORACE *are alone, they become awkward and self-conscious.*]

REGINA [*Laughs awkwardly*]: Well. Here we are. It's been a long time. [HORACE *smiles.*] Five months. You know, Horace, I wanted to come and be with you in the hospital, but I didn't know where my duty was. Here, or with you. But you know how much I *wanted* to come.

HORACE: That's kind of you, Regina. There was no need to come.

REGINA: Oh, but there was. Five months lying there all by yourself, no kinfolks, no friends. Don't try to tell me you didn't have a bad time of it.

HORACE: I didn't have a bad time. [*As she shakes her head, he becomes insistent.*] No, I didn't, Regina. Oh, at first when I— when I heard the news about myself—but after I got used to that, I liked it there.

REGINA: You *liked* it? [*Coldly.*] Isn't that strange. You liked it so well you didn't want to come home?

HORACE: That's not the way to put it. [*Then, kindly, as he sees her turn her head away.*] But there I was and I got kind of used to it, kind of to like lying there and thinking. [*Smiles.*] I never had much time to think before. And time's become valuable to me.

REGINA: It sounds almost like a holiday.

HORACE [*Laughs*]: It was, sort of. The first holiday I've had since I was a little kid.

REGINA: And here I was thinking you were in pain and—

HORACE [*Quietly*]: I was in pain.

REGINA: And instead you were having a holiday! A holiday of thinking. Couldn't you have done that here?

HORACE: I wanted to do it before I came here. I was thinking about us.

REGINA: About us? About you and me? Thinking about you and me after all these years. [*Unpleasantly.*] You shall tell me everything you thought—some day.

HORACE [*There is silence for a minute*]: Regina. [*She turns to him.*] Why did you send Zan to Baltimore?

REGINA: Why? Because I wanted you home. You can't make anything suspicious out of that, can you?

HORACE: I didn't mean to make anything suspicious about it. [*Hesitantly, taking her hand.*] Zan said you wanted me to come home. I was so pleased at that and touched, it made me feel good.

REGINA [*Taking away her hand, turns*]: Touched that I should want you home?

HORACE [*Sighs*]: I'm saying all the wrong things as usual. Let's try to get along better. There isn't so much more time. Regina, what's all this crazy talk I've been hearing about Zan and Leo? Zan and Leo marrying?

REGINA [*Turning to him, sharply*]: Who gossips so much around here?

HORACE [*Shocked*]: Regina!

REGINA [*Annoyed, anxious to quiet him*]: It's some foolishness that Oscar thought up. I'll explain later. I have no intention of allowing any such arrangement. It was simply a way of keeping Oscar quiet in all this business I've been writing you about—

HORACE [*Carefully*]: What has Zan to do with any business of Oscar's? Whatever it is, you had better put it out of Oscar's head immediately. You know what I think of Leo.

REGINA: But there's no need to talk about it now.

HORACE: There is no need to talk about it ever. Not as long as I live. [HORACE *stops, slowly turns to look at her.*] As long as I live. I've been in a hospital for five months. Yet since I've been here you have not once asked me about—about my health. [*Then gently.*] Well, I suppose they've written you. I can't live very long.

REGINA [*Coldly*]: I've never understood why people have to talk about this kind of thing.

HORACE [*There is a silence. Then he looks up at her, his face cold*]: You misunderstand. I don't intend to gossip about my sickness. I thought it was only fair to tell you. I was not asking for your sympathy.

REGINA [*Sharply, turns to him*]: What do the doctors think caused your bad heart?

HORACE: What do you mean?

REGINA: They didn't think it possible, did they, that your fancy women may have—

HORACE [*Smiles unpleasantly*]: Caused my heart to be bad? I don't think that's the best scientific theory. You don't catch heart trouble in bed.

REGINA [*Angrily*]: I didn't think you did. I only thought you might catch a bad conscience—in bed, as you say.

HORACE: I didn't tell them about my bad conscience. Or about my fancy women. Nor did I tell them that my wife has not wanted me in bed with her for— [*Sharply.*] How long is it, Regina? [REGINA *turns to him.*] Ten years? Did you bring me home for this, to make me feel guilty again? That means you want something. But you'll not make me feel guilty any more. My "thinking" has made a difference.

REGINA: I see that it has. [*She looks towards dining-room door. Then comes to him, her manner warm and friendly.*] It's foolish for us to fight this way. I didn't mean to be unpleasant. I was stupid.

HORACE [*Wearily*]: God knows I didn't either. I came home wanting so much not to fight, and then all of a sudden there we were. I got hurt and—

REGINA [*Hastily*]: It's all my fault. I didn't ask about—about your illness because I didn't want to remind you of it. Anyway I never believe doctors when they talk about— [*Brightly.*] when they talk like that.

HORACE [*Not looking at her*]: Well, we'll try our best with each other. [*He rises.*]

REGINA [*Quickly*]: I'll try. Honestly, I will. Horace, Horace, I know you're tired but, but—couldn't you stay down here a few minutes longer? I want Ben to tell you something.

HORACE: Tomorrow.

REGINA: I'd like to now. It's very important to me. It's very important to all of us. [*Gaily, as she moves toward dining room.*] Important to your beloved daughter. She'll be a very great heiress—

HORACE: Will she? That's nice.

REGINA [*Opens doors*]: Ben, are you finished breakfast?

HORACE: Is this the mill business I've had so many letters about?

REGINA [*To* BEN]: Horace would like to talk to you now.

HORACE: Horace would not like to talk to you now. I am very tired, Regina—

REGINA [*Comes to him*]: Please. You've said we'll try our best with each other. I'll try. Really, I will. Please do this for me now. You will see what I've done while you've been away. How I watched your interests. [*Laughs gaily.*] And I've done very well too. But things can't be delayed any longer. Everything must be settled this week— [HORACE *sits down.* BEN *enters.* OSCAR *has stayed in the dining room, his head turned to watch them.* LEO *is pretending to read the newspaper.*] Now you must tell Horace all about it. Only be quick because he is very tired and must go to bed. [HORACE *is looking up at her. His face hardens as she speaks.*] But I think your news will be better for him than all the medicine in the world.

BEN [*Looking at* HORACE]: It could wait. Horace may not feel like talking today.

REGINA: What an old faker you are! You know it can't wait. You know it must be finished this week. You've been just as anxious for Horace to get here as I've been.

BEN [*Very jovial*]: I suppose I have been. And why not? Horace has done Hubbard Sons many a good turn. Why shouldn't I be anxious to help him now?

REGINA [*Laughs*]: Help him! Help him when you need him, that's what you mean.

BEN: What a woman you married, Horace. [*Laughs awkwardly when* HORACE *does not answer.*] Well, then I'll make it quick. You know what I've been telling you for years. How I've always said that every one of us little Southern business men had great things—[*Extends his arm.*]—right beyond our finger tips. It's been my dream: my dream to make those fingers grow longer. I'm a lucky man, Horace, a lucky man. To dream and to live to get what you've dreamed of. That's *my* idea of a lucky man. [*Looks at his fingers as his arm drops slowly.*] For thirty years I've cried bring the cotton mills to the cotton. [HORACE *opens medicine bottle.*] Well, finally I got up nerve to go to Marshall Company in Chicago.

HORACE: I know all this. [*He takes the medicine.* REGINA *rises, steps to him.*]

BEN: Can I get you something?

HORACE: Some water, please.

REGINA [*Turns quickly*]: Oh, I'm sorry. Let me. [*Brings him a glass of water. He drinks as they wait in silence.*] You feel all right now?

HORACE: Yes. You wrote me. I know all that.

[OSCAR *enters from dining room.*]

REGINA [*Triumphantly*]: But you don't know that in the last few days Ben has agreed to give us—you, I mean—a much larger share.

HORACE: Really? That's very generous of him.

BEN [*Laughs*]: It wasn't so generous of me. It was smart of Regina.

REGINA [*As if she were signaling* HORACE]: I explained to Ben that perhaps you hadn't answered his letters because you didn't think he was offering you enough, and that the time was getting short and you could guess how much he needed you—

HORACE [*Smiles at her, nods*]: And I could guess that he wants to keep control in the family?

REGINA [*To* BEN, *triumphantly*]: Exactly. [*To* HORACE.] So I did a little bargaining for you and convinced my brothers they weren't the only Hubbards who had a business sense.

HORACE: Did you have to convince them of that? How little people know about each other! [*Laughs.*] But you'll know better about Regina next time, eh, Ben? [BEN, REGINA, HORACE *laugh together.* OSCAR'S *face is angry.*] Now let's see. We're getting a bigger share. [*Looking at* OSCAR.] Who's getting less?

BEN: Oscar.

HORACE: Well, Oscar, you've grown very unselfish. What's happened to you?

[LEO *enters from dining room.*]

BEN [*Quickly, before* OSCAR *can answer*]: Oscar doesn't mind. Not worth fighting about now, eh, Oscar?

OSCAR [*Angrily*]: I'll get mine in the end. You can be sure of that. I've got my son's future to think about.

HORACE [*Sharply*]: Leo? Oh, I see. [*Puts his head back, laughs.* REGINA *looks at him nervously.*] I am beginning to see. Everybody will get theirs.

BEN: I knew you'd see it. Seventy-five thousand, and that seventy-five thousand will make you a million.

REGINA [*Steps to table, leaning forward*]: It will, Horace, it will.

HORACE: I believe you. [*After a second.*] Now I can understand Oscar's self-sacrifice, but what did you have to promise Marshall Company besides the money you're putting up?

BEN: They wouldn't take promises. They wanted guarantees.

HORACE: Of what?

BEN [*Nods*]: Water power. Free and plenty of it.

HORACE: You got them that, of course.

BEN: Cheap. You'd think the Governor of a great state would make his price a little higher. From pride, you know. [HORACE *smiles.* BEN *smiles.*] Cheap wages. "What do you mean by cheap wages?" I say to Marshall. "Less than Massachusetts," he says to me, "and that averages eight a week." "Eight a week! By God," I tell him, "*I'd* work for eight a week myself." Why, there ain't a mountain white or a town nigger but wouldn't give his right arm for three silver dollars every week, eh, Horace?

HORACE: Sure. And they'll take less than that when you get around to playing them off against each other. You can save a little money that way, Ben. [*Angrily.*] And make them hate each other just a little more than they do now.

REGINA: What's all this about?

BEN [*Laughs*]: There'll be no trouble from anybody, white or black. Marshall said that to me. "What about strikes? That's all we've had in Massachusetts for the last three years." I say to him, "What's a strike? I never heard of one. Come South, Marshall. We got good folks and we don't stand for any fancy fooling."

HORACE: You're right. [*Slowly.*] Well, it looks like you made a good deal for yourselves, and for Marshall, too. [*To* BEN.] Your father used to say he made the thousands and you boys would make the millions. I think he was right. [*Rises.*]

REGINA [*They are all looking at* HORACE. *She laughs nervously*]: Millions for *us*, too.

HORACE: Us? You and me? I don't think so. We've got enough money, Regina. We'll just sit by and watch the boys grow rich. [*They watch* HORACE *tensely as he begins to move towards the staircase. He passes* LEO, *looks at him for a second.*] How's everything at the bank, Leo?

LEO: Fine, sir. Everything is fine.

HORACE: How are all the ladies in Mobile? [HORACE *turns to* REGINA, *sharply.*] Whatever made you think I'd let Zan marry—

REGINA: Do you mean that you are turning this down? Is it possible that's what you mean?

BEN: No, that's not what he means. Turning down a fortune. Horace is tired. He'd rather talk about it tomorrow—

REGINA: We can't keep putting it off this way. Oscar must be in Chicago by the end of the week with the money and contracts.

OSCAR [*Giggles, pleased*]: Yes, sir. Got to be there end of the week. No sense going without the money.

REGINA [*Tensely*]: I've waited long enough for your answer. I'm not going to wait any longer.

HORACE [*Very deliberately*]: I'm very tired now, Regina.

BEN [*Hastily*]: Now, Horace probably has his reasons. Things he'd like explained. Tomorrow will do. I can—

REGINA [*Turns to* BEN, *sharply*]: I want to know his reasons now! [*Turns back to* HORACE.]

HORACE [*As he climbs the steps*]: I don't know them all myself. Let's leave it at that.

REGINA: We shall not leave it at that! We have waited for you here like children. Waited for you to come home.

HORACE: So that you could invest my money. So this is why you wanted me home? Well, I had hoped— [*Quietly.*] If you are disappointed, Regina, I'm sorry. But I must do what I think best. We'll talk about it another day.

REGINA: We'll talk about it now. Just you and me.

HORACE [*Looks down at her. His voice is tense*]: Please, Regina. It's been a hard trip. I don't feel well. Please leave me alone now.

REGINA [*Quietly*]: I want to talk to you, Horace. I'm coming up. [*He looks at her for a minute, then moves on again out of sight. She begins to climb the stairs.*]

BEN [*Softly.* REGINA *turns to him as he speaks*]: Sometimes it is better to wait for the sun to rise again. [*She does not answer.*] And sometimes, as our mother used to tell you. [REGINA *starts up stairs.*] it's unwise for a good-looking woman to frown. [BEN *rises, moves towards stairs.*] Softness and a smile do more to the heart of men— [*She disappears.* BEN *stands looking up the stairs. There is a long silence. Then, suddenly,* OSCAR *giggles.*]

OSCAR: Let us hope she'll change his mind. Let us hope. [*After a second* BEN *crosses to table, picks up his newspaper.* OSCAR *looks at* BEN. *The silence makes* LEO *uncomfortable.*]

LEO: The paper says twenty-seven cases of yellow fever in New Orleans. Guess the flood-waters caused it. [*Nobody pays attention.*] Thought they were building the levees high enough. Like the niggers always say: a man born of woman can't build nothing high enough for the Mississippi. [*Gets no answer. Gives an embarrassed laugh.*]

[*Upstairs there is the sound of voices. The voices are not loud, but* BEN, OSCAR, LEO *become conscious of them.* LEO *crosses to landing, looks up, listens.*]

OSCAR [*Pointing up*]: Now just suppose she don't change his mind? Just suppose he keeps on refusing?

BEN [*Without conviction*]: He's tired. It was a mistake to talk to him today. He's a sick man, but he isn't a crazy one.

OSCAR [*Giggles*]: But just suppose he is crazy. What then?

BEN [*Puts down his paper, peers at* OSCAR]: Then we'll go outside for the money. There's plenty who would give it.

OSCAR: And plenty who will want a lot for what they give. The ones who are rich enough to give will be smart enough to want. That means we'd be working for them, don't it, Ben?

BEN: You don't have to tell me the things I told you six months ago.

OSCAR: Oh, you're right not to worry. She'll change his mind. She always has. [*There is a silence. Suddenly* REGINA'S *voice becomes louder and sharper. All of them begin to listen now. Slowly* BEN *rises, goes to listen by the staircase.* OSCAR, *watching him, smiles. As they listen* REGINA'S *voice becomes very loud.* HORACE'S *voice is no longer heard.*] Maybe. But I don't believe it. I never did believe he was going in with us.

BEN [*Turning on him*]: What the hell do you expect me to do?

OSCAR [*Mildly*]: Nothing. You done your almighty best. Nobody could blame you if the whole thing just dripped away right through our fingers. You can't do a thing. But there may be something I could do for us. [OSCAR *rises.*] Or, I might better say, Leo could do for us. [BEN *stops, turns, looks at* OSCAR. LEO *is staring at* OSCAR.] Ain't that true, son? Ain't it true you might be able to help your own kinfolks?

LEO [*Nervously taking a step to him*]: Papa, I—

BEN [*Slowly*]: How would he help us, Oscar?

OSCAR: Leo's got a friend. Leo's friend owns eighty-eight thousand dollars in Union Pacific bonds. [BEN *turns to look at* LEO.] Leo's friend don't look at the bonds much—not for five or six months at a time.

BEN [*After a pause*]: Union Pacific. Uh, huh. Let me understand. Leo's friend would—would lend him these bonds and he—

OSCAR [*Nods*]: Would be kind enough to lend them to us.

BEN: Leo.

LEO [*Excited, comes to him*]: Yes, sir?

BEN: When would your friend be wanting the bonds back?

LEO [*Very nervous*]: I don't know. I—well, I—

OSCAR [*Sharply. Steps to him*]: You told me he won't look at them until Fall—

LEO: Oh, that's right. But I—not till Fall. Uncle Horace never—

BEN [*Sharply*]: Be still.

OSCAR [*Smiles at* LEO]: Your uncle doesn't wish to know your friend's name.

LEO [*Starts to laugh*]: That's a good one. Not know his name—

OSCAR: Shut up, Leo! [LEO *turns away slowly, moves to table.* BEN *turns to* OSCAR.] He won't look at them again until September. That gives us five months. Leo will return the bonds in three months. And we'll have no trouble raising the money once the mills are going up. Will Marshall accept bonds?

[BEN *stops to listen to sudden sharp voices from above. The voices are now very angry and very loud.*]

BEN [*Smiling*]: Why not? Why not? [*Laughs.*] Good. We are lucky. We'll take the loan from Leo's friend—I think he will make a safer partner than our sister. [*Nods towards stairs. Turns to* LEO.] How soon can you get them?

LEO: Today. Right now. They're in the safe-deposit box and—

BEN [*Sharply*]: I don't want to know where they are.

OSCAR [*Laughs*]: We will keep it secret from you. [*Pats* BEN'S *arm.*]

BEN [*Smiles*]: Good. Draw a check for our part. You can take the night train for Chicago. Well, Oscar [*Holds out his hand.*], good luck to us.

OSCAR: Leo will be taken care of?

LEO: I'm entitled to Uncle Horace's share. I'd enjoy being a partner—

BEN [*Turns to stare at him*]: You would? You can go to hell, you little— [*Starts towards* LEO.]

OSCAR [*Nervously*]: Now, now. He didn't mean that. I only want to be sure he'll get something out of all this.

BEN: Of course. We'll take care of him. We won't have any trouble about that. I'll see you at the store.

OSCAR [*Nods*]: That's settled then. Come on, son. [*Starts for door.*]

LEO [*Puts out his hand*]: I didn't mean just that. I was only going to say what a great day this was for me and— [BEN *ignores his hand.*]

BEN: Go on.

[LEO *looks at him, turns, follows* OSCAR *out.* BEN *stands where he is, thinking. Again the voices upstairs can be heard.* REGINA'S *voice is high and furious.* BEN *looks up, smiles, winces at the noise.*]

ALEXANDRA [*Upstairs*]: Mama—Mama—don't . . . [*The noise of running footsteps is heard and* ALEXANDRA *comes running down the steps, speaking as she comes.*] Uncle Ben! Uncle Ben! Please go up. Please make Mama stop. Uncle Ben, he's sick, he's so sick. How can Mama talk to him like that— please, make her stop. She'll—

BEN: Alexandra, you have a tender heart.

ALEXANDRA [*Crying*]: Go on up, Uncle Ben, please—

[*Suddenly the voices stop. A second later there is the sound of a door being slammed.*]

BEN: Now you see. Everything is over. Don't worry. [*He starts for the door.*] Alexandra, I want you to tell your mother how sorry I am that I had to leave. And don't worry so, my dear. Married folk frequently raise their voices, unfortunately. [*He starts to put on his hat and coat as* REGINA *appears on the stairs.*]

ALEXANDRA [*Furiously*]: How can you treat Papa like this? He's sick. He's very sick. Don't you know that? I won't let you.

REGINA: Mind your business, Alexandra. [*To* BEN. *Her voice is cold and calm.*] How much longer can you wait for the money?

BEN [*Putting on his coat*]: He has refused? My, that's too bad.

REGINA: He will change his mind. I'll find a way to make him. What's the longest you can wait now?

BEN: I could wait until next week. But I can't wait until next week. [*He giggles, pleased at the joke.*] I could but I can't. Could and can't. Well, I must go now. I'm very late—

REGINA [*Coming downstairs towards him*]: You're not going. I want to talk to you.

BEN: I was about to give Alexandra a message for you. I wanted to tell you that Oscar is going to Chicago tonight, so we can't be here for our usual Friday supper.

REGINA [*Tensely*]: Oscar is going to Chi— [*Softly.*] What do you mean?

BEN: Just that. Everything is settled. He's going on to deliver to Marshall—

REGINA [*Taking a step to him*]: I demand to know what— You are lying. You are trying to scare me. *You haven't got the money.* How could you have it? You can't have— [BEN *laughs.*] You will wait until I—

[HORACE *comes into view on the landing.*]

BEN: You are getting out of hand. Since when do I take orders from you?

REGINA: Wait, you— [BEN *stops.*] How *can* he go to Chicago? Did a ghost arrive with the money? [BEN *starts for the hall.*] I don't believe you. Come back here. [REGINA *starts after him.*] Come back here, you— [*The door slams. She stops in the doorway, staring, her fists clenched. After a pause she turns slowly.*]

HORACE [*Very quietly*]: It's a great day when you and Ben cross swords. I've been waiting for it for years.

ALEXANDRA: Papa, Papa, please go back! You will—

HORACE: And so they don't need you, and so you will not have your millions, after all.

REGINA [*Turns slowly*]: You hate to see anybody live now, don't you? You hate to think that I'm going to be alive and have what I want.

HORACE: I should have known you'd think that was the reason.

REGINA: Because you're going to die and you know you're going to die.

ALEXANDRA [*Shrilly*]: Mama! Don't— Don't listen, Papa. Just don't listen. Go away—

HORACE: Not to keep you from getting what you want. Not even partly that. [*Holding to the rail.*] I'm sick of you, sick of this house, sick of my life here. I'm sick of your brothers and their dirty tricks to make a dime. There must be better ways of getting rich than cheating niggers on a pound of bacon. Why should I give you the money? [*Very angrily.*] To pound the bones of this town to make dividends for you to spend? You wreck the town, you and your brothers, *you* wreck the town and live on it. Not me. Maybe it's easy for the dying to be honest. But it's not my fault I'm dying. [ADDIE *enters, stands at door quietly.*] I'll do no more harm now. I've done enough. I'll die my own way. And I'll do it without making the world any worse. I leave that to you.

REGINA [*Looks up at him slowly, calmly*]: I hope you die. I hope you die soon. [*Smiles.*] I'll be waiting for you to die.

ALEXANDRA [*Shrieking*]: Papa! Don't— Don't listen— Don't—

ADDIE: Come here, Zan. Come out of this room.

[ALEXANDRA *runs quickly to* ADDIE, *who holds her.* HORACE *turns slowly and starts upstairs.*]

Curtain

ACT THREE

SCENE—*Same as Act One. Two weeks later. It is late afternoon and it is raining.*

AT RISE: HORACE *is sitting near the window in a wheel chair. On the table next to him is a safe-deposit box, and a small bottle of medicine.* BIRDIE *and* ALEXANDRA *are playing the piano. On a chair is a large sewing basket.*

BIRDIE [*Counting for* ALEXANDRA]: One and two and three and four. One and two and three and four. [*Nods—turns to* HORACE.] We once played together, Horace. Remember?

HORACE [*Has been looking out of the window*]: What, Birdie?

BIRDIE: We played together. You and me.

ALEXANDRA: Papa used to play?

BIRDIE: Indeed he did. [ADDIE *appears at the door in a large kitchen apron. She is wiping her hands on a towel.*] He played the fiddle and very well, too.

ALEXANDRA [*Turns to smile at* HORACE]: I never knew—

ADDIE: Where's your mama?

ALEXANDRA: Gone to Miss Safronia's to fit her dresses.

[ADDIE *nods, starts to exit.*]

HORACE: Addie.

ADDIE: Yes, Mr. Horace.

HORACE [*Speaks as if he had made a sudden decision*]: Tell Cal to get on his things. I want him to go an errand.

[ADDIE *nods, exits.* HORACE *moves nervously in his chair, looks out of the window.*]

ALEXANDRA [*Who has been watching him*]: It's too bad it's been raining all day, Papa. But you can go out in the yard tomorrow. Don't be restless.

HORACE: I'm not restless, darling.

BIRDIE: I remember so well the time we played together, your papa and me. It was the first time Oscar brought me here to supper. I had never seen all the Hubbards together before, and you know what a ninny I am and how shy. [*Turns to look at* HORACE.] You said you could play the fiddle and you'd be much obliged if I'd play with you. *I* was obliged to *you*, all right, all right. [*Laughs when he does not answer her.*] Horace, you haven't heard a word I've said.

HORACE: Birdie, when did Oscar get back from Chicago?

BIRDIE: Yesterday. Hasn't he been here yet?

ALEXANDRA [*Stops playing*]: No. Neither has Uncle Ben since—since that day.

BIRDIE: Oh, I didn't know it was *that* bad. Oscar never tells me anything—

HORACE [*Smiles, nods*]: The Hubbards have had their great quarrel. I knew it would come some day. [*Laughs.*] It came.

ALEXANDRA: It came. It certainly came all right.

BIRDIE [*Amazed*]: But Oscar was in such a good humor when he got home, I didn't—

HORACE: Yes, I can understand that.

[ADDIE *enters carrying a large tray with glasses, a carafe of elderberry wine and a plate of cookies, which she puts on the table.*]

ALEXANDRA: Addie! A party! What for?

ADDIE: Nothing for. I had the fresh butter, so I made the cakes, and a little elderberry does the stomach good in the rain.

BIRDIE: Isn't this nice! A party just for us. Let's play party music, Zan.

[ALEXANDRA *begins to play a gay piece.*]

ADDIE [*To* HORACE, *wheeling his chair to center*]: Come over here, Mr. Horace, and don't be thinking so much. A glass of elderberry will do more good.

[ALEXANDRA *reaches for a cake.* BIRDIE *pours herself a glass of wine.*]

ALEXANDRA: Good cakes, Addie. It's nice here. Just us. Be nice if it could always be this way.

BIRDIE [*Nods happily*]: Quiet and restful.

ADDIE: Well, it won't be that way long. Little while now, even sitting here, you'll hear the red bricks going into place. The next day the smoke'll be pushing out the chimneys and by church time that Sunday every human born of woman will be living on chicken. That's how Mr. Ben's been telling the story.

HORACE [*Looks at her*]: They believe it that way?

ADDIE: Believe it? They use to believing what Mr. Ben orders. There ain't been so much talk around here since Sherman's army didn't come near.

HORACE [*Softly*]: They are fools.

ADDIE [*Nods, sits down with the sewing basket*]: You ain't born in the South unless you're a fool.

BIRDIE [*Has drunk another glass of wine*]: But we didn't play together after that night. Oscar said he didn't like me to play on the piano. [*Turns to* ALEXANDRA.] You know what he said that night?

ALEXANDRA: Who?

BIRDIE: Oscar. He said that music made him nervous. He said he just sat and waited for the next note. [ALEXANDRA *laughs.*] He wasn't poking fun. He meant it. Ah, well— [*She finishes her glass, shakes her head.* HORACE *looks at her, smiles.*] Your papa don't like to admit it, but he's been mighty kind to me all these years. [*Running the back of her hand along his sleeve.*] Often he'd step in when somebody said something and once— [*She stops, turns away, her face still.*] Once he stopped Oscar from— [*She stops, turns. Quickly.*] I'm sorry I said that. Why, here I am so happy and yet I think about bad things. [*Laughs nervously.*] That's not right, now, is it? [*She pours a drink.* CAL *appears in the door. He has on an old coat and is carrying a torn umbrella.*]

ALEXANDRA: Have a cake, Cal.

CAL [*Comes in, takes a cake*]: Yes'm. You want me, Mr. Horace?

HORACE: What time is it, Cal?

CAL: 'Bout ten minutes before it's five.

HORACE: All right. Now you walk yourself down to the bank.

CAL: It'll be closed. Nobody'll be there but Mr. Manders, Mr. Joe Horns, Mr. Leo—

HORACE: Go in the back way. They'll be at the table, going over the day's business. [*Points to the deposit box.*] See that box?

CAL [*Nods*]: Yes, sir.

HORACE: You tell Mr. Manders that Mr. Horace says he's much obliged to him for bringing the box, it arrived all right.

CAL [*Bewildered*]: He know you got the box. He bring it

himself Wednesday. I opened the door to him and he say, "Hello, Cal, coming on to summer weather."

HORACE: You say just what I tell you. Understand?

[BIRDIE *pours another drink, stands at table.*]

CAL: No, sir. I ain't going to say I understand. I'm going down and tell a man he give you something he already know he give you, and you say "understand."

HORACE: Now, Cal.

CAL: Yes, sir. I just going to say you obliged for the box coming all right. I ain't going to understand it, but I'm going to say it.

HORACE: And tell him I want him to come over here after supper, and to bring Mr. Sol Fowler with him.

CAL [*Nods*]: He's to come after supper and bring Mr. Sol Fowler, your attorney-*at*-law, with him.

HORACE [*Smiles*]: That's right. Just walk right in the back room and say your piece. [*Slowly.*] In front of everybody.

CAL: Yes, sir. [*Mumbles to himself as he exits.*]

ALEXANDRA [*Who has been watching* HORACE]: Is anything the matter, Papa?

HORACE: Oh, no. Nothing.

ADDIE: Miss Birdie, that elderberry going to give you a headache spell.

BIRDIE [*Beginning to be drunk. Gaily*]: Oh, I don't think so. I don't think it will.

ALEXANDRA [*As* HORACE *puts his hand to his throat*]: Do you want your medicine, Papa?

HORACE: No, no. I'm all right, darling.

BIRDIE: Mama used to give me elderberry wine when I was a little girl. For hiccoughs. [*Laughs.*] You know, I don't think people get hiccoughs any more. Isn't that funny? [BIRDIE *laughs.* HORACE *and* ALEXANDRA *laugh.*] I used to get hiccoughs just when I shouldn't have.

ADDIE [*Nods*]: And nobody gets growing pains no more. That is funny. Just as if there was some style in what you get. One year an ailment's stylish and the next year it ain't.

BIRDIE [*Turns*]: I remember. It was my first big party, at Lionnet I mean, and I was so excited, and there I was with hiccoughs and Mama laughing. [*Softly. Looking at carafe.*] Mama always laughed. [*Picks up carafe.*] A big party, a lovely dress from Mr. Worth in Paris, France, and hiccoughs. [*Pours drink.*] My brother pounding me on the back and Mama with the elderberry bottle, laughing at me. Everybody was on their way to come, and I was such a ninny, hiccoughing away. [*Drinks.*] You know, that was the first day I ever saw Oscar Hubbard. The Ballongs were selling their horses and he was going there to buy. He passed and lifted his hat—we could see him from the window—and my brother, to tease Mama, said maybe we should have invited the Hubbards to the party. He said Mama didn't like them because they kept a store, and he said that was old-fashioned of her. [*Her face lights up.*] And then, and *then,* I saw Mama angry for the first time in my life. She said that wasn't the reason. She said she was old-fashioned, but not that way. She said she was old-fashioned enough not to like people who killed animals they couldn't use, and who made their money charging awful interest to poor, ignorant niggers and cheating them on what they bought. She was very angry, Mama was. I had never seen her face like that. And then suddenly she laughed and said, "Look, I've frightened Birdie out of the hiccoughs." [*Her head drops. Then softly.*] And so she had. They were all gone. [*Moves to sofa, sits.*]

ADDIE: Yeah, they got mighty well off cheating niggers. Well, there are people who eat the earth and eat all the people on it like in the Bible with the locusts. Then there are people who stand around and watch them eat it. [*Softly.*] Sometimes I think it ain't right to stand and watch them do it.

BIRDIE [*Thoughtfully*]: Like I say, if we could only go back to Lionnet. Everybody'd be better there. They'd be good and kind. I like people to be kind. [*Pours drink.*] Don't you, Horace; don't you like people to be kind?

HORACE: Yes, Birdie.

BIRDIE [*Very drunk now*]: Yes, that was the first day I ever saw Oscar. Who would have thought— [*Quickly.*] You all want to know something? Well, I don't like Leo. My very own son, and I don't like him. [*Laughs, gaily.*] My, I guess I even like Oscar more.

ALEXANDRA: Why did you marry Uncle Oscar?

ADDIE [*Sharply*]: That's no question for you to be asking.

HORACE [*Sharply*]: Why not? She's heard enough around here to ask anything.

ALEXANDRA: Aunt Birdie, why did you marry Uncle Oscar?

BIRDIE: I don't know. I thought I liked him. He was kind to me and I thought it was because he liked me too. But that wasn't the reason— [*Wheels on* ALEXANDRA.] Ask why *he* married *me*. I can tell you that: He's told it to me often enough.

ADDIE [*Leaning forward*]: Miss Birdie, don't—

BIRDIE [*Speaking very rapidly, tensely*]: My family was good and the cotton on Lionnet's fields was better. Ben Hubbard wanted the cotton and [*Rises.*] Oscar Hubbard married it for him. He was kind to me, then. He used to smile at me. He hasn't smiled at me since. Everybody knew that's what he married me for. [ADDIE *rises.*] Everybody but me. Stupid, stupid me.

ALEXANDRA [*To* HORACE, *holding his hand, softly*]: I see. [*Hesitates.*] Papa, I mean—when you feel better couldn't we go away? I mean, by ourselves. Couldn't we find a way to go—

HORACE: Yes, I know what you mean. We'll try to find a way. I promise you, darling.

ADDIE [*Moves to* BIRDIE]: Rest a bit, Miss Birdie. You get talking like this you'll get a headache and—

BIRDIE [*Sharply, turning to her*]: I've never had a headache in my life. [*Begins to cry hysterically.*] You know it as well as I do. [*Turns to* ALEXANDRA.] I never had a headache, Zan. That's a lie they tell for me. I drink. All by myself, in my own room, by myself, I drink. Then, when they want to hide it, they say, "Birdie's got a headache again"—

ALEXANDRA [*Comes to her quickly*]: Aunt Birdie.

BIRDIE [*Turning away*]: Even you won't like me now. You won't like me any more.

ALEXANDRA: I love you. I'll always love you.

BIRDIE [*Furiously*]: Well, don't. Don't love me. Because in twenty years you'll just be like me. They'll do all the same things to you. [*Begins to laugh hysterically.*] You know what? In twenty-two years I haven't had a whole day of happiness. Oh, a little, like today with you all. But never a single, whole day. I say to myself, if only I had one more *whole* day, then— [*The laugh stops.*] And that's the way you'll be. And you'll trail after them, just like me, hoping they won't be so mean that day or say something to make you feel so bad—only you'll be worse off because you haven't got my Mama to remember— [*Turns away, her head drops. She stands quietly, swaying a little, holding onto the sofa.* ALEXANDRA *leans down, puts her cheek on* BIRDIE'S *arm.*]

ALEXANDRA [*To* BIRDIE]: I guess we were all trying to make a happy day. You know, we sit around and try to pretend nothing's happened. We try to pretend we are not here. We make believe we are just by ourselves, some place else, and it doesn't seem to work. [*Kisses* BIRDIE'S *hand.*] Come now, Aunt Birdie, I'll walk you home. You and me. [*She takes* BIRDIE'S *arm. They move slowly out.*]

BIRDIE [*Softly as they exit*]: You and me.

ADDIE [*After a minute*]: Well. First time I ever heard Miss Birdie say a word. [HORACE *looks at her.*] Maybe it's good for her. I'm just sorry Zan had to hear it. [HORACE *moves his head as if he were uncomfortable.*] You feel bad, don't you? [*He shrugs.*]

HORACE: So you didn't want Zan to hear? It would be nice to let her stay innocent, like Birdie at her age. Let her listen now. Let her see everything. How else is she going to know that she's got to get away? I'm trying to show her that, I'm trying, but I've only got a little time left. She can even hate me when I'm dead, if she'll only learn to hate and fear this.

ADDIE: Mr. Horace—

HORACE: Pretty soon there'll be nobody to help her but you.

ADDIE [*Crossing to him*]: What can I do?

HORACE: Take her away.

ADDIE: How can I do that? Do you think they'd let me just go away with her?

HORACE: I'll fix it so they can't stop you when you're ready to go. You'll go, Addie?

ADDIE [*After a second, softly*]: Yes, sir. I promise. [*He touches her arm, nods.*]

HORACE [*Quietly*]: I'm going to have Sol Fowler make me a new will. They'll make trouble, but you make Zan stand firm and Fowler'll do the rest. Addie, I'd like to leave you something for yourself. I always wanted to.

ADDIE [*Laughs*]: Don't you do that, Mr. Horace. A nigger woman in a white man's will! I'd never get it nohow.

HORACE: I know. But upstairs in the armoire drawer there's seventeen hundred dollar bills. It's money left from my trip. It's in an envelope with your name. It's for you.

ADDIE: Seventeen hundred dollar bills! My God, Mr. Horace, I won't know how to count up that high. [*Shyly.*] It's mighty kind and good of you. I don't know what to say for thanks—

CAL [*Appears in doorway*]: I'm back. [*No answer.*] I'm back.

ADDIE: So we see.

HORACE: Well?

CAL: Nothing. I just went down and spoke my piece. Just like you told me. I say, "Mr. Horace he thank you mightily for the safe box arriving in good shape and he say you come right after supper to his house and bring Mr. Attorney-at-law Sol Fowler with you." Then I wipe my hands on my coat. Every time I ever told a lie in my whole life, I wipe my hands right after. Can't help doing it. Well, while I'm wiping my hands, Mr. Leo jump up and say to me, "What box? What you talking about?"

HORACE [*Smiles*]: Did he?

CAL: And Mr. Leo say he got to leave a little early cause he got something to do. And then Mr. Manders say Mr. Leo should sit right down and finish up his work and stop acting like somebody made him Mr. President. So he sit down. Now, just like I told you, Mr. Manders was mighty surprised with the message because he knows right well he brought the box— [*Points to box, sighs.*] But he took it all right. Some men take everything easy and some do not.

HORACE [*Puts his head back, laughs*]: Mr. Leo was telling the truth; he *has* got something to do. I hope Manders don't keep him too long. [*Outside there is the sound of voices.* CAL *exits.* ADDIE *crosses quickly to* HORACE, *puts basket on table, begins to wheel his chair towards the stairs. Sharply.*] No. Leave me where I am.

ADDIE: But that's Miss Regina coming back.

HORACE [*Nods, looking at door*]: Go away, Addie.

ADDIE [*Hesitates*]: Mr. Horace. Don't talk no more today. You don't feel well and it won't do no good—

HORACE [*As he hears footsteps in the hall*]: Go on. [*She looks at him for a second, then picks up her sewing from table and exits as* REGINA *comes in from hall.* HORACE'S *chair is now so placed that he is in front of the table with the medicine.* REGINA *stands in the hall, shakes umbrella, stands it in the corner, takes off her cloak and throws it over the banister. She stares at* HORACE.]

REGINA [*As she takes off her gloves*]: We had agreed that you were to stay in your part of this house and I in mine. This room is *my* part of the house. Please don't come down here again.

HORACE: I won't.

REGINA [*Crosses towards bell-cord*]: I'll get Cal to take you upstairs.

HORACE [*Smiles*]: Before you do I want to tell you that after all, we have invested our money in Hubbard Sons and Marshall, Cotton Manufacturers.

REGINA [*Stops, turns, stares at him*]: What are you talking about? You haven't seen Ben— When did you change your mind?

HORACE: I didn't change my mind. *I* didn't invest the money. [*Smiles.*] It was invested for me.

REGINA [*Angrily*]: What—?

HORACE: I had eighty-eight thousand dollars' worth of Union Pacific bonds in that safe-deposit box. They are not there now. Go and look. [*As she stares at him, he points to the box.*] Go and look, Regina. [*She crosses quickly to the box, opens it.*] Those bonds are as negotiable as money.

REGINA [*Turns back to him*]: What kind of joke are you playing now? Is this for my benefit?

HORACE: I don't look in that box very often, but three days ago, on Wednesday it was, because I had made a decision—

REGINA: I want to know what you are talking about.

HORACE [*Sharply*]: Don't interrupt me again. Because I had made a decision, I sent for the box. The bonds were gone. Eighty-eight thousand dollars gone. [*He smiles at her.*]

REGINA [*After a moment's silence, quietly*]: Do you think I'm crazy enough to believe what you're saying?

HORACE [*Shrugs*]: Believe anything you like.

REGINA [*Stares at him, slowly*]: Where did they go to?

HORACE: They are in Chicago. With Mr. Marshall, I should guess.

REGINA: What did they do? Walk to Chicago? Have you really gone crazy?

HORACE: Leo took the bonds.

REGINA [*Turns sharply then speaks softly, without conviction*]: I don't believe it.

HORACE [*Leans forward*]: I wasn't there but I can guess what happened. This fine gentleman, to whom you were willing to marry your daughter, took the keys and opened the box. You remember that the day of the fight Oscar went to Chicago? Well, he went with my bonds that his son Leo had stolen for him. [*Pleasantly.*] And for Ben, of course, too.

REGINA [*Slowly, nods*]: When did you find out the bonds were gone?

HORACE: Wednesday night.

REGINA: I thought that's what you said. Why have you waited three days to do anything? [*Suddenly laughs.*] This *will* make a fine story.

HORACE [*Nods*]: Couldn't it?

REGINA [*Still laughing*]: A fine story to hold over their heads. How could they be such fools? [*Turns to him.*]

HORACE: But I'm not going to hold it over their heads.

REGINA [*The laugh stops*]: What?

HORACE [*Turns his chair to face her*]: I'm going to let them keep the bonds—as a loan from you. An eighty-eight-thousand-dollar loan; they should be grateful to you. They will be, I think.

REGINA [*Slowly, smiles*]: I see. You are punishing me. But I won't let you punish me. If you won't do anything, I will. Now. [*She starts for door.*]

HORACE: You won't do anything. Because you can't. [REGINA *stops.*] It won't do you any good to make trouble because I shall simply say that I lent them the bonds.

REGINA [*Slowly*]: You would do that?

HORACE: Yes. For once in your life I am tying your hands. There is nothing for you to do. [*There is silence. Then she sits down.*]

REGINA: I see. You are going to lend them the bonds and let them keep all the profit they make on them, and there is nothing I can do about it. Is that right?

HORACE: Yes.

REGINA [*Softly*]: Why did you say that I was making this gift?

HORACE: I was coming to that. I am going to make a new will, Regina, leaving you eighty-eight thousand dollars in Union Pacific bonds. The rest will go to Zan. It's true that your brothers have borrowed your share for a little while. After my death I advise you to talk to Ben and Oscar. They won't admit anything and Ben, I think, will be smart enough to see that he's safe. Because I knew about the theft and said nothing. Nor will I say anything as long as I live. Is that clear to you?

REGINA [*Nods, softly, without looking at him*]: You will not say anything as long as you live.

HORACE: That's right. And by that time they will probably have replaced your bonds, and then they'll belong to you and nobody but us will ever know what happened. [*Stops, smiles.*] They'll be around any minute to see what I am going to do. I took good care to see that word reached Leo. They'll be mighty relieved to know I'm going to do nothing and Ben will thing it all a capital joke on you. And that will be the end of that. There's nothing you can do to them, nothing you can do to me.

REGINA: You hate me very much.

HORACE: No.

REGINA: Oh, I think you do. [*Puts her head back, sighs.*] Well, we haven't been very good together. Anyway, I don't hate you either. I have only contempt for you. I've always had.

HORACE: From the very first?

REGINA: I think so.

HORACE: I was in love with *you*. But why did *you* marry *me*?

REGINA: I was lonely when I was young.

HORACE: *You* were lonely?

REGINA: Not the way people usually mean. Lonely for all the things I wasn't going to get. Everybody in this house was so busy and there was so little place for what I wanted. I wanted the world. Then, and then— [*Smiles.*] Papa died and left the money to Ben and Oscar.

HORACE: And you married me?

REGINA: Yes, I thought— But I was wrong. You were a small-town clerk then. You haven't changed.

HORACE [*Nods, smiles*]: And that wasn't what you wanted.

REGINA: No. No, it wasn't what I wanted. [*Pauses, leans back, pleasantly.*] It took me a little while to find out I had made a mistake. As for you—I don't know. It was almost as if I couldn't stand the kind of man you were— [*Smiles, softly.*] I used to lie there at night, praying you wouldn't come near—

HORACE: Really? It was as bad as that?

REGINA [*Nods*]: Remember when I went to Doctor Sloan and I told you he said there was something the matter with me and that you shouldn't touch me any more?

HORACE: I remember.

REGINA: But you believed it. I couldn't understand that. I couldn't understand that anybody could be such a soft fool. That was when I began to despise you.

HORACE [*Puts his hand to his throat, looks at the bottle of medicine on table*]: Why didn't you leave me?

REGINA: I told you I married you for something. It turned out it was only for this. [*Carefully.*] This wasn't what I wanted, but it was something. I never thought about it much but if I had [HORACE *puts his hand to his throat.*] I'd have known that you would die before I would. But I couldn't have known that you would get heart trouble so early and so bad. I'm lucky, Horace. I've always been lucky. [HORACE *turns slowly to the medicine.*] I'll be lucky again. [HORACE *looks at her. Then he puts his hand to his throat. Because he cannot reach the bottle he moves the chair closer. He reaches for the medicine, takes out the cork, picks up the spoon. The bottle slips and smashes on the table. He draws in his breath, gasps.*]

HORACE: Please. Tell Addie— The other bottle is upstairs. [REGINA *has not moved. She does not move now. He stares at her. Then, suddenly as if he understood, he raises his voice. It is a panic-stricken whisper, too small to be heard outside the room.*] Addie! Addie! Come— [*Stops as he hears the softness of his voice. He makes a sudden, furious spring from the chair to the stairs, taking the first few steps as if he were a desperate runner. On the fourth step he slips, gasps, grasps the rail, makes a great effort to reach the landing. When he reaches the landing, he is on his knees. His knees give way, he falls on the landing, out of view.* REGINA *has not turned during his climb up the stairs. Now she waits a second. Then she goes below the landing, speaks up.*]

REGINA: Horace. Horace. [*When there is no answer, she turns, calls.*] Addie! Cal! Come in here. [*She starts up the steps.* ADDIE *and* CAL *appear. Both run towards the stairs.*] He's had an attack. Come up here. [*They run up the steps quickly.*]

CAL: My God. Mr. Horace—

[*They cannot be seen now.*]

REGINA [*Her voice comes from the head of the stairs*]: Be still, Cal. Bring him in here.

[*Before the footsteps and the voices have completely died away,* ALEXANDRA *appears in the hall door, in her raincloak and hood. She comes into the room, begins to unfasten the cloak, suddenly looks around, sees the empty wheel chair, stares, begins to move swiftly as if to look in the dining room. At the same moment* ADDIE *runs down the stairs.* ALEXANDRA *turns and stares up at* ADDIE.]

ALEXANDRA: Addie! What?

ADDIE [*Takes* ALEXANDRA *by the shoulders*]: I'm going for the doctor. Go upstairs. [ALEXANDRA *looks at her, then quickly breaks away and runs up the steps.* ADDIE *exits. The stage is empty for a minute. Then the front doorbell begins to ring. When there is no answer, it rings again. A second later* LEO *appears in the hall, talking as he comes in.*]

LEO [*Very nervous*]: Hello. [*Irritably.*] Never saw any use ringing a bell when a door was open. If you are going to ring a bell, then somebody should answer it. [*Gets in the room, looks around, puzzled, listens, hears no sound.*] Aunt Regina. [*He moves around restlessly.*] Addie. [*Waits.*] Where the hell— [*Crosses to the bell cord, rings it impatiently, waits, gets no answer, calls.*] Cal! Cal! [CAL *appears on the stair landing.*]

CAL [*His voice is soft, shaken*]: Mr. Leo. Miss Regina says you stop that screaming noise.

LEO [*Angrily*]: Where is everybody?

CAL: Mr. Horace he got an attack. He's bad. Miss Regina says you stop that noise.

LEO: Uncle Horace— What— What happened? [CAL *starts down the stairs, shakes his head, begins to move swiftly off.* LEO *looks around wildly.*] But when— You seen Mr. Oscar or Mr. Ben? [CAL *shakes his head. Moves on.* LEO *grabs him by the arm.*] Answer me, will you?

CAL: No, I ain't seen 'em. I ain't got time to answer you. I got to get things. [CAL *runs off.*]

LEO: But what's the matter with him? When did this happen— [*Calling after* CAL.] You'd think Papa'd be some place where you could find him. I been chasing him all afternoon.

[OSCAR *and* BEN *come into the room, talking excitedly.*]

OSCAR: I hope it's not a bad attack.

BEN: It's the first one he's had since he came home.

LEO: Papa, I've been looking all over town for you and Uncle Ben—

BEN: Where is he?

OSCAR: Addie said it was sudden.

BEN [*To* LEO]: Where is he? When did it happen?

LEO: Upstairs. Will you listen to me, please? I been looking for you for—

OSCAR [*To* BEN]: You think we should go up? [BEN, *looking up the steps, shakes his head.*]

BEN: I don't know. I don't know.

OSCAR [*Shakes his head*]: But he was all right—

LEO [*Yelling*]: *Will you listen to me?*

OSCAR [*Sharply*]: What is the matter with you?

LEO: I been trying to tell you. I been trying to find you for an hour—

OSCAR: Tell me what?

LEO: Uncle Horace knows about the bonds. He knows about them. He's had the box since Wednesday—

BEN [*Sharply*]: Stop shouting! What the hell are you talking about?

LEO [*Furiously*]: I'm telling you he knows about the bonds. Ain't that clear enough—

OSCAR [*Grabbing* LEO'S *arm*]: You God-damn fool! Stop screaming!

BEN: Now what happened? Talk quietly.

LEO: You heard me. Uncle Horace knows about the bonds. He's known since Wednesday.

BEN [*After a second*]: How do you know that?

LEO: Because Cal comes down to Manders and says the box came O.K. and—

OSCAR [*Trembling*]: That might not mean a thing—

LEO [*Angrily*]: No? It might not, huh? Then he says Manders should come here tonight and bring Sol Fowler with him. I guess that don't mean a thing either.

OSCAR [*To* BEN]: Ben— What— Do you think he's seen the—

BEN [*Motions to the box*]: There's the box. [*Both* OSCAR *and* LEO *turn sharply.* LEO *makes a leap to the box.*] You ass. Put it down. What are you going to do with it, eat it?

LEO: I'm going to— [*Starts.*]

BEN [*Furiously*]: Put it down. Don't touch it again. Now sit down and shut up for a minute.

OSCAR: Since Wednesday. [*To* LEO.] You said he had it since Wednesday. Why didn't he say something— [*To* BEN.] I don't understand—

LEO [*Taking a step*]: I can put it back. I can put it back before anybody knows.

BEN [*Who is standing at the table, softly*]: He's had it since Wednesday. Yet he hasn't said a word to us.

OSCAR: *Why? Why?*

LEO: What's the difference why? He was getting ready to say plenty. He was going to say it to Fowler tonight—

OSCAR [*Angrily*]: Be still. [*Turns to* BEN, *looks at him, waits.*]

BEN [*After a minute*]: I don't believe that.

LEO [*Wildly*]: *You* don't believe it? What do I care what *you* believe? I do the dirty work and then—

BEN [*Turning his head sharply to* LEO]: I'm remembering that. I'm remembering that, Leo.

OSCAR: What do you mean?

LEO: You—

BEN [*To* OSCAR]: If you don't shut that little fool up, I'll show you what I mean. For some reason he knows, but he don't say a word.

OSCAR: Maybe he didn't know that *we*—

BEN [*Quickly*]: That *Leo*— He's no fool. Does Manders know the bonds are missing?

LEO: How could I tell? I was half crazy. I don't think so. Because Manders seemed kind of puzzled and—

OSCAR: But we got to find out— [*He breaks off as* CAL *comes into the room carrying a kettle of hot water.*]

BEN: How is he, Cal?

CAL: I don't know, Mr. Ben. He was bad. [*Going towards stairs.*]

OSCAR: But when did it happen?

CAL [*Shrugs*]: He wasn't feeling bad early. [ADDIE *comes in quickly from the hall.*] Then there he is next thing on the landing, fallen over, his eyes tight—

ADDIE [*To* CAL]: Dr. Sloan's over at the Ballongs. Hitch the buggy and go get him. [*She takes the kettle and cloths from him, pushes him, runs up the stairs.*] Go on. [*She disappears. *CAL *exits.*]

BEN: Never seen Sloan anywhere when you need him.

OSCAR [*Softly*]: Sounds bad.

LEO: He would have told *her* about it. Aunt Regina. He would have told his own wife—

BEN [*Turning to* LEO]: Yes, he might have told her. But they weren't on such pretty terms and maybe he didn't. Maybe he didn't. [*Goes quickly to* LEO.] Now, listen to me. If she doesn't know, it may work out all right. If she does know, you're to say he lent you the bonds.

LEO: Lent them to me! Who's going to believe that?

BEN: Nobody.

OSCAR [*To* LEO]: Don't you understand? It can't do no harm to say it—

LEO: Why should I say he lent them to me? Why not to you? [*Carefully.*] Why not to Uncle Ben?

BEN [*Smiles*]: Just because he didn't lend them to me. Remember that.

LEO: But all he has to do is say he didn't lend them to me—

BEN [*Furiously*]: But for some reason, he doesn't seem to be talking, does he?

[*There are footsteps above. They all stand looking at the stairs.* REGINA *begins to come slowly down.*]

BEN: What happened?

REGINA: He's had a bad attack.

OSCAR: Too bad. I'm so sorry we weren't here when—when Horace needed us.

BEN: When *you* needed us.

REGINA [*Looks at him*]: Yes.

BEN: How is he? Can we—can we go up?

REGINA [*Shakes her head*]: He's not conscious.

OSCAR [*Pacing around*]: It's that—it's that bad? Wouldn't you think Sloan could be found quickly, just once, just once?

REGINA: I don't think there is much for him to do.

BEN: Oh, don't talk like that. He's come through attacks before. He will now.

[REGINA *sits down. After a second she speaks softly.*]

REGINA: Well. We haven't seen each other since the day of our fight.

BEN [*Tenderly*]: That was nothing. Why, you and Oscar and I used to fight when we were kids.

OSCAR [*Hurriedly*]: Don't you think we should go up? Is there anything we can do for Horace—

BEN: You don't feel well. Ah—

REGINA [*Without looking at them*]: No, I don't. [*Slight pause.*] Horace told me about the bonds this afternoon. [*There is an immediate shocked silence.*]

LEO: The bonds. What do you mean? What bonds? What—

BEN [*Looks at him furiously. Then to* REGINA]: The Union Pacific bonds? *Horace's* Union Pacific bonds?

REGINA: Yes.

OSCAR [*Steps to her, very nervously*]: Well. Well what— what about them? What—what could he say?

REGINA: He said that Leo had stolen the bonds and given them to you.

OSCAR [*Aghast, very loudly*]: That's ridiculous, Regina, absolutely—

LEO: I don't know what you're talking about. What would I— Why—

REGINA [*Wearily to* BEN]: Isn't it enough that he stole them from me? Do I have to listen to this in the bargain?

OSCAR: You are talking—

LEO: I didn't steal anything. I don't know why—

REGINA [*To* BEN]: Would you ask them to stop that, please? [*There is silence for a minute.* BEN *glowers at* OSCAR *and* LEO.]

BEN: Aren't we starting at the wrong end, Regina? What did Horace tell you?

REGINA [*Smiles at him*]: He told me that Leo had stolen the bonds.

LEO: I didn't steal—

REGINA: Please. Let me finish. Then he told me that he was going to pretend that he had lent them to you [LEO *turns sharply to* REGINA, *then looks at* OSCAR, *then looks back at*

REGINA.] as a present from me—to my brothers. He said there was nothing I could do about it. He said the rest of his money would go to Alexandra. That is all. [*There is a silence.* OSCAR *coughs,* LEO *smiles slyly.*]

LEO [*Taking a step to her*]: I told you he had lent them— I could have told you—

REGINA [*Ignores him, smiles sadly at* BEN]: So I'm very badly off, you see. [*Carefully.*] But Horace said there was nothing I could do about it as long as he was alive to say he had lent you the bonds.

BEN: You shouldn't feel that way. It can all be explained, all be adjusted. It isn't as bad—

REGINA: So you, at least, are willing to admit that the bonds were stolen?

BEN [OSCAR *laughs nervously*]: I admit no such thing. It's possible that Horace made up that part of the story to tease you— [*Looks at her.*] Or perhaps to punish you. Punish you.

REGINA [*Sadly*]: It's not a pleasant story. I feel bad, Ben, naturally. I hadn't thought—

BEN: Now you shall have the bonds safely back. That was the understanding, wasn't it, Oscar?

OSCAR: Yes.

REGINA: I'm glad to know that. [*Smiles.*] Ah, I had greater hopes—

BEN: Don't talk that way. That's foolish. [*Looks at his watch.*] I think we ought to drive out for Sloan ourselves. If we can't find him we'll go over to Senateville for Doctor Morris. And don't think I'm dismissing this other business. I'm not. We'll have it all out on a more appropriate day.

REGINA [*Looks up, quietly*]: I don't think you had better go yet. I think you had better stay and sit down.

BEN: We'll be back with Sloan.

REGINA: Cal has gone for him. I don't want you to go.

BEN: Now don't worry and—

REGINA: You will come back in this room and sit down. I have something more to say.

BEN [*Turns, comes towards her*]: Since when do I take orders from you?

REGINA [*Smiles*]: You don't—yet. [*Sharply.*] Come back, Oscar. You too, Leo.

OSCAR [*Sure of himself, laughs*]: My dear Regina—

BEN [*Softly, pats her hand*]: Horace has already clipped your wings and very wittily. Do I have to clip them, too? [*Smiles at her.*] You'd get farther with a smile, Regina. I'm a soft man for a woman's smile.

REGINA: I'm smiling, Ben. I'm smiling because you are quite safe while Horace lives. But I don't think Horace will live. And if he doesn't live I shall want seventy-five per cent in exchange for the bonds.

BEN [*Steps back, whistles, laughs*]: Greedy! What a greedy girl you are! You want so much of everything.

REGINA: Yes. And if I don't get what I want I am going to put all three of you in jail.

OSCAR [*Furiously*]: You're mighty crazy. Havihg just admitted—

BEN: And on what evidence would you put Oscar and Leo in jail?

REGINA [*Laughs, gaily*]: Oscar, listen to him. He's getting ready to swear that it was you and Leo! What do you say to that? [OSCAR *turns furiously towards* BEN.] Oh, don't be angry, Oscar. I'm going to see that he goes in with you.

BEN: Try anything you like, Regina. [*Sharply.*] And now we can stop all this and say good-bye to you. [ALEXANDRA *comes slowly down the steps.*] It's his money and he's obviously willing to let us borrow it. [*More pleasantly.*] Learn to make threats when you can carry them through. For how many years have I told you a good-looking woman gets more by being soft and appealing? Mama used to tell you that. [*Looks at his watch.*] Where the hell is Sloan? [*To* OSCAR.] Take the buggy and— [*As* BEN *turns to* OSCAR, *he sees* ALEXANDRA. *She walks stiffly. She goes slowly to the lower window, her head bent. They all turn to look at her.*]

OSCAR [*After a second, moving toward her*]: What? Alexandra— [*She does not answer. After a second,* ADDIE *comes slowly down the stairs, moving as if she were very tired. At foot of steps, she looks at* ALEXANDRA, *then turns and slowly crosses to door and exits.* REGINA *rises.* BEN *looks nervously at* ALEXANDRA, *at* REGINA.]

OSCAR [*As* ADDIE *passes him, irritably to* ALEXANDRA]: Well,

what is— [*Turns into room—sees* ADDIE *at foot of steps.*]
—what's? [BEN *puts up a hand, shakes his head.*] My God, I
didn't know—who *could* have known—I didn't know he was
that sick. Well, well—I— [REGINA *stands quietly, her back to
them.*]

BEN [*Softly, sincerely*]: Seems like yesterday when he first
came here.

OSCAR [*Sincerely, nervously*]: Yes, that's true. [*Turns to*
BEN.] The whole town loved him and respected him.

ALEXANDRA [*Turns*]: Did you love him, Uncle Oscar?

OSCAR: Certainly, I— What a strange thing to ask! I—

ALEXANDRA: Did you love him, Uncle Ben?

BEN [*Simply*]: He had—

ALEXANDRA [*Suddenly starts to laugh very loudly*]: And you,
Mama, did you love him, too?

REGINA: I know what you feel, Alexandra, but please try to
control yourself.

ALEXANDRA [*Still laughing*]: I'm trying, Mama. I'm trying
very hard.

BEN: Grief makes some people laugh and some people cry.
It's better to cry, Alexandra.

ALEXANDRA [*The laugh has stopped. Tensely moves toward*
REGINA]: What was Papa doing on the staircase?

[BEN *turns to look at* ALEXANDRA.]

REGINA: Please go and lie down, my dear. We all need time
to get over shocks like this. [ALEXANDRA *does not move.* RE-
GINA'S *voice becomes softer, more insistent.*] Please go, Alexandra.

ALEXANDRA: No, Mama. I'll wait. I've got to talk to you.

REGINA: Later. Go and rest now.

ALEXANDRA [*Quietly*]: I'll wait, Mama. I've plenty of time.

REGINA [*Hesitates, stares, makes a half shrug, turns back to*
BEN]: As I was saying. Tomorrow morning I am going up to
Judge Simmes. I shall tell him about Leo.

BEN [*Motioning toward* ALEXANDRA]: Not in front of the
child, Regina. I—

REGINA [*Turns to him. Sharply*]: I didn't ask her to stay.
Tomorrow morning I go to Judge Simmes—

OSCAR: And what proof? What proof of all this—

REGINA [*Turns sharply*]: None. I won't need any. The bonds are missing and they are with Marshall. That will be enough. If it isn't, I'll add what's necessary.

BEN: I'm sure of that.

REGINA [*Turns to* BEN]: You can be quite sure.

OSCAR: We'll deny—

REGINA: Deny your heads off. You couldn't find a jury that wouldn't weep for a woman whose brothers steal from her. And you couldn't find twelve men in this state you haven't cheated and hate you for it.

OSCAR: What kind of talk is this? You couldn't do anything like that! We're your own brothers. [*Points upstairs.*] How can you talk that way when upstairs not five minutes ago—

REGINA [*Slowly*]: There are people who can never go back, who must finish what they start. I am one of those people, Oscar. [*After a slight pause.*] Where was I? [*Smiles at* BEN.] Well, they'll convict you. But I won't care much if they don't. [*Leans forward, pleasantly.*] Because by that time you'll be ruined. I shall also tell my story to Mr. Marshall, who likes me, I think, and who will not want to be involved in your scandal. A respectable firm like Marshall and Company. The deal would be off in an hour. [*Turns to them angrily.*] And you know it. Now I don't want to hear any more from any of you. *You'll do no more bargaining in this house.* I'll take my seventy-five per cent and we'll forget the story forever. That's one way of doing it, and the way I prefer. You know me well enough to know that I don't mind taking the other way.

BEN [*After a second, slowly*]: None of us have ever known you well enough, Regina.

REGINA: You're getting old, Ben. Your tricks aren't as smart as they used to be. [*There is no answer. She waits, then smiles.*] All right. I take it that's settled and I get what I asked for.

OSCAR [*Furiously to* BEN]: Are you going to let her do this—

BEN [*Turns to look at him, slowly*]: You have a suggestion?

REGINA [*Puts her arms above her head, stretches, laughs*]: No, he hasn't. All right. Now, Leo, I have forgotten that you ever saw the bonds. [*Archly, to* BEN *and* OSCAR.] And as long as you boys both behave yourselves, I've forgotten that we ever talked about them. You can draw up the necessary papers to-morrow. [BEN *laughs.* LEO *stares at him, starts for door. Exits.*

OSCAR *moves towards door angrily.* REGINA *looks at* BEN, *nods, laughs with him. For a second,* OSCAR *stands in the door, looking back at them. Then he exits.*]

REGINA: You're a good loser, Ben. I like that.

BEN [*He picks up his coat, then turns to her*]: Well, I say to myself, what's the good? You and I aren't like Oscar. We're not sour people. I think that comes from a good digestion. Then, too, one loses today and wins tomorrow. I say to myself, years of planning and I get what I want. Then I don't get it. But I'm not discouraged. The century's turning, the world is open. Open for people like you and me. Ready for us, waiting for us. After all this is just the beginning. There are hundreds of Hubbards sitting in rooms like this throughout the country. All their names aren't Hubbard, but they are all Hubbards and they will own this country some day. We'll get along.

REGINA [*Smiles*]: I think so.

BEN: Then, too, I say to myself, things may change. [*Looks at* ALEXANDRA.] I agree with Alexandra. What is a man in a wheel chair doing on a staircase? I ask myself that.

REGINA [*Looks up at him*]: And what do you answer?

BEN: I have no answer. But maybe some day I will. Maybe never, but maybe some day. [*Smiles. Pats her arm.*] When I do, I'll let you know. [*Goes towards hall.*]

REGINA: When you do, write me. I will be in Chicago. [*Gaily.*] Ah, Ben, if Papa had only left me his money.

BEN: I'll see you tomorrow.

REGINA: Oh, yes. Certainly. You'll be sort of working for me now.

BEN [*As he passes* ALEXANDRA, *smiles*]: Alexandra, you're turning out to be a right interesting girl. [*Looks at* REGINA.] Well, good night all. [*He exits.*]

REGINA [*Sits quietly for a second, stretches, turns to look at* ALEXANDRA]: What do you want to talk to me about, Alexandra?

ALEXANDRA [*Slowly*]: I've changed my mind. I don't want to talk. There's nothing to talk about now.

REGINA: You're acting very strange. Not like yourself. You've had a bad shock today. I know that. And you loved Papa, but you must have expected this to come some day. You knew how sick he was.

ALEXANDRA: I knew. We all knew.

REGINA: It will be good for you to get away from here. Good for me, too. Time heals most wounds, Alexandra. You're young, you shall have all the things I wanted. I'll make the world for you the way I wanted it to be for me. [*Uncomfortably.*] Don't sit there staring. You've been around Birdie so much you're getting just like her.

ALEXANDRA [*Nods*]: Funny. That's what Aunt Birdie said today.

REGINA [*Nods*]: Be good for you to get away from all this. [ADDIE *enters.*]

ADDIE: Cal is back, Miss Regina. He says Dr. Sloan will be coming in a few minutes.

REGINA: We'll go in a few weeks. A few weeks! That means two or three Saturdays, two or three Sundays. [*Sighs.*] Well, I'm very tired. I shall go to bed. I don't want any supper. Put the lights out and lock up. [ADDIE *moves to the piano lamp, turns it out.*] You go to your room, Alexandra. Addie will bring you something hot. You look very tired. [*Rises. To* ADDIE.] Call me when Dr. Sloan gets here. I don't want to see anybody else. I don't want any condolence calls tonight. The whole town will be over.

ALEXANDRA: Mama, I'm not coming with you. I'm not going to Chicago.

REGINA [*Turns to her*]: You're very upset, Alexandra.

ALEXANDRA [*Quietly*]: I mean what I say. With all my heart.

REGINA: We'll talk about it tomorrow. The morning will make a difference.

ALEXANDRA: It won't make any difference. And there isn't anything to talk about. I am going away from you. Because I want to. Because I know Papa would want me to.

REGINA [*Puzzled, careful, polite*]: You *know* your papa wanted you to go away from me?

ALEXANDRA: Yes.

REGINA [*Softly*]: And if I say no?

ALEXANDRA [*Looks at her*]: Say it, Mama, say it. And see what happens.

REGINA [*Softly, after a pause*]: And if I make you stay?

ALEXANDRA: That would be foolish. It wouldn't work in the end.

REGINA: You're very serious about it, aren't you? [*Crosses to stairs.*] Well, you'll change your mind in a few days.

ALEXANDRA: You only change your mind when you want to. And I won't want to.

REGINA [*Going up the steps*]: Alexandra, I've come to the end of my rope. Somewhere there has to be what I want, too. Life goes too fast. Do what you want; think what you want; go where you want. I'd like to keep you with me, but I won't make you stay. Too many people used to make me do too many things. No, I won't make you stay.

ALEXANDRA: You couldn't, Mama, because I want to leave here. As I've never wanted anything in my life before. Because now I understand what Papa was trying to tell me. [*Pause.*] All in one day: Addie said there were people who ate the earth and other people who stood around and watched them do it. And just now Uncle Ben said the same thing. Really, he said the same thing. [*Tensely.*] Well, tell him for me, Mama, I'm not going to stand around and watch you do it. Tell him I'll be fighting as hard as he'll be fighting [*Rises.*] some place where people don't just stand around and watch.

REGINA: Well, you have spirit, after all. I used to think you were all sugar water. We don't have to be bad friends. I don't want us to be bad friends, Alexandra. [*Starts, stops, turns to* ALEXANDRA.] Would you like to come and talk to me, Alexandra? Would you—would you like to sleep in my room tonight?

ALEXANDRA [*Takes a step towards her*]: Are you afraid, Mama? [REGINA *does not answer. She moves slowly out of sight.* ADDIE *comes to* ALEXANDRA, *presses her arm.*]

The Curtain Falls

Tennessee Williams

THE GLASS MENAGERIE

Nobody, not even the rain, has such small hands.
E. E. CUMMINGS

THE CHARACTERS

AMANDA WINGFIELD [*the mother*]: A little woman of great but confused vitality clinging frantically to another time and place. Her characterization must be carefully created, not copied from type. She is not paranoiac, but her life is paranoia. There is much to admire in Amanda, and as much to love and pity as there is to laugh at. Certainly she has endurance and a kind of heroism, and though her foolishness makes her unwittingly cruel at times, there is tenderness in her slight person.

LAURA WINGFIELD [*her daughter*]: Amanda, having failed to establish contact with reality, continues to live vitally in her illusions, but Laura's situation is even graver. A childhood illness has left her crippled, one leg slightly shorter than the other, and held in a brace. This defect need not be more than suggested on the stage. Stemming from this, Laura's separation increases till she is like a piece of her own glass collection, too exquisitely fragile to move from the shelf.

TOM WINGFIELD [*her son*]: And the narrator of the play. A poet with a job in a warehouse. His nature is not remorseless, but to escape from a trap he has to act without pity.

JIM O'CONNOR [*the gentleman caller*]: A nice, ordinary, young man.

SCENE

AN ALLEY IN ST. LOUIS

PART I. Preparation for a Gentleman Caller.
PART II. The Gentleman calls.

Time: Now and the Past.

PRODUCTION NOTES

Being a "memory play," *The Glass Menagerie* can be presented with unusual freedom of convention. Because of its considerably delicate or tenuous material, atmospheric touches and subtleties of direction play a particularly important part. Expressionism and all other unconventional techniques in drama have only one valid aim, and that is a closer approach to truth. When a play employs unconventional techniques, it is not, or certainly shouldn't be, trying to escape its responsibility of dealing with reality, or interpreting experience, but is actually or should be attempting to find a closer approach, a more penetrating and vivid expression of things as they are. The straight realistic play with its genuine frigidaire and authentic ice-cubes, its characters that speak exactly as its audience speaks, corresponds to the academic landscape and has the same virtue of a photographic likeness. Everyone should know nowadays the unimportance of the photographic in art: that truth, life, or reality is an organic thing which the poetic imagination can represent or suggest, in essence, only through transformation, through changing into other forms than those which were merely present in appearance.

These remarks are not meant as a preface only to this particular play. They have to do with a conception of a new, plastic theatre which must take the place of the exhausted theatre of realistic conventions if the theatre is to resume vitality as a part of our culture.

THE SCREEN DEVICE

There is *only one important difference between the original and acting version of the play* and that is the *omission* in the latter of the device which I tentatively included in my *original* script. This device was the use of a screen on which were projected magic-lantern slides bearing images or titles. I do not regret the omission of this device from the present Broadway production. The extraordinary power of Miss Taylor's performance made it suitable to have the utmost simplicity in the physical production. But I think it may be interesting to some readers to see how this device was conceived. So I am putting it into the published manuscript. These images and legends, projected from behind, were cast on a section of wall between the front-room and dining-room areas, which should be indistinguishable from the rest when not in use.

The purpose of this will probably be apparent. It is to give accent to certain values in each scene. Each scene contains a particular point (or several) which is structurally the most important. In an episodic play, such as this, the basic structure or narrative line may be obscured from the audience; the effect may seem fragmentary rather than architectural. This may not be the fault of the play so much as a lack of attention in the audience. The legend or image upon the screen will strengthen the effect of what is merely allusion in the writing and allow the primary point to be made more simply and lightly than if the entire responsibility were on the spoken lines. Aside from this structural value, I think the screen will have a definite emotional appeal, less definable but just as important. An imaginative producer or director may invent many other uses for this device than those indicated in the present script. In fact the possibilities of the device seem much larger to me than the instance of this play can possibly utilize.

THE MUSIC

Another extra-literary accent in this play is provided by the use of music. A single recurring tune, "The Glass Menagerie," is used to give emotional emphasis to suitable passages. This tune is like circus music, not when you are on the grounds or in the immediate vicinity of the parade, but when you are at some distance and very likely thinking of something else. It seems under those circumstances to continue almost interminably and it weaves in and out of your preoccupied consciousness; then it is the lightest, most delicate music in the world and perhaps the saddest. It expresses the surface vivacity of life with the underlying strain of immutable and inexpressible sorrow. When you look at a piece of delicately spun glass you think of two things: how beautiful it is and how easily it can be broken. Both of those ideas should be woven into the recurring tune, which dips in and out of the play as if it were carried on a wind that changes. It serves as a thread of connection and allusion between the narrator with his separate point in time and space and the subject of his story. Between each episode it returns as reference to the emotion, nostalgia, which is the first condition of the play. It is primarily LAURA's music and therefore comes out most clearly when the play focuses upon her and the lovely fragility of glass which is her image.

THE LIGHTING

The lighting in the play is not realistic. In keeping with the atmosphere of memory, the stage is dim. Shafts of light are focused on selected areas or actors, sometimes in contradistinction to what is the apparent center. For instance, in the quarrel scene between TOM and AMANDA, in which LAURA has no active part, the clearest pool of light is on her figure. This is also true of the supper scene, when her silent figure on the sofa should remain the visual center. The light upon LAURA should be distinct from the others, having a peculiar pristine clarity such as light used in early religious portraits of female saints or madonnas. A certain correspondence to light in religious paintings, such as El Greco's, where the figures are radiant in atmosphere that is relatively dusky, could be effectively used throughout the play. [It will also permit a more effective use of the screen.] A free, imaginative use of light can be of enormous value in giving a mobile, plastic quality to plays of a more or less static nature.

T. W.

SCENE I

The Wingfield apartment is in the rear of the building, one of those vast hive-like conglomerations of cellular living-units that flower as warty growths in overcrowded urban centers of lower middle-class population and are symptomatic of the impulse of this largest and fundamentally enslaved section of American society to avoid fluidity and differentiation and to exist and function as one interfused mass of automatism.

The apartment faces an alley and is entered by a fire-escape, a structure whose name is a touch of accidental poetic truth, for all of these huge buildings are always burning with the slow and implacable fires of human desperation. The fire-escape is included in the set—that is, the landing of it and steps descending from it.

The scene is memory and is therefore nonrealistic. Memory takes a lot of poetic license. It omits some details; others are exaggerated, according to the emotional value of the articles it touches, for memory is seated predominantly in the heart. The interior is therefore rather dim and poetic.

At the rise of the curtain, the audience is faced with the dark, grim rear wall of the Wingfield tenement. This building, which runs parallel to the footlights, is flanked on both sides by dark, narrow alleys which run into murky canyons of tangled clotheslines, garbage cans and the sinister lattice-work of neighboring fire-escapes. It is up and down these side alleys that exterior entrances and exits are made, during the play. At the end of TOM'S opening commentary, the dark tenement wall slowly reveals (by means of a transparency) the interior of the ground floor Wingfield apartment.

Downstage is the living room, which also serves as a sleeping room for LAURA, the sofa unfolding to make her bed. Upstage, center, and divided by a wide arch or second pro-scenium with transparent faded portieres (or second curtain), is the dining room. In an old-fashioned what-not in the living room are seen scores of transparent glass animals. A blown-up photograph of the father hangs on the wall of the living room, facing the audience, to the left of the archway. It is the face of a very handsome young man in a doughboy's First World War cap. He is gallantly smiling, ineluctably smiling, as if to say, "I will be smiling forever."

The audience hears and sees the opening scene in the dining room through both the transparent fourth wall of the building and the transparent gauze portieres of the dining-room arch. It is during this revealing scene that the fourth wall slowly ascends, out of sight. This transparent exterior wall is not brought down again until the very end of the play, during TOM'S *final speech.*

The narrator is an undisguised convention of the play. He takes whatever license with dramatic convention as is convenient to his purposes.

TOM *enters dressed as a merchant sailor from alley, stage left, and strolls across the front of the stage to the fire-escape. There he stops and lights a cigarette. He addresses the audience.*

TOM: Yes, I have tricks in my pocket, I have things up my sleeve. But I am the opposite of a stage magician. He gives you illusion that has the appearance of truth. I give you truth in the pleasant disguise of illusion.

To begin with, I turn back time. I reverse it to that quaint period, the thirties, when the huge middle class of America was matriculating in a school for the blind. Their eyes had failed them, or they had failed their eyes, and so they were having their fingers pressed forcibly down on the fiery Braille alphabet of a dissolving economy.

In Spain there was revolution. Here there was only shouting and confusion.

In Spain there was Guernica. Here there were disturbances of labor, sometimes pretty violent, in otherwise peaceful cities such as Chicago, Cleveland, Saint Louis . . .

This is the social background of the play.

[MUSIC.]

The play is memory.

Being a memory play, it is dimly lighted, it is sentimental, it is not realistic.

In memory everything seems to happen to music. That explains the fiddle in the wings.

I am the narrator of the play, and also a character in it.

The other characters are my mother, Amanda, my sister, Laura, and a gentleman caller who appears in the final scenes.

He is the most realistic character in the play, being an emissary from a world of reality that we were somehow set apart from.

But since I have a poet's weakness for symbols, I am using this character also as a symbol; he is the long delayed but always expected something that we live for.

There is a fifth character in the play who doesn't appear except in this larger-than-life-size photograph over the mantel.

This is our father who left us a long time ago.

He was a telephone man who fell in love with long distances; he gave up his job with the telephone company and skipped the light fantastic out of town . . .

The last we heard of him was a picture post-card from Mazatlan, on the Pacific coast of Mexico, containing a message of two words—

"Hello— Good-bye!" and no address.

I think the rest of the play will explain itself. . . .

[AMANDA's *voice becomes audible through the portieres.*]

[LEGEND ON SCREEN: "OU SONT LES NEIGES."]

[*He divides the portieres and enters the upstage area.*]

[AMANDA *and* LAURA *are seated at a drop-leaf table. Eating is indicated by gestures without food or utensils.* AMANDA *faces the audience.* TOM *and* LAURA *are seated in profile.*]

[*The interior has lit up softly and through the scrim we see* AMANDA *and* LAURA *seated at the table in the upstage area.*]

AMANDA [*Calling*]: Tom?

TOM: Yes, Mother.

AMANDA: We can't say grace until you come to the table!

TOM: Coming, Mother. [*He bows slightly and withdraws, reappearing a few moments later in his place at the table.*]

AMANDA [*To her son*]: Honey, don't *push* with your *fingers*. If you have to push with something, the thing to push with is a crust of bread. And chew—chew! Animals have sections in their stomachs which enable them to digest food without mastication, but human beings are supposed to chew their food before they swallow it down. Eat food leisurely, son, and really enjoy it. A well-cooked meal has lots of delicate flavors that have to be held in the mouth for appreciation. So chew your food and give your salivary glands a chance to function!

[TOM *deliberately lays his imaginary fork down and pushes his chair back from the table.*]

TOM: I haven't enjoyed one bite of this dinner because of your constant directions on how to eat it. It's you that make me rush through meals with your hawk-like attention to every bite I take. Sickening—spoils my appetite—all this discussion of—animals' secretion—salivary glands—mastication!

AMANDA [*Lightly*]: Temperament like a Metropolitan star! [*He rises and crosses downstage.*] You're not excused from the table.

TOM: I'm getting a cigarette.

AMANDA: You smoke too much.

[LAURA *rises.*]

LAURA: I'll bring in the blanc mange.

[*He remains standing with his cigarette by the portieres during the following.*]

AMANDA [*Rising*]: No, sister, no, sister—you be the lady this time and I'll be the darky.

LAURA: I'm already up.

AMANDA: Resume your seat, little sister—I want you to stay fresh and pretty—for gentlemen callers!

LAURA: I'm not expecting any gentlemen callers.

AMANDA [*Crossing out to kitchenette. Airily*]: Sometimes they come when they are least expected! Why, I remember one Sunday afternoon in Blue Mountain— [*Enters kitchenette.*]

TOM: I know what's coming!

LAURA: Yes. But let her tell it.

TOM: Again?

LAURA: She loves to tell it.

[AMANDA *returns with bowl of dessert.*]

AMANDA: One Sunday afternoon in Blue Mountain—your

mother received—*seventeen!*—gentlemen callers! Why, sometimes there weren't chairs enough to accommodate them all. We had to send the nigger over to bring in folding chairs from the parish house.

TOM: [*Remaining at portieres*]: How did you entertain those gentlemen callers?

AMANDA: I understood the art of conversation!

TOM: I bet you could talk.

AMANDA: Girls in those days *knew* how to talk, I can tell you.

TOM: Yes?

[IMAGE: AMANDA AS A GIRL ON A PORCH, GREETING CALLERS.]

AMANDA: They knew how to entertain their gentlemen callers. It wasn't enough for a girl to be possessed of a pretty face and a graceful figure—although I wasn't slighted in either respect. She also needed to have a nimble wit and a tongue to meet all occasions.

TOM: What did you talk about?

AMANDA: Things of importance going on in the world! Never anything coarse or common or vulgar. [*She addresses* TOM *as though he were seated in the vacant chair at the table though he remains by portieres. He plays this scene as though he held the book.*] My callers were gentlemen—all! Among my callers were some of the most prominent young planters of the Mississippi Delta—planters and sons of planters!

[TOM *motions for music and a spot of light on* AMANDA.]

[*Her eyes lift, her face glows, her voice becomes rich and elegiac.*]

[SCREEN LEGEND: "OU SONT LES NEIGES."]

There was young Champ Laughlin who later became vice-president of the Delta Planters Bank.

Hadley Stevenson who was drowned in Moon Lake and left his widow one hundred and fifty thousand in Government bonds.

There were the Cutrere brothers, Wesley and Bates. Bates was one of my bright particular beaux! He got in a quarrel with that wild Wainwright boy. They shot it out on the floor of Moon Lake Casino. Bates was shot through the stomach. Died in the ambulance on his way to Memphis. His widow was also well-provided for, came into eight or ten thousand acres, that's all. She married him on the rebound—never loved her—carried my picture on him the night he died!

And there was that boy that every girl in the Delta had set her cap for! That beautiful, brilliant young Fitzhugh boy from Greene County!

TOM: What did he leave his widow?

AMANDA: He never married! Gracious, you talk as though all of my old admirers had turned up their toes to the daisies!

TOM: Isn't this the first you've mentioned that still survives?

AMANDA: That Fitzhugh boy went North and made a fortune —came to be known as the Wolf of Wall Street! He had the Midas touch, whatever he touched turned to gold!

And I could have been Mrs. Duncan J. Fitzhugh, mind you! But—I picked your *father!*

LAURA [*Rising*]: Mother, let me clear the table.

AMANDA: No, dear, you go in front and study your typewriter chart. Or practice your shorthand a little. Stay fresh and pretty!—It's almost time for our gentlemen callers to start arriving. [*She flounces girlishly toward the kitchenette.*] How many do you suppose we're going to entertain this afternoon?

[TOM *throws down the paper and jumps up with a groan.*]

LAURA [*Alone in the dining room*]: I don't believe we're going to receive any, Mother.

AMANDA [*Reappearing, airily*]: What? No one—not one? You must be joking! [LAURA *nervously echoes her laugh. She slips in a fugitive manner through the half-open portieres and draws them gently behind her. A shaft of very clear light is thrown on her face against the faded tapestry of the curtains.* MUSIC: "THE GLASS MENAGERIE" UNDER FAINTLY. *Lightly.*] Not one gentleman caller? It can't be true! There must be a flood, there must have been a tornado!

LAURA: It isn't a flood, it's not a tornado, Mother. I'm just not popular like you were in Blue Mountain. . . . [TOM *utters another groan.* LAURA *glances at him with a faint, apologetic smile. Her voice catching a little.*] Mother's afraid I'm going to be an old maid.

THE SCENE DIMS OUT WITH "GLASS MENAGERIE" MUSIC

SCENE II

"Laura, Haven't You Ever Liked Some Boy?"

On the dark stage the screen is lighted with the image of blue roses.

Gradually LAURA'S *figure becomes apparent and the screen goes out.*

The music subsides.

LAURA *is seated in the delicate ivory chair at the small claw-foot table.*

She wears a dress of soft violet material for a kimono—her hair tied back from her forehead with a ribbon.

She is washing and polishing her collection of glass.

AMANDA *appears on the fire-escape steps. At the sound of her ascent,* LAURA *catches her breath, thrusts the bowl of ornaments away and seats herself stiffly before the diagram of the typewriter keyboard as though it held her spellbound.*

Something has happened to AMANDA. *It is written in her face as she climbs to the landing: a look that is grim and hopeless and a little absurd.*

She has on one of those cheap or imitation velvety-looking cloth coats with imitation fur collar. Her hat is five or six years old, one of those dreadful cloche hats that were worn in the late twenties and she is clasping an enormous black patent-leather pocketbook with nickel clasps and initials. This is her full-dress outfit, the one she usually wears to the D.A.R.

Before entering she looks through the door.

She purses her lips, opens her eyes very wide, rolls them upward and shakes her head.

Then she slowly lets herself in the door. Seeing her mother's expression LAURA *touches her lips with a nervous gesture.*

LAURA: Hello, Mother, I was— [*She makes a nervous gesture toward the chart on the wall.* AMANDA *leans against the shut door and stares at* LAURA *with a martyred look.*]

AMANDA: Deception? Deception? [*She slowly removes her hat and gloves, continuing the sweet suffering stare. She lets the hat and gloves fall on the floor—a bit of acting.*]

LAURA [*Shakily*]: How was the D.A.R. meeting? [AMANDA

slowly opens her purse and removes a dainty white handkerchief which she shakes out delicately and delicately touches to her lips and nostrils.] Didn't you go to the D.A.R. meeting, Mother?

AMANDA [*Faintly, almost inaudibly*]:—No.—No. [*Then more forcibly.*] I did not have the strength—to go to the D. A. R. In fact, I did not have the courage! I wanted to find a hole in the ground and hide myself in it forever! [*She crosses slowly to the wall and removes the diagram of the typewriter keyboard. She holds it in front of her for a second, staring at it sweetly and sorrowfully—then bites her lips and tears it in two pieces.*]

LAURA [*Faintly*]: Why did you do that, Mother? [AMANDA *repeats the same procedure with the chart of the Gregg Alphabet.*] Why are you—

AMANDA: Why? Why? How old are you, Laura?

LAURA: Mother, you know my age.

AMANDA: I thought that you were an adult; it seems that I was mistaken. [*She crosses slowly to the sofa and sinks down and stares at* LAURA.]

LAURA: Please don't stare at me, Mother.

[AMANDA *closes her eyes and lowers her head. Count ten.*]

AMANDA: What are we going to do, what is going to become of us, what is the future?

[*Count ten.*]

LAURA: Has something happened, Mother? [AMANDA *draws a long breath and takes out the handkerchief again. Dabbing process.*] Mother, has—something happened?

AMANDA: I'll be all right in a minute, I'm just bewildered— [*Count five.*]—by life. . . .

LAURA: Mother, I wish that you would tell me what's happened!

AMANDA: As you know, I was supposed to be inducted into my office at the D.A.R. this afternoon. [IMAGE: A SWARM OF TYPEWRITERS.] But I stopped off at Rubicam's business college to speak to your teachers about your having a cold and ask them what progress they thought you were making down there.

LAURA: Oh. . . .

AMANDA: I went to the typing instructor and introduced myself as your mother. She didn't know who you were. Wingfield, she said. We don't have any such student enrolled at the school!

I assured her she did, that you had been going to classes since early in January.

"I wonder," she said, "if you could be talking about that terribly shy little girl who dropped out of school after only a few days' attendance?"

"No," I said, "Laura, my daughter, has been going to school every day for the past six weeks!"

"Excuse me," she said. She took the attendance book out and there was your name, unmistakably printed, and all the dates you were absent until they decided that you had dropped out of school.

I still said, "No, there must have been some mistake! There must have been some mix-up in the records!"

And she said, "No—I remember her perfectly now. Her hands shook so that she couldn't hit the right keys! The first time we gave a speed-test, she broke down completely—was sick at the stomach and almost had to be carried into the wash-room! After that morning she never showed up any more. We phoned the house but never got any answer—while I was working at Famous and Barr, I suppose, demonstrating those— Oh!"

I felt so weak I could barely keep on my feet!

I had to sit down while they got me a glass of water!

Fifty dollars' tuition, all of our plans—my hopes and ambitions for you—just gone up the spout, just gone up the spout like that. [LAURA *draws a long breath and gets awkwardly to her feet. She crosses to the victrola and winds it up.*] What are you doing?

LAURA: Oh! [*She releases the handle and returns to her seat.*]

AMANDA: Laura, where have you been going when you've gone out pretending that you were going to business college?

LAURA: I've just been going out walking.

AMANDA: That's not true.

LAURA: It is. I just went walking.

AMANDA: Walking? Walking? In winter? Deliberately courting pneumonia in that light coat? Where did you walk to, Laura?

LAURA: All sorts of places—mostly in the park.

AMANDA: Even after you'd started catching that cold?

LAURA: It was the lesser of two evils, Mother. [IMAGE: WINTER SCENE IN PARK.] I couldn't go back up. I—threw up— on the floor!

AMANDA: From half past seven till after five every day you mean to tell me you walked around in the park, because you wanted to make me think that you were still going to Rubicam's Business College?

LAURA: It wasn't as bad as it sounds. I went inside places to get warmed up.

AMANDA: Inside where?

LAURA: I went in the art museum and the bird-houses at the Zoo. I visited the penguins every day! Sometimes I did without lunch and went to the movies. Lately I've been spending most of my afternoons in the Jewel-box, that big glass house where they raise the tropical flowers.

AMANDA: You did all this to deceive me, just for deception? [LAURA *looks down*.] Why?

LAURA: Mother, when you're disappointed, you get that awful suffering look on your face, like the picture of Jesus' mother in the museum!

AMANDA: Hush!

LAURA: I couldn't face it.

[*Pause. A whisper of strings.*]
[LEGEND: "THE CRUST OF HUMILITY."]

AMANDA [*Hopelessly fingering the huge pocketbook*]: So what are we going to do the rest of our lives? Stay home and watch the parades go by? Amuse ourselves with the glass menagerie, darling? Eternally play those worn-out phonograph records your father left as a painful reminder of him?

We won't have a business career—we've given that up because it gave us nervous indigestion! [*Laughs wearily*.] What is there left but dependency all our lives? I know so well what becomes of unmarried women who aren't prepared to occupy a position. I've seen such pitiful cases in the South—barely tolerated spinsters living upon the grudging patronage of sister's husband or brother's wife!—stuck away in some little mouse-trap of a room—encouraged by one in-law to visit another— little birdlike women without any nest—eating the crust of humility all their life!

Is that the future that we've mapped out for ourselves?

I swear it's the only alternative I can think of!
It isn't a very pleasant alternative, is it?
Of course—some girls *do marry.*
[LAURA *twists her hands nervously.*]
Haven't you ever liked some boy?

LAURA: Yes. I liked one once. [*Rises.*] I came across his picture a while ago.

AMANDA [*With some interest*]: He gave you his picture?

LAURA: No, it's in the year-book.

AMANDA [*Disappointed*]: Oh—a high-school boy.

[SCREEN IMAGE: JIM AS HIGH-SCHOOL HERO BEARING A SILVER CUP.]

LAURA: Yes. His name was Jim. [LAURA *lifts the heavy annual from the claw-foot table.*] Here he is in *The Pirates of Penzance.*

AMANDA [*Absently*]: The what?

LAURA: The operetta the senior class put on. He had a wonderful voice and we sat across the aisle from each other Mondays, Wednesdays and Fridays in the Aud. Here he is with the silver cup for debating! See his grin?

AMANDA [*Absently*]: He must have had a jolly disposition.

LAURA: He used to call me—Blue Roses.

[IMAGE: BLUE ROSES.]

AMANDA: Why did he call you such a name as that?

LAURA: When I had that attack of pleurosis—he asked me what was the matter when I came back. I said pleurosis—he thought that I said Blue Roses! So that's what he always called me after that. Whenever he saw me, he'd holler, "Hello, Blue Roses!" I didn't care for the girl that he went out with. Emily Meisenbach. Emily was the best-dressed girl at Soldan. She never struck me, though, as being sincere . . . It says in the Personal Section—they're engaged. That's—six years ago! They must be married by now.

AMANDA: Girls that aren't cut out for business careers usually wind up married to some nice man. [*Gets up with a spark of revival.*] Sister, that's what you'll do!

[LAURA *utters a startled, doubtful laugh. She reaches quickly for a piece of glass.*]

LAURA: But, Mother—

AMANDA: Yes? [*Crossing to photograph.*]

LAURA: [*In a tone of frightened apology*]: I'm —crippled!
[IMAGE: SCREEN.]

AMANDA: Nonsense! Laura, I've told you never, never to use
that word. Why, you're not crippled, you just have a little
defect—hardly noticeable, even! When people have some slight
disadvantage like that, they cultivate other things to make up
for it—develop charm—and vivacity—and—*charm!* That's all
you have to do! [*She turns again to the photograph.*] One thing
your father had *plenty of*—was *charm!*

[TOM *motions to the fiddle in the wings.*]

THE SCENE FADES OUT WITH MUSIC

SCENE III

LEGEND ON SCREEN: "AFTER THE FIASCO—"
TOM *speaks from the fire-escape landing.*

TOM: After the fiasco at Rubicam's Business College, the idea
of getting a gentleman caller for Laura began to play a more
and more important part in Mother's calculations.

It became an obsession. Like some archetype of the universal
unconscious, the image of the gentleman caller haunted our
small apartment. . . .

[IMAGE: YOUNG MAN AT DOOR WITH FLOWERS.]

An evening at home rarely passed without some allusion to
this image, this spectre, this hope. . . .

Even when he wasn't mentioned, his presence hung in Mother's preoccupied look and in my sister's frightened, apologetic
manner—hung like a sentence passed upon the Wingfields!

Mother was a woman of action as well as words.

She began to take logical steps in the planned direction.

Late that winter and in the early spring—realizing that
extra money would be needed to properly feather the nest
and plume the bird—she conducted a vigorous campaign on
the telephone, roping in subscribers to one of those magazines
for matrons called *The Home-maker's Companion,* the type of
journal that features the serialized sublimations of ladies of
letters who think in terms of delicate cup-like breasts, slim,

tapering waists, rich, creamy thighs, eyes like wood-smoke in autumn, fingers that soothe and caress like strains of music, bodies as powerful as Etruscan sculpture.

[SCREEN IMAGE: GLAMOR MAGAZINE COVER.]

[AMANDA *enters with phone on long extension cord. She is spotted in the dim stage.*]

AMANDA: Ida Scott? This is Amanda Wingfield!

We *missed* you at the D.A.R. last Monday!

I said to myself: She's probably suffering with that sinus condition! How is that sinus condition?

Horrors! Heaven have mercy!—You're a Christian martyr, yes, that's what you are, a Christian martyr!

Well, I just now happened to notice that your subscription to the *Companion's* about to expire! Yes, it expires with the next issue, honey!—just when that wonderful new serial by Bessie Mae Hopper is getting off to such an exciting start. Oh, honey, it's something that you can't miss! You remember how *Gone With the Wind* took everybody by storm? You simply couldn't go out if you hadn't read it. All everybody *talked* was Scarlet O'Hara. Well, this is a book that critics already compare to *Gone With the Wind*. It's the *Gone With the Wind* of the post-World War generation!—What?—Burning?—Oh, honey, don't let them burn, go take a look in the oven and I'll hold the wire! Heavens—I think she's hung up!

DIM OUT

[LEGEND ON SCREEN: "YOU THINK I'M IN LOVE WITH CONTINENTAL SHOEMAKERS?"]

[*Before the stage is lighted, the violent voices of* TOM *and* AMANDA *are heard.*]

[*They are quarreling behind the portieres. In front of them stands* LAURA *with clenched hands and panicky expression.*]

[*A clear pool of light on her figure throughout this scene.*]

TOM: What in Christ's name am I—

AMANDA [*Shrilly*]: Don't you use that—

TOM: Supposed to do!

AMANDA: Expression! Not in my—

TOM: Ohhh!

AMANDA: Presence! Have you gone out of your senses?

TOM: I have, that's true, *driven* out!

AMANDA: What is the matter with you, you—big—big—IDIOT!

TOM: Look!—I've got *no thing*, no single thing—

AMANDA: Lower your voice!

TOM: In my life here that I can call my OWN! Everything is—

AMANDA: Stop that shouting!

TOM: Yesterday you confiscated my books! You had the nerve to—

AMANDA: I took that horrible novel back to the library—yes! That hideous book by that insane Mr. Lawrence. [TOM *laughs wildly.*] I cannot control the output of diseased minds or people who cater to them— [TOM *laughs still more wildly.*] BUT I WON'T ALLOW SUCH FILTH BROUGHT INTO MY HOUSE! No, no, no, no, no!

TOM: House, house! Who pays rent on it, who makes a slave of himself to—

AMANDA [*Fairly screeching*]: Don't you DARE to—

TOM: No, no, *I* mustn't say things! *I've* got to just—

AMANDA: Let me tell you—

TOM: I don't want to hear any more! [*He tears the portieres open. The upstage area is lit with a turgid smoky red glow.*]

[AMANDA'S *hair is in metal curlers and she wears a very old bathrobe, much too large for her slight figure, a relic of the faithless Mr. Wingfield.*]

[*An upright typewriter and a wild disarray of manuscripts are on the drop-leaf table. The quarrel was probably precipitated by* AMANDA'S *interruption of his creative labor. A chair lying overthrown on the floor.*]

[*Their gesticulating shadows are cast on the ceiling by the fiery glow.*]

AMANDA: You *will* hear more, you—

TOM: No, I won't hear more, I'm going out!

AMANDA: You come right back in—

TOM: Out, out, out! Because I'm—

AMANDA: Come back here, Tom Wingfield! I'm not through talking to you!

TOM: Oh, go—

LAURA [*Desperately*]:—Tom!

AMANDA: You're going to listen, and no more insolence from you! I'm at the end of my patience!

[*He comes back toward her.*]

TOM: What do you think I'm at? Aren't I supposed to have any patience to reach the end of, Mother? I know, I know. It seems unimportant to you, what I'm *doing*—what I *want* to do —having a little *difference* between them! You don't think that—

AMANDA: I think you've been doing things that you're ashamed of. That's why you act like this. I don't believe that you go every night to the movies. Nobody goes to the movies night after night. Nobody in their right minds goes to the movies as often as you pretend to. People don't go to the movies at nearly midnight, and movies don't let out at two A.M. Come in stumbling. Muttering to yourself like a maniac! You get three hours' sleep and then go to work. Oh, I can picture the way you're doing down there. Moping, doping, because you're in no condition.

TOM [*Wildly*]: No, I'm in no condition!

AMANDA: What right have you got to jeopardize your job? Jeopardize the security of us all? How do you think we'd manage if you were—

TOM: Listen! You think I'm crazy *about* the *warehouse?* [*He bends fiercely toward her slight figure.*] You think I'm in love with the Continental Shoemakers? You think I want to spend fifty-five *years* down there in that—*celotex interior!* with— *fluorescent—tubes!* Look! I'd rather somebody picked up a crowbar and battered out my brains—than go back mornings! I *go!* Every time you come in yelling that God damn *"Rise and Shine!" "Rise and Shine!"* I say to myself, "How *lucky dead* people are!" But I get up. I *go!* For sixty-five dollars a month I give up all that I dream of doing and being *ever!* And you say self—*self's* all I ever think of. Why, listen, if self is what I thought of, Mother, I'd be where he is—GONE! [*Pointing to father's picture.*] As far as the system of transportation reaches! [*He starts past her. She grabs his arm.*] Don't grab at me, Mother!

AMANDA: Where are you going?

TOM: I'm going to the *movies!*

AMANDA: I don't believe that lie!

TOM [*Crouching toward her, overtowering her tiny figure. She backs away, gasping*]: I'm going to opium dens! Yes, opium dens, dens of vice and criminals' hang-outs, Mother. I've joined the Hogan gang, I'm a hired assassin, I carry a tommy-gun in a violin case! I run a string of cat-houses in the Valley! They call me Killer, Killer Wingfield, I'm leading a double-life, a simple, honest warehouse worker by day, by night a dynamic *czar* of the *underworld, Mother.* I go to gambling casinos, I spin away fortunes on the roulette table! I wear a patch over one eye and a false mustache, sometimes I put on green whiskers. On those occasions they call me—*El Diablo!* Oh, I could tell you things to make you sleepless! My enemies plan to dynamite this place. They're going to blow us all sky-high some night! I'll be glad, very happy, and so will you! You'll go up, up on a broomstick, over Blue Mountain with seventeen gentlemen callers! You ugly —babbling old—*witch.* . . . [*He goes through a series of violent, clumsy movements, seizing his overcoat, lunging to the door, pulling it fiercely open. The women watch him, aghast. His arm catches in the sleeve of the coat as he struggles to pull it on. For a moment he is pinioned by the bulky garment. With an outraged groan he tears the coat off again, splitting the shoulder of it, and hurls it across the room. It strikes against the shelf of* LAURA'S *glass collection, there is a tinkle of shattering glass.* LAURA *cries out as if wounded.*]

[MUSIC. LEGEND: "THE GLASS MENAGERIE."]

LAURA [*Shrilly*]: My glass!—menagerie. . . . [*She covers her face and turns away.*]

[*But* AMANDA *is still stunned and stupefied by the "ugly witch" so that she barely notices this occurrence. Now she recovers her speech.*]

AMANDA [*In an awful voice*]: I won't speak to you—until you apologize! [*She crosses through portieres and draws them together behind her.* TOM *is left with* LAURA. LAURA *clings weakly to the mantel with her face averted.* TOM *stares at her stupidly for a moment. Then he crosses to shelf. Drops awkwardly on his knees to collect the fallen glass, glancing at* LAURA *as if he would speak but couldn't.*]

"The Glass Menagerie" steals in as

THE SCENE DIMS OUT

SCENE IV

The interior is dark. Faint light in the alley.

A deep-voiced bell in a church is tolling the hour of five as the scene commences.

TOM *appears at the top of the alley. After each solemn boom of the bell in the tower, he shakes a little noise-maker or rattle as if to express the tiny spasm of man in contrast to the sustained power and dignity of the Almighty. This and the unsteadiness of his advance make it evident that he has been drinking.*

As he climbs the few steps to the fire-escape landing light steals up inside. LAURA *appears in night-dress, observing* TOM'S *empty bed in the front room.*

TOM *fishes in his pockets for door-key, removing a motley assortment of articles in the search, including a perfect shower of movie-ticket stubs and an empty bottle. At last he finds the key, but just as he is about to insert it, it slips from his fingers. He strikes a match and crouches below the door.*

TOM [*Bitterly*]: One crack—and it falls through!

[LAURA *opens the door.*]

LAURA: Tom! Tom, what are you doing?

TOM: Looking for a door-key.

LAURA: Where have you been all this time?

TOM: I have been to the movies.

LAURA: All this time at the movies?

TOM: There was a very long program. There was a Garbo picture and a Mickey Mouse and a travelogue and a newsreel and a preview of coming attractions. And there was an organ solo and a collection for the milk-fund—simultaneously—which ended up in a terrible fight between a fat lady and an usher!

LAURA [*Innocently*]: Did you have to stay through everything?

TOM: Of course! And, oh, I forgot! There was a big stage show! The headliner on this stage show was Malvolio the Magician. He performed wonderful tricks, many of them, such as pouring water back and forth between pitchers. First it turned to wine and then it turned to beer and then it turned to whiskey. I know it was whiskey it finally turned into because he needed somebody to come up out of the audience to help him, and I came up—both shows! It was Kentucky Straight Bourbon. A very generous fellow, he gave souvenirs. [*He pulls from his back pocket a shimmering rainbow-colored scarf.*] He gave me this. This is his magic scarf. You can have it, Laura. You wave it over a canary cage and you get a bowl of gold-fish. You wave it over the gold-fish bowl and they fly away canaries. . . . But the wonderfullest trick of all was the coffin trick. We nailed him into a coffin and he got out of the coffin without removing one nail. [*He has come inside.*] There is a trick that would come in handy for me—get me out of this 2 by 4 situation! [*Flops onto bed and starts removing shoes.*]

LAURA: Tom—Shhh!

TOM: What're you shushing me for?

LAURA: You'll wake up Mother.

TOM: Goody, goody! Pay 'er back for all those "Rise an' Shines." [*Lies down, groaning.*] You know it don't take much intelligence to get yourself into a nailed-up coffin, Laura. But who in hell ever got himself out of one without removing one nail?

[*As if in answer, the father's grinning photograph lights up.*]

SCENE DIMS OUT

[*Immediately following: The church bell is heard striking six. At the sixth stroke the alarm clock goes off in* AMANDA'S *room, and after a few moments we hear her calling: "Rise and Shine! Rise and Shine! Laura, go tell your brother to rise and shine!"*]

TOM [*Sitting up slowly*]: I'll rise—but I won't shine.

[*The light increases.*]

AMANDA: Laura, tell your brother his coffee is ready.

[LAURA *slips into front room.*]

LAURA: Tom!—It's nearly seven. Don't make Mother nervous. [*He stares at her stupidly. Beseechingly.*] Tom, speak to Mother this morning. Make up with her, apologize, speak to her!

TOM: She won't to me. It's her that started not speaking.

LAURA: If you just say you're sorry she'll start speaking.

TOM: Her not speaking—is that such a tragedy?

LAURA: Please—please!

AMANDA [*Calling from kitchenette*]: Laura, are you going to do what I asked you to do, or do I have to get dressed and go out myself?

LAURA: Going, going—soon as I get on my coat! [*She pulls on a shapeless felt hat with nervous, jerky movement, pleadingly glancing at* TOM. *Rushes awkwardly for coat. The coat is one of* AMANDA'S, *inaccurately made-over, the sleeves too short for* LAURA.] Butter and what else?

AMANDA [*Entering upstage*]: Just butter. Tell them to charge it.

LAURA: Mother, they make such faces when I do that.

AMANDA: Sticks and stones can break our bones, but the expression on Mr. Garfinkel's face won't harm us! Tell your brother his coffee is getting cold.

LAURA [*At door*]: Do what I asked you, will you, will you, Tom?

[*He looks sullenly away.*]

AMANDA: Laura, go now or just don't go at all!

LAURA [*Rushing out*]: Going—going! [*A second later she cries out.* TOM *springs up and crosses to door.* AMANDA *rushes anxiously in.* TOM *opens the door.*]

TOM: Laura?

LAURA: I'm all right. I slipped, but I'm all right.

AMANDA [*Peering anxiously after her*]: If anyone breaks a leg on those fire-escape steps, the landlord ought to be sued for every cent he possesses! [*She shuts door. Remembers she isn't speaking and returns to other room.*]

[*As* TOM *enters listlessly for his coffee, she turns her back to him and stands rigidly facing the window on the gloomy gray vault of the areaway. Its light on her face with its aged but childish features is cruelly sharp, satirical as a Daumier print.*]

[MUSIC UNDER: "AVE MARIA."]

[TOM *glances sheepishly but sullenly at her averted figure and slumps at the table. The coffee is scalding hot; he sips it and gasps and spits it back in the cup. At his gasp,* AMANDA *catches her breath and half turns. Then catches herself and turns back to window.*]

[TOM *blows on his coffee, glancing sidewise at his mother.*

She clears her throat. TOM *clears his. He starts to rise. Sinks back down again, scratches his head, clears his throat again.* AMANDA *coughs.* TOM *raises his cup in both hands to blow on it, his eyes staring over the rim of it at his mother for several moments. Then he slowly sets the cup down and awkwardly and hesitantly rises from the chair.*]

TOM [*Hoarsely*]: Mother. I—I apologize, Mother. [AMANDA *draws a quick, shuddering breath. Her face works grotesquely. She breaks into childlike tears.*] I'm sorry for what I said, for everything that I said, I didn't mean it.

AMANDA [*Sobbingly*]: My devotion has made me a witch and so I make myself hateful to my children!

TOM: *No,* you *don't.*

AMANDA: I worry so much, don't sleep, it makes me nervous!

TOM [*Gently*]: I understand that.

AMANDA: I've had to put up a solitary battle all these years. But you're my right-hand bower! Don't fall down, don't fail!

TOM [*Gently*]: I try, Mother.

AMANDA [*With great enthusiasm*]: Try and you will SUCCEED! [*The notion makes her breathless.*] Why, you—you're just *full* of natural endowments! Both of my children—they're *unusual* children! Don't you think I know it? I'm so—*proud!* Happy and —feel I've—so much to be thankful for but— Promise me one thing, Son!

TOM: What, Mother?

AMANDA: Promise, son, you'll—never be a drunkard!

TOM [*Turns to her grinning*]: I will never be a drunkard, Mother.

AMANDA: That's what frightened me so, that you'd be drinking! Eat a bowl of Purina!

TOM: Just coffee, Mother.

AMANDA: Shredded wheat biscuit?

TOM: No. No, Mother, just coffee.

AMANDA: You can't put in a day's work on an empty stomach. You've got ten minutes—don't gulp! Drinking too-hot liquids makes cancer of the stomach. . . . Put cream in.

TOM: No, thank you.

AMANDA: To cool it.

TOM: No! No, thank you, I want it black.

AMANDA: I know, but it's not good for you. We have to do

all that we can to build ourselves up. In these trying times we
live in, all that we have to cling to is—each other. . . . That's
why it's so important to— Tom, I— I sent out your sister
so I could discuss something with you. If you hadn't spoken I
would have spoken to you. [*Sits down.*]

TOM [*Gently*]: What is it, Mother, that you want to discuss?

AMANDA: *Laura!*

[TOM *puts his cup down slowly.*]

[LEGEND ON SCREEN: "LAURA."]

[MUSIC: "THE GLASS MENAGERIE."]

TOM: —Oh.—Laura . . .

AMANDA [*Touching his sleeve*]: You know how Laura is. So
quiet but—still water runs deep! She notices things and I think
she—broods about them. [TOM *looks up.*] A few days ago I
came in and she was crying.

TOM: What about?

AMANDA: You.

TOM: Me?

AMANDA: She has an idea that you're not happy here.

TOM: What gave her that idea?

AMANDA: What gives her any idea? However, you do act
strangely. I—I'm not criticizing, understand *that!* I know your
ambitions do not lie in the warehouse, that like everybody in the
whole wide world—you've had to—make sacrifices, but—Tom
—Tom—life's not easy, it calls for—Spartan endurance!
There's so many things in my heart that I cannot describe to
you! I've never told you but I—*loved* your father. . . .

TOM [*Gently*]: I know that, Mother.

AMANDA: And you—when I see you taking after his ways!
Staying out late—and—well, you *had* been drinking the night
you were in that—terrifying condition! Laura says that you
hate the apartment and that you go out nights to get away from
it! Is that true, Tom?

TOM: No. You say there's so much in your heart that you
can't describe to me. That's true of me, too. There's so much in
my heart that I can't describe to *you!* So let's respect each
other's—

AMANDA: But, why—*why,* Tom—are you always so *restless?*
Where do you *go* to, nights?

TOM: I—go to the movies.

AMANDA: Why do you go to the movies so much, Tom?

TOM: I go to the movies because—I like adventure. Adventure is something I don't have much of at work, so I go to the movies.

AMANDA: But, Tom, you go to the movies *entirely* too *much!*

TOM: I like a lot of adventure.

[AMANDA *looks baffled, then hurt. As the familiar inquisition resumes he becomes hard and impatient again.* AMANDA *slips back into her querulous attitude toward him.*]

[IMAGE ON SCREEN: SAILING VESSEL WITH JOLLY ROGER.]

AMANDA: Most young men find adventure in their careers.

TOM: Then most young men are not employed in a warehouse.

AMANDA: The world is full of young men employed in warehouses and offices and factories.

TOM: Do all of them find adventure in their careers?

AMANDA: They do or they do without it! Not everybody has a craze for adventure.

TOM: Man is by instinct a lover, a hunter, a fighter, and none of those instincts are given much play at the warehouse!

AMANDA: Man is by instinct! Don't quote instinct to me! Instinct is something that people have got away from! It belongs to animals! Christian adults don't want it!

TOM: What do Christian adults want, then, Mother?

AMANDA: Superior things! Things of the mind and the spirit! Only animals have to satisfy instincts! Surely your aims are somewhat higher than theirs! Than monkeys—pigs—

TOM: I reckon they're not.

AMANDA: You're joking. However, that isn't what I wanted to discuss.

TOM [*Rising*]: I haven't much time.

AMANDA [*Pushing his shoulders*]: Sit down.

TOM: You want me to punch in red at the warehouse, Mother?

AMANDA: You have five minutes. I want to talk about Laura.

[LEGEND: "PLANS AND PROVISIONS."]

TOM: All right! What about Laura?

AMANDA: We have to be making some plans and provisions for her. She's older than you, two years, and nothing has happened. She just drifts along doing nothing. It frightens me terribly how she just drifts along.

TOM: I guess she's the type that people call home girls.

AMANDA: There's no such type, and if there is, it's a pity!
That is unless the home is hers, with a husband!

TOM: What?

AMANDA: Oh, I can see the handwriting on the wall as plain
as I see the nose in front of my face! It's terrifying!

More and more you remind me of your father! He was out
all hours without explanation!—Then *left! Good-bye!*
And me with the bag to hold. I saw that letter you got from
the Merchant Marine. I know what you're dreaming of. I'm
not standing here blindfolded.

Very well, then. Then *do* it!

But not till there's somebody to take your place.

TOM: What do you mean?

AMANDA: I mean that as soon as Laura has got somebody to
take care of her, married, a home of her own, independent—
why, then you'll be free to go wherever you please, on land, on
sea, whichever way the wind blows you!

But until that time you've got to look out for your sister. I
don't say me because I'm old and don't matter! I say for your
sister because she's young and dependent.

I put her in business college—a dismal failure! Frightened
her so it made her sick at the stomach.

I took her over to the Young People's League at the church.
Another fiasco. She spoke to nobody, nobody spoke to her. Now
all she does is fool with those pieces of glass and play those
worn-out records. What kind of a life is that for a girl to lead?

TOM: What can I do about it?

AMANDA: Overcome selfishness!

Self, self, self is all that you ever think of!

[TOM *springs up and crosses to get his coat. It is ugly and
bulky. He pulls on a cap with earmuffs.*]

Where is your muffler? Put your wool muffler on! [*He
snatches it angrily from the closet and tosses it around his neck
and pulls both ends tight.*] Tom! I haven't said what I had
in mind to ask you.

TOM: I'm too late to—

AMANDA [*Catching his arm—very importunately. Then
shyly*]: Down at the warehouse, aren't there some—nice young
men?

TOM: No!

AMANDA: There *must* be—*some* . . .

TOM: Mother—

[*Gesture.*]

AMANDA: Find out one that's clean-living—doesn't drink and —ask him out for sister!

TOM: What?

AMANDA: For *sister!* To *meet!* Get *acquainted!*

TOM [*Stamping to door*]: Oh, my *go-osh!*

AMANDA: Will you? [*He opens door. Imploringly.*] Will you? [*He starts down.*] Will you? *Will* you, dear?

TOM [*Calling back*]: YES!

[AMANDA *closes the door hesitantly and with a troubled but faintly hopeful expression.*]

[SCREEN IMAGE: GLAMOR MAGAZINE COVER.]

[*Spot* AMANDA *at phone.*]

AMANDA: Ella Cartwright? This is Amanda Wingfield!

How are you, honey?

How is that kidney condition?

[*Count five.*]

Horrors!

[*Count five.*]

You're a Christian martyr, yes, honey, that's what you are, a Christian martyr!

Well, I just now happened to notice in my little red book that your subscription to the *Companion* has just run out! I knew that you wouldn't want to miss out on the wonderful serial starting in this new issue. It's by Bessie Mae Hopper. the first thing she's written since *Honeymoon for Three.*

Wasn't that a strange and interesting story? Well, this one is even lovelier, I believe. It has a sophisticated, society background. It's all about the horsey set on Long Island!

FADE OUT

SCENE V

LEGEND ON SCREEN: "ANNUNCIATION." *Fade with music.*

It is early dusk of a spring evening. Supper has just been finished in the Wingfield apartment. AMANDA *and* LAURA *in light-colored dresses are removing dishes from the table, in the upstage area, which is shadowy, their movements formalized almost as a dance or ritual, their moving forms as pale and silent as moths.*

TOM, *in white shirt and trousers, rises from the table and crosses toward the fire-escape.*

AMANDA [*As he passes her*]: Son, will you do me a favor?

TOM: What?

AMANDA: Comb your hair! You look so pretty when your hair is combed! [TOM *slouches on sofa with evening paper. Enormous caption "Franco Triumphs."*] There is only one respect in which I would like you to emulate your father.

TOM: What respect is that?

AMANDA: The care he always took of his appearance. He never allowed himself to look untidy. [*He throws down the paper and crosses to fire-escape.*] Where are you going?

TOM: I'm going out to smoke.

AMANDA: You smoke too much. A pack a day at fifteen cents a pack. How much would that amount to in a month? Thirty times fifteen is how much, Tom? Figure it out and you will be astounded at what you could save. Enough to give you a night-school course in accounting at Washington U! Just think what a wonderful thing that would be for you, Son!

[TOM *is unmoved by the thought.*]

TOM: I'd rather smoke. [*He steps out on landing, letting the screen door slam.*]

AMANDA [*Sharply*]: I know! That's the tragedy of it. . . . [*Alone, she turns to look at her husband's picture.*]

[DANCE MUSIC: "ALL THE WORLD IS WAITING FOR THE SUNRISE!"]

TOM [*To the audience*]: Across the alley from us was the Paradise Dance Hall. On evenings in spring the windows and doors were open and the music came outdoors. Sometimes the lights were turned out except for a large glass sphere that hung from the ceiling. It would turn slowly about and filter the dusk with delicate rainbow colors. Then the orchestra played a waltz or a tango, something that had a slow and sensuous rhythm. Couples would come outside, to the relative privacy of the alley.

You could see them kissing behind ash-pits and telephone poles.

This was the compensation for lives that passed like mine, without any change or adventure.

Adventure and change were imminent in this year. They were waiting around the corner for all these kids.

Suspended in the mist over Berchtesgaden, caught in the folds of Chamberlain's umbrella—

In Spain there was Guernica!

But here there was only hot swing music and liquor, dance halls, bars, and movies, and sex that hung in the gloom like a chandelier and flooded the world with brief, deceptive rainbows. . . .

All the world was waiting for bombardments!

[AMANDA *turns from the picture and comes outside.*]

AMANDA [*Sighing*]: A fire-escape landing's a poor excuse for a porch. [*She spreads a newspaper on a step and sits down, gracefully and demurely as if she were settling into a swing on a Mississippi veranda.*] What are you looking at?

TOM: The moon.

AMANDA: Is there a moon this evening?

TOM: It's rising over Garfinkel's Delicatessen.

AMANDA: So it is! A little silver slipper of a moon. Have you made a wish on it yet?

TOM: Um-hum.

AMANDA: What did you wish for?

TOM: That's a secret.

AMANDA: A secret, huh? Well, I won't tell mine either. I will be just as mysterious as you.

TOM: I bet I can guess what yours is.

AMANDA: Is my head so transparent?

TOM: You're not a sphinx.

AMANDA: No, I don't have secrets. I'll tell you what I wished for on the moon. Success and happiness for my precious children! I wish for that whenever there's a moon, and when there isn't a moon, I wish for it, too.

TOM: I thought perhaps you wished for a gentleman caller.

AMANDA: Why do you say that?

TOM: Don't you remember asking me to fetch one?

AMANDA: I remember suggesting that it would be nice for

your sister if you brought home some nice young man from the warehouse. I think that I've made that suggestion more than once.

TOM: Yes, you have made it repeatedly.

AMANDA: Well?

TOM: We are going to have one.

AMANDA: *What?*

TOM: A gentleman caller!

[THE ANNUNCIATION IS CELEBRATED WITH MUSIC.]

[AMANDA *rises.*]

[IMAGE ON SCREEN: CALLER WITH BOUQUET.]

AMANDA: You mean you have asked some nice young man to come over?

TOM: Yep. I've asked him to dinner.

AMANDA: You really did?

TOM: I did!

AMANDA: You did, and did he—*accept?*

TOM: He did!

AMANDA: Well, well—well, well! That's—lovely!

TOM: I thought that you would be pleased.

AMANDA: It's definite, then?

TOM: Very definite.

AMANDA: Soon?

TOM: Very soon.

AMANDA: For heaven's sake, stop putting on and tell me some things, will you?

TOM: What things do you want me to tell you?

AMANDA: *Naturally* I would like to know when he's *coming!*

TOM: He's coming tomorrow.

AMANDA: *Tomorrow?*

TOM: Yep. Tomorrow.

AMANDA: But, Tom!

TOM: Yes, Mother?

AMANDA: Tomorrow gives me no time!

TOM: Time for what?

AMANDA: Preparations! Why didn't you phone me at once, as soon as you asked him, the minute that he accepted? Then, don't you see, I could have been getting ready!

TOM: You don't have to make any fuss.

AMANDA: Oh, Tom, Tom, Tom, of course I have to make

a fuss! I want things nice, not sloppy! Not thrown together. I'll certainly have to do some fast thinking, won't I?

TOM: I don't see why you have to think at all.

AMANDA: You just don't know. We can't have a gentleman caller in a pig-sty! All my wedding silver has to be polished, the monogrammed table linen ought to be laundered! The windows have to be washed and fresh curtains put up. And how about clothes? We have to *wear* something, don't we?

TOM: Mother, this boy is no one to make a fuss over!

AMANDA: Do you realize he's the first young man we've introduced to your sister?

It's terrible, dreadful, disgraceful that poor little sister has never received a single gentleman caller! Tom, come inside! [*She opens the screen door.*]

TOM: What for?

AMANDA: I want to ask you some things.

TOM: If you're going to make such a fuss, I'll call it off, I'll tell him not to come!

AMANDA: You certainly won't do anything of the kind. Nothing offends people worse than broken engagements. It simply means I'll have to work like a Turk! We won't be brilliant, but we will pass inspection. Come on inside. [TOM *follows, groaning.*] Sit down.

TOM: Any particular place you would like me to sit?

AMANDA: Thank heavens I've got that new sofa! I'm also making payments on a floor lamp I'll have sent out! And put the chintz covers on, they'll brighten things up! Of course I'd hoped to have these walls re-papered. . . . What is the young man's name?

TOM: His name is O'Connor.

AMANDA: That, of course, means fish—tomorrow is Friday! I'll have that salmon loaf—with Durkee's dressing! What does he do? He works at the warehouse?

TOM: Of course! How else would I—

AMANDA: Tom, he—doesn't drink?

TOM: Why do you ask me that?

AMANDA: Your father *did!*

TOM: Don't get started on that!

AMANDA: He *does* drink, then?

TOM: Not that I know of!

AMANDA: Make sure, be certain! The last thing I want for my daughter's a boy who drinks!

TOM: Aren't you being a little bit premature? Mr. O'Connor has not yet appeared on the scene!

AMANDA: But will tomorrow. To meet your sister, and what do I know about his character? Nothing! Old maids are better off than wives of drunkards!

TOM: Oh, my God!

AMANDA: Be still!

TOM [*Leaning forward to whisper*]: Lots of fellows meet girls whom they don't marry!

AMANDA: Oh, talk sensibly, Tom—and don't be sarcastic! [*She has gotten a hairbrush.*]

TOM: What are you doing?

AMANDA: I'm brushing that cow-lick down!

What is this young man's position at the warehouse?

TOM: [*Submitting grimly to the brush and the interrogation*]: This young man's position is that of a shipping clerk, Mother.

AMANDA: Sounds to me like a fairly responsible job, the sort of a job *you* would be in if you just had more *get-up*.

What is his salary? Have you any idea?

TOM: I would judge it to be approximately eighty-five dollars a month.

AMANDA: Well—not princely, but—

TOM: Twenty more than I make.

AMANDA: Yes, how well I know! But for a family man, eighty-five dollars a month is not much more than you can just get by on. . . .

TOM: Yes, but Mr. O'Connor is not a family man.

AMANDA: He might be, mightn't he? Some time in the future?

TOM: I see. Plans and provisions.

AMANDA: You are the only young man that I know of who ignores the fact that the future becomes the present, the present the past, and the past turns into everlasting regret if you don't plan for it!

TOM: I will think that over and see what I can make of it.

AMANDA: Don't be supercilious with your mother! Tell me some more about this—what do you call him?

TOM: James D. O'Connor. The D. is for Delaney.

AMANDA: Irish on *both* sides! *Gracious!* And doesn't drink?

TOM: Shall I call him up and ask him right this minute?

AMANDA: The only way to find out about those things is to make discreet inquiries at the proper moment. When I was a girl in Blue Mountain and it was suspected that a young man drank, the girl whose attentions he had been receiving, if any girl *was,* would sometimes speak to the minister of his church, or rather her father would if her father was living, and sort of feel him out on the young man's character. That is the way such things are discreetly handled to keep a young woman from making a tragic mistake!

TOM: Then how did you happen to make a tragic mistake?

AMANDA: That innocent look of your father's had everyone fooled!

He *smiled*—the world was *enchanted!*

No girl can do worse than put herself at the mercy of a handsome appearance!

I hope that Mr. O'Connor is not too good-looking.

TOM: No, he's not too good-looking. He's covered with freckles and hasn't too much of a nose.

AMANDA: He's not right-down homely, though?

TOM: Not right-down homely. Just medium homely, I'd say.

AMANDA: Character's what to look for in a man.

TOM: That's what I've always said, Mother.

AMANDA: You've never said anything of the kind and I suspect you would never give it a thought.

TOM: Don't be so suspicious of me.

AMANDA: At least I hope he's the type that's up and coming.

TOM: I think he really goes in for self-improvement.

AMANDA: What reason have you to think so?

TOM: He goes to night school.

AMANDA [*Beaming*]: Splendid! What does he do, I mean study?

TOM: Radio engineering and public speaking!

AMANDA: Then he has visions of being advanced in the world!

Any young man who studies public speaking is aiming to have an executive job some day!

And radio engineering? A thing for the future!

Both of these facts are very illuminating. Those are the sort of things that a mother should know concerning any young man who comes to call on her daughter. Seriously or—not.

TOM: One little warning. He doesn't know about Laura. I didn't let on that we had dark ulterior motives. I just said, why don't you come and have dinner with us? He said okay and that was the whole conversation.

AMANDA: I bet it was! You're eloquent as an oyster.

However, he'll know about Laura when he gets here. When he sees how lovely and sweet and pretty she is, he'll thank his lucky stars he was asked to dinner.

TOM: Mother, you mustn't expect too much of Laura.

AMANDA: What do you mean?

TOM: Laura seems all those things to you and me because she's ours and we love her. We don't even notice she's crippled any more.

AMANDA: Don't say crippled! You know that I never allow that word to be used!

TOM: But face facts, Mother. She is and—that's not all—

AMANDA: What do you mean "not all"?

TOM: Laura is very different from other girls.

AMANDA: I think the difference is all to her advantage.

TOM: Not quite all—in the eyes of others—strangers—she's terribly shy and lives in a world of her own and those things make her seem a little peculiar to people outside the house.

AMANDA: Don't say peculiar.

TOM: Face the facts. She is.

[THE DANCE-HALL MUSIC CHANGES TO A TANGO THAT HAS A MINOR AND SOMEWHAT OMINOUS TONE.]

AMANDA: In what way is she peculiar—may I ask?

TOM [*Gently*]: She lives in a world of her own—a world of —little glass ornaments, Mother. . . . [*Gets up.* AMANDA *remains holding brush, looking at him, troubled.*] She plays old phonograph records and—that's about all— [*He glances at himself in the mirror and crosses to door.*]

AMANDA [*Sharply*]: Where are you going?

TOM: I'm going to the movies. [*Out screen door.*]

AMANDA: Not to the movies, every night to the movies! [*Follows quickly to screen door.*] I don't believe you always go to the movies! [*He is gone.* AMANDA *looks worriedly after him for a moment. Then vitality and optimism return and she turns from the door. Crossing to portieres.*] Laura! Laura! [LAURA *answers from kitchenette.*]

LAURA: Yes, Mother.

AMANDA: Let those dishes go and come in front! [LAURA *appears with dish towel. Gaily.*] Laura, come here and make a wish on the moon!

[SCREEN IMAGE: MOON.]

LAURA [*Entering*]: Moon—moon?

AMANDA: A little silver slipper of a moon. Look over your left shoulder, Laura, and make a wish!

[LAURA *looks faintly puzzled as if called out of sleep.* AMANDA *seizes her shoulders and turns her at an angle by the door.*] Now!

Now, darling, *wish!*

LAURA: What shall I wish for, Mother?

AMANDA [*Her voice trembling and her eyes suddenly filling with tears*]: Happiness! Good fortune!

[*The violin rises and the stage dims out.*]

CURTAIN

SCENE VI

IMAGE: HIGH SCHOOL HERO.

TOM: And so the following evening I brought Jim home to dinner. I had known Jim slightly in high school. In high school Jim was a hero. He had tremendous Irish good nature and vitality with the scrubbed and polished look of white chinaware. He seemed to move in a continual spotlight. He was a star in basketball, captain of the debating club, president of the senior class and the glee club and he sang the male lead in the annual light operas. He was always running or bounding, never just walking. He seemed always at the point of defeating the law of gravity. He was shooting with such velocity through his adolescence that you would logically expect him to arrive at nothing short of the White House by the time he was thirty. But Jim apparently ran into more interference after his graduation from Soldan. His speed had definitely slowed. Six years after he left high school he was holding a job that wasn't much better than mine.

[IMAGE: CLERK.]

He was the only one at the warehouse with whom I was on

friendly terms. I was valuable to him as someone who could remember his former glory, who had seen him win basketball games and the silver cup in debating. He knew of my secret practice of retiring to a cabinet of the wash-room to work on poems when business was slack in the warehouse. He called me Shakespeare. And while the other boys in the warehouse regarded me with suspicious hostility, Jim took a humorous attitude toward me. Gradually his attitude affected the others, their hostility wore off and they also began to smile at me as people smile at an oddly fashioned dog who trots across their path at some distance.

I knew that Jim and Laura had known each other at Soldan, and I had heard Laura speak admiringly of his voice. I didn't know if Jim remembered her or not. In high school Laura had been as unobtrusive as Jim had been astonishing. If he did remember Laura, it was not as my sister, for when I asked him to dinner, he grinned and said, "You know, Shakespeare, I never thought of you as having folks!"

He was about to discover that I did. . . .

[LIGHT UPSTAGE.]

[LEGEND ON SCREEN: "THE ACCENT OF A COMING FOOT."]

[*Friday evening. It is about five o'clock of a late spring evening which comes "scattering poems in the sky."*]

[*A delicate lemony light is in the Wingfield apartment.*]

[AMANDA *has worked like a Turk in preparation for the gentleman caller. The results are astonishing. The new floor lamp with its rose-silk shade is in place, a colored paper lantern conceals the broken light fixture in the ceiling, new billowing white curtains are at the windows, chintz covers are on chairs and sofa, a pair of new sofa pillows make their initial appearance.*]

[*Open boxes and tissue paper are scattered on the floor.*]

[LAURA *stands in the middle with lifted arms while* AMANDA *crouches before her, adjusting the hem of the new dress, devout and ritualistic. The dress is colored and designed by memory. The arrangement of* LAURA'S *hair is changed; it is softer and more becoming. A fragile, unearthly prettiness has come out in* LAURA: *she is like a piece of translucent glass touched by light, given a momentary radiance, not actual, not lasting.*]

AMANDA [*Impatiently*]: Why are you trembling?

LAURA: Mother, you've made me so nervous!

AMANDA: How have I made you nervous?

LAURA: By all this fuss! You make it seem so important!

AMANDA: I don't understand you, Laura. You couldn't be satisfied with just sitting home, and yet whenever I try to arrange something for you, you seem to resist it. [*She gets up.*] Now take a look at yourself.

No, wait! Wait just a moment—I have an idea!

LAURA: What is it now?

[AMANDA *produces two powder puffs which she wraps in handkerchiefs and stuffs in* LAURA'S *bosom.*]

LAURA: Mother, what are you doing?

AMANDA: They call them "Gay Deceivers"!

LAURA: I won't wear them!

AMANDA: You will!

LAURA: Why should I?

AMANDA: Because, to be painfully honest, your chest is flat.

LAURA: You make it seem like we were setting a trap.

AMANDA: All pretty girls are a trap, a pretty trap, and men expect them to be.

[LEGEND: "A PRETTY TRAP."]

Now look at yourself, young lady. This is the prettiest you will ever be!

I've got to fix myself now! You're going to be surprised by your mother's appearance! [*She crosses through portieres, humming gaily.*]

[LAURA *moves slowly to the long mirror and stares solemnly at herself.*]

[*A wind blows the white curtains inward in a slow, graceful motion and with a faint, sorrowful sighing.*]

AMANDA [*Off stage*]: It isn't dark enough yet. [LAURA *turns slowly before the mirror with a troubled look.*]

[LEGEND ON SCREEN: "THIS IS MY SISTER: CELEBRATE HER WITH STRINGS!" MUSIC.]

AMANDA [*Laughing, off*]: I'm going to show you something. I'm going to make a spectacular appearance!

LAURA: What is it, Mother?

AMANDA: Possess your soul in patience—you will see!

Something I've resurrected from that old trunk! Styles haven't changed so terribly much after all. . . .

[*She parts the portieres.*]

Now just look at your mother!

[*She wears a girlish frock of yellowed voile with a blue silk sash. She carries a bunch of jonquils—the legend of her youth is nearly revived. Feverishly.*]

This is the dress in which I led the cotillion. Won the cake-walk twice at Sunset Hill, wore one spring to the Governor's ball in Jackson!

See how I sashayed around the ballroom, Laura?

[*She raises her skirt and does a mincing step around the room.*]

I wore it on Sundays for my gentlemen callers! I had it on the day I met your father—

I had malaria fever all that spring. The change of climate from East Tennessee to the Delta—weakened resistance—I had a little temperature all the time—not enough to be serious—just enough to make me restless and giddy!—Invitations poured in—parties all over the Delta!—"Stay in bed," said Mother, "you have fever!"—but I just wouldn't.—I took quinine but kept on going, going!—Evenings, dances!—After-noons, long, long rides! Picnics—lovely!—So lovely, that country in May.—All lacy with dogwood, literally flooded with jonquils!—That was the spring I had the craze for jonquils. Jonquils became an absolute obsession. Mother said, "Honey, there's no more room for jonquils." And still I kept on bringing in more jonquils. Whenever, wherever I saw them, I'd say, "Stop! Stop! I see jonquils!" I made the young men help me gather the jonquils! It was a joke, Amanda and her jonquils! Finally there were no more vases to hold them, every available space was filled with jonquils. No vases to hold them? All right, I'll hold them myself! And then I—[*She stops in front of the picture. MUSIC.*] met your father!

Malaria fever and jonquils and then—this—boy. . . .

[*She switches on the rose-colored lamp.*]

I hope they get here before it starts to rain.

[*She crosses upstage and places the jonquils in bowl on table.*]

I gave your brother a little extra change so he and Mr. O'Connor could take the service car home.

LAURA [*With altered look*]: What did you say his name was?

AMANDA: O'Connor.

LAURA: What is his first name?

AMANDA: I don't remember. Oh, yes, I do. It was—Jim!

[LAURA *sways slightly and catches hold of a chair.*]

[LEGEND ON SCREEN: "NOT JIM!"]

LAURA [*Faintly*]: Not—Jim!

AMANDA: Yes, that was it, it was Jim! I've never known a Jim that wasn't nice!

[MUSIC: OMINOUS.]

LAURA: Are you sure his name is Jim O'Connor?

AMANDA: Yes. Why?

LAURA: Is he the one that Tom used to know in high school?

AMANDA: He didn't say so. I think he just got to know him at the warehouse.

LAURA: There was a Jim O'Connor we both knew in high school—[*Then, with effort.*] If that is the one that Tom is bringing to dinner—you'll have to excuse me, I won't come to the table.

AMANDA: What sort of nonsense is this?

LAURA: You asked me once if I'd ever liked a boy. Don't you remember I showed you this boy's picture?

AMANDA: You mean the boy you showed me in the year book?

LAURA: Yes, that boy.

AMANDA: Laura, Laura, were you in love with that boy?

LAURA: I don't know, Mother. All I know is I couldn't sit at the table if it was him!

AMANDA: It won't be him! It isn't the least bit likely. But whether it is or not, you will come to the table. You will not be excused.

LAURA: I'll have to be, Mother.

AMANDA: I don't intend to humor your silliness, Laura. I've had too much from you and your brother, both!

So just sit down and compose yourself till they come. Tom has forgotten his key so you'll have to let them in, when they arrive.

LAURA [*Panicky*]: Oh, Mother—*you* answer the door!

AMANDA [*Lightly*]: I'll be in the kitchen—busy!

LAURA: Oh, Mother, please answer the door, don't make me do it!

AMANDA [*Crossing into kitchenette*]: I've got to fix the dressing for the salmon. Fuss, fuss—silliness!—over a gentleman caller!

[*Door swings shut.* LAURA *is left alone.*]

[LEGEND: "TERROR!"]

[*She utters a low moan and turns off the lamp—sits stiffly on the edge of the sofa, knotting her fingers together.*]

[LEGEND ON SCREEN: "THE OPENING OF A DOOR!"]

[TOM *and* JIM *appear on the fire-escape steps and climb to landing. Hearing their approach,* LAURA *rises with a panicky gesture. She retreats to the portieres.*]

[*The doorbell.* LAURA *catches her breath and touches her throat. Low drums.*]

AMANDA [*Calling*]: Laura, sweetheart! The door!

[LAURA *stares at it without moving.*]

JIM: I think we just beat the rain.

TOM: Uh-huh. [*He rings again, nervously.* JIM *whistles and fishes for a cigarette.*]

AMANDA [*Very, very gaily*]: Laura, that is your brother and Mr. O'Connor! Will you let them in, darling?

[LAURA *crosses toward kitchenette door.*]

LAURA [*Breathlessly*]: Mother—you go to the door!

[AMANDA *steps out of kitchenette and stares furiously at* LAURA. [*She points imperiously at the door.*]

LAURA: Please, please!

AMANDA [*In a fierce whisper*]: What is the matter with you, you silly thing?

LAURA [*Desperately*]: Please, you answer it, *please!*

AMANDA: I told you I wasn't going to humor you, Laura. Why have you chosen this moment to lose your mind?

LAURA: Please, please, please, you go!

AMANDA: You'll have to go to the door because I can't!

LAURA [*Despairingly*]: I can't either!

AMANDA: *Why?*

LAURA: I'm *sick!*

AMANDA: I'm sick, too—of your nonsense! Why can't you

and your brother be normal people? Fantastic whims and behavior!

[TOM *gives a long ring.*]

Preposterous goings on! Can you give me one reason—[*Calls out lyrically.*] COMING! JUST ONE SECOND!—why you should be afraid to open a door? Now you answer it, Laura!

LAURA: Oh, oh, oh . . . [*She returns through the portieres. Darts to the victrola and winds it frantically and turns it on.*]

AMANDA: Laura Wingfield, you march right to that door!

LAURA: Yes—yes, Mother!

[*A faraway, scratchy rendition of "Dardanella" softens the air and gives her strength to move through it. She slips to the door and draws it cautiously open.*]

[TOM *enters with the caller,* JIM O'CONNOR.]

TOM: Laura, this is Jim. Jim, this is my sister, Laura.

JIM [*Stepping inside*]: I didn't know that Shakespeare had a sister!

LAURA [*Retreating stiff and trembling from the door*]: How —how do you do?

JIM [*Heartily extending his hand*]: Okay!

[LAURA *touches it hesitantly with hers.*]

JIM: Your hand's *cold*, Laura!

LAURA: Yes, well—I've been playing the victrola. . . .

JIM: Must have been playing classical music on it! You ought to play a little hot swing music to warm you up!

LAURA: Excuse me—I haven't finished playing the victrola. . . . [*She turns awkwardly and hurries into the front room. She pauses a second by the victrola. Then catches her breath and darts through the portieres like a frightened deer.*]

JIM [*Grinning*]: What was the matter?

TOM: Oh—with Laura? Laura is—terribly shy.

JIM: Shy, huh? It's unusual to meet a shy girl nowadays. I don't believe you ever mentioned you had a sister.

TOM: Well, now you know. I have one. Here is the *Post Dispatch*. You want a piece of it?

JIM: Uh-huh.

TOM: What piece? The comics?

JIM: Sports! [*Glances at it.*] Ole Dizzy Dean is on his bad behavior.

TOM [*Disinterest*]: Yeah? [*Lights cigarette and crosses back to fire-escape door.*]

JIM: Where are *you* going?

TOM: I'm going out on the terrace.

JIM [*Goes after him*]: You know, Shakespeare—I'm going to sell you a bill of goods!

TOM: What goods?

JIM: A course I'm taking.

TOM: Huh?

JIM: In public speaking! You and me, we're not the warehouse type.

TOM: Thanks—that's good news.

But what has public speaking got to do with it?

JIM: It fits you for—executive positions!

TOM: Awww.

JIM: I tell you it's done a helluva lot for me.

[IMAGE: EXECUTIVE AT DESK.]

TOM: In what respect?

JIM: In every! Ask yourself what is the difference between you an' me and men in the office down front? Brains?—No!—Ability?—No! Then what? Just one little thing—

TOM: What is that one little thing?

JIM: Primarily it amounts to—social poise! Being able to square up to people and hold your own on any social level!

AMANDA [*Off stage*]: Tom?

TOM: Yes, Mother?

AMANDA: Is that you and Mr. O'Connor?

TOM: Yes, Mother.

AMANDA: Well, you just make yourselves comfortable in there.

TOM: Yes, Mother.

AMANDA: Ask Mr. O'Connor if he would like to wash his hands.

JIM: Aw, no—no—thank you—I took care of that at the warehouse. Tom—

TOM: Yes?

JIM: Mr. Mendoza was speaking to me about you.

TOM: Favorably?

JIM: What do you think?

TOM: Well—

JIM: You're going to be out of a job if you don't wake up.

TOM: I am waking up—

JIM: You show no signs.

TOM: The signs are interior.

[IMAGE ON SCREEN: THE SAILING VESSEL WITH JOLLY ROGER AGAIN.]

TOM: I'm planning to change. [*He leans over the rail speaking with quiet exhilaration. The incandescent marquees and signs of the first-run movie houses light his face from across the alley. He looks like a voyager.*] I'm right at the point of committing myself to a future that doesn't include the warehouse and Mr. Mendoza or even a night-school course in public speaking.

JIM: What are you gassing about?

TOM: I'm tired of the movies.

JIM: Movies!

TOM: Yes, movies! Look at them— [*A wave toward the marvels of Grand Avenue.*] All of those glamorous people— having adventures—hogging it all, gobbling the whole thing up! You know what happens? People go to the *movies* instead of *moving!* Hollywood characters are supposed to have all the adventures for everybody in America, while everybody in America sits in a dark room and watches them have them! Yes, until there's a war. That's when adventure becomes available to the masses! *Everyone's* dish, not only Gable's! Then the people in the dark room come out of the dark room to have some adventures themselves—Goody, goody!—It's our turn now, to go to the South Sea Islands—to make a safari—to be exotic, far-off!—But I'm not patient. I don't want to wait till then. I'm tired of the *movies* and I am *about* to *move!*

JIM [*Incredulously*]: Move?

TOM: Yes.

JIM: When?

TOM: Soon!

JIM: Where? Where?

[THEME THREE MUSIC SEEMS TO ANSWER THE QUESTION, WHILE TOM THINKS IT OVER. HE SEARCHES AMONG HIS POCKETS.]

TOM: I'm starting to boil inside. I know I seem dreamy, but inside—well, I'm boiling!—Whenever I pick up a shoe, I shud-

der a little thinking how short life is and what I am doing!—
Whatever that means, I know it doesn't mean shoes—except as
something to wear on a traveler's feet! [*Finds paper.*] Look—

JIM: What?

TOM: I'm a member.

JIM [*Reading*]: The Union of Merchant Seamen.

TOM: I paid my dues this month, instead of the light bill.

JIM: You will regret it when they turn the lights off.

TOM: I won't be here.

JIM: How about your mother?

TOM: I'm like my father. The bastard son of a bastard! See
how he grins? And he's been absent going on sixteen years!

JIM: You're just talking, you drip. How does your mother feel
about it?

TOM: Shhh!—Here comes Mother! Mother is not acquainted
with my plans!

AMANDA [*Enters portieres*]: Where are you all?

TOM: On the terrace, Mother.

[*They start inside. She advances to them.* TOM *is distinctly
shocked at her appearance. Even* JIM *blinks a little. He is
making his first contact with girlish Southern vivacity and
in spite of the night-school course in public speaking is somewhat thrown off the beam by the unexpected outlay of social
charm.*]

[*Certain responses are attempted by* JIM *but are swept
aside by* AMANDA'S *gay laughter and chatter.* TOM *is embarrassed but after the first shock* JIM *reacts very warmly.
Grins and chuckles, is altogether won over.*]

[IMAGE: AMANDA AS A GIRL.]

AMANDA [*Coyly smiling, shaking her girlish ringlets*]: Well,
well, well, so this is Mr. O'Connor. Introductions entirely un-
necessary. I've heard so much about you from my boy. I finally
said to him, Tom—good gracious!—why don't you bring this
paragon to supper? I'd like to meet this nice young man at the
warehouse!—Instead of just hearing you sing his praises so
much!

I don't know why my son is so stand-offish—that's not Southern behavior!

Let's sit down and—I think we could stand a little more

air in here! Tom, leave the door open. I felt a nice fresh breeze a moment ago. Where has it gone to?

Mmm, so warm already! And not quite summer, even. We're going to burn up when summer really gets started.

However, we're having—we're having a very light supper. I think light things are better fo' this time of year. The same as light clothes are. Light clothes an' light food are what warm weather calls fo'. You know our blood gets so thick during th' winter—it takes a while fo' us to *adjust* ou'selves!—when the season changes . . .

It's come so quick this year. I wasn't prepared. All of a sudden—heavens! Already summer!—I ran to the trunk an' pulled out this light dress— Terribly old! Historical almost! But feels so good—so good an' co-ol, y' know. . . .

TOM: Mother—

AMANDA: Yes, honey?

TOM: How about—supper?

AMANDA: Honey, you go ask Sister if supper is ready! You know that Sister is in full charge of supper!

Tell her you hungry boys are waiting for it.

[*To* JIM.]

Have you met Laura?

JIM: She—

AMANDA: Let you in? Oh, good, you've met already! It's rare for a girl as sweet an' pretty as Laura to be domestic! But Laura is, thank heavens, not only pretty but also very domestic. I'm not at all. I never was a bit. I never could make a thing but angel-food cake. Well, in the South we had so many servants. Gone, gone, gone. All vestige of gracious living! Gone completely! I wasn't prepared for what the future brought me. All of my gentlemen callers were sons of planters and so of course I assumed that I would be married to one and raise my family on a large piece of land with plenty of servants. But man proposes—and woman accepts the proposal!—To vary that old, old saying a little bit—I married no planter! I married a man who worked for the telephone company!— That gallantly smiling gentleman over there! [*Points to the picture.*] A telephone man who—fell in love with long distance! —Now he travels and I don't even know where!—But what am I going on for about my—tribulations?

Tell me yours—I hope you don't have any!
Tom?

TOM [*Returning*]: Yes, Mother?

AMANDA: Is supper nearly ready?

TOM: It looks to me like supper is on the table.

AMANDA: Let me look— [*She rises prettily and looks through portieres.*] Oh, lovely!—But where is Sister?

TOM: Laura is not feeling well and she says that she thinks she'd better not come to the table.

AMANDA: What?—Nonsense!—Laura? Oh, Laura!

LAURA [*Off stage, faintly*]: Yes, Mother.

AMANDA: You really must come to the table. We won't be seated until you come to the table!
Come in, Mr. O'Connor. You sit over there, and I'll—
Laura? Laura Wingfield!
You're keeping us waiting, honey! We can't say grace until you come to the table!

[*The back door is pushed weakly open and* LAURA *comes in. She is obviously quite faint, her lips trembling, her eyes wide and staring. She moves unsteadily toward the table.*]

[LEGEND: "TERROR!"]

[*Outside a summer storm is coming abruptly. The white curtains billow inward at the windows and there is a sorrowful murmur and deep blue dusk.*]

[LAURA *suddenly stumbles—she catches at a chair with a faint moan.*]

TOM: Laura!

AMANDA: Laura!

[*There is a clap of thunder.*]

[LEGEND: "AH!"]

[*Despairingly.*]

Why, Laura, you *are* sick, darling! Tom, help your sister into the living room, dear!
Sit in the living room, Laura—rest on the sofa.
Well!

[*To the gentleman caller.*]

Standing over the hot stove made her ill!—I told her that it was just too warm this evening, but—

[TOM *comes back in.* LAURA *is on the sofa.*]

Is Laura all right now?

TOM: Yes.

AMANDA: What *is* that? Rain? A nice cool rain has come up!
[*She gives the gentleman caller a frightened look.*]
I think we may—have grace—now . . .
[TOM *looks at her stupidly.*]
Tom, honey—you say grace!

TOM: Oh . . .
"For these and all thy mercies—"
[*They bow their heads,* AMANDA *stealing a nervous glance
at* JIM. *In the living room* LAURA, *stretched on the sofa,
clenches her hand to her lips, to hold back a shuddering sob.*]
God's Holy Name be praised—

THE SCENE DIMS OUT

SCENE VII

A SOUVENIR.
*Half an hour later. Dinner is just being finished in the upstage
area which is concealed by the drawn portieres.*

As the curtain rises LAURA *is still huddled upon the sofa, her
feet drawn under her, her head resting on a pale blue pillow,
her eyes wide and mysteriously watchful. The new floor lamp
with its shade of rose-colored silk gives a soft, becoming light
to her face, bringing out the fragile, unearthly prettiness
which usually escapes attention. There is a steady murmur
of rain, but it is slackening and stops soon after the scene
begins; the air outside becomes pale and luminous as the
moon breaks out.*

*A moment after the curtain rises, the lights in both rooms
flicker and go out.*

JIM: Hey, there, Mr. Light Bulb!
[AMANDA *laughs nervously.*]
[LEGEND: "SUSPENSION OF A PUBLIC SERVICE."]

AMANDA: Where was Moses when the lights went out? Ha-ha.
Do you know the answer to that one, Mr. O'Connor?

JIM: No, Ma'am, what's the answer?

AMANDA: In the dark!
[JIM *laughs appreciatively.*]

Everybody sit still. I'll light the candles. Isn't it lucky we have them on the table? Where's a match? Which of you gentlemen can provide a match?

JIM: Here.

AMANDA: Thank you, sir.

JIM: Not at all, Ma'am!

AMANDA: I guess the fuse has burnt out. Mr. O'Connor, can you tell a burnt-out fuse? I know I can't and Tom is a total loss when it comes to mechanics.

[SOUND: GETTING UP: VOICES RECEDE A LITTLE TO KITCHENETTE.]

Oh, be careful you don't bump into something. We don't want our gentleman caller to break his neck. Now wouldn't that be a fine howdy-do?

JIM: Ha-ha!

Where is the fuse-box?

AMANDA: Right here next to the stove. Can you see anything?

JIM: Just a minute.

AMANDA: Isn't electricity a mysterious thing?

Wasn't it Benjamin Franklin who tied a key to a kite?

We live in such a mysterious universe, don't we? Some people say that science clears up all the mysteries for us. In my opinion it only creates more!

Have you found it yet?

JIM: No, Ma'am. All these fuses look okay to me.

AMANDA: Tom!

TOM: Yes, Mother?

AMANDA: That light bill I gave you several days ago. The one I told you we got the notices about?

[LEGEND: "HA!"]

TOM: Oh.—Yeah.

AMANDA: You didn't neglect to pay it by any chance?

TOM: Why, I—

AMANDA: Didn't! I might have known it!

JIM: Shakespeare probably wrote a poem on that light bill, Mrs. Wingfield.

AMANDA: I might have known better than to trust him with it! There's such a high price for negligence in this world!

JIM: Maybe the poem will win a ten-dollar prize.

AMANDA: We'll just have to spend the remainder of the

evening in the nineteenth century, before Mr. Edison made the Mazda lamp!

JIM: Candlelight is my favorite kind of light.

AMANDA: That shows you're romantic! But that's no excuse for Tom.

Well, we got through dinner. Very considerate of them to let us get through dinner before they plunged us into everlasting darkness, wasn't it, Mr. O'Connor?

JIM: Ha-ha!

AMANDA: Tom, as a penalty for your carelessness you can help me with the dishes.

JIM: Let me give you a hand.

AMANDA: Indeed you will not!

JIM: I ought to be good for something.

AMANDA: Good for something? [*Her tone is rhapsodic.*]

You? Why, Mr. O'Connor, nobody, *nobody's* given me this much entertainment in years—as you have!

JIM: Aw, now, Mrs. Wingfield!

AMANDA: I'm not exaggerating, not one bit! But Sister is all by her lonesome. You go keep her company in the parlor!

I'll give you this lovely old candelabrum that used to be on the altar at the church of the Heavenly Rest. It was melted a little out of shape when the church burnt down. Lightning struck it one spring. Gypsy Jones was holding a revival at the time and he intimated that the church was destroyed because the Episcopalians gave card parties.

JIM: Ha-ha.

AMANDA: And how about you coaxing Sister to drink a little wine? I think it would be good for her! Can you carry both at once?

JIM: Sure. I'm Superman!

AMANDA: Now, Thomas, get into this apron!

[*The door of kitchenette swings closed on* AMANDA'S *gay laughter; the flickering light approaches the portieres.*]

[LAURA *sits up nervously as he enters. Her speech at first is low and breathless from the almost intolerable strain of being alone with a stranger.*]

[THE LEGEND: "I DON'T SUPPOSE YOU REMEMBER ME AT ALL!"]

[*In her first speeches in this scene, before* JIM'S *warmth*] *overcomes her paralyzing shyness,* LAURA'S *voice is thin and breathless as though she has just run up a steep flight of stairs.*]

[JIM's *attitude is gently humorous. In playing this scene it should be stressed that while the incident is apparently unimportant, it is to* LAURA *the climax of her secret life.*]

JIM: Hello, there, Laura.

LAURA [*Faintly*]: Hello. [*She clears her throat.*]

JIM: How are you feeling now? Better?

LAURA: Yes. Yes, thank you.

JIM: This is for you. A little dandelion wine. [*He extends it toward her with extravagant gallantry.*]

LAURA: Thank you.

JIM: Drink it—but don't get drunk!

[*He laughs heartily.* LAURA *takes the glass uncertainly; laughs shyly.*]

Where shall I set the candles?

LAURA: Oh—oh, anywhere . . .

JIM: How about here on the floor? Any objections?

LAURA: No.

JIM: I'll spread a newspaper under to catch the drippings. I like to sit on the floor. Mind if I do?

LAURA: Oh, no.

JIM: Give me a pillow?

LAURA: What?

JIM: A pillow!

LAURA: Oh . . . [*Hands him one quickly.*]

JIM: How about you? Don't you like to sit on the floor?

LAURA: Oh—yes.

JIM: Why don't you, then?

LAURA: I—will.

JIM: Take a pillow! [LAURA *does. Sits on the other side of the candelabrum.* JIM *crosses his legs and smiles engagingly at her.*] I can't hardly see you sitting way over there.

LAURA: I can—see you.

JIM: I know, but that's not fair, I'm in the limelight. [LAURA *moves her pillow closer.*] Good! Now I can see you! Comfortable?

LAURA: Yes.

JIM: So am I. Comfortable as a cow! Will you have some gum?

LAURA: No, thank you.

JIM: I think that I will indulge, with your permission. [*Musingly unwraps it and holds it up.*] Think of the fortune made by the guy that invented the first piece of chewing gum. Amazing, huh? The Wrigley Building is one of the sights of Chicago. —I saw it summer before last when I went up to the Century of Progress. Did you take in the Century of Progress?

LAURA: No, I didn't.

JIM: Well, it was quite a wonderful exposition. What impressed me most was the Hall of Science. Gives you an idea of what the future will be in America, even more wonderful than the present time is! [*Pause. Smiling at her.*] Your brother tells me you're shy. Is that right, Laura?

LAURA: I—don't know.

JIM: I judge you to be an old-fashioned type of girl. Well, I think that's a pretty good type to be. Hope you don't think I'm being too personal—do you?

LAURA [*Hastily, out of embarrassment*]: I believe I *will* take a piece of gum, if you—don't mind. [*Clearing her throat.*] Mr. O'Connor, have you—kept up with your singing?

JIM: Singing? Me?

LAURA: Yes. I remember what a beautiful voice you had.

JIM: When did you hear me sing?

[VOICE OFF STAGE IN THE PAUSE.]

VOICE [*Off stage*]:

> O blow, ye winds, heigh-ho,
> A-roving I will go!
> I'm off to my love
> With a boxing glove—
> Ten thousand miles away!

JIM: You say you've heard me sing?

LAURA: Oh, yes! Yes, very often . . . I don't suppose—you remember me—at all?

JIM [*Smiling doubtfully*]: You know I have an idea I've seen you before. I had that idea soon as you opened the door. It seemed almost like I was about to remember your name. But the name that I started to call you—wasn't a name! And so I stopped myself before I said it.

LAURA: Wasn't it—Blue Roses?

JIM [*Springs up. Grinning*]: Blue Roses!—My gosh, yes—
Blue Roses!

That's what I had on my tongue when you opened the door!
Isn't it funny what tricks your memory plays? I didn't connect you with high school somehow or other.

But that's where it was; it was high school. I didn't even
know you were Shakespeare's sister!

Gosh, I'm sorry.

LAURA: I didn't expect you to. You—barely knew me!

JIM: But we did have a speaking acquaintance, huh?

LAURA: Yes, we—spoke to each other.

JIM: When did you recognize me?

LAURA: Oh, right away!

JIM: Soon as I came in the door?

LAURA: When I heard your name I thought it was probably
you. I knew that Tom used to know you a little in high school.
So when you came in the door—

Well, then I was—sure.

JIM: Why didn't you *say* something, then?

LAURA [*Breathlessly*]: I didn't know what to say, I was—
too surprised!

JIM: For goodness' sakes! You know, this sure is funny!

LAURA: Yes! Yes, isn't it, though . . .

JIM: Didn't we have a class in something together?

LAURA: Yes, we did.

JIM: What class was that?

LAURA: It was—singing—Chorus!

JIM: Aw!

LAURA: I sat across the aisle from you in the Aud.

JIM: Aw.

LAURA: Mondays, Wednesdays and Fridays.

JIM: Now I remember—you always came in late.

LAURA: Yes, it was so hard for me, getting upstairs. I had
that brace on my leg—it clumped so loud!

JIM: I never heard any clumping.

LAURA [*Wincing at the recollection*]: To me it sounded like
—thunder!

JIM: Well, well, well, I never even noticed.

LAURA: And everybody was seated before I came in I had to

walk in front of all those people. My seat was in the back row. I had to go clumping all the way up the aisle with everyone watching!

JIM: You shouldn't have been self-conscious.

LAURA: I know, but I was. It was always such a relief when the singing started.

JIM: Aw, yes, I've placed you now! I used to call you Blue Roses. How was it that I got started calling you that?

LAURA: I was out of school a little while with pleurosis. When I came back you asked me what was the matter. I said I had pleurosis—you thought I said Blue Roses. That's what you always called me after that!

JIM: I hope you didn't mind.

LAURA: Oh, no—I liked it. You see, I wasn't acquainted with many—people. . . .

JIM: As I remember you sort of stuck by yourself.

LAURA: I—I—never have had much luck at—making friends.

JIM: I don't see why you wouldn't.

LAURA: Well, I—started out badly.

JIM: You mean being—

LAURA: Yes, it sort of—stood between me—

JIM: You shouldn't have let it!

LAURA: I know, but it did, and—

JIM: You were shy with people!

LAURA: I tried not to be but never could—

JIM: Overcome it?

LAURA: No, I—I never could!

JIM: I guess being shy is something you have to work out of kind of gradually.

LAURA [Sorrowfully]: Yes—I guess it—

JIM: Takes time!

LAURA: Yes—

JIM: People are not so dreadful when you know them. That's what you have to remember! And everybody has problems, not just you, but practically everybody has got some problems.

You think of yourself as having the only problems, as being the only one who is disappointed. But just look around you and you will see lots of people as disappointed as you are. For instance, I hoped when I was going to high school that I would be further along at this time, six years later, than I am now—

You remember that wonderful write-up I had in *The Torch?*

LAURA: Yes! [*She rises and crosses to table.*]

JIM: It said I was bound to succeed in anything I went into! [LAURA *returns with the annual.*] Holy Jeez! *The Torch!* [*He accepts it reverently. They smile across it with mutual wonder.* LAURA *crouches beside him and they begin to turn through it.* LAURA's *shyness is dissolving in his warmth.*]

LAURA: Here you are in *The Pirates of Penzance!*

JIM [*Wistfully*]: I sang the baritone lead in that operetta.

LAURA [*Raptly*]: So—*beautifully!*

JIM [*Protesting*]: Aw—

LAURA: Yes, yes—beautifully—beautifully!

JIM: You heard me?

LAURA: All three times!

JIM: No!

LAURA: Yes!

JIM: All three performances?

LAURA [*Looking down*]: Yes.

JIM: Why?

LAURA: I—wanted to ask you to—autograph my program.

JIM: Why didn't you ask me to?

LAURA: You were always surrounded by your own friends so much that I never had a chance to.

JIM: You should have just—

LAURA: Well, I—thought you might think I was—

JIM: Thought I might think you was—what?

LAURA: Oh—

JIM [*With reflective relish*]: I was beleaguered by females in those days.

LAURA: You were terribly popular!

JIM: Yeah—

LAURA: You had such a—friendly way—

JIM: I was spoiled in high school.

LAURA: Everybody—liked you!

JIM: Including you?

LAURA: I—yes, I—I did, too— [*She gently closes the book in her lap.*]

JIM: Well, well, well!—Give me that program, Laura. [*She hands it to him. He signs it with a flourish.*] There you are— better late than never!

LAURA: Oh, I—what a—surprise!

JIM: My signature isn't worth very much right now.
But some day—maybe—it will increase in value!
Being disappointed is one thing and being discouraged is
something else. I am disappointed but I am not discouraged
I'm twenty-three years old.
How old are you?

LAURA: I'll be twenty-four in June.

JIM: That's not old age!

LAURA: No, but—

JIM: You finished high school?

LAURA [*With difficulty*]: I didn't go back.

JIM: You mean you dropped out?

LAURA: I made bad grades in my final examinations. [*She
rises and replaces the book and the program. Her voice
strained.*] How is—Emily Meisenbach getting along?

JIM: Oh, that kraut-head!

LAURA: Why do you call her that?

JIM: That's what she was.

LAURA: You're not still—going with her?

JIM: I never see her.

LAURA: It said in the Personal Section that you were—engaged!

JIM: I know, but I wasn't impressed by that—propaganda!

LAURA: It wasn't—the truth?

JIM: Only in Emily's optimistic opinion!

LAURA: Oh—

[LEGEND: "WHAT HAVE YOU DONE SINCE HIGH SCHOOL?"]

[JIM *lights a cigarette and leans indolently back on his
elbows smiling at* LAURA *with a warmth and charm which
lights her inwardly with altar candles. She remains by the
table and turns in her hands a piece of glass to cover her
tumult.*]

JIM [*After several reflective puffs on a cigarette*]: What have
you done since high school? [*She seems not to hear him.*] Huh?
[LAURA *looks up.*] I said what have you done since high school,
Laura?

LAURA: Nothing much.

JIM: You must have been doing something these six long
years.

LAURA: Yes.

JIM: Well, then, such as what?

LAURA: I took a business course at business college—

JIM: How did that work out?

LAURA: Well, not very—well—I had to drop out, it gave me—indigestion—

[JIM *laughs gently.*]

JIM: What are you doing now?

LAURA: I don't do anything—much. Oh, please don't think I sit around doing nothing! My glass collection takes up a good deal of time. Glass is something you have to take good care of.

JIM: What did you say—about glass?

LAURA: Collection I said—I have one— [*She clears her throat and turns away again, acutely shy.*]

JIM [*Abruptly*]: You know what I judge to be the trouble with you?

Inferiority complex! Know what that is? That's what they call it when someone low-rates himself!

I understand it because I had it, too. Although my case was not so aggravated as yours seems to be. I had it until I took up public speaking, developed my voice, and learned that I had an aptitude for science. Before that time I never thought of myself as being outstanding in any way whatsoever!

Now I've never made a regular study of it, but I have a friend who says I can analyze people better than doctors that make a profession of it. I don't claim that to be necessarily true, but I can sure guess a person's psychology, Laura! [*Takes out his gum.*] Excuse me, Laura. I always take it out when the flavor is gone. I'll use this scrap of paper to wrap it in. I know how it is to get it stuck on a shoe.

Yep—that's what I judge to be your principal trouble. A lack of confidence in yourself as a person. You don't have the proper amount of faith in yourself. I'm basing that fact on a number of your remarks and also on certain observations I've made. For instance that clumping you thought was so awful in high school. You say that you even dreaded to walk into class. You see what you did? You dropped out of school, you gave up an education because of a clump, which as far as I know was practically non-existent! A little physical defect is what you have.

Hardly noticeable even! Magnified thousands of times by imagination!

You know what my strong advice to you is? Think of yourself as *superior* in some way!

LAURA: In what way would I think?

JIM: Why, man alive, Laura! Just look about you a little. What do you see? A world full of common people! All of 'em born and all of 'em going to die!

Which of them has one-tenth of your good points! Or mine! Or anyone else's, as far as that goes—Gosh!

Everybody excels in some one thing. Some in many!

[*Unconsciously glances at himself in the mirror.*]

All you've got to do is discover in *what!*

Take me, for instance.

[*He adjusts his tie at the mirror.*]

My interest happens to lie in electro-dynamics. I'm taking a course in radio engineering at night school, Laura, on top of a fairly responsible job at the warehouse. I'm taking that course and studying public speaking.

LAURA: Ohhhh.

JIM: Because I believe in the future of television!

[*Turning back to her.*]

I wish to be ready to go up right along with it. Therefore I'm planning to get in on the ground floor. In fact I've already made the right connections and all that remains is for the industry itself to get under way! Full steam—

[*His eyes are starry.*]

*Knowledge—*Zzzzzp! *Money—*Zzzzzzp!—*Power!*

That's the cycle democracy is built on!

[*His attitude is convincingly dynamic.* LAURA *stares at him, even her shyness eclipsed in her absolute wonder. He suddenly grins.*]

I guess you think I think a lot of myself!

LAURA: No—o-o-o, I—

JIM: Now how about you? Isn't there something you take more interest in than anything else?

LAURA: Well, I do—as I said—have my—glass collection—

[*A peal of girlish laughter from the kitchen.*]

JIM: I'm not right sure I know what you're talking about. What kind of glass is it?

LAURA: Little articles of it, they're ornaments mostly!

Most of them are little animals made out of glass, the tiniest little animals in the world. Mother calls them a glass menagerie!

Here's an example of one, if you'd like to see it!

This one is one of the oldest. It's nearly thirteen.

[MUSIC: "THE GLASS MENAGERIE."]

[*He stretches out his hand.*]

Oh, be careful—if you breathe, it breaks!

JIM: I'd better not take it. I'm pretty clumsy with things.

LAURA: Go on, I trust you with him!

[*Places it in his palm.*]

There now—you're holding him gently!

Hold him over the light, he loves the light! You see how the light shines through him?

JIM: It sure does shine!

LAURA: I shouldn't be partial, but he is my favorite one.

JIM: What kind of a thing is this one supposed to be?

LAURA: Haven't you noticed the single horn on his forehead?

JIM: A unicorn, huh?

LAURA: Mmm-hmmm!

JIM: Unicorns, aren't they extinct in the modern world?

LAURA: I know!

JIM: Poor little fellow, he must feel sort of lonesome.

LAURA [*Smiling*]: Well, if he does he doesn't complain about it. He stays on a shelf with some horses that don't have horns and all of them seem to get along nicely together.

JIM: How do you know?

LAURA [*Lightly*]: I haven't heard any arguments among them!

JIM [*Grinning*]: No arguments, huh? Well, that's a pretty good sign!

Where shall I set him?

LAURA: Put him on the table. They all like a change of scenery once in a while!

JIM [*Stretching*]: Well, well, well, well—

Look how big my shadow is when I stretch!

LAURA: Oh, oh, yes—it stretches across the ceiling!

JIM [*Crossing to door*]: I think it's stopped raining. [*Opens fire-escape door.*] Where does the music come from?

LAURA: From the Paradise Dance Hall across the alley.

JIM: How about cutting the rug a little, Miss Wingfield?

LAURA: Oh, I—

JIM: Or is your program filled up? Let me have a look at it. [*Grasps imaginary card.*] Why, every dance is taken! I'll just have to scratch some out. [WALTZ MUSIC: "LA GOLONDRINA."] Ahhh, a waltz! [*He executes some sweeping turns by himself then holds his arms toward* LAURA.]

LAURA [*Breathlessly*]: I—can't dance!

JIM: There you go, that inferiority stuff!

LAURA: I've never danced in my life!

JIM: Come on, try!

LAURA: Oh, but I'd step on you!

JIM: I'm not made out of glass.

LAURA: How—how—how do we start?

JIM: Just leave it to me. You hold your arms out a little.

LAURA: Like this?

JIM: A little bit higher. Right. Now don't tighten up, that's the main thing about it—relax.

LAURA [*Laughing breathlessly*]: It's hard not to.

JIM: Okay.

LAURA: I'm afraid you can't budge me.

JIM: What do you bet I can't? [*He swings her into motion.*]

LAURA: Goodness, yes, you can!

JIM: Let yourself go, now, Laura, just let yourself go.

LAURA: I'm—

JIM: Come on!

LAURA: Trying!

JIM: Not so stiff— Easy does it!

LAURA: I know but I'm—

JIM: Loosen th' backbone! There now, that's a lot better.

LAURA: Am I?

JIM: Lots, lots better! [*He moves her about the room in a clumsy waltz.*]

LAURA: Oh, my!

JIM: Ha-ha!

LAURA: Oh, my goodness!

JIM: Ha-ha-ha! [*They suddenly bump into the table.* JIM *stops.*] What did we hit on?

LAURA: Table.

JIM: Did something fall off it? I think—

LAURA: Yes.

JIM: I hope that it wasn't the little glass horse with the horn!

LAURA: Yes.

JIM: Aw, aw, aw. Is it broken?

LAURA: Now it is just like all the other horses.

JIM: It's lost its—

LAURA: Horn!

It doesn't matter. Maybe it's a blessing in disguise.

JIM: You'll never forgive me. I bet that that was your favorite piece of glass.

LAURA: I don't have favorites much. It's no tragedy, Freckles. Glass breaks so easily. No matter how careful you are. The traffic jars the shelves and things fall off them.

JIM: Still I'm awfully sorry that I was the cause.

LAURA [*Smiling*]: I'll just imagine he had an operation. The horn was removed to make him feel less—freakish!

[*They both laugh.*]

Now he will feel more at home with the other horses, the ones that don't have horns. . . .

JIM: Ha-ha, that's very funny!

[*Suddenly serious.*]

I'm glad to see that you have a sense of humor.

You know—you're—well—very different!

Surprisingly different from anyone else I know!

[*His voice becomes soft and hesitant with a genuine feeling.*]

Do you mind me telling you that?

[LAURA *is abashed beyond speech.*]

I mean it in a nice way . . .

[LAURA *nods shyly, looking away.*]

You make me feel sort of—I don't know how to put it!

I'm usually pretty good at expressing things, but—

This is something that I don't know how to say!

[LAURA *touches her throat and clears it—turns the broken unicorn in her hands.*]

[*Even softer.*]

Has anyone ever told you that you were pretty?

[PAUSE: MUSIC.]

[LAURA *looks up slowly, with wonder, and shakes her head.*]

Well, you are! In a very different way from anyone else.

And all the nicer because of the difference, too.

[*His voice becomes low and husky.* LAURA *turns away, nearly faint with the novelty of her emotions.*]

I wish that you were my sister. I'd teach you to have some confidence in yourself. The different people are not like other people, but being different is nothing to be ashamed of. Because other people are not such wonderful people. They're one hundred times one thousand. You're one times one! They walk all over the earth. You just stay here. They're common as—weeds, but—you—well, you're—*Blue Roses!*

[IMAGE ON SCREEN: BLUE ROSES.]

[MUSIC CHANGES.]

LAURA: But blue is wrong for—roses . . .

JIM: It's right for you!—You're—pretty!

LAURA: In what respect am I pretty?

JIM: In all respects—believe me! Your eyes—your hair—are pretty! Your hands are pretty!

[*He catches hold of her hand.*]

You think I'm making this up because I'm invited to dinner and have to be nice. Oh, I could do that! I could put on an act for you, Laura, and say lots of things without being very sincere. But this time I am. I'm talking to you sincerely. I happened to notice you had this inferiority complex that keeps you from feeling comfortable with people. Somebody needs to build your confidence up and make you proud instead of shy and turning away and—blushing—

Somebody—ought to—

Ought to—*kiss* you, Laura!

[*His hand slips slowly up her arm to her shoulder.*]

[MUSIC SWELLS TUMULTUOUSLY.]

[*He suddenly turns her about and kisses her on the lips.*]

   [*When he releases her,* LAURA *sinks on the sofa with a bright, dazed look.*]

[JIM *backs away and fishes in his pocket for a cigarette.*]

[LEGEND ON SCREEN: "SOUVENIR."]

Stumble-john!

[*He lights the cigarette, avoiding her look.*]

   [*There is a peal of girlish laughter from* AMANDA *in the kitchen.*]

   [LAURA *slowly raises and opens her hand. It still contains the little broken glass animal. She looks at it with a tender, bewildered expression.*]

Stumble-john!

I shouldn't have done that— That was way off the beam. You don't smoke, do you?

[*She looks up, smiling, not hearing the question.*]

[*He sits beside her a little gingerly. She looks at him speechlessly—waiting.*]

[*He coughs decorously and moves a little farther aside as he considers the situation and senses her feelings, dimly, with perturbation.*]

[*Gently.*]

Would you—care for a—mint?

[*She doesn't seem to hear him but her look grows brighter even.*]

Peppermint—Life-Saver?

My pocket's a regular drug store—wherever I go . . .

[*He pops a mint in his mouth. Then gulps and decides to make a clean breast of it. He speaks slowly and gingerly.*]

Laura, you know, if I had a sister like you, I'd do the same thing as Tom. I'd bring out fellows and—introduce her to them. The right type of boys of a type to—appreciate her.

Only—well—he made a mistake about me.

Maybe I've got no call to be saying this. That may not have been the idea in having me over. But what if it was?

There's nothing wrong about that. The only trouble is that in my case—I'm not in a situation to—do the right thing.

I can't take down your number and say I'll phone.

I can't call up next week and—ask for a date.

I thought I had better explain the situation in case you—misunderstood it and—hurt your feelings. . . .

[*Pause.*]

[*Slowly, very slowly,* LAURA's *look changes, her eyes returning slowly from his to the ornament in her palm.*]

[AMANDA *utters another gay laugh in the kitchen.*]

LAURA [*Faintly*]: You—won't—call again?

JIM: No, Laura, I can't.

[*He rises from the sofa.*]

As I was just explaining, I've—got strings on me.

Laura, I've—been going steady!

I go out all of the time with a girl named Betty. She's a home-girl like you, and Catholic, and Irish, and in a great many ways we—get along fine.

I met her last summer on a moonlight boat trip up the river to Alton, on the *Majestic*.

Well—right away from the start it was—love!

[LEGEND: LOVE!]

[LAURA *sways slightly forward and grips the arm of the sofa. He fails to notice, now enrapt in his own comfortable being.*]

Being in love has made a new man of me!

[*Leaning stiffly forward, clutching the arm of the sofa,* LAURA *struggles visibly with her storm. But* JIM *is oblivious, she is a long way off.*]

The power of love is really pretty tremendous!

Love is something that—changes the whole world, Laura!

[*The storm abates a little and* LAURA *leans back. He notices her again.*]

It happened that Betty's aunt took sick, she got a wire and had to go to Centralia. So Tom—when he asked me to dinner— I naturally just accepted the invitation, not knowing that you —that he—that I—

[*He stops awkwardly.*]

Huh—I'm a stumble-john!

[*He flops back on the sofa.*]

[*The holy candles in the altar of* LAURA'S *face have been snuffed out. There is a look of almost infinite desolation.*]

[JIM *glances at her uneasily.*]

I wish that you would—say something. [*She bites her lip which was trembling and then bravely smiles. She opens her hand again on the broken glass ornament. Then she gently takes his hand and raises it level with her own. She carefully places the unicorn in the palm of his hand, then pushes his fingers closed upon it.*] What are you—doing that for? You want me to have him?—Laura? [*She nods.*] What for?

LAURA: A—souvenir . . .

[*She rises unsteadily and crouches beside the victrola to wind it up.*]

[LEGEND ON SCREEN: "THINGS HAVE A WAY OF TURNING OUT SO BADLY!"]

[OR IMAGE: "GENTLEMAN CALLER WAVING GOOD-BYE!—GAILY."]

[*At this moment* AMANDA *rushes brightly back in the front room. She bears a pitcher of fruit punch in an old-fashioned cut-glass pitcher and a plate of macaroons. The plate has a gold border and poppies painted on it.*]

AMANDA: Well, well, well! Isn't the air delightful after the shower? I've made you children a little liquid refreshment.

[*Turns gaily to the gentleman caller.*]

Jim, do you know that song about lemonade?

"Lemonade, lemonade
Made in the shade and stirred with a spade—
Good enough for any old maid!"

JIM [*Uneasily*]: Ha-ha! No—I never heard it.

AMANDA: Why, Laura! You look so serious!

JIM: We were having a serious conversation.

AMANDA: Good! Now you're better acquainted!

JIM [*Uncertainly*]: Ha-ha! Yes.

AMANDA: You modern young people are much more serious-minded than my generation. I was so gay as a girl!

JIM: You haven't changed, Mrs. Wingfield.

AMANDA: Tonight I'm rejuvenated! The gaiety of the occasion, Mr. O'Connor!

[*She tosses her head with a peal of laughter. Spills lemonade.*]

Oooo! I'm baptizing myself!

JIM: Here—let me—

AMANDA [*Setting the pitcher down*]: There now. I discovered we had some maraschino cherries. I dumped them in, juice and all!

JIM: You shouldn't have gone to that trouble, Mrs. Wingfield.

AMANDA: Trouble, trouble? Why, it was loads of fun!

Didn't you hear me cutting up in the kitchen? I bet your ears were burning! I told Tom how outdone with him I was for keeping you to himself so long a time! He should have brought you over much, much sooner! Well, now that you've found your way, I want you to be a very frequent caller! Not just occasional but all the time.

Oh, we're going to have a lot of gay times together! I see them coming!

Mmm, just breathe that air! So fresh, and the moon's so pretty!

I'll skip back out—I know where my place is when young folks are having a—serious conversation!

JIM: Oh, don't go out, Mrs. Wingfield. The fact of the matter is I've got to be going.

AMANDA: Going, now? You're joking! Why, it's only the shank of the evening, Mr. O'Connor!

JIM: Well, you know how it is.

AMANDA: You mean you're a young workingman and have to keep workingmen's hours. We'll let you off early tonight. But only on the condition that next time you stay later.

What's the best night for you? Isn't Saturday night the best night for you workingmen?

JIM: I have a couple of time-clocks to punch, Mrs. Wingfield. One at morning, another one at night!

AMANDA: My, but you *are* ambitious! You work at night, too?

JIM: No, Ma'am, not work but—Betty! [*He crosses deliberately to pick up his hat. The band at the Paradise Dance Hall goes into a tender waltz.*]

AMANDA: Betty? Betty? Who's—Betty!

[*There is an ominous cracking sound in the sky.*]

JIM: Oh, just a girl. The girl I go steady with! [*He smiles charmingly. The sky falls.*]

[LEGEND: "THE SKY FALLS."]

AMANDA [*A long-drawn exhalation*]: Ohhhh . . . Is it a serious romance, Mr. O'Connor?

JIM: We're going to be married the second Sunday in June.

AMANDA: Ohhhh—how nice!

Tom didn't mention that you were engaged to be married.

JIM: The cat's not out of the bag at the warehouse yet.

You know how they are. They call you Romeo and stuff like that.

[*He stops at the oval mirror to put on his hat. He carefully shapes the brim and the crown to give a discreetly dashing effect.*]

It's been a wonderful evening, Mrs. Wingfield. I guess this is what they mean by Southern hospitality.

AMANDA: It really wasn't anything at all.

JIM: I hope it don't seem like I'm rushing off. But I promised Betty I'd pick her up at the Wabash depot, an' by the time I get my jalopy down there her train'll be in. Some women are pretty upset if you keep 'em waiting.

AMANDA: Yes, I know— The tyranny of women!
[*Extends her hand.*]
Good-bye, Mr. O'Connor.

I wish you luck—and happiness—and success! All three of them, and so does Laura!—Don't you, Laura?

LAURA: Yes!

JIM [*Taking her hand*]: Good-bye, Laura. I'm certainly going to treasure that souvenir. And don't you forget the good advice I gave you.
[*Raises his voice to a cheery shout.*]
So long, Shakespeare!

Thanks again, ladies— Good night!
[*He grins and ducks jauntily out.*]

   [*Still bravely grimacing,* AMANDA *closes the door on the gentleman caller. Then she turns back to the room with a puzzled expression. She and* LAURA *don't dare to face each other.* LAURA *crouches beside the victrola to wind it.*]

AMANDA [*Faintly*]: Things have a way of turning out so badly.

I don't believe that I would play the victrola.

Well, well—well—

Our gentleman caller was engaged to be married!

Tom!

TOM [*From back*]: Yes, Mother?

AMANDA: Come in here a minute. I want to tell you something awfully funny.

TOM [*Enters with macaroon and a glass of lemonade*]: Has the gentleman caller gotten away already?

AMANDA: The gentleman caller has made an early departure. What a wonderful joke you played on us!

TOM: How do you mean?

AMANDA: You didn't mention that he was engaged to be married.

TOM: Jim? Engaged?

AMANDA: That's what he just informed us.

TOM: I'll be jiggered! I didn't know about that.

AMANDA: That seems very peculiar.

TOM: What's peculiar about it?

AMANDA: Didn't you call him your best friend down at the warehouse?

TOM: He is, but how did I know?

AMANDA: It seems extremely peculiar that you wouldn't know your best friend was going to be married!

TOM: The warehouse is where I work, not where I know things about people!

AMANDA: You don't know things anywhere! You live in a dream; you manufacture illusions!

[*He crosses to door.*]

Where are you going?

TOM: I'm going to the movies.

AMANDA: That's right, now that you've had us make such fools of ourselves. The effort, the preparations, all the expense! The new floor lamp, the rug, the clothes for Laura! All for what? To entertain some other girl's fiancé!

Go to the movies, go! Don't think about us, a mother deserted, an unmarried sister who's crippled and has no job! Don't let anything interfere with your selfish pleasure!

Just go, go, go—to the movies!

TOM: All right, I will! The more you shout about my selfishness to me the quicker I'll go, and I won't go to the movies!

AMANDA: Go, then! Then go to the moon—you selfish dreamer!

[TOM *smashes his glass on the floor. He plunges out on the fire-escape, slamming the door.* LAURA *screams—cut by door.*]

[*Dance-hall music up.* TOM *goes to the rail and grips it desperately, lifting his face in the chill white moonlight penetrating the narrow abyss of the alley.*]

[LEGEND ON SCREEN: "AND SO GOOD-BYE . . ."]

[TOM'S *closing speech is timed with the interior pantomime. The interior scene is played as though viewed through sound-proof glass.* AMANDA *appears to be making a comforting speech to* LAURA *who is huddled upon the sofa. Now that we cannot hear the mother's speech, her silliness is gone and she has dignity and tragic beauty.* LAURA'S *dark hair hides her face until at the end of the speech she lifts it to smile at her mother.* AMANDA'S *gestures are slow and graceful, almost dancelike, as she comforts the daughter. At the end of her speech she glances a moment at the father's picture—then withdraws through the portieres. At the close of* TOM'S *speech,* LAURA *blows out the candles, ending the play.*]

TOM: I didn't go to the moon, I went much further—for time is the longest distance between two places—

Not long after that I was fired for writing a poem on the lid of a shoe-box.

I left Saint Louis. I descended the steps of this fire-escape for a last time and followed, from then on, in my father's footsteps, attempting to find in motion what was lost in space—

I traveled around a great deal. The cities swept about me like dead leaves, leaves that were brightly colored but torn away from the branches.

I would have stopped, but I was pursued by something.

It always came upon me unawares, taking me altogether by surprise. Perhaps it was a familiar bit of music. Perhaps it was only a piece of transparent glass—

Perhaps I am walking along a street at night, in some strange city, before I have found companions. I pass the lighted window of a shop where perfume is sold. The window is filled with pieces of colored glass, tiny transparent bottles in delicate colors, like bits of a shattered rainbow.

Then all at once my sister touches my shoulder. I turn around and look into her eyes . . .

Oh, Laura, Laura, I tried to leave you behind me, but I am more faithful than I intended to be!

I reach for a cigarette, I cross the street, I run into the movies or a bar, I buy a drink, I speak to the nearest stranger—anything that can blow your candles out!

[LAURA *bends over the candles.*]

—for nowadays the world is lit by lightning! Blow out your candles, Laura—and so good-bye. . . .

[*She blows the candles out.*]

THE SCENE DISSOLVES

Thomas Heggen
and
Joshua Logan

MISTER ROBERTS

FOR
NEDDA

CHARACTERS

CHIEF JOHNSON

LIEUTENANT (JG) ROBERTS

DOC

DOWDY

THE CAPTAIN

INSIGNA

MANNION

LINDSTROM

STEFANOWSKI

WILEY

SCHLEMMER

REBER

ENSIGN PULVER

DOLAN

GERHART

PAYNE

LIEUTENANT ANN GIRARD

SHORE PATROLMAN

MILITARY POLICEMAN

SHORE PATROL OFFICER

SEAMEN, FIREMEN AND OTHERS

SCENE

Aboard the U.S. Navy Cargo Ship, *AK 601*, operating in the back areas of the Pacific

Time: A few weeks before V-E Day until a few weeks before V-J Day

NOTE: In the U.S. Navy, all officers below the rank of Commander are addressed as "Mister."

ACT ONE

SCENE I

The curtain rises on the main set, which is the amidships section of a navy cargo ship. The section of the ship shown is the house, and the deck immediately forward of the house. Dominating center stage is a covered hatch. The house extends on an angle to the audience from downstage left to upstage right. At each side is a passageway leading to the after part of the ship. Over the passageways on each side are twenty-millimeter gun tubs; ladders lead up to each tub. In each passageway and hardly visible to the audience is a steep ladder leading up to a bridge. Downstage right is a double bitt. At the left end of the hatch cover is an opening. This is the entrance to the companionway which leads to the crew's compartment below. The lower parts of two kingposts are shown against the house. A life raft is also visible. A solid metal rail runs from stage right and disappears behind the house. Upstage center is the door to the Captain's cabin. The pilothouse with its many portholes is indicated on the bridge above. On the flying bridge are the usual nautical furnishings: a searchlight and two ventilators. Over the door is a loudspeaker. There is a porthole to the left of the door and two portholes to the right. These last two look into the Captain's cabin.

The only object which differentiates this ship from any other navy cargo ship is a small scrawny palm tree, potted in a five-gallon can, standing to the right of the Captain's cabin door. On the container, painted in large white letters, is the legend: "PROP.T OF CAPTAIN, KEEP AWAY."

At rise, the lighting indicates that it is shortly after dawn. The stage is empty and there is no indication of life other than the sound of snoring from below.

CHIEF JOHNSON, *a bulging man about forty, enters through passageway upstage left. He wears dungaree shirt and pants*

343

and a chief petty officer's cap. He is obviously chewing tobacco, and he starts down the hatchway, notices the palm tree, crosses to the Captain's door cautiously, peering into the porthole to see that he is not being watched, then deliberately spits into the palm tree container. He wipes his mouth smugly and shuffles over to the hatch. There he stops, takes out his watch and looks at it, then disappears down the hatchway. A shrill whistle is heard.

JOHNSON [*Offstage—in a loud singsong voice which is obviously just carrying out a ritual*]: Reveille . . . Hit the deck . . . Greet the new day . . . [*The whistle is heard again.*] Reveille . . .

INSIGNA [*Offstage*]: Okay, Chief, you done your duty—now get your big fat can out of here!

[JOHNSON *reappears at the head of hatchway calling back.*]

JOHNSON: Just thought you'd like to know about reveille. And you're going to miss chow again.

STEFANOWSKI [*Offstage*]: Thanks, Chief. Now go back to bed and stop bothering us.

[*His duty done,* JOHNSON, *still chewing, shuffles across the stage and disappears. There is a brief moment of silence, then the snoring is resumed below.*]

[*After a moment,* ROBERTS *enters from the passageway at right. He wears khaki shirt and trousers and an officer's cap. On each side of his collar he wears the silver bar indicating the rank of Lieutenant (junior grade). He carries a rumpled piece of writing paper in his left hand, on which there is a great deal of writing and large black marks indicating that much has been scratched out. He walks slowly to the bitt, concentrating, then stands a moment looking out right. He suddenly gets an idea and goes to hatch cover, sitting and writing on the paper.* DOC *enters from the left passageway.* DOC *is between thirty-five and forty and he wears khakis and an officer's fore-and-aft cap; he wears medical insignia and the bars of Lieutenant (senior grade) on his collar. A stethoscope sticks out of his hip pocket. He is wiping the sweat off his neck with his handkerchief as he crosses above hatch cover. He stops as he sees* ROBERTS.]

DOC: That you, Doug?

ROBERTS [*Wearily, looking up*]: Hello, Doc. What are you doing up?

DOC: I heard you were working cargo today so I thought I'd get ready. On days when there's any work to be done I can always count on a big turnout at sick call.

ROBERTS [*Smiles*]: Oh, yeah.

DOC: I attract some very rare diseases on cargo days. That day they knew you were going to load five ships I was greeted by six more cases of beriberi—double beriberi this time. So help me, I'm going down to the ship's library and throw that old copy of *Moby Dick* overboard!

[*He sits on hatch cover.*]

ROBERTS: What are you giving them these days for double beriberi?

DOC: Aspirin—what else? [*He looks at* ROBERTS.] Is there something wrong, Doug?

ROBERTS [*Preoccupied*]: No.

DOC [*Lying back on the hatch*]: We missed you when you went on watch last night. I gave young Ensign Pulver another drink of alcohol and orange juice and it inspired him to relate further sexual feats of his. Some of them bordered on the supernatural!

ROBERTS: I don't doubt it. Did he tell you how he conquered a forty-five-year-old virgin by the simple tactic of being the first man in her life to ask her a direct question?

DOC: No. Last night he was more concerned with quantity. It seems that on a certain cold and wintry night in November, 1939—a night when most of us mortal men would have settled for a cup of cocoa—he rendered pregnant three girls in Washington, D. C., caught the 11:45 train, and an hour later performed the same service for a young lady in Baltimore.

ROBERTS [*Laughing*]: Oh, my God!

DOC: I'm not sure what to do with young Pulver. I'm thinking of reporting his record to the American Medical Association.

ROBERTS: Why don't you just get him a job as a fountain in Radio City?

DOC: Don't be too hard on him, Doug. He thinks you are approximately God. . . . Say, there *is* something wrong, isn't there?

ROBERTS: I've been up all night, Doc.

DOC: What is it? What's the matter?

ROBERTS: I saw something last night when I was on watch that just about knocked me out.

DOC [*Alarmed*]: What happened?

ROBERTS [*With emotion*]: I was up on the bridge. I was just standing there looking out to sea. I couldn't bear to look at that island any more. All of a sudden I noticed something. Little black specks crawling over the horizon. I looked through the glasses and it was a formation of our ships that stretched for miles! Carriers and battleships and cans—a whole task force, Doc!

DOC: Why didn't you break me out? I've never seen a battleship!

ROBERTS: They came on and they passed within half a mile of that reef! Carriers so big they blacked out half the sky! And battlewagons sliding along—dead quiet! I could see the men on the bridges. And this is what knocked me out, Doc. Somehow— I thought I was on those bridges—I thought I was riding west across the Pacific. I watched them until they were out of sight, Doc— and I was right there on those bridges all the time.

DOC: I know how that must have hurt, Doug.

ROBERTS: And then I looked down from our bridge and saw our Captain's palm tree! [*Points at palm tree, then bitterly.*] Our trophy for superior achievement! The Admiral John J. Finchley award for delivering more toothpaste and toilet paper than any other Navy cargo ship in the safe area of the Pacific. [*Taking letter from pocket and handing it to* DOC.] Read this, Doc—see how it sounds.

DOC: What is it?

ROBERTS: My application for transfer. I've been rewriting it ever since I got off watch last night.

DOC: O God, not another one!

ROBERTS: This one's different—I'm trying something new, Doc—a stronger wording. Read it carefully.

[DOC *looks for a moment skeptically, then noticing the intensity in his face decides to read the letter.*]

DOC [*Reading*]: "From: Lieutenant (jg) Douglas Roberts
To: Bureau of Naval Personnel
16 April 1945

Subject: Change of Duty, Request for . . ."
[*He looks up.*]
Boy, this is sheer poetry.

ROBERTS [*Rises nervously*]: Go on, Doc.

DOC [*Reads on*]: "For two years and four months I have served aboard this vessel as Cargo Officer. I feel that my continued service aboard can only reduce my own usefulness to the Navy and increase disharmony aboard this ship."

[*He looks at* ROBERTS *and rises.* ROBERTS *looks back defiantly.*]

ROBERTS: How about *that!*

DOC [*Whistles softly, then continues*]: "It is therefore urgently requested that I be ordered to combat duty, preferably aboard a destroyer."

ROBERTS [*Tensely, going to* DOC]: What do you say, Doc? I've got a chance, haven't I?

DOC: Listen, Doug, you've been sending in a letter every week for God knows how long . . .

ROBERTS: Not like this . . .

DOC: . . . and every week the Captain has screamed like a stuck pig, *dis*approved your letters and forwarded them that way. . . .

ROBERTS: That's just my point, Doc. He *does* forward them. They go through the chain of command all the way up to the Bureau . . . Just because the Captain doesn't . . .

DOC: Doug, the Captain of a Navy ship is the most absolute monarch left in this world!

ROBERTS: I know that.

DOC: If he endorsed your letter "approved" you'd get your orders in a minute . . .

ROBERTS: Naturally, but I . . .

[*Turns away from* DOC.]

DOC: . . . but "disapproved," you haven't got a prayer. You're stuck on this old bucket, Doug. Face it!

ROBERTS [*Turns quickly back*]: Well, grant me this much, Doc. That one day I'll find the perfect wording and one human guy way up on top will read those words and say, "Here's a poor son-of-a-bitch screaming for help. Let's put him on a fighting ship!"

DOC [*Quietly*]: Sure . . .

ROBERTS [*After a moment*]: I'm not kidding myself, am I, Doc? I've got a chance, haven't I?

DOC: Yes, Doug, you've got a chance. It's about the same chance as putting your letter in a bottle and dropping it in the ocean . . .

ROBERTS [*Snatching letter from* DOC]: But it's still a chance, goddammit! It's still a chance!

[ROBERTS *stands looking out to sea.* DOC *watches him for a moment then speaks gently.*]

DOC: I wish you hadn't seen that task force, Doug. [*Pauses.*] Well, I've got to go down to my hypochondriacs.

[*He goes off slowly through passageway.*]

[ROBERTS *is still staring out as* DOWDY *enters from the hatchway. He is a hard-bitten man between thirty-five and forty and is wearing dungarees and no hat. He stands by hatchway with a cup of coffee in his hand.*]

DOWDY: Morning, Mister Roberts.

ROBERTS: Good morning, Dowdy.

DOWDY: Jeez, it's even hotter up here than down in that mess-hall! [*He looks off.*] Look at that cruddy island . . . smell it! It's so hot it *already* smells like a hog pen. Think we'll get out of here today, sir?

[ROBERTS *takes* DOWDY'S *cup as he speaks and drinks from it, then hands it back.*]

ROBERTS: I don't know, Dowdy. There's one LCT coming alongside for supplies . . . [*Goes to hatchway, looks down.*] Are they getting up yet?

DOWDY [*Also looking down hatch*]: Yeah, they're starting to stumble around down there—the poor punch-drunk bastards. Mister Roberts, when are you going to the Captain again and ask him to give this crew a liberty? These guys ain't been off the ship for over a year except on duty.

ROBERTS: Dowdy, the last time I asked him was last night.

DOWDY: What'd he say?

ROBERTS: He said "No."

DOWDY: We gotta get these guys ashore! They're going Asi-atic! [*Pause.*] Will you see him anyhow, Mister Roberts—just once more?

ROBERTS: You know I will, Dowdy. [*Hands* DOWDY *the let-*

ter.] In the meantime, have Dolan type that up for me. [*He starts off right.*]

DOWDY [*Descending hatchway*]: Oh, your letter. Yes, sir!

ROBERTS [*Calling over his shoulder*]: Then will you bring a couple of men back aft? [*He exits through passageway.*]

DOWDY: Okay, Mister Roberts. [*He disappears down hatchway. He is heard below.*] All right, you guys in there. Finish your coffee and get up on deck. Stefanowski, Insigna, off your tails . . .

[*After a moment the center door opens and the* CAPTAIN *appears wearing pajamas and bathrobe and his officer's cap. He is carrying water in an engine-room oil can. He waters the palm tree carefully, looks at it for a moment tenderly and goes back into his cabin. After a moment,* DOWDY'S *voice is heard from the companionway and he appears followed by members of the crew.*]

DOWDY: All right, let's go! Bring me those glasses, Schlemmer. [SCHLEMMER *exits by ladder to the bridge. Other men appear from the hatchway. They are* INSIGNA, STEFANOWSKI, MANNION, WILEY, REBER *and* LINDSTROM—*all yawning, buttoning pants, tucking in shirts and, in general, being comatose. The men do not appear to like one another very much at this hour— least of all* INSIGNA *and* MANNION.] All right, I got a little recreation for you guys. Stefanowski, you take these guys and get this little rust patch here. [*He hands* STEFANOWSKI *an armful of scrapers and wire brushes, indicating a spot on the deck.* STEFANOWSKI *looks at instruments dully, then distributes them to the men standing near him.* SCHLEMMER *returns from the bridge, carrying four pairs of binoculars and a spy glass. He drops them next to* INSIGNA *who is sitting on the hatch.*] Insigna, I got a real special job for you. You stay right here and clean these glasses.

INSIGNA: Ah, let me work up forward, Dowdy. I don't want to be around this crud, Mannion.

MANNION: Yeah, Dowdy. Take Insigna with you!

DOWDY: Shut up, I'm tired of you two bellyaching! [*Nodding to others to follow him.*] All right, let's go, Reber . . . Schlemmer.

[DOWDY, REBER *and* SCHLEMMER *leave through passageway right. The others sit in sodden silence.* LINDSTROM *wan-*

ders slowly over to INSIGNA. *He picks up spy glass and examines it. He holds the large end toward him and looks into it.*]

LINDSTROM: Hey, look! I can see myself!

STEFANOWSKI: Terrifying, ain't it?

[INSIGNA *takes the spy glass from him and starts polishing it.* LINDSTROM *removes his shoe and feels inside it, then puts it back on.*]

MANNION [*After a pause*]: Hey, what time is it in San Francisco?

INSIGNA [*Scornfully*]: *When?*

MANNION: Anybody ask you? [*Turns to* WILEY.] What time would it be there?

WILEY: I don't know. I guess about midnight last night.

STEFANOWSKI [*Studying scraper in his hand*]: I wonder if you could get sent back to the States if you cut off a finger.

[*Nobody answers.*]

INSIGNA [*Looking offstage*]: Hey, they got a new building on that island. Fancy—two stories . . .

[*Nobody shows any curiosity.*]

MANNION: You know, I had a girl in San Francisco wore flowers in her hair—instead of hats. Never wore a hat . . .

[*Another sodden pause.*]

INSIGNA [*Holding spy glass*]: Hey, Stefanowski! Which end of this you look through?

STEFANOWSKI: It's optional, Sam. Depends on what size eyeball you've got.

[INSIGNA *idly looks through spy glass at something out right. Another pause.*]

INSIGNA: Hey, the Japs must've took over this island—there's a red and white flag on that new building.

MANNION: Japs! We never been within five thousand miles of a Jap! Japs! You hear that, Wiley?

WILEY: Yeah, smart, ain't he?

MANNION: Japs! That's a hospital flag!

INSIGNA: Anybody ask you guys? [*Nudging* LINDSTROM *and pointing to the other group.*] The goldbrick twins! [*Looks through spy glass.*] Hey, they got a fancy hospital . . . big windows and . . . [*Suddenly rises, gasping at what he sees.*]

STEFANOWSKI: What's the matter, Sam?

INSIGNA: Oh, my God! She's bare-assed!

STEFANOWSKI: *She!*

INSIGNA: Taking a shower . . . in that bathroom . . . that nurse . . . upstairs window!

[*Instantly the others rush to hatch cover, grab binoculars and stand looking out right.*]

WILEY: She's a blonde—see!

LINDSTROM: I never seen such a beautiful girl!

MANNION: She's sure taking a long time in that shower!

WILEY: Yeah, honey, come on over here by the window!

INSIGNA: Don't you do it, honey! You take your time!

STEFANOWSKI: There's another one over by the washbasin—taking a shampoo.

INSIGNA [*Indignantly*]: Yeah. But why the hell don't she take her bathrobe off! That's a stupid goddamn way to take a shampoo!

[*For a moment the men watch in silent vigilance.*]

STEFANOWSKI: Ah-hah!

WILEY: She's coming out of the shower!

MANNION: She's coming over to the window! [*A pause.*] Kee-ri-mi-ny!

[*For a moment the men stand transfixed, their faces radiant. They emit rapturous sighs. That is all.*]

LINDSTROM: Aw, she's turning around the other way!

MANNION: What's that red mark she's got . . . there?

INSIGNA [*Authoritatively*]: That's a birthmark!

MANNION [*Scornfully*]: Birthmark!

INSIGNA: What do you think it is, wise guy?

MANNION: Why, that's paint! She's sat in some red paint!

INSIGNA: Sat in some red paint! I'm tellin' you, that's a birth-mark!

MANNION: Did you ever see a birthmark down there?

INSIGNA [*Lowers his spy glass, turns to* MANNION]: Why, you stupid jerk! I had an uncle once had a birthmark right down . . .

WILEY: Aww!

[INSIGNA *and* MANNION *return quickly to their glasses.*]

STEFANOWSKI [*Groaning*]: She's put her bathrobe on!

MANNION: Hey, she's got the same color bathrobe as that stupid bag taking the shampoo!

[*The four men notice something and exclaim in unison.*]

INSIGNA: Bag, hell! Look at her now with her head out of the water . . .

LINDSTROM: She's just as beautiful as the other one . . .

STEFANOWSKI: They look exactly alike with those bathrobes on. Maybe they're twins.

MANNION: That's my girl on the right—the one with the red birthmark.

INSIGNA: You stupid crud, the one with the birthmark's on the left!

MANNION: The hell she is . . .

[MANNION *and* INSIGNA *again lower their glasses.*]

INSIGNA: The hell she ain't . . .

WILEY: Awwww!

[MANNION *and* INSIGNA *quickly drop their argument and look.*]

STEFANOWSKI: They're both leaving the bathroom together. . . .

[*The men are dejected again.*]

LINDSTROM: Hey, there ain't no one in there now!

STEFANOWSKI [*Lowering his glasses*]: Did you figure that out all by yourself?

[*He looks through his glasses again.*]

MANNION [*After a pause*]: Come on, girls, let's go!

WILEY: Yeah. Who's next to take a nice zippy shower?

INSIGNA [*After a pause*]: They must think we got nothing better to do than stand here!

LINDSTROM: These glasses are getting heavy!

STEFANOWSKI: Yeah. We're wasting manpower. Let's take turns, okay? [*The others agree.*] All right, Mannion, you take it first.

[MANNION *nods, crosses and sits on bitt, keeping watch with his binoculars. The others pick up their scrapers and wire brushes.*]

INSIGNA [*Watching* MANNION]: I don't trust that crud.

LINDSTROM: Gee, I wish we was allowed to get over to that island. We could get a closer look.

STEFANOWSKI: No, Lindstrom. They'd see us and pull the shades down.

LINDSTROM: No, they wouldn't. We could cover ourselves

with leaves and make out like we was bushes—and sneak up on them—like them Japs we seen in that movie . . . [*He starts to sneak around front of hatch, holding his wire brush before his face.* STEFANOWSKI *hears a noise from the* CAPTAIN'S *cabin and quickly warns the others.*]

STEFANOWSKI: Flash Red! [*The men immediately begin working in earnest as the* CAPTAIN, *now in khaki, enters. He stands for a moment, looking at them, and then wanders over to the group scraping the rust patch to inspect their work. Then, satisfied that they are actually working, he starts toward passageway. He sees* MANNION, *sitting on the bitt, looking through his glasses and smiling. The* CAPTAIN *goes over and stands beside him, looking off in the same direction.* STEFANOWSKI *tries frantically to signal a warning to* MANNION *by beating out code with his scraper.* MANNION *suddenly sees the* CAPTAIN *and quickly lowers his glasses and pretends to clean them, alternately wiping the lenses and holding them up to his eyes to see that they are clean. The* CAPTAIN *watches him suspiciously for a moment, then he exits by the ladder to the bridge.* STEFANOWSKI *rises and looks up ladder to make certain the* CAPTAIN *has gone.*] Flash White! [*He turns and looks at* MANNION.] Hey, Mannion. Anyone in there yet?

MANNION [*Watching something happily through glasses*]: No, not yet!

INSIGNA [*Picks up spy glass and looks, and rises quickly*]: Why, you dirty, miserable cheat!

[*Instantly all the men are at the glasses.*]

LINDSTROM: There's one in there again!

STEFANOWSKI: The hell with her—she's already got her clothes on!

INSIGNA: And there she goes! [*Slowly lowers his glass, turning to* MANNION *threateningly.*] Why, you lousy, cheating crud!

MANNION [*Idly swinging his glasses*]: That ain't all. I seen three!

STEFANOWSKI: You lowdown Peeping Tom!

LINDSTROM [*Hurt*]: Mannion, that's a real dirty trick.

INSIGNA: What's the big idea?

MANNION: Who wants to know?

INSIGNA: *I* want to know! And you're damn well going to tell me!

MANNION: You loud-mouthed little bastard! Why don't you make me?

INSIGNA: You're damn right I will. Right now! [*He swings on* MANNION *as* LINDSTROM *steps clumsily between them.*]

LINDSTROM: Hey, fellows! Fellows!

INSIGNA: No wonder you ain't got a friend on this ship . . . except this crud, Wiley. [*He jerks his head in direction of* WILEY *who stands behind him on hatch cover.* WILEY *takes him by shoulder and whirls him around.*]

WILEY: What'd you say?

STEFANOWSKI [*Shoving* WILEY]: You heard him!

[MANNION *jumps on hatch cover to protect* WILEY *from* STEFANOWSKI. INSIGNA *rushes at* MANNION *and for a moment they are all in a clinch.* LINDSTROM *plows up on the hatch and breaks them apart. The men have suddenly formed into two camps—*MANNION *and* WILEY *on one side,* INSIGNA *and* STEFANOWSKI *facing them.* LINDSTROM *is just an accessory, but stands prepared to intervene if necessary.*]

MANNION [*To* WILEY]: Look at them two! Everybody on the ship hates their guts! The two moochingest, no-good loud-nouths on the ship!

[STEFANOWSKI *starts for* MANNION *but* INSIGNA *pulls him back and steps menacingly toward* MANNION.]

INSIGNA: Why, you slimy, lying son-of-a-bitch!

[*Suddenly* MANNION *hits* INSIGNA, *knocking him down. He jumps on* INSIGNA *who catches* MANNION *in the chest with his feet and hurls him back.* WILEY *and* STEFANOWSKI *start fighting with* LINDSTROM, *attempting to break them apart.* MANNION *rushes back at* INSIGNA. INSIGNA *sidesteps* MAN-NION'S *lunge and knocks him to the deck.* INSIGNA *falls on him. They wrestle to their feet and stand slugging. At this point* ROBERTS *and* DOWDY *run on from passageway.* ROBERTS *flings* INSIGNA *and* MANNION *apart.* DOWDY *separates the others.*]

ROBERTS: Break it up! Break it up, I tell you!

[INSIGNA *and* MANNION *rush at each other.* ROBERTS *and* DOWDY *stop them.*]

DOWDY: Goddamn you guys, break it up!

ROBERTS: All right! What's going on?

INSIGNA [*Pointing at* MANNION]: This son-of-a-bitch here . . .

ROBERTS: Did you hear me?

MANNION [*To* INSIGNA]: Shut your mouth!

DOWDY: Shut up, both of you!

INSIGNA: Slimy son-of-a-bitch! [*Picks up scraper and lunges at* MANNION *again.* ROBERTS *throws him back.*]

ROBERTS: I said to cut it out! Did you hear me? [*Wheels on* MANNION.] That goes for you too! [*Includes entire group.*] I'm going to give it to the first one who opens his mouth! [*The men stand subdued, breathing hard from the fight.*] Now get to work! All of you! [*They begin to move sullenly off right.*] Mannion, you and the rest get to work beside number two! And, Insigna, take those glasses way up to the bow and work on them! Stefanowski, keep those two apart.

STEFANOWSKI: Yes, sir.

[*The men exit.* ROBERTS *and* DOWDY *look after them.*]

DOWDY [*Tightly*]: You seen that, Mister Roberts. Well, last night down in the compartment I stopped three of them fights —worse than that. They've got to have a liberty, Mister Roberts.

ROBERTS: They sure do. Dowdy, call a boat for me, will you? I'm going ashore.

DOWDY: What are you going to do?

ROBERTS: I just got a new angle.

DOWDY: Are you going over the Captain's head?

ROBERTS: No, I'm going around his end—I hope. Get the lead out, Dowdy. [*He exits left as* DOWDY *goes off right and the lights*

Fade Out

[*During the darkness, voices can be heard over the squawk-box saying:*]

Now hear this . . . now hear this. Sweepers, man your brooms. Clean sweep-down fore and aft. Sweep-down all ladders and all passageways. Do *not* throw trash over the fantail.

Now, all men on report will see the master-at-arms for assignment to extra duty.

Now hear this . . . now hear this. Because in violation of

the Captain's orders, a man has appeared on deck without a shirt on, there will be no movies again tonight—by order of the Captain.

SCENE II

The lights dim up revealing the stateroom of PULVER *and* ROB-ERTS. *Two lockers are shown, one marked "Ensign F. T. Pulver," the other marked "Lt. (jg) D. A. Roberts." There is a double bunk along the bulkhead right. A desk with its end against the bulkhead left has a chair at either side. There is a porthole in the bulkhead above it. Up center, right of* PULVER'S *locker is a washbasin over which is a shelf and a medicine chest. The door is up center.*

An officer is discovered with his head inside ROBERTS' *locker, throwing skivvy shirts over his shoulder as he searches for something.* DOLAN, *a young, garrulous, brash yeoman, second class, enters. He is carrying a file folder.*

DOLAN: Here's your letter, Mister Roberts. [*He goes to the desk, taking fountain pen from his pocket.*] I typed it up. Just sign your old John Henry here and I'll take it in to the Captain . . . then hold your ears. [*No answer.*] Mister Roberts! [PULVER'S *head appears from the locker.*] Oh, it's only you, Mister Pulver. What are you doing in Mister Roberts' locker?

PULVER [*Hoarsely*]: Dolan, look in there, will you? I know there's a shoe box in there, but I can't find it.

[DOLAN *looks in the locker.*]

DOLAN: There ain't no shoe box in there, Mister Pulver.

PULVER: They've stolen it! There's nothing they'll stop at now. They've broken right into the sanctity of a man's own locker. [*He sits in chair at desk.*]

DOLAN [*Disinterested*]: Ain't Mister Roberts back from the island yet?

PULVER: No.

DOLAN: Well, as soon as he gets back, will you ask him to sign this baby?

PULVER: What is it?

DOLAN: What is it! It's the best damn letter Mister Roberts

writ yet. It's going to blow the Old Man right through the overhead. And them big shots at the Bureau are going to drop their
drawers too. This letter is liable to get him transferred.

PULVER: Yeah, lemme see it.

DOLAN [*Handing letter to* PULVER]: Get a load of that last
paragraph. Right here.

PULVER [*Reading with apprehension*]: ". . . increase disharmony aboard this ship . . ."

DOLAN [*Interrupting gleefully*]: Won't that frost the Old
Man's knockers? I can't wait to jab this baby in the Old Man's
face. Mr. Pulver, you know how he gets sick to his stomach
when he gets extra mad at Mister Roberts—well, when I deliver
this letter I'm going to take along a wastebasket! Let me know
when Mister Roberts gets back.

[DOLAN *exits.* PULVER *continues reading the letter with
great dismay. He hears* ROBERTS *and* DOC *talking in the passageway, offstage, and quickly goes to his bunk and hides the
letter under a blanket. He goes to the locker and is replacing
skivvy shirts as* ROBERTS *and* DOC *enter.*]

ROBERTS: . . . so after the fight I figured I had to do something and do it quick!

DOC: What did you do over on the island, Doug?

ROBERTS [*Sitting in chair and searching through desk
drawer*]: Hey, Frank, has Dolan been in here yet with my
letter?

PULVER [*Innocently*]: I don't know, Doug boy. I just came
in here myself.

DOC: You don't know anybody on the island, do you, Doug?

ROBERTS: Yes. The Port Director—the guy who decides where
to send this ship next. He confided to me that he used to drink
a quart of whiskey every day of his life. So this morning when
I broke up that fight it came to me that he might just possibly
sell his soul for a quart of Scotch.

PULVER [*Rises*]: Doug, you didn't give that shoe box to the
Port Director!

ROBERTS: I did. "Compliments of the Captain."

DOC: You've had a quart of Scotch in a shoe box?

ROBERTS: Johnny Walker! I was going to break it out the day
I got off this ship—Resurrection Day!

PULVER: Oh, my God! It's really gone! [*He sinks to the bunk.*]

DOC: Well, did the Port Director say he'd send us to a Liberty Port?

ROBERTS: Hell, no. He took the Scotch and said, "Don't bother me, Roberts. I'm busy." The rummy!

PULVER: How could you do it!

DOC: Well, where there's a rummy, there's hope. Maybe when he gets working on that Scotch he'll mellow a little.

PULVER: You gave that bottle to a goddamn *man!*

ROBERTS: Man! Will you name me another sex within a thousand miles . . . [PULVER, *dejected, goes up to porthole.*] What the hell's eating you anyway, Frank?

[DOC *crosses to bunk. He sees two fancy pillows on bottom bunk, picks up one and tosses it to* ROBERTS. *He picks up the other.*]

DOC: Well, look here. Somebody seems to be expecting company!

ROBERTS: Good Lord!

DOC [*Reads lettering on pillowcase*]: "Toujours l'amour . . . Souvenir of San Diego . . . Oh, you kid!"

ROBERTS [*Reading from his pillowcase*]: "Tonight or never . . . Compliments of Allis-Chalmers, Farm Equipment . . . We plow deep while others sleep." [*He looks at* DOC, *then rises.*] Doc—that new hospital over there hasn't got nurses, has it?

DOC: Nurses! It didn't have yesterday!

PULVER [*Turning from porthole*]: It has today!

DOC: But how did you find out they were there?

PULVER [*Trying to recall*]: Now let me think . . . it just came to me all of a sudden. This morning it was so hot I was just lying on my bunk—thinking . . . There wasn't a breath of air. And then, all of a sudden, a funny thing happened. A little breeze came up and I took a big deep breath and said to myself, "Pulver boy, there's women on that island."

ROBERTS: Doc, a thing like this could make a bird dog self-conscious as hell.

PULVER [*Warming up*]: They just flew in last night. There's eighteen of them—all brunettes except for two beautiful blondes —twin sisters! I'm working on one of those. I asked her out to the ship for lunch and she said she was kind of tired. So then I got kind of desperate and turned on the old personality—and I said, "Ain't there anything in the world that'll make you come out to the ship with me?" And she said, "Yes, there is, one thing and one thing only—" [*Crosses to* ROBERTS, *looks at him accusingly.*] "A good stiff drink of Scotch!" [*He sinks into the chair.*]

ROBERTS [*After a pause*]: I'm sorry, Frank. I'm really sorry. Your first assignment in a year. [*He pats* PULVER *on the shoulder.*]

PULVER: I figured I'd bring her in here . . . I fixed it up real cozy . . . [*Fondling pillow on desk.*] . . . and then I was going to throw a couple of fast slugs of Scotch into her and . . . but, hell, without the Scotch, she wouldn't . . . she just wouldn't, that's all.

ROBERTS [*After a pause*]: Doc, let's make some Scotch!

DOC: Huh?

ROBERTS: As naval officers we're supposed to be resourceful. Frank here's got a great opportunity and I've let him down. Let's fix him up!

DOC: Right! [*He goes to desk.* ROBERTS *begins removing bottles from medicine chest.*] Frank, where's the rest of that alcohol we were drinking last night?

PULVER [*Pulling a large vinegar bottle half filled with colorless liquid from the wastebasket and handing it to* DOC]: Hell, that ain't even the right color.

DOC [*Taking the bottle*]: Quiet! [*Thinks deeply.*] Color . . . [*With sudden decision*] Coca-Cola! Have you got any?

ROBERTS: I haven't seen a Coke in four months—no, by God, it's five months!

PULVER: Oh, what the hell! [*He rises, crosses to bunk, reaches under mattress of top bunk and produces a bottle of Coca-Cola. The others watch him.* DOC *snatches the bottle.* PULVER *says apologetically.*] I forgot I had it.

[DOC *opens the bottle and is about to pour the Coca-Cola into the vinegar bottle when he suddenly stops.*]

DOC: Oh—what shade would you like? Cutty Sark . . . Haig and Haig . . . Vat 69 . . .

PULVER [*Interested*]: I told her Johnny Walker.

DOC: Johnny Walker it is! [*He pours some of the Coca-Cola into the bottle.*]

ROBERTS [*Looking at color of the mixture*]: Johnny Walker Red Label!

DOC: Red Label!

PULVER: It may look like it—but it won't taste like it!

ROBERTS: Doc, what does Scotch taste like?

DOC: Well, it's a little like . . . uh . . . it tastes like . . .

ROBERTS: Do you know what it's always tasted a little like to me? Iodine.

DOC [*Shrugs as if to say "Of course" and rises. He takes dropper from small bottle of iodine and flicks a drop in the bottle*]: One drop of iodine—for taste. [*Shakes the bottle and pours some in glass.*]

PULVER: Lemme taste her, Doc!

DOC [*Stops him with a gesture*]: No. This calls for a medical opinion. [*Takes a ceremonial taste while the others wait for his verdict.*]

PULVER: How about it?

DOC: We're on the right track! [*Sets glass down. Rubs hands professionally.*] Now we need a little something extra—for age! What've you got there, Doug?

ROBERTS [*Reading labels of bottles on desk*]: Bromo-Seltzer . . . Wildroot Wave Set . . . Eno Fruit Salts . . . Kreml Hair Tonic . . .

DOC: Kreml! It has a coal-tar base! And it'll age the hell out of it! [*Pours a bit of Kreml into mixture. Shakes bottle solemnly.*] One drop Kreml for age. [*Sets bottle on desk, looks at wrist watch for a fraction of a second.*] That's it! [*Pours drink into glass.* PULVER *reaches for it.* ROBERTS *pushes his arm aside and tastes it.*]

ROBERTS: By God, it does taste a little like Scotch!

[PULVER *again reaches for glass.* DOC *pushes his arm aside and takes a drink.*]

DOC: By God, it does!

[PULVER *finally gets glass and takes a quick sip.*]

PULVER: It's delicious. That dumb little blonde won't know the difference.

DOC [*Hands the bottle to* PULVER]: Here you are, Frank. Doug and I have made the Scotch. The *nurse* is your department.

[PULVER *takes the bottle and hides it under the mattress, then replaces the pillows.*]

PULVER [*Singing softly*]: Won't know the difference . . . won't know the difference. [DOC *starts to drink from Coca-Cola bottle as* PULVER *comes over and snatches it from his hand.*] Thanks, Doc. [*Puts cap on the bottle and hides it under the mattress. Turns and faces the others.*] Thanks, Doug. Jeez, you guys are wonderful to me.

ROBERTS [*Putting bottles back in medicine chest*]: Don't mention it, Frank. I think you almost deserve it.

PULVER: You do—really? Or are you just giving me the old needle again? What do you really think of me, Doug—honestly?

ROBERTS [*Turning slowly to face* PULVER]: Frank, I like you. No one can get around the fact that you're a hell of a likable guy.

PULVER [*Beaming*]: Yeah—yeah . . .

ROBERTS: *But* . . .

PULVER: But what?

ROBERTS: But I also think you are the most hapless . . . lazy . . . disorganized . . . and, in general, the most lecherous person I've ever known in my life.

PULVER: I am not.

ROBERTS: Not what?

PULVER: I'm not disorganized—for one thing.

ROBERTS: Have you ever in your life finished anything you started out to do? You sleep sixteen hours a day. You pretend you want me to improve your mind and you've never even finished a book I've given you to read!

PULVER: I finished *God's Little Acre,* Doug boy!

ROBERTS: I didn't give you that! [*To* DOC.] He's been reading *God's Little Acre* for over a year! [*Takes dog-eared book from* PULVER's *bunk.*] He's underlined every erotic passage, and added exclamation points—and after a certain pornographic climax, he's inserted the words "well written." [*To* PULVER.] You're the Laundry and Morale Officer and I doubt if you've ever seen the Laundry.

PULVER: I was down there only last week.

ROBERTS: And you're scared of the Captain.

PULVER: I'm not scared of the Captain.

ROBERTS: Then why do you hide in the passageway every time you see him coming? I doubt if he even knows you're on board. You're scared of him.

PULVER: I am not. I'm scared of myself—I'm scared of what I might do to him.

ROBERTS [*Laughing*]: What you might do to him! Doc, he lies in his sack all day long and bores me silly with great moronic plots against the Captain and he's never carried out one.

PULVER: I haven't, huh.

ROBERTS: No, Frank, you haven't. What happened to your idea of plugging up the line of the Captain's sanitary system? "I'll make it overflow," you said. "I'll make a backwash that'll lift him off the throne and knock him clean across the room."

PULVER: I'm workin' on that. I thought about it for half an hour—yesterday.

ROBERTS: Half an hour! There's only one thing you've thought about for half an hour in your life! And what about those marbles that you were going to put in the Captain's overhead—so they'd roll around at night and keep him awake?

PULVER: Now you've gone too far. Now you've asked for it. [*Goes to bunk and produces small tin box from under mattress. Crosses to* ROBERTS *and shakes it in his face. Opens it.*] What does that look like? Five marbles! I'm collecting marbles all the time. I've got one right here in my pocket! [*Takes marble from pocket, holds it close to* ROBERTS' *nose, then drops it in box. Closes box.*] Six marbles! [*Puts box back under mattress, turns defiantly to* ROBERTS.] I'm looking for marbles all day long!

ROBERTS: Frank, you asked me what I thought of you. Well, I'll tell you! The day you finish one thing you've started out to do, the day you actually put those marbles in the Captain's overhead, and then have the guts to knock on his door and say, "Captain, I put those marbles there," that's the day I'll have some respect for you—that's the day I'll look up to you as a man. Okay?

PULVER [*Belligerently*]: Okay!

[ROBERTS *goes to the radio and turns it up. While he is listening,* DOC *and* PULVER *exchange worried looks.*]

RADIO VOICE: . . . intersecting thirty miles north of Hanover.

At the same time, General George S. Patton's Third Army continues to roll unchecked into Southern Germany. The abrupt German collapse brought forth the remark from a high London official that the end of the war in Europe is only weeks away—maybe days . . .

[ROBERTS *turns off radio.*]

ROBERTS: Where the hell's Dolan with that letter! [*Starts toward the door.*] I'm going to find him.

PULVER: Hey, Doug, wait! Listen! [ROBERTS *pauses at the door.*] I wouldn't send in that letter if I were you!

ROBERTS: What do you mean—*that* letter!

PULVER [*Hastily*]: I mean any of those letters you been writin'. What are you so nervous about anyway?

ROBERTS: Nervous!

PULVER: I mean about getting off this ship. Hell, this ain't such a bad life. Look, Doug. We're a threesome, aren't we—you and Doc and me? Share and share alike! Now look, I'm not going to keep those nurses all to myself. Soon as I get my little nursie organized today, I'm going to start working on her twin sister—for you.

ROBERTS: All right, Frank.

PULVER: And then I'm going to scare up something for you too, Doc. And in the meantime you've got a lot of work to do, Doug boy—improvin' my mind and watching my grammar. And speaking of grammar, you better watch your grammar. You're going to get in trouble, saying things like "disharmony aboard this ship!" [ROBERTS *looks at* PULVER *quickly.* PULVER *catches himself.*] I mean just in case you ever said anything like "disharmony aboard this ship" . . . or . . . uh . . . "harmony aboard this ship" or . . .

ROBERTS: Where's that letter?

PULVER: I don't know, Doug boy . . . [*As* ROBERTS *steps toward him, he quickly produces the letter from the blanket.*] Here it is, Doug.

ROBERTS [*Snatching the letter*]: What's the big idea!

[ROBERTS *goes to desk, reading and preparing to sign the letter.* PULVER *follows him.*]

PULVER: I just wanted to talk to you before you signed it. You can't send it in that way—it's too strong! Don't sign that letter, Doug, please don't! They'll transfer you and you'll get your ass shot off. You're just running a race with death, isn't he, Doc? It's stupid to keep asking for it like that. The Doc says so too. Tell him what you said to me last night, Doc—about how stupid he is.

ROBERTS [*Coldly, to* DOC]: Yes, Doc, maybe you'd like to tell me to my face.

DOC [*Belligerently*]: Yes, I would. Last night I asked you why you wanted to fight this war. And you said: anyone who doesn't fight it is only half-alive. Well, I thought that over and I've decided that's just a crock, Doug—just a crock.

ROBERTS: I take it back, Doc. After seeing my task force last night I don't even feel half-alive.

DOC: You are stupid! And I can prove it! You quit medical school to get into this thing when you could be saving lives today. Why? Do you even know yourself?

ROBERTS: Has it ever occurred to you that the guys who fight this war might also be saving lives . . . yours and mine, for instance! Not just putting men together again, but *keeping* them together! Right now I'd rather practice that kind of medicine— Doctor!

DOC [*Rising*]: Well, right now, that's exactly what you're doing.

ROBERTS: What, for God's sake!

DOC: Whether you like it or not, this sorry old bucket does a necessary job. And you're the guy who keeps her lumbering along. You keep this crew working cargo, and more than that —you keep them *alive*. It might just be that right here, on this bucket, you're deeper and more truly in this war than you ever would be anywhere else.

ROBERTS: Oh, Jesus, Doc. In a minute, you'll start quoting Emerson.

DOC: *That* is a lousy thing to say!

ROBERTS: We've got nothing to do with the war. Maybe that's why we're on this ship—because we're not good enough to fight. [*Then quietly with emotion.*] Maybe there's some omniscient son-of-a-bitch who goes down the line of all the servicemen and picks out the ones to send into combat, the ones whose glands secrete enough adrenalin, or whose great-great-grandfathers weren't afraid of the dark or something. The rest of us are packed off to ships like this where we can't do any harm.

DOC: What is it you want to be—a hero or something?

ROBERTS [*Shocked*]: Hero! My God, Doc! You haven't heard a word I said! Look, Doc, the war's way out there! I'm here. I don't want to be here—I want to be out there. I'm sick and tired of being a lousy spectator. I just happen to believe in this thing. I've got to feel I'm *good* enough to be in it—to *participate!*

DOC: Good enough! Doug, you're good enough! You just don't have the opportunity. That's mostly what physical heroism is—opportunity. It's a reflex. I think seventy-five out of a hundred young males have that reflex. If you put any one of them—say, even Frank Thurlow Pulver, here—in a B-29 over Japan, do you know what you'd have?

ROBERTS: No, by God, I don't.

DOC: You'd have Pulver, the Congressional Medal of Honor winner! You'd have Pulver, who, singlehanded, shot down twenty-three attacking Zeroes, then with his bare hands held together the severed wing struts of his plane, and with his bare feet successfully landed the mortally wounded plane on his home field. [PULVER *thinks this over.*] Hell, it's a reflex. It's like the knee jerk. Strike the patella tendon of any human being and you produce the knee jerk. Look. [*He illustrates on* PULVER. *There is no knee jerk. He strikes again—still no reaction.*]

PULVER: What's the matter, Doc?

DOC: Nothing. But stay out of B-29's, will you, Frank?

ROBERTS: You've made your point very vividly, Doc. But I still want to get into this thing. I've got to get into it! And I'm going to keep on sending in these letters until I do.

DOC: I know you are, Doug.

ROBERTS [*Signs the letter. Then to* DOC]: I haven't got much time. I found that out over on the island. That task force I saw last night is on its way to start our last big push in the Pacific. And it went by me, Doc. I've got to catch it. [*He exits.*]

PULVER [*After a pause*]: Doc, what are you going to give Doug on his birthday?

DOC: I hadn't thought of giving him anything.

PULVER: You know what? I'm gonna show him he's got old Pulver figured out all wrong. [*Pulls small cardboard roll from under mattress.*] Doc, what does that look like?

DOC: Just what it is—the cardboard center of a roll of toilet paper.

PULVER: I suppose it doesn't look like a firecracker.

DOC: Not a bit like a firecracker.

PULVER [*Taking a piece of string from the bunk*]: I suppose that doesn't look like a fuse.

DOC [*Rising and starting off*]: No, that looks like a piece of string. [*He walks slowly out of the room.* PULVER *goes on.*]

PULVER: Well, you just wait till old Pulver gets through with it! I'm going to get me some of that black powder from the gunner's mate. No, by God, this isn't going to be any peanut firecracker—I'm going to pack this old thing full of that stuff they use to blow up bridges, that fulminate of mercury stuff. And then on the night of Doug's birthday, I'm going to throw it under the Old Man's bunk. Bam—bam—bam! [*Knocks on* ROBERTS' *locker, opens it.*] Captain, it is I, Ensign Pulver. I just threw that firecracker under your goddamn bunk. [*He salutes as the lights*

Fade Out

[*In the darkness we hear the sound of a winch and shouted orders:*]

LCT OFFICER: On the AK—where do you want us?

AK VOICE: Starboard side, up for'd—alongside number two!

LCT OFFICER: Shall we use our fenders or yours?

AK VOICE: No, we'll use ours! Stand off till we finish with the barge!

SCENE III

The curtain rises and the lights dim up on the deck. ROBERTS *stands on the hatch cover.* SCHLEMMER, GERHART *and another seaman are sitting on the hatch cover. They are tired and hot. A cargo net, filled with crates, is disappearing off right. Off-stage we hear the shouts of men working cargo. Two officers walk across the stage. Everyone's shirt is wet with perspiration.*

ROBERTS [*Calling through megaphone*]: Okay—take it away—that's all for the barge. On the LCT—I'll give you a bow line.

LCT OFFICER [*Offstage*]: Okay, Lieutenant.

ROBERTS [*To crew*]: Get a line over!

DOWDY [*Offstage*]: Yes, sir!

REBER [*Off right*]: Heads up on the LCT!

ROBERTS: That's good. Make it fast.

[PAYNE, *wearing the belt of a messenger, enters from companionway as* DOWDY *enters from right.*]

PAYNE: Mister Roberts, the Captain says not to give this LCT any fresh fruit. He says he's going to keep what's left for his own mess.

ROBERTS: Okay, okay . . .

PAYNE: Hold your hat, Mister Roberts. I just saw Dolan go in there with your letter. [*He grins and exits as* ROBERTS *smiles at* DOWDY.]

DOWDY: Here's the list of what the LCT guy wants.

ROBERTS [*Reading rapidly*]: One ton dry stores . . . quarter-ton frozen food . . . one gross dungarees . . . twenty cartons toothpaste . . . two gross skivvy shirts . . . Okay, we can give him all that.

DOWDY: Can these guys take their shirts off while we're working?

ROBERTS: Dowdy, you know the Captain has a standing order . . .

DOWDY: Mister Roberts, Corcoran just passed out from the heat.

ROBERTS [*Looks at men who wait for his decision*]: Hell, yes, take 'em off. [DOWDY *exits*. SCHLEMMER, REBER *and seaman remove shirts saying "Thanks,* MISTER ROBERTS" *and exit right.* ROBERTS *calls through megaphone.*] LCT, want to swap movies? We've got a new one.

LCT [*Offstage*]: What's that?

ROBERTS: *Charlie Chan at the Opera.*

LCT [*Offstage*]: No, thanks, we've seen that three times!

ROBERTS: What you got?

LCT [*Offstage*]: Hoot Gibson in *Riders of the Range.*

ROBERTS: Sorry I brought the subject up.

DOWDY [*Entering from right*]: All set, Mister Roberts.

LCT [*Offstage*]: Lieutenant, one thing I didn't put on my list because I wanted to ask you—you couldn't spare us any fresh fruit, could you?

ROBERTS: You all out?

LCT [*Offstage*]: We haven't seen any for two months.

ROBERTS [*To* DOWDY]: Dowdy, give 'em a couple of crates of oranges.

DOWDY: Yes, sir.

ROBERTS: Compliments of the Captain.

DOWDY: Aye-aye, sir. [*He exits.*]

ROBERTS [*To* LCT]: Here comes your first sling-load! [*There is the grinding sound of a winch. With hand-signals* ROBERTS *directs placing of the sling-load. Then he shouts:*] Watch that line!

[DOWDY'S *voice is heard offstage:*]

DOWDY: Slack off, you dumb bastards! Slack off!

[PAYNE *enters.* ROBERTS *turns to him sharply.*]

ROBERTS: What!

PAYNE: The Captain wants to see you, Mister Roberts.

DOWDY [*Offstage*]: Goddammit, there it goes! You've parted the line!

ROBERTS: Get a fender over! Quick! [*To* PAYNE.] You go tell the Captain I'm busy! [PAYNE *exits.* ROBERTS *calls offstage.*] Get a line over—his bow's coming in!

REBER [*Offstage*]: Heads up!

GERHART [*Offstage*]: Where shall we secure?

DOWDY [*Offstage*]: Secure here!

ROBERTS: No. Take it around the bitt!

DOWDY [*Offstage*]: Around the bitt!

ROBERTS: That's too much! Give him some slack this time! [*Watches intently.*] That's good. Okay, let's give him the rest of his cargo.

GERHART [*Entering quickly and pointing toward companionway*]: Flash Red! [*He exits. The* CAPTAIN *enters, followed by* PAYNE *and* DOLAN.]

CAPTAIN: All right, Mister! Let's have this out right here and now! What do you mean—telling me you're busy!

ROBERTS: We parted a line, Captain. You didn't want me to leave the deck with this ship coming in on us?

CAPTAIN: You're damn right I want you to leave the deck. When I tell you I want to see you, I mean *now,* Mister! I mean jump! Do you understand?

[*At this point a group of men, attracted by the noise, crowd*

*in. They are naked to the waist. They pretend they are work-
ing, but actually they are listening to the* CAPTAIN'S *fight
with* ROBERTS.]

ROBERTS: Yes, Captain. I'll remember that next time.

CAPTAIN: You're damn right you'll remember it! Dont *ever*
tell me you're too busy to see me! Ever! [ROBERTS *doesn't
answer. The* CAPTAIN *points to the letter he is carrying.*] By
God, you think you're pretty cute with this letter, don't you?
You're trying to get me in bad with the Admiral, ain't you?
Ain't you?

ROBERTS: No, I'm not, Captain.

CAPTAIN: Then what do you mean by writing "disharmony
aboard this ship"?

ROBERTS: Because it's true, Captain.

[*The men grin at each other.*]

CAPTAIN: Any disharmony on this ship is my own doing!

ROBERTS: That's true too, Captain.

CAPTAIN: Damn right it's true. And it ain't gonna be in any
letter that leaves this ship. Any criticism of this ship stays on
this ship. I got a reputation with the Admiral and I ain't gonna
lose it on account of a letter written by some smart-alec college
officer. Now you retype that letter and leave out that disharmony crap and I'll send it in. But this is the last one, understand?

ROBERTS: Captain, every man in the Navy has the right to
send in a request for transfer . . . and no one can change the
wording. That's in Navy regs.

CAPTAIN [*After a pause*]: How about that, Dolan?

DOLAN: That's what it says, sir.

CAPTAIN: This goddamn Navy! I never put up with crap like
that in the merchant service. All right, I'll send this one in as
it is—*dis*approved, like I always do. But there's one thing I
don't have to do and that's send in a letter that ain't been
written. And, Mister, I'm tellin' you here and now—you ain't
gonna write any more. You bring one next week and you'll regret
it the rest of your life. You got a job right here and, Mister, you
ain't *never* going to leave this ship. Now get on with your work.
[*He looks around and notices the men. He shouts.*] Where are
your shirts?

ROBERTS: Captain, I . . .

CAPTAIN: Shut up! *Answer me, where are your shirts?* [*They stare at him.*] Get those shirts on in a goddamn quick hurry.

[*The men pick up their shirts, then pause, looking at* ROBERTS.]

ROBERTS: Captain, it was so hot working cargo, I . . .

CAPTAIN [*Shouting louder*]: I told you to shut up! [*To the men.*] I'm giving you an order: get those shirts on!

[*The men do not move.*]

ROBERTS [*Quietly*]: I'm sorry. Put your shirts on.

[*The men put on their shirts. There is a pause while the* CAPTAIN *stares at the men. Then he speaks quietly:*]

CAPTAIN: Who's the Captain of this ship? By God, that's the rankest piece of insubordination I've seen. You've been getting pretty smart playing grab-ass with Roberts here . . . but now you've gone too far. I'm givin' you a little promise—I ain't never gonna forget this. And in the meantime, every one of you men who disobeyed my standing order and appeared on deck without a shirt—every one—is on report, do you hear? On report!

ROBERTS: Captain, you're not putting these men on report.

CAPTAIN: What do you mean—I'm not!

ROBERTS: I'm responsible. I gave them permission.

CAPTAIN: You disobeyed my order?

ROBERTS: Yes, sir. It was too hot working cargo in the sun. One man passed out.

CAPTAIN: I don't give a damn if fifty men passed out. I gave an order and you disobeyed it.

LCT [*Offstage*]: Thanks a million for the oranges, Lieutenant.

CAPTAIN [*To* ROBERTS]: Did you give that LCT fresh fruit?

ROBERTS: Yes, sir. We've got plenty, Captain. They've been out for two months.

CAPTAIN: I've taken all the crap from you that I'm going to. You've just got yourself ten days in your room. Ten days, Mister! Ten days!

ROBERTS: Very well, Captain. Do you relieve me here?

CAPTAIN: You're damn right, I relieve you. You can go to your room for ten days! See how you like that!

LCT [*Offstage*]: We're waiting on you, Lieutenant. We gotta shove off.

[ROBERTS *gives the megaphone to the* CAPTAIN *and starts*

off. The CAPTAIN *looks in direction of the* LCT *then calls to* ROBERTS.]

CAPTAIN: Where do you think you're going?

ROBERTS [*Pretending surprise*]: To my room, Captain!

CAPTAIN: Get back to that cargo! I'll let you know when you have ten days in your room and you'll damn well know it! You're going to stay right here and do your job! [ROBERTS *crosses to the crew. The* CAPTAIN *slams the megaphone into* ROBERTS' *stomach.* PULVER *enters around the corner of the house, sees the* CAPTAIN *and starts to go back. The* CAPTAIN *sees* PULVER *and shouts:*] Who's that? Who's that officer there?

PULVER [*Turning*]: Me, sir?

CAPTAIN: Yes, you. Come here, boy. [PULVER *approaches in great confusion and can think of nothing better to do than salute. This visibly startles the* CAPTAIN.] Why, you're one of my officers!

PULVER: Yes, sir.

CAPTAIN: What's your name again?

PULVER: Ensign Pulver, sir. [*He salutes again. The* CAPTAIN, *amazed, returns the salute, then says for the benefit of* ROBERTS *and the crew:*]

CAPTAIN: By God, I'm glad to see one on this ship knows how to salute. [*Then to* PULVER.] Pulver . . . oh, yes . . . Pulver. How is it I never see you around?

PULVER [*Terrified*]: I've wondered about that myself, sir.

CAPTAIN: What's your job?

PULVER [*Trembling*]: Officer in charge of laundry and morale, sir.

CAPTAIN: How long you been aboard?

PULVER: Fourteen months, sir.

CAPTAIN: Fourteen months! You spend most of your time down in the laundry, eh?

PULVER: Most of the time, sir. Yes, sir.

[ROBERTS *turns his face to hide his laughter.*]

CAPTAIN: Well, you do a good job, Pulver, and . . . you know I'd like to see more of you. Why don't you have lunch with me in my cabin today?

PULVER: Oh, I can't today.

CAPTAIN: Can't? Why not?

PULVER: I'm on my way over to the hospital on the island.
I've got to go pick up a piece . . . of medical equipment.

ROBERTS [*Calling over*]: Why, I'll take care of that, Frank.

CAPTAIN: That's right, Roberts. You finish here and you go
over and fetch it.

ROBERTS: Yes, sir. [*He nods and turns away grinning.*]

CAPTAIN [*To* PULVER]: Well, how about it?

PULVER: This is something I've got to take care of myself, sir.
If you don't mind, sir.

CAPTAIN: Well, some other time then.

PULVER: Yes, sir. Thank you, sir.

CAPTAIN: Okay, Pulver.

[*The* CAPTAIN *baits another salute from* PULVER, *then
exits.* PULVER *watches him go, then starts to sneak off.*]

ROBERTS [*Grinning and mimicking the* CAPTAIN]: Oh, boy!
[PULVER *stops uneasily.* ROBERTS *salutes him.*] I want to see
more of you, Pulver!

PULVER [*Furiously*]: That son-of-a-bitch! Pretending he
doesn't know me! [*He looks at watch and exits.* ROBERTS *turns
laughing to the crew who are standing rather solemnly.*]

DOWDY [*Quietly*]: Nice going, Mister Roberts.

SCHLEMMER: It was really beautiful the way you read the
Old Man off!

GERHART: Are you going to send in that letter next week,
Mister Roberts?

ROBERTS: Are we, Dolan?

DOLAN: You're damn right we are! And I'm the baby who's
going to deliver it!

SCHLEMMER: He said he'd fix you good. What do you think
he'll do?

REBER: You got a promotion coming up, haven't you?

SCHLEMMER: Yeah. Could he stop that or something?

DOLAN: Promotion! This is Mister Roberts. You think he
gives a good hoot-in-hell about another lousy stripe?

ALL: Yeah.

GERHART: Hey, Mister Roberts, can I take the letter in next
week?

DOLAN [*Indignantly*]: You can like hell! That's my job—
isn't it, Mister Roberts?

GERHART: Can I, Mister Roberts?

ROBERTS: I'm afraid I've promised that job to Dolan.

DOLAN [*Pushing* GERHART *away*]: You heard him. [*To* ROBERTS.] We gotta write a really hot one next week.

ROBERTS: Got any asbestos paper? [*He starts off, the men follow happily as the lights*

Fade Out

SCENE IV

The lights come up immediately on the main set. REBER *and* GERHART *enter from right passageway. As they get around the corner of the house, they break into a run.* REBER *dashes off through left passageway.*

GERHART [*Excitedly, descending hatchway*]: Hey, Schlemmer! Schlemmer!

[MISS GIRARD, *a young, attractive, blonde Army nurse, and* PULVER *enter from right passageway.*]

PULVER: Well, here it is.

MISS GIRARD: This is a ship?

PULVER: Unh-hunh.

MISS GIRARD: My sister and I flew over some warships on our way out from the States and they looked so busy—men running around like mad.

PULVER: It's kinda busy sometimes up on deck.

MISS GIRARD: Oh, you mean you've seen a lot of action?

PULVER: Well, I sure as hell haven't had much in the last year . . . Oh, battle action! Yeah . . . Yeah . . .

MISS GIRARD: Then you must have a lot of B.F. on here.

PULVER: Hunh?

MISS GIRARD: You know—battle fatigue?

PULVER: Yeah, we have a lot of that.

MISS GIRARD: Isn't that too bad! But they briefed us to expect a lot of that out here. [*Pause.*] Say, you haven't felt any yourself, have you?

PULVER: I guess I had a little touch of it . . . just a scratch.

MISS GIRARD: You know what you should do then? You should sleep more.

PULVER: Yeah.

MISS GIRARD: What's your job on the ship?

PULVER: Me? I'm . . . Executive Officer . . .

MISS GIRARD: But I thought that Executive Officers had to be at least a . . .

PULVER: Say, you know what I was thinking? That we should have that little old drink of Scotcharoo right now—

MISS GIRARD: I think so too. You know, I just love Scotch. I've just learned to drink it since I've joined the Army. But I'm already an absolute connoisseur.

PULVER [*Dismayed*]: Oh, you are?

MISS GIRARD: My twin sister has a nickname for me that's partly because I like a particular brand of Scotch . . . [*Giggles.*] and partly because of a little personal thing about me that you wouldn't understand. Do you know what she calls me? "Red Label!" [*They both laugh.*] What are you laughing at? You don't know what I'm talking about—and what's more you never will.

PULVER: What I was laughing about is—that's the kind I've got.

MISS GIRARD: Red Label! Oh, you're God's gift to a thirsty nurstie! But where can we drink it? This is a Navy ship . . . isn't it?

PULVER: Oh, yeah, yeah, we'll have to be careful . . . We mustn't be seen . . . Lemme see, where shall we go . . . [*Considers.*] I have it! We'll go back to my cabin. Nobody'd bother us there.

MISS GIRARD: Oh, you're what our outfit calls an operator. But you look harmless to me.

PULVER: Oh, I don't know about that.

MISS GIRARD: What's your first name—Harmless?

PULVER: Frank.

MISS GIRARD: Hello, Frank. Mine's Ann.

PULVER: Hello, Ann.

MISS GIRARD: All right. We'll have one nice little sip in your room.

PULVER: Right this way. [*They start off toward left passageway.* INSIGNA, MANNION, STEFANOWSKI, WILEY *and* LINDSTROM *enter from right, carrying the spy glass and binoculars.* STEFANOWSKI *trips on hatch cover.* MISS GIRARD *and* PULVER *turn.*] Hello, Mannion . . . Insigna . . . Stefanowski . . .

MANNION [*Hoarsely*]: Hello, Mister Pulver . . .

PULVER: This is—Lieutenant Girard.

[*The men murmur a greeting.*]

MISS GIRARD: What're you all doing with those glasses?

INSIGNA: We're . . . cleaning them. [*Suddenly pulls out shirt tail and begins lamely polishing spy glass. The others follow his example. More men crowd onto the stage.*]

PULVER: Well, don't work too hard . . . [*They turn to leave, but find themselves hemmed in by the men.*] It's getting a little stuffy up here, I guess we better . . .

[ROBERTS *enters, very excited, carrying a piece of paper and a small book.*]

ROBERTS [*Entering*]: Hey, Insigna . . . Mannion . . . get a load of this . . . Hey, Frank . . . [*He stops short seeing* MISS GIRARD.]

PULVER: Hiya, Doug boy! This is Ann Girard—Doug Roberts.

ROBERTS: How do you do?

MISS GIRARD [*Beaming*]: How do you do? You're Frank's roommate. He's told me all about you.

ROBERTS: Really?

MISS GIRARD: What are you doing on this ship?

ROBERTS: Now there you've got me.

MISS GIRARD: No, I mean what's your job? Like Frank here is Executive Officer.

ROBERTS: Oh, I'm just the Laundry and Morale Officer.

MISS GIRARD: Why, that's wonderful—I've just been made Laundry and Morale Officer in our outfit!

PULVER: Oh, for Christ's sake!

[MANNION *and* INSIGNA *begin an argument in whispers.*]

MISS GIRARD: Maybe we can get together and compare notes.

ROBERTS: I'd enjoy that very much.

PULVER [*Attempting to usher* MISS GIRARD *off*]: Look, Doug. Will you excuse us? We're going down to have a little drink.

MISS GIRARD: Frank, I don't think that's very nice. Aren't you going to ask Doug to join us?

PULVER: Hell, no—I mean—he doesn't like Scotch.

ROBERTS: That's right, Miss Girard. I stay true to alcohol and orange juice.

PULVER: Come on, Ann . . .

MISS GIRARD: Wait a minute! A lot of the girls at the hospital swear by alcohol and orange juice. We ought to all get together and have a party in our new dayroom.

INSIGNA [*To* MANNION]: I bet you fifty bucks . . .

[STEFANOWSKI *moves* INSIGNA *and* MANNION *away from* MISS GIRARD.]

MISS GIRARD: Seems to be an argument.

PULVER: Yeah.

MISS GIRARD: Well, anyhow, we're fixing up a new dayroom. [*She looks offstage.*] Look, you can see it! The hospital! And there's our new dormitory! That first window . . .

[PULVER *takes glasses from* WILEY *to look at island.*]

INSIGNA [*To* MANNION, *his voice rising*]: All right, I got a *hundred* bucks says that's the one with the birthmark on her ass.

[*There is a terrible silence.* MISS GIRARD, *after a moment, takes the glasses from* PULVER *and looks at the island. After a moment she lowers the glasses and speaks to* PULVER.]

MISS GIRARD: Frank, I won't be able to have lunch with you after all. Would you call the boat, please? [*To* ROBERTS.] Goodbye, Doug. It was nice knowing you. You see, I promised the girls I'd help them hang some curtains and I think we'd better get started right away. Good-bye, everybody. [*To* MANNION.] Oh, what's your name again?

INSIGNA: Mine?

MISS GIRARD: No. Yours.

MANNION: Mine? [MISS GIRARD *nods.*] Mannion.

MISS GIRARD: Well, Mannion. I wouldn't take that bet if I were you because you'd lose a hundred bucks. [*To* PULVER.] Come on, Harmless. [*She exits, followed by a bewildered* PULVER. *The men watch her off.* STEFANOWSKI *throws his cap on the ground in anger.*]

MANNION [*To* INSIGNA]: You loud-mouthed little bastard! Now you've gone and done it!

ROBERTS: Shut up! Insigna, how did you . . .

INSIGNA: We seen her taking a bath.

LINDSTROM: Through these glasses, Mister Roberts! We could see everything!

STEFANOWSKI [*Furious*]: You heard what she said—she's going to hang some curtains.

MANNION: Yeah . . .

LINDSTROM: Gee, them nurses was pretty to look at. [*He sighs. There is a little tragic moment.*]

ROBERTS: She's got a ten-minute boat ride. You've still got ten minutes.

WILEY: It wouldn't be any fun when you know you're going to be rushed.

LINDSTROM: This was the first real good day this ship has ever had. But it's all over now.

ROBERTS: Well, maybe you've got time then to listen to a little piece of news . . . [*He reads from the paper in his hands.*] "When in all respects ready for sea, on or about 1600 today, the *AK 601* will proceed at ten knots via points X-Ray, Yolk and Zebra to Elysium Island, arriving there in seven days and reporting to the Port Director for cargo assignment." [*Emphatically.*] "During its stay in Elysium, the ship will make maximum use of the recreational facilities of this port."

[*The men look up in slow surprise and disbelief.*]

STEFANOWSKI: But that means liberty!

LINDSTROM: That don't mean liberty, Mister Roberts?

ROBERTS: That's exactly what it means!

INSIGNA [*Dazed*]: Somebody must've been drunk to send us to a Liberty Port!

[ROBERTS *nods.*]

LINDSTROM: Has the Old Man seen them orders?

ROBERTS: He saw them before I did. [*Now the men are excited.*]

WILEY: Elysium! Where's that?

MANNION: Yeah! Where's that, Mister Roberts?

[*The men crowd around* ROBERTS *as he sits on the hatch.*]

ROBERTS [*Reading from guide-book.*] "Elysium is the largest of the Limbo Islands. It is often referred to as the 'Polynesian Paradise.' Vanilla, sugar, cocoa, coffee, copra, mother-of-pearl, phosphates and rum are the chief exports."

INSIGNA: Rum! Did you hear that? [*He gooses* LINDSTROM.]

LINDSTROM: Cut that out!

[DOLAN *gooses* INSIGNA.]

INSIGNA: Cut that out!

MANNION: Shut up!

ROBERTS: "Elysium City, its capital, is a beautiful metropolis of palm-lined boulevards, handsome public buildings and colorful stucco homes. Since 1900, its population has remained remarkably constant at approximately 30,000.

INSIGNA: I'll fix that!

[*The men shout him down.*]

ROBERTS: That's all there is here. If you want the real dope on Elysium, there's one man on this ship who's been there.

STEFANOWSKI: Who's that?

MANNION: Who?

ROBERTS: Dowdy!

[*The men run off wildly in every direction, shouting for* DOWDY. *The call is taken up all over the ship.* ROBERTS *listens to them happily, then notices a pair of binoculars. He looks toward the island for a moment, shrugs and is lifting the binoculars to his eyes as the lights*

Fade Out

SCENE V

During the darkness we can hear the exciting strains of Polynesian music.

The lights come up slowly through a porthole, casting a strong late-afternoon shaft of light onto motionless white figures. It is the enlisted men's compartment below decks. Except for a few not yet fully dressed, the men are all in white uniforms. The compartment is a crowded place with three-tiered bunks against the bulkheads. Most of the men are crowded around the porthole, downstage left. The men who cannot see are listening to the reports of INSIGNA, *who is standing on a bench, looking out the porthole. The only man who is not galvanized with excitement is* DOWDY, *who sits calmly on a bench, downstage center, reading a magazine—* True Detective.

GERHART [*To* INSIGNA]: What do you see now, Sam?

INSIGNA: There's a lot of little boats up forward—up around the bow.

PAYNE: What kind of boats?

INSIGNA: They're little sort of canoes and they're all filled up with flowers and stuff. And there's women in them boats, paddling them . . .

PAYNE: Are they coming down this way?

INSIGNA: Naw. They're sticking around the bow.

STEFANOWSKI: Sam, where's that music coming from?

INSIGNA: There's a great big canoe up there and it's all filled with fat bastards with flowers in their ears playing little old gittars . . .

SCHLEMMER: Why the hell can't we go up on deck? That's what I'd like to know!

LINDSTROM: When are we going ashore! That's what I'd like to know!

[INSIGNA *suddenly laughs.*]

PAYNE: What is it, Sam?

INSIGNA: I wish you could see this . . .

[CHIEF JOHNSON *enters, looking knowingly at the men, shakes his head and addresses* DOWDY.]

JOHNSON: Same story in here, eh? Every porthole this side of the ship!

DOWDY: They're going to wear themselves down to a nub before they ever get over there . . .

LINDSTROM [*Takes coin from pocket and thrusts it at* INSIGNA]: Hey, Sam, here's another penny. Make them kids down below dive for it.

INSIGNA [*Impatiently*]: All right! [*Throws coin out the port.*] Heads up, you little bastards!

[*The men watch tensely.*]

LINDSTROM: Did he get that one too?

INSIGNA: Yeah . . .

[*The men relax somewhat.*]

LINDSTROM: Them kids don't ever miss!

INSIGNA: Hey, Dowdy—where's that little park again? Where you said all the good-looking women hang out?

DOWDY: For the last time—you see that big hill over there to the right . . .

INSIGNA: Yeah.

DOWDY: You see a big church . . . with a street running off to the left of it.

INSIGNA: Yeah.

DOWDY: Well, you go up that street three blocks . . .

INSIGNA: Yeah, I'm there.

DOWDY: That's the park.

INSIGNA: Well, I'll be damned . . .

LINDSTROM: Hey, show me that park, Sam?

[*The other men gather around* INSIGNA, *asking to see the park.*]

INSIGNA [*The authority now*]: All right, you bastards, line up. I'll show you where the women hang out.

[*The men form a line and each steps up to the porthole where* INSIGNA *points out the park.*]

JOHNSON [*To* DOWDY]: Smell that shoe polish? These guys have gone nuts!

DOWDY: I went down the ship's store the other day to buy a bar of soap and, do you know, they been sold out for a week! No soap, no Listerine, no lilac shaving lotion—hell, they even sold eighteen jars of Mum! Now these bastards are bootlegging it! They're gettin' ten bucks for a used jar of Mum!

[REBER, *wearing the messenger's belt, enters. The men greet him excitedly.*]

STEFANOWSKI: What's the word on liberty, Reber? Is the Old Man still asleep?

MANNION: Yeah, what's the word?

REBER: I just peeked in on him. He's snoring like a baby.

GERHART: Jeez, how any guy can sleep at a time like this!

INSIGNA: I'll get him up! I'm going up there and tap on his door! [*Picks up a heavy lead pipe.*]

DOWDY [*Grabbing* INSIGNA]: Like hell you are! You're going to stay right here and pray! You're going to pray that he wakes up feeling good and decides he's kept you guys sweating long enough!

MANNION: That's telling the little crud!

[INSIGNA *and* MANNION *threaten each other.*]

REBER: Hey, Lindstrom. I got good news for you. You can take them whites off.

LINDSTROM: I ain't got the duty *tonight?*

REBER: That's right. You and Mister Roberts got the duty tonight—the twelve to four watch. The Exec just posted the list . . . [*He is interrupted by the sound of static on the squawk box. Instantly all men turn toward it eagerly.*]

DOLAN [*On squawk box*]: Now hear this! Now hear this!

WILEY: Here we go! Here we go!

STEFANOWSKI [*Imitating the squawk box*]: Liberty . . . will com-mence . . . immediately!

GERHART: Quiet!

DOLAN [*On squawk box*]: Now hear this! The Captain's messenger will report to the Captain's cabin on the double!

REBER: My God! He's awake! [*He runs out.*]

PAYNE: Won't be long now!

WILEY: Get going, Mannion! Get into those whites! We're going to be the first ones over the side!

MANNION: Hell, yes! Give me a hand!

[*Now there is a general frenzy of preparation—the men put the last-minute touches to shoes, hair, uniforms.*]

GERHART [*Singing to the tune of "California, Here I Come"*]: Ee-liss-ee-um, here I come! . . . Ta-ta-ta-ta-*ta*-da-tah . . .

SCHLEMMER [*To* GERHART]: Watch where you're going! You stepped on my shine!

INSIGNA: Schlemmer . . . Stef . . . Gerhart . . . come here! [*These men gather around him.* LINDSTROM *remains unhappily alone.*] Now listen! Stefanowski and me are going to work alone for the first hour and a half! But if you pick up something first . . . [*Produces small map from his pocket.*] We'll be working up and down this street here . . .

[*They study the map. Now the squawk box is clicked on again. All the men stand rigid, listening.*]

DOLAN [*On squawk box*]: Now hear this! Now hear this! The Captain is now going to make a personal announcement.

[*Sound of squawk-box switch.*]

CAPTAIN [*On squawk box*]: Goddammit, how does this thing work? [*Sound of squawk-box switch again.*] This is the Captain speaking. I just woke up from a little nap and I got a surprise. I found out there were men on this ship who were expecting liberty. [*At this point, the lights start dimming until the entire scene is blacked out. The speech continues throughout the darkness. Under the* CAPTAIN'S *speech the strains of Polynesian music can be heard.*] Now I don't know how such a rumor got around, but I'd like to clear it up right now. You see, it's like this. Because of cargo requirements and security conditions which has just come to my personal attention there will be no liberty as long as we're in this here port. And one other thing—

as long as we're here, no man will wear white uniforms. Now I would like to repeat for the benefit of complete understanding and clearness, NO LIBERTY. That is all.

SCENE VI

The lights come up on the CAPTAIN'S *cabin. Against the left bulkhead is a settee. A chair is placed center. Up center is the only door. The* CAPTAIN *is seated behind his desk, holding a watch in one hand and the microphone in the other, in an attitude of waiting. Just over the desk and against the right bulkhead is a ship's intercommunication board. There is a wall-safe in the right bulkhead. After a moment there is a knock on the door.*

CAPTAIN: Come in, Mister Roberts. [*As* ROBERTS *enters, the* CAPTAIN *puts the microphone on the desk.*] Thirty-eight seconds. Pretty good time! You see, I been expectin' you ever since I made my little announcement.

ROBERTS: Well, as long as you're expecting me, what about it—when does this crew get liberty?

CAPTAIN: Well, in the first place, just kinda hold your tongue. And in the second place, sit down.

ROBERTS: There's no time to sit down. When are you going to let this crew go ashore?

CAPTAIN: I'm not. This wasn't my idea—coming to a Liberty Port. One of my officers arranged it with a certain Port Director—gave him a bottle of Scotch whiskey—compliments of the Captain. And the Port Director was kind enough to send me a little thank-you note along with our orders. Sit down, Mister Roberts. [ROBERTS *sits.*] Don't worry about it. I'm not going to make trouble about that wasted bottle of Scotch. I'll admit I was a little pre-voked about not being consulted. Then I got to thinking maybe we oughta come to this port anyway so's you and me could have a little talk.

ROBERTS: You can make all the trouble you want, Captain, but let's quit wasting time. Don't you hear that music? Don't you know it's tearing those guys apart? They're breakable, Captain! I promise you!

CAPTAIN: That's enough! I've had enough of your fancy

educated talk. [*Rises, goes to* ROBERTS.] Now you listen to me. I got two things I want to show you. [*He unlocks the wall-safe, opens it and takes out a commander's cap with gold braid "scrambled eggs" on the visor.*] You see that? That's the cap of a full commander. I'm gonna wear that cap some day and you're going to help me. [*Replaces cap in safe, goes back to* ROBERTS.] I guess there's no harm in telling you that you helped me get that palm tree by working cargo. Now don't let this go to your head, but when Admiral Finchley gave me that award, he said, "You got a good Cargo Officer, Morton; keep him at it, you're going places." So I went out and bought that hat. There's nothing gonna stand between me and that hat—certainly not you. Now last week you wrote a letter that said "disharmony aboard this ship." I told you there wasn't going to be any more letters. But what do I find on my desk this morning . . . [*Taking letter from desk.*] Another one. It says "friction between myself and the Commanding Officer." That ain't gonna go in, Mister.

ROBERTS: How are you going to stop it, Captain?

CAPTAIN: I ain't, you are. [*Goes to his chair and sits.*] Just how much do you want this crew to have a liberty anyhow? Enough to stop this "disharmony"? To stop this "friction"? [*Leans forward.*] Enough to get out of the habit of writing letters ever? Because that's the only way this crew is ever gonna get ashore. [*Leans back.*] Well, we've had our little talk. What do you say?

ROBERTS [*After a moment*]: How did you get in the Navy? How did you get on our side? You're what I joined to fight *against*. You ignorant, arrogant, ambitious . . . [*Rises.*] jackass! Keeping a hundred and sixty-seven men in prison because you got a palm tree for the work *they* did. I don't know which I hate worse—you or that other malignant growth that stands outside your door!

CAPTAIN: Why, you goddamn . . .

ROBERTS: How did you ever get command of a ship? I realize that in wartime they have to scrape the bottom of the barrel, but where the hell did they ever scrape you up?

CAPTAIN [*Shouting*]: There's just one thing left for you, by God—a general court-martial.

ROBERTS: That suits me fine. Court-martial me!

CAPTAIN: By God, you've got it!

ROBERTS: I'm asking for it!

CAPTAIN: You don't have to ask for it, you've got it now!

ROBERTS: If I can't get transferred off here, I'll get court-martialed off! I'm fed up! But you'll need a witness. Send for your messenger. He's down below. I'll say it all again in front of him. [*Pauses.*] Go on, call in Reber! [*The* CAPTAIN *doesn't move.*] Go on, call him. [*Still the* CAPTAIN *doesn't move.*] Do you want me to call him?

CAPTAIN: No. [*He walks upstage, then turns to* ROBERTS.] I think you're a pretty smart boy. I may not talk very good, Mister, but I know how to take care of smart boys. Let me tell you something. Let me tell you a little secret. I hate your guts, you college son-of-a-bitch! You think you're better than I am! You think you're better because you've had everything handed to you! Let me tell you something, Mister—I've worked since I was ten years old, and all my life I've known you superior bastards. I knew you people when I was a kid in Boston and I worked in eating-places and you ordered me around. . . . "Oh, bus-boy! My friend here seems to have thrown up on the table. Clean it up, please." I started going to sea as a steward and I worked for you then . . . "Steward, take my magazine out to the deck chair!" . . . "Steward, I don't like your looks. Please keep out of my way as much as possible!" Well, I took that crap! I took that for years from pimple-faced bastards who weren't good enough to wipe my nose! And now I don't have to take it any more! There's a war on, by God, and I'm the Captain and you can wipe my nose! The worst thing I can do to you is to keep you on this ship! And that's where you're going to stay! Now get out of here! [*He goes to his chair and sits.* ROBERTS *moves slowly toward the door. He hears the music, goes to the porthole and listens. Then he turns to the* CAPTAIN.]

ROBERTS: Can't you hear that music, Captain?

CAPTAIN: Yeah, I hear it. [*Busies himself at desk, ignoring* ROBERTS.]

ROBERTS: Don't you know those guys below can hear it too? Oh, my God.

CAPTAIN: Get out of here.

[*After a moment,* ROBERTS *turns from the porthole and slumps against the* CAPTAIN'S *locker. His face is strained.*]

ROBERTS: What do you want for liberty, Captain?

CAPTAIN: I want plenty. You're through writin' letters—ever.

ROBERTS: Okay.

CAPTAIN: That's not all. You're through givin' me trouble. You're through talkin' back to me in front of the crew. You ain't even gonna open your mouth—except in civil answer. [ROBERTS *doesn't answer.*] Mister Roberts, you know that if you don't take my terms I'll let you out that door and that's the end of any hope for liberty.

ROBERTS: Is that all, Captain?

CAPTAIN: No. Anyone know you're in here?

ROBERTS: No one.

CAPTAIN: Then you won't go blabbin' about this to anyone ever. It might not sound so good. And besides I don't want you to take credit for gettin' this crew ashore.

ROBERTS: Do you think I'm doing this for credit? Do you think I'd *let* anyone know about this?

CAPTAIN: I gotta be sure.

ROBERTS: You've got my word, that's all.

CAPTAIN [*After a pause*]: Your word. Yes, you college fellas make a big show about keeping your word.

ROBERTS: How about it, Captain. Is it a deal?

CAPTAIN: Yeah. [ROBERTS *picks up the microphone, turns on a switch and thrusts the microphone at the* CAPTAIN.] Now hear this. This is the Captain speaking. I've got some further word on security conditions in this port and so it gives me great pleasure to tell you that liberty, for the starboard section . . .

ROBERTS [*Covering the microphone with his hand*]: For the entire crew, goddammit.

CAPTAIN: Correction: Liberty for the entire crew will commence immediately.

[ROBERTS *turns off the microphone. After a moment we hear the shouts of the crew.* ROBERTS *goes up to porthole. The* CAPTAIN *leans back on his chair. A song, "Roll Me Over," is started by someone and is soon taken up by the whole crew.*]

ROBERTS [*Looking out of the porthole. He is excited and happy*]: Listen to those crazy bastards. Listen to them.

[*The crew continues to sing with increasing volume. Now
the words can be distinguished:*
>Roll me over in the clover,
>Roll me over, lay me down
>And do it again.*]

The Curtain Falls

ACT TWO

SCENE I

*The curtain rises on the main set. It is now 3:45 A.M. The night
is pitch-black, but we can see because of a light over the head
of the gangway, where a temporary desk has been rigged;
a large ship's logbook lies open on this desk. A small table
on which are hospital supplies is at left of the door.*

At rise, ROBERTS, DOC, LINDSTROM, JOHNSON *and four* SEA-
MEN *are discovered onstage.* LINDSTROM, *in web belt, is writing in the log.* ROBERTS *is standing with a pile of yellow slips in
his hand; he wears the side-arms of the Officer of the Deck.*
JOHNSON *and a* SEAMAN *are standing near the hatchway,
holding the inert body of another* SEAMAN, *who has court
plaster on his face. Two more* SEAMEN *lie on the hatch cover
where* DOC *is kneeling, bandaging one of them. As the curtain
rises we hear the sound of a siren off right. Everyone turns
and looks—that is, everyone who is conscious.*

LINDSTROM: Here's another batch, Mister Roberts—a whole
paddy wagon full. And this one's an Army paddy wagon.

ROBERTS: We haven't filed away this batch yet. [*To* DOC.]
Hurry up, Doc.

JOHNSON [*To* DOC, *indicating body he is carrying*]: Where do
we put number twenty-three here, Doc? Sick bay or what?

DOC: Just put him to bed. His condition's only critical.

JOHNSON [*Carrying* SEAMAN *off*]: They just roll out of their bunks, Doc. Now I'm stacking 'em on the deck down there— I'm on the third layer already.

VOICE [*Offstage*]: Okay, Lieutenant! All set down here! You ready?

ROBERTS [*Calling offstage—and giving hand signal*]: Okay! [*To* DOC.] Here they come, Doc! Heads up!

SHORE PATROLMAN'S VOICE [*Offstage*]: Lieutenant!

ROBERTS: Oh, not you again!

SHORE PATROLMAN'S VOICE [*Offstage*]: I got a bunch of real beauties for you this time.

ROBERTS [*Calling offstage*]: Can they walk?

SHORE PATROLMAN'S VOICE [*Offstage*]: Just barely!

ROBERTS [*Calling*]: Then send 'em up.

LINDSTROM: Man, oh, man, what a liberty! We got the record now, Mister Roberts! This makes the seventh batch since we went on watch!

[*The sound of a cargo winch and a voice offstage singing the Army Air Corps song are heard.* ROBERTS *is looking offstage.*]

ROBERTS [*Signaling*]: Looks like a real haul this time. Schlemmer, look out!

LINDSTROM: Schlemmer, look out!

ROBERTS: Okay, Doc. [DOC *and* ROBERTS *lift the two bodies from the hatch cover and deposit them farther upstage. At this moment, the cargo net appears, loaded with bodies in once-white uniforms and leis. Riding on top of the net is* SCHLEMMER, *wearing a lei and singing "Off We Go into the Wild Blue Yonder."*] Let her in easy . . .

LINDSTROM: Let her in easy . . .

[*The net is lowered onto the hatch cover and* LINDSTROM *detaches it from the hook. All start untangling bodies.*]

ROBERTS: Well, they're peaceful anyhow.

[*At this point a* SHORE PATROLMAN *enters from the gangway.*]

SHORE PATROLMAN [*Handing* ROBERTS *a sheaf of yellow slips*]: For your collection. [*Points down gangway.*] Take a look at them.

ROBERTS [*Looks offstage*]: My God, what did they do?

SHORE PATROLMAN: They done all right, Lieutenant. Six of them busted into a formal dance and took on a hundred and twenty-eight Army bastards. [*Calls off.*] All right, let's go!

[STEFANOWSKI, REBER, WILEY, PAYNE *and* MANNION, *with his arm around* INSIGNA, *straggle on—a frightening sight— followed by a* MILITARY POLICEMAN. INSIGNA'S *uniform is torn to shreds.* MANNION *is clad in a little diaper of crepe paper. All have bloody faces and uniforms. A few bear souvenirs—a Japanese lantern, leis, Army caps, a Shore Patrol band, etc. They throw perfunctory salutes to the colors, then murmur a greeting to* ROBERTS.]

MILITARY POLICEMAN: Duty Officer?

ROBERTS: That's right.

MILITARY POLICEMAN [*Salutes*]: Colonel Middleton presents his compliments to the Captain and wishes him to know that these men made a shambles out of the Colonel's testimonial dinner-dance.

ROBERTS: Is this true, Insigna?

INSIGNA: That's right, Mister Roberts. A shambles. [*To* MANNION.] Ain't that right, Killer?

MANNION: That's right, Mister Roberts.

ROBERTS: You men crashed a dance for Army personnel?

MANNION: Yes, sir! And they made us feel unwelcome! [*To* INSIGNA.] Didn't they, Slugger?

ROBERTS: Oh, they started a fight, eh?

WILEY: No, sir! *We* started it!

STEFANOWSKI: We finished it too! [*To* MILITARY POLICEMAN.] Tell Mister Roberts how many of you Army bastards are in the hospital.

MANNION: Go on.

MILITARY POLICEMAN: Thirty-eight soldiers of the United States Army have been hospitalized. And the Colonel himself has a very bad bruise on his left shin!

PAYNE: *I* did that, Mister Roberts.

MILITARY POLICEMAN: And that isn't all, Lieutenant. There were young ladies present—fifty of them. Colonel Middleton had been lining them up for a month, from the best families of Elysium. And he had personally guaranteed their safety this evening. Well, sir . . .

ROBERTS: Well?

MILITARY POLICEMAN: Two of those young ladies got somewhat mauled, one actually got a black eye, six of them got their clothes torn off and then went screaming off into the night and they haven't been heard from since. What are you going to do about it, Lieutenant?

ROBERTS: Well, I'm due to get relieved here in fifteen minutes —I'll be glad to lead a search party.

MILITARY POLICEMAN: No, sir. The Army's taking care of that end. The Colonel will want to know what punishment you're going to give these men.

ROBERTS: Tell the Colonel that I'm sure our Captain will think of something.

MILITARY POLICEMAN: But . . .

ROBERTS: That's all, Sergeant.

MILITARY POLICEMAN [*Salutes*]: Thank you, sir. [*He goes off.*]

SHORE PATROLMAN: Lieutenant, I been pretty sore at your guys up till now—we had to put on ten extra Shore Patrolmen on account of this ship. But if you knew Colonel "Chicken" Middleton—well, I'd be willing to do this every night. [*To the men.*] So long, fellows!

[*The men call "So long." SHORE PATROLMAN exits, saluting ROBERTS and quarter-deck.*]

ROBERTS: Well, what've you got to say for yourselves?

STEFANOWSKI [*After a moment*]: Okay if we go ashore again, Mister Roberts?

ROBERTS [*To LINDSTROM*]: Is this the first time for these guys?

LINDSTROM [*Showing log*]: Yes, sir, they got a clean record —they only been brought back once.

ROBERTS: What do you say, Doc?

[*The men turn eagerly to DOC.*]

DOC: Anybody got a fractured skull?

MEN: No.

DOC: Okay, you pass the physical.

ROBERTS: Go down and take a shower first and get into some clothes.

[*The men rush to the hatchway.*]

STEFANOWSKI: We still got time to get back to that dance!

[*As they descend hatchway, INSIGNA pulls crepe paper*

from around MANNION *as he is halfway down the hatchway.*]

ROBERTS: How you feeling, Doc?

DOC: These alcohol fumes are giving me a cheap drunk—otherwise pretty routine. When do you get relieved, Doug? [*Takes box from table and gestures for men to remove table. They carry it off.*]

ROBERTS: Soon as Carney gets back from the island. Any minute now.

DOC: What are you grinning like a skunk for?

ROBERTS: Nothing. I always grin like a skunk. What have you got in the box?

DOC [*Descending hatchway—holding up small packet he has taken from the box*]: Little favors from the Doc. I'm going to put one in each man's hand and when he wakes up he'll find pinned to his shirt full instructions for its use. I think it'll save me a lot of work later on. [*His head disappears.*]

LINDSTROM: I wish Gerhart would get back here and relieve me. I've got to get over to that island before it runs out of women.

[DOLAN *enters from gangway.*]

DOLAN: Howdy, Mister Roberts! I'm drunk as a goat! [*Pulls a goat aboard.*] Show him how drunk I am. Mister Roberts, when I first saw her she was eatin', and you know, she just eat her way into my heart. She was eatin' a little old palm tree and I thought to myself, our ship needs a mascot. [*He points out palm tree to goat.*] There you are, kid. Chow!

[ROBERTS *blocks his way.*]

ROBERTS: Wait a minute . . . wait a minute. What's her name?

DOLAN: I don't know, sir.

ROBERTS: She's got a name plate.

DOLAN: Oh, so she has . . . her name is . . . [*Reads from tag on goat's collar.*] . . . Property Of.

ROBERTS: What's her last name?

DOLAN: Her last name . . . [*Reads again.*] Rear Admiral Wentworth.

[*Approaching siren is heard offstage.*]

ROBERTS: Okay, Dolan, hit the sack. I'll take care of her.

DOLAN: Okay, Mister Roberts. [*Descends hatchway.*] See that she gets a good square meal. [*He points to the* CAPTAIN'S *palm tree and winks, then disappears.* GERHART *enters from gangway.*]

LINDSTROM: Gerhart! [LINDSTROM *frantically removes his web belt and shoves it at* GERHART.]

GERHART: Okay, okay—you're relieved.

LINDSTROM [*Tosses a fast salute to* ROBERTS *and says in one breath*]: Requestpermissiontogoashore! [*He hurries down gangway.*

[SHORE PATROLMAN *enters from gangway.*]

SHORE PATROLMAN: Lieutenant, has one of your men turned up with a . . . [*Sees goat and takes leash.*] Oh, Thanks. [*To goat.*] Come on, come on, your papa over there is worried about you. [*Pulls goat down gangway.*]

GERHART: Where's your relief, Mister Roberts?

ROBERTS [*Sitting on hatch*]: He'll be along any minute. How was your liberty, Gerhart?

[GERHART *grins. So does* ROBERTS. DOC *enters from hatchway.*]

DOC: What are you looking so cocky about anyway?

ROBERTS: Am I looking cocky? Maybe it's because for the first time since I've been on this ship, I'm seeing a crew.

DOC: What do you think you've been living with all this time?

ROBERTS: Just a hundred and sixty-seven separate guys. There's a big difference, Doc. Now these guys are bound together. You saw Insigna and Mannion. Doc, I think these guys are strong enough now to take all the miserable, endless days ahead of us. I only hope I'm strong enough.

DOC: Doug, tomorrow you and I are going over there and take advantage of the groundwork that's been laid tonight. You and I are going to have ourselves a liberty.

[PULVER *enters slowly from the gangway and walks across the stage.* DOC *calls* ROBERTS' *attention to him.*]

ROBERTS: Hello, Frank. How was your liberty?

[PULVER *half turns, shrugs and holds up seven fingers, then exits. A* SHORE PATROL OFFICER *enters from the gangway and calls offstage. He speaks with a Southern accent.*]

SHORE PATROL OFFICER: That's your post and that's your post. You know what to do. [*He salutes the quarter-deck, then* ROBERTS.] Officer of the Deck? [ROBERTS *nods. The* SHORE PATROL OFFICER *hesitates a moment.*] I hope you don't mind but

I've stationed two of my men at the foot of the gangway. I'm sorry but this ship is restricted for the rest of its stay in Elysium. Your Captain is to report to the Island Commander at seven o'clock this morning. I'd recommend that he's there on time. The Admiral's a pretty tough cookie when he's mad, and he's madder now than I've ever seen him.

ROBERTS: What in particular did this?

SHORE PATROL LIEUTENANT: A little while ago six men from your ship broke into the home of the French Consul and started throwing things through the plate-glass living-room window. We found some of the things on the lawn: a large world globe, a small love seat, a lot of books and a bust of Balzac—the French writer. We also found an Army private first class who was unconscious at the time. He claims they threw him too.

ROBERTS: Through the window?

SHORE PATROL LIEUTENANT: That's right! It seems he took them there for a little joke. He didn't tell them it was the Consul's house; he said it was a—what we call in Alabama—a cat-house. [ROBERTS *and* DOC *nod.*] Be sure that your Captain is there at seven o'clock sharp. If it makes you feel any better, Admiral Wentworth says this is the worst ship he's ever seen in his entire naval career. [*Laughs, then salutes.*] Good night, Lieutenant.

ROBERTS [*Returning salute*]: Good night.

[*The* SHORE PATROL LIEUTENANT *exits down gangway— saluting the quarter-deck.*]

GERHART: Well, there goes the liberty. That was sure a wham-bam-thank you, ma'am!

DOC: Good night. [*He exits through left passageway.*]

GERHART: But, by God, it was worth it. That liberty was worth anything!

ROBERTS: I think you're right, Gerhart.

GERHART: Hunh?

ROBERTS: I think you're right.

GERHART: Yeah. [*He smiles.* ROBERTS *looks over the log.* GERHART *whistles softly to himself* "Roll Me Over" *as the lights slowly*

Fade Out

During the darkness we hear JOHNSON *shouting:*

JOHNSON: All right, fall in for muster. Form two ranks. And pipe down.

SCENE II

The lights come up, revealing the deck. Morning sunlight. A group of men, right and left, in orderly formation. They are talking.

JOHNSON: 'Ten-shun!

[*The command is relayed through the ship. The* CAPTAIN *enters from his cabin, followed by* ROBERTS. *The* CAPTAIN *steps up on the hatch cover.* ROBERTS *starts to fall in with the men.*]

CAPTAIN [*Calling to* ROBERTS *and pointing to a place beside himself on hatch cover*]: Over here, Roberts. [ROBERTS *takes his place left of* CAPTAIN.] We're being kicked out of this port. I had a feeling this liberty was a bad idea. That's why we'll never have one again. We're going to erase this blot from my record if we have to work twenty-four hours a day. We're going to move even more cargo than we've ever moved before. And if there ain't enough cargo work, Mister Roberts here is gonna find some. Isn't that right, Mister Roberts? [ROBERTS *doesn't answer.*] Isn't that right, Mister Roberts?

ROBERTS: Yes, sir.

CAPTAIN: I'm appointing Mister Roberts here and now to see that you men toe the line. And I can't think of a more honorable man for the job. He's a man who keeps his word no matter what. [*Turns to* ROBERTS.] Now, Roberts, if you do a good job—and if the Admiral begins to smile on us again—there might be something in it for you. What would you say if that little silver bar on your collar got a twin brother some day? [ROBERTS *is startled. The* CAPTAIN *calls offstage.*] Officer of the Deck!

OFFSTAGE VOICE: Yes, sir!

CAPTAIN [*To* ROBERTS]: You wasn't expectin' that, was you? [*Calling offstage.*] Get ready to sail!

OFFSTAGE VOICE: Aye-aye, sir!

CAPTAIN: You men are dismissed!

JOHNSON: Fall out!

[*The men fall out. Some exit. A little group forms down-stage.*]

CAPTAIN: Wait a minute! Wait a minute! Roberts, take these men here back aft to handle lines. And see that they work up a sweat. [ROBERTS *and men look at him.*] Did you hear me, Roberts? I gave you an order!

ROBERTS [*Carefully*]: Yes, Captain. I heard you.

CAPTAIN: How do you answer when I give an order?

ROBERTS [*After a pause*]: Aye-aye, sir.

CAPTAIN: That's more like it . . . that's more like it! [*He exits into his cabin.*]

STEFANOWSKI: What'd he mean, Mister Roberts?

ROBERTS: I don't know. Just what he said, I guess.

GERHART: What'd you let him give you all that guff for?

DOLAN [*Stepping up on hatch, carrying a file folder*]: Because he's tired, that's why. He had the mid-watch last night. Your tail'd be dragging too if you had to handle all them customers.

ROBERTS: Come on. Let's get going . . .

DOLAN: Wait a minute, Mister Roberts. Something come for you in the mail this morning—a little love letter from the Bureau. [*Pulls out paper from file folder.*] Get a load of this! [*Reads.*] "To All Ships and Stations: Heightened war offensive has created urgent need aboard combat ships for experienced officers. [*He clicks his teeth and winks at* ROBERTS.] All commanding officers are hereby directed to forward with their endorsements all applications for transfer from officers with twenty-four months' sea duty." [ROBERTS *grabs the directive and reads it.* DOLAN *looks at* ROBERTS *and smiles.*] You got twenty-nine months—you're the only officer aboard that has. Mister Roberts, the Old Man is hanging on the ropes from the working-over the Admiral give him. All he needs to flatten him is one more little jab. And here it is. Your letter. I typed it up. [*He pulls out triplicate letters from file cover—then a fountain pen which he offers to* ROBERTS.] Sign it and I'll take it in—

MANNION: Go on, sign it, Mister Roberts. He'll take off like a bird.

DOLAN: What're you waitin' for, Mister Roberts?

ROBERTS [*Handing directive back to* DOLAN]: I'll want to look it over first, Dolan. Come on, let's get going.

DOLAN: There's nothing to look over. This is the same letter we wrote yesterday—only quoting this new directive.

ROBERTS: Look, Dolan, I'm tired. And I told you I wanted—

DOLAN: You ain't too tired to sign your name!

ROBERTS [*Sharply*]: Take it easy, Dolan. I'm not going to sign it. So take it easy! [*Turns to exit right, finds himself blocked by crew.*] Did you hear me? Let's get going! [*Exits.*]

STEFANOWSKI: What the hell's come over him?

[*They look at one another.*]

INSIGNA: Aye-aye, sir—for Christ's sake!

MANNION [*After a moment*]: Come on. Let's get going.

DOLAN [*Bitterly*]: "Take it easy . . . take it easy!"

[*The men start to move off slowly as the lights*

Fade Out

During the darkness we hear a radio. There is considerable static.

AMERICAN BROADCASTER: Still, of course, we have no official word from the Headquarters of the Supreme Allied Command in Europe. I repeat, there is no official announcement yet. The report that the war in Europe has ended has come from only one correspondent. It has not been confirmed by other correspondents or by SHAEF headquarters. But here is one highly intriguing fact—that report has not been denied either in Washington or in SHAEF headquarters in Europe. IT HAS NOT BEEN DENIED. Right now in those places the newsmen are crowded, waiting to flash to the world the announcement of V-E Day.

SCENE III

The lights come up on ROBERTS' *and* PULVER'S *cabin.* DOC, *at the desk, and* PULVER, *up in his bunk, are listening to the radio.*

PULVER: Turn that damn thing off, Doc. Has Doug ever said anything to you about wanting a promotion?

DOC: Of course not. I doubt if he's even conscious of what rank he is.

PULVER: You can say that again!

DOC: I doubt if he's even conscious of what rank he is.

PULVER: That's what I said. He doesn't even think about a promotion. The only thing he thinks about is the war news—up in the radio shack two weeks now—all day long—listening with a headset, reading all the bulletins . . . Anyone who says he's bucking for another stripe is a dirty liar.

DOC: Who says he is, Frank?

PULVER: Insigna, Mannion and some of the other guys. I heard them talking outside the porthole. They were talking loud on purpose so I could hear them—they must've guessed I was lying here on my bunk. What's happened to Doug anyway, Doc?

DOC: How would I know! He's spoken about ten words to me in as many days. But I'm damn well going to find out.

PULVER: He won't talk, Doc. This morning I followed him all around the room while he was shaving. I begged him to talk to me. I says, "You're a fellow who needs a friend and here I am." And I says, "What's all this trouble you're having with the crew? You tell me and I'll fix it up like that." And then I give him some real good advice—I says, "Keep your chin up," and things like that. And then do you know what he did? He walked out of the room just as though I wasn't here.

[*There is a knock on the door.*]

DOC: Come in.

[DOWDY *enters.*]

DOWDY: Doc, Mister Pulver—could we see you officers a minute?

DOC: Sure. [GERHART *and* LINDSTROM *enter, closing the door.*] What is it?

DOWDY: Tell them what happened, Gerhart.

GERHART: Well, sir, I sure don't like to say this but . . . Mister Roberts just put Dolan on report.

LINDSTROM: Me and Gerhart seen him.

PULVER: On report!

GERHART: Yes, sir. Tomorrow morning Dolan has to go up before the Captain—on account of Mister Roberts.

LINDSTROM: On account of Mister Roberts.

GERHART: And we was wondering if you officers could get him to take Dolan off report before . . . well, before—

DOC: Before what, Gerhart?

GERHART: Well, you see, the guys are all down in the compartment, talking about it. And they're saying some pretty rough things about Mister Roberts. Nobody just ever expected to see him put a man on report and . . .

LINDSTROM: He ain't gonna turn out to be like an officer, is he, Doc?

DOWDY: Lindstrom . . .

LINDSTROM: Oh, I didn't mean you, Doc . . . or even you, Mister Pulver!

DOC: That's all right, Lindstrom. What was this trouble with Dolan?

DOWDY: This letter business again!

GERHART: Yes, sir. Dolan was just kiddin' him about not sending in any more letters. And all of a sudden Mister Roberts turned just white and yelled, "Shut up, Dolan. Shut your goddamn mouth. I've had enough." And Dolan naturally got snotty back at him and Mister Roberts put him right on report.

LINDSTROM: Right on report.

[ROBERTS *enters*.]

PULVER: Hello, Doug boy. Aren't you listening to the war news?

DOWDY: All right, Doctor. We'll get that medical store room cleaned out tomorrow.

[DOWDY, GERHART *and* LINDSTROM *leave*.]

PULVER: We thought you were up in the radio shack.

ROBERTS [*To* PULVER]: Don't you want to go down to the wardroom and have a cup of coffee?

PULVER [*Jumping down from bunk*]: Sure. I'll go with you.

ROBERTS: I don't want any. Why don't you go ahead?

PULVER: Nah. [*He sits back on bunk. There is another little pause.*]

ROBERTS: Will you go on out anyway? I want to talk to Doc.

PULVER [*Rising and crossing to door*]: All right, I will. I'm going for a cup of coffee. [*Stops, turns and gets cap from top of locker.*] No! I'm going up to the radio shack. You aren't the only one interested in the war news. [*He exits.*]

ROBERTS [*With emotion*]: Doc, transfer me, will you? [DOC *looks at him.*] Transfer me to the hospital on this next island! You can do it. You don't need the Captain's approval! Just put me ashore for examination—say there's something wrong with my eyes or my feet or my head, for Christ's sake! You can trump up something!

DOC: What good would that do?

ROBERTS: Plenty! I could lie around that hospital for a couple of weeks. The ship would have sailed—I'd have missed it! I'd be off this ship. Will you do it, Doc?

DOC: Doug, why did you put Dolan on report just now?

ROBERTS [*Angrily*]: I gave him an order and he didn't carry it out fast enough to suit me. [*Glares at* DOC, *who just studies him.* ROBERTS *rises and paces right.*] No, that's not true. It was the war. I just heard the news. The war is ending and I couldn't get to it and there was Dolan giving me guff about something— and all of a sudden I hated him. I hated all of them. I was sick of the sullen bastards staring at me as though I'd sold them down the river or something. If they think I'm bucking for a promotion—if they're stupid enough to think I'd walk ten feet across the room to get anything from that Captain, then I'm through with the whole damn ungrateful mob!

DOC: Does this crew owe you something?

ROBERTS: What the hell do you mean by that?

DOC: You talk as if they did. [ROBERTS *rises and crosses to bunk.*]

ROBERTS [*Quietly*]: That's exactly how I'm talking. I didn't realize it but that's exactly the way I've been feeling. Oh, Jesus, that shows you how far gone I am, Doc. I've been taking something out on them. I've been blaming them for something that . . .

DOC: What, Doug? Something what? You've made some sort of an agreement with the Captain, haven't you, Doug!

ROBERTS [*Turns*]: Agreement? I don't know what you mean. Will you transfer me, Doc?

DOC: Not a chance, Doug. I could never get away with it— you know that.

ROBERTS: Oh, my God!

PULVER [*Offstage*]: Doug! Doc! [*Entering.*] Listen to the radio, you uninformed bastards! Turn it up!

[ROBERTS *reaches over and turns up the radio. The excited voice of an announcer can be heard.*]

ANNOUNCER: . . . this broadcast to bring you a special news

flash! The war is over in Europe! THE WAR IS OVER IN EUROPE! [ROBERTS *grasps* DOC'S *arm in excitement.*] Germany has surrendered unconditionally to the Allied Armies. The surrender was signed in a schoolhouse in the city of Rheims . . .

[ROBERTS *stands staring.* DOC *turns off the radio. For a moment there is silence, then:*]

DOC: I would remind you that there's still a minor skirmish here in the Pacific.

ROBERTS: I'll miss that one too. But to hell with me. This is the greatest day in the world. We're going to celebrate. How about it, Frank?

PULVER: Yeah, Doug. We've got to celebrate!

DOC [*Starting to pull alcohol from waste basket*]: What'll it be—alcohol and orange juice or orange juice and alcohol?

ROBERTS: No, that's not good enough.

PULVER: Hell, no, Doc! [*He looks expectantly at* ROBERTS.]

ROBERTS: We've got to think of something that'll lift this ship right out of the water and turn it around the other way.

[PULVER *suddenly rises to his feet.*]

PULVER [*Shouting*]: Doug! Oh, my God, why didn't I think of this before. Doug! Doc! You're going to blow your tops when you hear the idea I got! Oh, Jesus, what a wonderful idea! It's the only thing to do. It's the only thing in the whole world to do! That's all! Doug, you said I never had any ideas. You said I never finished anything I started. Well, you're wrong—tonight you're wrong! I thought of something and I finished it. I was going to save it for your birthday, but I'm going to give it to you tonight, because we gotta celebrate . . .

ROBERTS [*Waves his hands in* PULVER'S *face for attention*]: Wait a minute, Frank! What is it?

PULVER: A firecracker, by God. [*He reaches under his mattress and pulls out a large, wobbly firecracker which has been painted red.*] We're gonna throw a firecracker under the Old Man's bunk. Bam-bam-bam! Wake up, you old son-of-a-bitch, IT'S V-E DAY!

ROBERTS [*Rising*]: Frank!

PULVER: Look at her, Doc. Ain't it a beauty? Ain't that the greatest hand-made, hand-painted, hand-packed firecracker you ever saw?

ROBERTS [*Smiling and taking firecracker*]: Yes, Frank. That's the most beautiful firecracker I ever saw in my life. But will it work?

PULVER: Sure it'll work. At least, I think so.

ROBERTS: Haven't you tested it? It's got to work, Frank, it's just got to work!

PULVER: I'll tell you what I'll do. I'll take it down to the laundry and test it—that's my laboratory, the laundry. I got all the fixings down there—powder, fuses, everything, all hid behind the soapflakes. And if this one works, I can make another one in two minutes.

ROBERTS: Okay, Frank. Take off. We'll wait for you here. [PULVER *starts off.*] Be sure you got enough to make it loud. What'd you use for powder?

PULVER: Loud! This ain't a popgun. This is a firecracker. I used fulminate of mercury. I'll be right back. [*He runs out.*]

ROBERTS: Fulminate of mercury! That stuff's murder! Do you think he means it?

DOC [*Taking alcohol bottle from waste basket*]: Of course not. Where could he get fulminate of mercury?

ROBERTS: I don't know. He's pretty resourceful. Where did he get the clap last year?

DOC: How about a drink, Doug? [*He pours alcohol and orange juice into two glasses.*]

ROBERTS: Right! Doc, I been living with a genius. This makes it all worth while—the whole year and a half he spent in his bunk. How else could you celebrate V-E Day? A firecracker under the Old Man's bunk! The silly little son-of-a-bitch!

DOC [*Handing* ROBERTS *a drink*]: Here you are, Doug. [DOC *holds the drink up in a toast.*] To better days!

ROBERTS: Okay. And to a great American, Frank Thurlowe Pulver . . . Soldier . . . Statesman . . . Scientist . . .

DOC: Friend of the Working Girl . . .

[*Suddenly there is a tremendous explosion.* DOC *and* ROBERTS *clutch at the desk.*]

ROBERTS: Oh, my God!

DOC: He wasn't kidding! That's fulminate of mercury!

CAPTAIN [*Offstage*]: What was that?

[ROBERTS *and* DOC *rush to porthole, listening.*]

JOHNSON [*Offstage*]: I don't know, Captain. I'll find out!

[*We hear the sounds of running feet.*]

ROBERTS: Doc, we've got to go down and get him.

DOC: This may be pretty bad, Doug.

[*They turn to start for the door when suddenly a figure hurtles into the room and stops. For a moment it looks like a combination scarecrow and snowman but it is* PULVER— *his uniform tattered; his knees, arms and face blackened; he is covered with soapsuds and his eyes are shining with excitement.* ROBERTS *stares in amazement.*]

PULVER: Jeez, that stuff's terrific!

DOC: Are you all right?

PULVER: I'm great! Gee, you should've been there!

ROBERTS: You aren't burned—or anything?

PULVER: Hell, no. But the laundry's kinda beat up. The mangle's on the other side of the room now. And there's a new porthole on the starboard side where the electric iron went through. And I guess a steam-line must've busted or something —I was up to my ass in lather. And soapflakes flyin' around—it was absolutely beautiful!

[*During these last lines,* DOC *has been making a brisk, professional examination.*]

DOC: It's a miracle. He isn't even scratched!

PULVER: Come on down and see it, Doug. It's a Winter Wonderland!

CAPTAIN [*Offstage*]: Johnson!

ROBERTS: Quiet!

JOHNSON [*Offstage*]: Yes, sir.

CAPTAIN [*Offstage*]: What was it?

JOHNSON [*Offstage*]: The laundry, Captain. A steam-line must've blew up.

PULVER [*Explaining*]: Steam-line came right out of the bulkhead. [*He demonstrates.*] Whish!'

CAPTAIN [*Offstage*]: How much damage?

JOHNSON [*Offstage*]: We can't tell yet, Captain. We can't get in there—the passageway is solid soapsuds.

PULVER: Solid soapsuds. [*He pantomimes walking blindly through soapsuds.*]

CAPTAIN [*Offstage*]: Tell those men to be more careful.

ROBERTS [*Excitedly*]: Frank, our celebration is just getting started. The night is young and our duty's clear.

PULVER: Yeah? What're we gonna do now, Doug?

ROBERTS: Get cleaned up and come with me.

PULVER: Where we goin' now, Doug?

ROBERTS: We're going down and get the rest of your stuff. You proved it'd work—you just hit the wrong target, that's all. We're going to make another firecracker, and put it where it really belongs.

PULVER [*Who has slowly wilted during* ROBERTS' *speech*]: The rest of my stuff was—in the laundry, Doug. It all went up. There isn't any more. I'm sorry, Doug. I'm awful sorry.

ROBERTS [*Sinks into chair*]: That's all right, Frank.

PULVER: Maybe I can scrounge some more tomorrow.

ROBERTS: Sure.

PULVER: You aren't sore at me, are you, Doug?

ROBERTS: What for?

PULVER: For spoilin' our celebration?

ROBERTS: Of course not.

PULVER: It was a good idea though, wasn't it, Doug?

ROBERTS: Frank, it was a great idea. I'm proud of you. It just didn't work, that's all. [*He starts for the door.*]

DOC: Where are you going, Doug?

ROBERTS: Out on deck.

PULVER: Wait'll I get cleaned up and I'll come with you.

ROBERTS: No, I'm going to turn in after that. [*To* PULVER.] It's okay, Frank. [*He exits.*]

[PULVER *turns pleadingly to* DOC.]

PULVER: He was happy there for a minute though, wasn't he, Doc? Did you see him laughing? He was happy as hell. [*Pause.*] We gotta do something for that guy, Doc. He's in bad shape. What's the matter with him anyhow, Doc. Did you find out?

DOC: No, he wouldn't tell me. But I know one thing he's feeling tonight and that's panic. Tonight he feels his war is dying before he can get to it. [DOC *goes to radio and turns up volume.*]

PULVER: I let him down. He wanted to celebrate and I let him down. [*He drops his head.*]

ANNOUNCER'S VOICE *on radio comes up as the lights*

Fade Out

[*During the darkness and under the first part of Scene IV we hear the voice of a British broadcaster:*]

BRITISH BROADCASTER: . . . we hope that the King and Queen will come out. The crowds are cheering—listen to them—and at any second now we hope to see Their Majesties. The color here is tremendous—everywhere rosettes, everywhere gay, red-white-and-blue hats. All the girls in their summer frocks on this lovely, mild, historic May evening. And although we celebrate with joyous heart the great victory, perhaps the greatest victory in the history of mankind, the underlying mood is a mood of thanksgiving. And now, I believe, they're coming. They haven't appeared but the crowd in the center are cheering madly. Handkerchiefs, flags, hands waving—HERE THEY COME! First, Her Majesty, the Queen, has come into view. Then the King in the uniform of an Admiral of the Fleet. The two Princesses standing on the balcony—listen to the crowd—

[*Sound of wild cheering.*]

[*This broadcast continues throughout the blackout and the next scene. Several times the station is changed, from a broadcast of the celebration in San Francisco to the speaker in New York and the band playing "The Stars and Stripes Forever" in Times Square.*]

SCENE IV

The lights dim up on the main set. It is a few minutes later, and bright moonlight. The ship is under way—this is indicated by the apparent movement of the stars, slowly up and down. A group of men are sitting on the hatch cover in a late bull session. They are INSIGNA, MANNION, DOLAN *and* STEFANOW-SKI. GERHART *stands over them; he has obviously just returned from some mission for the group.*

GERHART: I'm telling you, that's all it was. A steam pipe busted in the laundry—they're cleaning it up now. It ain't worth going to see.
[*The others make way for him and he sits down beside them.* INSIGNA *cocks his head toward the sound of the radio.*]
INSIGNA: What the hell's all the jabbering on the radio now?

MANNION: I don't know. Something about the King and Queen . . .

[*The men listen for a moment without curiosity; then, as the radio fades, they settle back in indolent positions.*]

INSIGNA: Well, anyhow, like I was telling you, this big sergeant in Elysium was scared to fight me! Tell 'em how big he was, Killer.

MANNION: Six foot seven or eight . . .

STEFANOWSKI: That sergeant's grown eight inches since we left Elysium . . . Did you see me when I swiped that Shore Patrol band and went around arresting guys? That Shore Patrol Lieutenant said I was the best man he had. I arrested forty-three guys, . . .

MANNION [*Smiles at* DOLAN *who is looking depressed*]: Come on, Dolan, don't let him get you down.

INSIGNA: Yeah, come on, Dolan.

[ROBERTS *enters. He looks at the men, who have their backs turned, hesitates, then goes slowly over to them.*]

GERHART [*Idly*]: What was them croquette things we had for chow tonight?

[STEFANOWSKI *looks up and notices* ROBERTS. *Instantly he sits upright.*]

STEFANOWSKI: Flash Red!

[*The men sit up. There is an embarrassed silence.*]

ROBERTS: Good evening. [*The men smile politely.* ROBERTS *is very embarrassed.*] Did you hear the news? The war's over in Europe.

MANNION [*Smiling*]: Yes, sir. We heard.

STEFANOWSKI [*Helping out the conversation*]: Sure. Maybe somebody'll get on the ball out here now . . .

[DOLAN *rises, starts down hatchway.*]

ROBERTS: Dolan, I guess I kind of blew my top tonight. I'm sorry. I'm taking you off report.

DOLAN: Whatever you want, sir . . . [*He looks ostentatiously at his watch and yawns.*] Well, I guess I'll hit the old sack . . . [*He goes down hatchway.*]

MANNION: Yeah, me too . . .

INSIGNA: Yeah . . .

GERHART: It's late as hell.

STEFANOWSKI: I didn't realize how late it was . . .

[*All the men get up, then go down the hatchway.* ROBERTS *stands looking after them. Now the radio is heard again.* ROBERTS *goes to hatchway and sits listening.*]

SPEAKER: . . . Our boys have won this victory today. But the rest is up to you. You and you alone must recognize our enemies: the forces of ambition, cruelty, arrogance and stupidity. You must recognize them, you must destroy them, you must tear them out as you would a malignant growth! And cast them from the surface of the earth!

[*The end of the speech is followed by a band playing "The Stars and Stripes Forever." ROBERTS' face lights up and a new determination is in it. He repeats the words "malignant growth." The band music swells. He marches to the palm tree, salutes it, rubs his hands together and, as the music reaches a climax, he jerks the palm tree, earth and all, from the container and throws it over the side. Then, as the music continues, loud and climactic, he brushes his hands together, shrugs, and walks casually off left singing the tune to himself.*]

[*For a moment the stage is empty. Then the lights go up in the* CAPTAIN'S *cabin. The door to the* CAPTAIN'S *cabin opens and the* CAPTAIN *appears. He is in pajamas and bathrobe, and in one hand he carries his watering can. He discovers the empty container. He looks at it, then plunges into his cabin. After a moment, the General Alarm is heard. It is a terrible clanging noise designed to rouse the dead. When the alarm stops, the* CAPTAIN'S *voice is heard, almost hysterical, over the squawk box.*]

CAPTAIN: General Quarters! General Quarters! Every man to his battle station on the double!

[JOHNSON, *in helmet and life jacket, scurries from hatchway into the* CAPTAIN'S *cabin.* WILEY *enters from right passageway and climbs into the right gun tub. Now men appear from all directions in various degrees of dress. The stage is filled with men frantically running everywhere, all wearing helmets and life preservers.*]

INSIGNA [*Appearing from hatchway*]: What happened? [*He

runs up the ladder and into the left gun tub. PAYNE *enters from left and starts to clumb up to left gun tub.*] Get the hell out of here, Payne. This ain't your gun—your gun's over there!

DOLAN [*Also trying to climb the ladder with* PAYNE]: Over there . . . over there . . .

[PAYNE *crosses to right gun tub.*]

REBER [*Entering from hatchway*]: What the hell happened?

SCHLEMMER: Are *we* in an air raid?

PAYNE: Submarine . . . must be a submarine!

GERHART: Hey, Wiley, what happened?

DOWDY [*Calling to someone on life raft*]: Hey, get away from that life raft. He didn't say abandon ship!

[*During the confusion,* STEFANOWSKI, *bewildered, emerges from the hatchway and wanders over to right gun tub.*]

STEFANOWSKI: Hey, Wiley, Wiley—you sure you're supposed to be up there?

WILEY: Yeah.

STEFANOWSKI [*Crossing to left gun tub*]: Hey, Sam. Are you supposed to be up there?

INSIGNA: Yeah, we was here last year!

STEFANOWSKI: Hey, Dowdy. Where the hell's my battle station?

DOWDY: I don't know where your battle station is! Look around!

[STEFANOWSKI *wanders aimlessly about.* WILEY, *in the gun tub right, is receiving reports of battle readiness from various parts of the ship:*]

WILEY: Twenty millimeters manned and ready. [*Pause.*] Engine room manned and ready. [*Pause.*] All battle stations manned and ready.

STEFANOWSKI [*Sitting on corner of hatch*]: Yeah, all but mine . . .

JOHNSON'S VOICE [*In* CAPTAIN'S *cabin*]: All battle stations manned and ready, Captain.

CAPTAIN'S VOICE: Give me that thing.

JOHNSON'S VOICE [*"On mike"—that is, speaking directly into squawk-box microphone. "Off mike" means speaking unintentionally into this live microphone*]: Attention . . . Attention . . . The Captain wishes to . . .

CAPTAIN'S VOICE [*Off mike*]: Give me that thing! [*On mike.*]

All right, who did it? Who did it? You're going to stay here all night until someone confesses. You're going to stay at those battle stations until hell freezes over until I find out who did it. It's an insult to the honor of this ship, by God! The symbol of our cargo record has been destroyed and I'm going to find out who did it if it takes all night! [*Off mike.*] Johnson, read me that muster list!

JOHNSON'S VOICE [*Reading muster list off mike*]: Abernathy . . .

MANNION

Symbol of our cargo record? What the hell's that?

CAPTAIN'S VOICE

No, not Abernathy . . .

JOHNSON'S VOICE

Baker . . .

[STEFANOWSKI *rises, sees empty container, kneels and ceremoniously bows to it.*]

CAPTAIN'S VOICE

No . . .

DOWDY

For God's sake, Stefanowski, find some battle station!

JOHNSON'S VOICE

Bartholomew . . . Becker . . . Billings . . . Carney . . . Daniels . . . Dexter . . . Ellison . . . Everman . . . Jenkins . . . Kelly . . . Kevin . . . Martin . . . Olsen . . . O'Neill . . .

CAPTAIN'S VOICE

No, not O'Neill . . .

JOHNSON'S VOICE

Pulver . . .

[STEFANOWSKI *points to empty container.* DOWDY *sees it and spreads the news to the men on left.* SCHLEMMER *sees it and tells the other men. Now from all parts of the ship men enter and jubilantly look at the empty container. Bits of soil fly into the air as the men group around the empty can.*]

CAPTAIN'S VOICE

No, not Pulver. He hasn't
the guts . . .

JOHNSON'S VOICE

Roberts . . .

CAPTAIN'S VOICE [*Roaring, off mike*]: Roberts! He's the one!
Get him up here!

JOHNSON'S VOICE [*On mike*]: Mister Roberts will report to
the Captain's cabin on the double!

[*The men rush back to their battle stations.*]

CAPTAIN'S VOICE: Get him up here, I tell you! Get him up
here . . .

JOHNSON'S VOICE [*On mike*]: Mister Roberts will report to
the Captain's cabin on the . . .

CAPTAIN [*Off mike*]: Give me that thing. [*On mike.*]
Roberts, you get up here in a goddamn quick hurry. Get up
here! Roberts, I'm giving you an order—get the lead out of
your pants.

[ROBERTS *appears from left passageway and, walking
slowly, enters the* CAPTAIN'S *cabin.*]

[*The men move onstage and* LINDSTROM *gets to a position on the ladder where he can look through the porthole
of the* CAPTAIN'S *cabin.*]

ROBERTS' VOICE: Did you want to see me, Captain?

CAPTAIN'S VOICE: You did it. You did it. Don't lie to me.
Don't stand there and lie to me. Confess it!

ROBERTS' VOICE: Confess what, Captain? I don't know what
you're talking about.

CAPTAIN'S VOICE: You know damn well what I'm talkin'
about because you did it. You've doublecrossed me—you've
gone back on your word!

ROBERTS' VOICE: No, I haven't, Captain.

CAPTAIN: Yes, by God, you have. I kept my part of the
bargain! I gave this crew liberty—I gave this crew liberty, by
God, but you've gone back on *your* word.

[DOWDY *takes off his helmet and looks at the men.*]

ROBERTS' VOICE: I don't see how you can say that, Captain. I
haven't sent in any more letters.

[DOLAN, *on gun tub ladder, catches* INSIGNA'S *eye.*]

CAPTAIN'S VOICE: I'm not talkin' about your goddamn sons-a-bitchin' letters. I'm talkin' about what you did tonight.

ROBERTS' VOICE: Tonight? I don't understand you, Captain. What do you think I did?

CAPTAIN: Quit saying that, goddammit, quit saying that. You know damn well what you did. You stabbed me in the back. You stabbed me in the back . . . aaa . . . aa . . .

JOHNSON'S VOICE: Captain! Get over to the washbasin, Captain!

CAPTAIN'S VOICE: Aaaaaaa . . .

INSIGNA: What the hell happened?

DOLAN: Quiet!

JOHNSON [*On mike*]: Will the Doctor please report to the Captain's cabin on the double?

[DOC *appears from left, pushing his way through the crowd, followed by two* MEDICAL CORPSMEN *wearing Red Cross brassards and carrying first-aid kits and a stretcher.* DOC *walks slowly; he is idly attaching a brassard and smoking a cigarette. He wears his helmet sloppily.*]

DOC: Gangway . . . gangway . . .

DOWDY: Hey, Doc, tell us what's going on.

DOC: Okay. Okay. [*He enters the* CAPTAIN'S *cabin followed by the* CORPSMEN *who leave stretcher leaning against the bulkhead. The door closes. There is a tense pause. The men gather around the cabin again.* LINDSTROM *is at the porthole.*]

REBER: Hey, Lindstrom, where's the Old Man?

LINDSTROM: He's sittin' in the chair—leaning way forward.

PAYNE: What's the Doc doin'?

LINDSTROM: He's holdin' the waste basket.

REBER: What waste basket?

LINDSTROM: The one the Old Man's got his head in. And he needs it too. [*Pause.*] They're helpin' him over to the couch. [*Pause.*] He's lying down there and they're takin' off his shoes. [*Pause.*] Look out, here they come.

[*The men break quickly and rush back to their battle stations. The door opens and* ROBERTS, DOC *and the* CORPSMEN *come out.*]

DOC [*To* CORPSMEN]: We won't need that stretcher. Sorry. [*Calls.*] Dowdy! Come here.

[DOWDY *comes down to* DOC. *He avoids* ROBERTS' *eyes.*]

ROBERTS: Dowdy, pass the word to the crew to secure from General Quarters.

DOC: And tell the men not to make any noise while they go to their bunks. The Captain's resting quietly now, and I think that's desirable.

ROBERTS: Pass the word, will you, Dowdy?

DOWDY: Yes, Mister Roberts. [*He passes the word to the crew who slowly start to leave their battle stations. They are obviously stalling.*]

DOC [*To* ROBERTS]: Got a cigarette? [ROBERTS *reaches in his pocket and offers* DOC *a cigarette. Then he lights* DOC's *cigarette.* DOC *notices the men stalling.*] Well, guess I'd better get back inside. I'll be down to see you after I get through. [*He enters cabin and stands there watching. The men move offstage, very slowly, saying "Good night, Mister Roberts," "Good night, sir." Suddenly* ROBERTS *notices that all the men are saying good night to him.*]

DOLAN [*Quietly*]: Good night, Mister Roberts. [ROBERTS *does not hear him.*] Good night, Mister Roberts.

ROBERTS: Good night, Dolan.

[DOLAN *smiles and exits down hatch.* ROBERTS *steps toward hatch, removes helmet, looks puzzled as the lights*

Fade Out

[*During the darkness, over the squawk box the following announcements are heard:*]

FIRST VOICE: Now hear this . . . Now hear this . . . C, E and S Divisions and all Pharmacist's Mates will air bedding today—positively!

SECOND VOICE: There is now available at the ship's store a small supply of peanut brittle. Ship's store will be open from 1300 to 1315.

THIRD VOICE: Now, Dolan, Yeoman Second Class, report to the radio shack immediately.

SCENE V

The lights come up on the stateroom of ROBERTS *and* PULVER. PULVER *is lying in the lower bunk.* DOC *is sitting at the desk with a glass and a bottle of grain alcohol in front of him.* ROBERTS *is tying up a sea bag. A small suitcase stands beside it. His locker is open and empty.* WILEY *picks up the sea bag.*

WILEY: Okay, Mister Roberts. I'll take these down to the gangway. The boat from the island should be out here any minute for you. I'll let you know.

ROBERTS: Thanks, Wiley.

WILEY [*Grinning*]: That's okay, Mister Roberts. Never thought you'd be taking this ride, did you? [*He exits with the bags.*]

ROBERTS: I'm going to be off this bucket before I even wake up.

DOC: They flying you all the way to the *Livingston?*

ROBERTS: I don't know. The radio dispatch just said I was transferred and travel by air if possible. I imagine it's all the way though. They're landing planes at Okinawa now and that's where my can is probably running around. [*Laughs a little.*] Listen to me, Doc—my can!

PULVER [*Studying map by* ROBERTS' *bunk*]: Okinawa! Jeez, you be might-y careful, Doug.

ROBERTS: Okay, Frank. This is *too* much to take, Doc. I even got a destroyer! The *Livingston!* That's one of the greatest cans out there.

PULVER: I know a guy on the *Livingston*. He don't think it's so hot.

DOLAN [*Entering. He has a file folder under his arm*]: Here you are, Mister Roberts. I typed up three copies of the radio dispatch. I've got to keep a copy and here's two for you. You're now officially detached from this here bucket. Let me be the first.

ROBERTS: Thanks, Dolan. [*They shake hands.* ROBERTS *takes papers, and looks at them.*] Dolan, how about these orders? I haven't sent in a letter for a month!

DOLAN [*Carefully*]: You know how the Navy works, Mister Roberts.

ROBERTS: Yeah, I know, but it doesn't seem . . .

DOLAN: Listen, Mister Roberts, I can tell you exactly what happened. Those guys at the Bureau need men for combat duty awful bad and they started looking through all the old letters and they just come across one of yours.

ROBERTS: Maybe—but still you'd think . . .

DOLAN: Listen, Mister Roberts. We can't stand here beating our gums! You better get cracking! You seen what it said there, "Proceed immediately." And the Old Man says if you ain't off of here in an hour, by God, he's going to throw you off!

ROBERTS: Is that all he said?

DOLAN: That's all he said.

ROBERTS [*Grinning at* DOC]: After fighting this for two years you'd think he'd say more than that . . .

CAPTAIN'S VOICE [*Offstage*]: Be careful of that one. Put it down easy.

DOC: What's that?

DOLAN: A new enlarged botanical garden. That's why he can't even be bothered about you today, Mister Roberts. Soon as we anchored this morning he sent Olsen over with a special detail —they dug up two palm trees . . . He's busy as a mother skunk now and you know what he's done—he's already set a twenty-four-hour watch on these new babies with orders to shoot to kill. [*To* PULVER.] That reminds me, Mister Pulver. The Captain wants to see you right away.

PULVER: Yeah? What about?

DOLAN: I don't know, sir. [*To* ROBERTS.] I'll be back to say good-bye, Mister Roberts. Come on, Mister Pulver. [*He exits.*]

PULVER [*Following* DOLAN *out*]: What the hell did I do with his laundry this week?

[ROBERTS *smiles as he starts putting on his black tie.*]

DOC: You're a happy son-of-a-bitch, aren't you?

ROBERTS: Yep. You're happy about it too, aren't you, Doc?

DOC: I think it's the only thing for you. [*Casually.*] What do you think of the crew now, Doug?

ROBERTS: We're all right now. I think they're nice guys— all of them.

DOC: Unh-hunh. And how do you think they feel about you?

ROBERTS: I think they like me all right . . . till the next guy comes along.

DOC: You don't think you're necessary to them?

ROBERTS [*Sitting on bunk*]: Hell, no. No officer's necessary to the crew, Doc.

DOC: Are you going to leave this ship believing that?

ROBERTS: That's nothing against them. A crew's too busy looking after themselves to care about anyone else.

DOC: Well, take a good, deep breath, Buster. [*He drinks some alcohol.*] What do you think got you your orders? Prayer and fasting? Sending in enough Wheatie box tops?

ROBERTS: My orders? Why, what Dolan said—one of my old letters turned up . . .

DOC: Bat crap! This crew got you transferred. They were so busy looking out for themselves that they took a chance of landing in prison for five years—any one of them. Since you couldn't send in a letter for transfer, they sent one in for you. Since they knew the Captain wouldn't sign it approved, they didn't bother him—they signed it for him.

ROBERTS: What do you mean? They forged the Captain's name?

DOC: That's right.

ROBERTS [*Rising*]: Doc! Who did? Which one of them?

DOC: That would be hard to say. You see, they had a mass meeting down in the compartment. They put guards at every door. They called it the Captain's-Name-Signing contest. And every man in this crew—a hundred and sixty-seven of them— signed the Captain's name on a blank sheet of paper. And then there were judges who compared these signatures with the Captain's and selected the one to go in. At the time there was some criticism of the decision on the grounds that the judges were drunk, but apparently, from the results, they chose well.

ROBERTS: How'd you find out about this, Doc?

DOC: Well, it was a great honor. I am the only officer aboard who does know. I was a contestant. I was also a judge. This double honor was accorded me because of my character, charm, good looks and because the medical department contributed four gallons of grain alcohol to the contest. [*Pauses.*] It was quite a thing to see, Doug. A hundred and sixty-seven guys with only one idea in their heads—to do something for Mister Roberts.

ROBERTS [*After a moment*]: I wish you hadn't told me, Doc. It makes me look pretty silly after what I just said. But I didn't mean it, Doc. I was afraid to say what I really feel. I love those bastards, Doc. I think they're the greatest guys on this earth. All of a sudden I feel that there's something wrong—something terribly wrong—about leaving them. God, what can I say to them?

DOC: You won't say anything—you don't even know. When you're safely aboard your new ship I'm supposed to write and tell you about it. And at the bottom of the letter, I'm supposed to say, "Thanks for the liberty, Mister Roberts. Thanks for everything."

ROBERTS: Jesus!

[PULVER *enters, downcast.*]

PULVER: I'm the new Cargo Officer. And that's not all—I got to have dinner with him tonight. He *likes* me!

[*There is a polite rap on the door.*]

DOC: Come in. [*Enter* PAYNE, REBER, GERHART, SCHLEMMER, DOLAN *and* INSIGNA, *all carrying canteen cups except* INSIGNA *whose cup is in his belt. He carries a large, red fire extinguisher.*] What's this?

INSIGNA: Fire and rescue party. Heard you had a fire in here.

[*All are looking at* ROBERTS.]

ROBERTS: No, but—since you're here—I—

INSIGNA: Hell, we got a false alarm then. Happens all the time. [*Sets extinguisher on desk.*] In that case, we might as well drink this stuff. Give me your glass, Mister Roberts, and I'll put a head on it—yours too, Doc. I got one for you, Mister Pulver. [*He fills their glasses from the fire extinguisher.*]

ROBERTS: What's in that, a new batch of jungle juice?

INSIGNA: Yeah, in the handy, new, portable container. Everybody loaded?

[*All nod.*]

DOLAN: Go ahead, Sam.

INSIGNA [*To* ROBERTS]: There's a story going around that you're leaving us. That right?

ROBERTS [*Carefully*]: That's right, Sam. And I . . .

INSIGNA: Well, we didn't want you to get away without hav-ing a little drink with us and we thought we ought to give you a little sort of going-away present. The fellows made it down in the machine shop. It ain't much but we hope you like it. [REBER *prompts him.*] We all sincerely hope you like it. [*Calls offstage.*] All right, you bastards, you can come in now.

[*Enter* LINDSTROM, MANNION, DOWDY *and* STEFANOWSKI. MANNION *is carrying a candy box. He walks over to* ROBERTS *shyly and hands him the box.*]

ROBERTS: What is it?

SCHLEMMER: Open it.

[ROBERTS *opens the box. There is a deep silence.*]

PULVER: What is it, Doug?

[ROBERTS *holds up the box. In it is a brass medal shaped like a palm tree attached to a piece of gaudy ribbon.*]

LINDSTROM: It's a palm tree, see.

DOLAN: It was Dowdy's idea.

DOWDY: Mannion here made it. He cut it out of sheet brass down in the machine shop.

INSIGNA: Mannion drilled the words on it too.

MANNION: Stefanowski thought up the words.

STEFANOWSKI [*Shoving* LINDSTROM *forward*]: Lindstrom gets credit for the ribbon from a box of candy that his sister-in-law sent him. Read the words, Mister Roberts.

ROBERTS [*With difficulty*]: "Order . . . order of . . ." [*He hands the medal to* DOC.]

DOC [*Rises and reads solemnly*]: "Order of the palm. To Lieutenant (jg) Douglas Roberts for action against the enemy, above and beyond the call of duty on the night of eight May 1945." [*He passes the medal back to* ROBERTS.]

ROBERTS [*After a moment—smiling*]: It's very nice but I'm afraid you've got the wrong guy.

[*The men turn to* DOWDY, *grinning.*]

DOWDY: We know that, but we'd kinda like for you to have it anyway.

ROBERTS: All right, I'll keep it.

[*The men beam. There is an awkward pause.*]

GERHART: Stefanowski thought up the words.

ROBERTS: They're fine words.

[WILEY *enters.*]

WILEY: The boat's here, Mister Roberts. I put your gear in. They want to shove off right away.

ROBERTS [*Rising*]: Thanks. We haven't had our drink yet.

REBER: No, we ain't.

[*All get to their feet.* ROBERTS *picks up his glass, looks at the crew, and everyone drinks.*]

ROBERTS: Good-bye, Doc.

DOC: Good-bye, Doug.

ROBERTS: And thanks, Doc.

DOC: Okay.

ROBERTS: Good-bye, Frank.

PULVER: Good-bye, Doug.

ROBERTS: Remember, I'm counting on you.

[PULVER *nods.* ROBERTS *turns to the crew and looks at them for a moment. Then he takes the medal from the box, pins it on his shirt, shows it to them, then gives a little gestured salute and exits as the lights*

Fade Out

During the darkness we hear voices making announcements over the squawk box:

FIRST VOICE: Now hear this . . . now hear this . . . Sweepers, man your brooms. Clean sweep-down fore and aft!

SECOND VOICE: Now hear this! All men put on report today will fall in on the quarter-deck—and form three ranks!

THIRD VOICE: Now hear this! All divisions will draw their mail at 1700—in the mess hall.

SCENE VI

The lights come up showing the main set at sunset. DOC *is sitting on the hatch, reading a letter.* MANNION, *wearing sidearms, is pacing up and down in front of the* CAPTAIN'S *cabin. On each side of the door is a small palm tree in a five-gallon can—on one can is painted in large white letters, "Keep Away"; on the other, "This Means You." After a moment,*

PULVER *enters from the left passageway, carrying a small packet of letters.*

PULVER: Hello, Mannion. Got your mail yet?

MANNION: No. I've got the palm tree watch.

PULVER: Oh. [*To* DOC.] What's your news, Doc?

DOC: My wife got some new wallpaper for the living room.

[PULVER *sits on hatch cover.* DOWDY *enters wearing work gloves.*]

DOWDY: Mister Pulver, we'll be finished with the cargo in a few minutes.

PULVER: How'd it go?

DOWDY: Not bad. I've got to admit you were right about Number Three hold. It worked easier out of there. Mister Pulver, I just found out what the Captain decided—he ain't going to show a movie again tonight.

PULVER: Why not?

DOWDY: He's still punishing us because he caught Reber without a shirt on two days ago. You've got to go in and see him.

PULVER: I did. I asked him to show a movie yesterday.

DOWDY: Mister Pulver, what the hell good does that do us today? You've got to keep needlin' that guy—I'm tellin' you.

PULVER: Don't worry. I'll take care of it in my own way.

DOWDY [*Going off, but speaking loud enough to be heard*]: Oh, God, no movie again tonight. [*He exits.* PULVER *starts looking at his packet of mail.*]

PULVER [*Looking at first letter*]: This is from my mother. All she ever says is stay away from Japan. [*He drops it on the hatch cover.*] This is from Alabama. [*Puts it in his pocket and pats it. Looks at third letter.*] Doc! This is from Doug!

DOC: Yeah? [PULVER *rips open the envelope.*] What does he say?

PULVER [*Reading*]: "This will be short and sweet, as we're shoving off in about two minutes . . ." [*Pauses and remarks.*] This is dated three weeks ago.

DOC: Does he say where he is?

PULVER: Yeah. He says: "My guess about the location of this ship was just exactly right." [*Looks up.*] That means he's around Okinawa all right! [*Reads on and chuckles.*] He's met Fornell. That's that friend of mine . . . a guy named Fornell I went to college with. Listen to this: "Fornell says that you and he used to load up your car with liquor in Omaha and then sell it at an indecent profit to the fraternity boys at Iowa City. How about that?" We did too. [*Smiles happily.*] "This part is for Doc." [DOC *gestures for him to read it.*] "I've been aboard this destroyer for two weeks now and we've already been through four air attacks. I'm in the war at last, Doc. I've caught up with that task force that passed me by. I'm glad to be here. I had to be here, I guess. But I'm thinking now of you, Doc, and you, Frank, and Dolan and Dowdy and Insigna and everyone else on that bucket—all the guys everywhere who sail from Tedium to Apathy and back again—with an occasional side trip to Monotony. This is a tough crew on here, and they have a wonderful battle record. But I've discovered, Doc, that the most terrible enemy of this war is the boredom that eventually becomes a faith and, therefore, a sort of suicide—and I know now that the ones who refuse to surrender to it are the strongest of all.

"Right now, I'm looking at something that's hanging over my desk: a preposterous hunk of brass attached to the most bilious piece of ribbon I've ever seen. I'd rather have it than the Congressional Medal of Honor. It tells me what I'll always be proudest of—that at a time in the world when courage counted most, I lived among a hundred and sixty-seven brave men.

"So, Doc, and especially you, Frank, don't let those guys down. Of course, I know that by this time they must be very happy because the Captain's overhead is filled with marbles and . . ." [*He avoids* DOC's *eyes.*] "Oh, hell, here comes the mail orderly. This has to go now. I'll finish it later. Meanwhile you bastards can write too, can't you?

"Doug."

DOC: Can I see that, Frank?

[PULVER *hands him the letter, looks at the front of his next letter and says quietly:*]

PULVER: Well, for God's sake, this is from Fornell!

DOC [*Reading* ROBERTS' *letter to himself*]: ". . . I'd rather have it than the Congressional Medal of Honor." I'm glad he found that out. [*He looks at* PULVER, *sensing something wrong.*] What's the matter? [PULVER *does not answer.*] What's the matter, Frank? [PULVER *looks at him slowly as* DOWDY *enters.*]

DOWDY: All done, Mister Pulver. We've secured the hatch cover. No word on the movie, I suppose.

DOC [*Louder, with terror*]: Frank, what is it?

PULVER: Mister Roberts is dead. [*Looks at letter.*] This is from Fornell . . . They took a Jap suicide plane. It killed everyone in a twin-forty battery and then it went on through and killed Doug and another officer in the wardroom. [*Pause.*] They were drinking coffee when it hit.

DOWDY [*Quietly*]: Mister Pulver, can I please give that letter to the crew?

DOC: No. [*Holding out* ROBERTS' *letter.*] Give them this one. It's theirs. [DOWDY *removes gloves and takes the letter from* DOC *and goes off.*] Coffee . . .

[PULVER *gets up restlessly.* DOC *stares straight ahead.* PULVER *straightens. He seems to grow. He walks casually over to* MANNION.]

PULVER [*In a friendly voice*]: Go on down and get your mail. I'll stand by for you.

MANNION [*Surprised*]: You will? Okay, thanks, Mister Pulver.

[MANNION *disappears down hatch. As soon as he exits* PULVER *very calmly jerks the rooted palms, one by one, from their containers and throws them over the side.* DOC *looks up to see* PULVER *pull second tree.* DOC *ducks as tree goes past him. Then* PULVER *knocks loudly on the* CAPTAIN'S *door.*]

CAPTAIN [*Offstage. His voice is very truculent*]: Yeah. Who is it?

PULVER: Captain, this is Ensign Pulver. I just threw your palm trees overboard. Now what's all this crap about no movie tonight? [*He throws the door open, banging it against the bulkhead, and is entering the* CAPTAIN'S *cabin as*

The Curtain Falls